TELEVISION MYTH
AND
THE AMERICAN MIND

TELEVISION MYTH *AND* THE AMERICAN MIND

HAL HIMMELSTEIN

PRAEGER SPECIAL STUDIES • PRAEGER SCIENTIFIC

New York • Philadelphia • Eastbourne, UK
Toronto • Hong Kong • Tokyo • Sydney

Library of Congress Cataloging in Publication Data

Himmelstein, Hal.
    Television myth and the American mind.

    Includes index.
    1. Television programs—United States—History and
criticism. 2. Television advertising—United States.
3. Television broadcasting—United States. I. Title
PN1992.3.U5H55 1984   302.2'345   84-11621
ISBN 0-03-062134-8 (alk. paper)
ISBN 0-03-062136-4 (pbk. : alk. paper)

Published in 1984 by Praeger Publishers
CBS Educational and Professional Publishing
a Division of CBS Inc.
521 Fifth Avenue, New York, NY 10175 USA

©1984 by Praeger Publishers

456789 052 987654321

Printed in the United States of America
on acid-free paper

For Larry Firestone

Acknowledgments

The motivation for writing this volume was supplied in large measure by my colleague and dear friend Charles Clift III, who encouraged me to develop a book which could be used in a basic television criticism course we were developing at Ohio University. His suggestions and critique of the general approach to the material and to specific ideas contained herein, as well as critiques from other colleagues, most notably George Korn, Drew McDaniel, James A. Anderson, and James Webster, have been invaluable.

One cannot grow intellectually in an academic environment without constant challenge from students, particularly those in graduate courses. During the book's preparation, four graduate students—David Sholle, Geoffrey Coward, Eric Kramer, and Omar Oliviera—provided particularly articulate challenges to my ideas; I am grateful for their curiosity, dogged questioning, and insights.

In one's past are those rarest of teachers who are truly inspired. My passion for the study of American institutions and cultural history was kindled by my first and perhaps most influential mentor, Harry Kluttz, who opened the doors to the larger American cultural and social arena at a time when a young high school student was undirected and generally bored with the oppressive atmosphere of schooling. His optimism for the future of the American artistic spirit was infectious, and, although I often find it hard to share that optimism as it relates to our popular arts, his openness to his students and his sharp mind have left a lasting impression, for which I remain in his debt. Later, as an undergraduate, I fell under the spell of historians John T. Alexander and Clifford S. Griffin at the University of Kansas. As a graduate student, I was led into the mysterious world of Marshall McLuhan and Harold Adams Innis by professor Peter Dart. Finally, Professor Sung Ho Kim introduced me to the complex law, politics, and ethics of international and inter-cultural relations. I eventually found my way on my own, having grown under the thoughtful and caring tutelage of these teachers. Homage is herewith offered to all.

Words on paper will not do justice to the efforts of my editor, Lynda Sharp, to bring this work to fruition. She provided continual support for the project, as she did with our previous book and offered numerous suggestions both for improvements in the theoretical arguments advanced, and for the inclusion of television programs I had overlooked. Her work in developing a coherent series of books in critical sociology and communications will prove invaluable to our discipline. My hope is that the work before you approaches the high standards she has set for the series. If it falls short, the responsibility rests, of course, with the author.

Finally, I wish to thank once again my wife, RoseAnne Spradlin, for her constant support, her patience, her critique of my ideas, and her permission to watch endless *Leave It To Beaver* and *Green Acres* reruns, local gospel hours, and an occasional prime time soap.

Table of Contents

Introduction

In Aldous Huxley's prophetic condemnation of industrial civilization and mass society, *Brave New World*, written five decades ago, the brilliant, solitary Bernard Marx and the vapid, highly socialized Lenina Crowne journey from the Other Place—a sterile, painless civilization of eternal youth, endless platitudes, indiscriminate sex without love, and the narcotizing drug *soma*, all controlled by leaders who feared that the "primitive" urges and the potential social power of the masses might undermine the smoothly operating industrial system they had built. They arrive at the Reservation—a dirty, dusty world of Indians, religious human sacrifice, ragged clothes, starving dogs, old age, maternal love, and monogomy. There they encounter a white woman, Linda, and her son, John, who have been living with the Indians for years although they have never been fully incorporated into the tribe because they exhibit qualities of the Other Place the Indians find reprehensible. Bernard and Lenina return to the Other Place with Linda and John, the latter becoming fondly known as "Mr. Savage," and they share in John's celebrityhood (John, young and virile, is clearly star material, while his haggard toothless mother is a pariah in the land of the beautiful people). But John's disdain for the shallow, plastic world of the Other Place leads to his eventual ostracism and suicide.

The Other Place was none other than Television Land. The Other Place eased the pain of physical and psychic dying with the "television box." "Television was left on, a running tap, from morning till night." Huxley's world of the future, in which industrialists are deities (substitute Ford for Lord), and citizens are drugged and contented, is an elaborately constructed metaphor for today's electronic world—a pastiche of psychic landscapes offering its citizens reassurance that through the purchase of the correct commodities and the proper respect for capitalist traditions and dominant authority life can be painless.

How close have we come to Huxley's vision? In what ways does television control the American mind? In whom and for what reasons is that control vested? This book attempts to map the contemporary electronic landscapes of American life through an interpretation of our dominant myths which provide the conceptual frames for today's television images. By understanding the construction of these myths we will come to a clearer comprehension of the social formations which are constantly reproduced by and are in turn reproducing the myths, for myths come from the culture and refer back to its history. And while myths seem natural and inevitable to those under their spell—"this is how life was, is, and should be"—a careful deconstruction of the myths will cast doubt on their inevitability and simultaneously open our vision to oppositional conceptions of social formation.

Huxley warned us of a world in which there was "no leisure from pleasure, not a moment to sit down and think . . . safe on the solid ground of daily labour and distraction."* Today, in advanced capitalist America, those in the middle and lower middle classes live out their dreams in such a world. Our television screens thrust an unending stream of commodities at us and assure us our way of life is both defensible and unthreatened. We have come to believe in the psychic television landscapes of Mayfield, Mayberry, Minneapolis, and midtown Manhattan, while ignoring those of Saigon, Harlem, and Fernwood.

---

*Aldous Huxley, *Brave New World* (New York: Harper & Row, 1939), p. 134.

1

TELEVISION MYTH
AND
THE AMERICAN MIND

Psychoanalyst Erich Fromm once described the world of the commercial as "a kind of sacred land in which [the] image of the beautiful, successful, energetic young man [and woman] is never touched . . . ." We live, said Fromm, in the "twilight of reality/fiction."[1] Images of eternal youth achieved through the consumption of miracle products, and the glamorous life that is the reward for personal success won through a combination of hard work and the right connections, are the stuff of the television dream world that provides the compensatory distractions necessary to make the mundane work routines and the inherently unequal social power relationships of everyday living seem more tolerable. The frames that circumscribe these waking dreams exist somewhere outside the realm of our control. They exist "out there," in the "twilight" of culture, manufactured for us. We uncritically accept these frames as we do the air we breathe. They seem natural to us—inevitable. They become *our* dreams.

The refinement of psychoanalytic techniques in the late nineteenth and twentieth centuries has made many in the academic community increasingly aware of some important connections between the individual's dream life and the culture's myth life. According to Fromm, both the dream and the myth are highly creative acts; both employ symbolic language; and both are reactions to significant experiences in the waking world. Most dreams reflect a significant personal experience of the preceding day, while myths reflect a significant cultural experience in the "timeless past"—the culture's prehistory—

1

that is always present in the contemporary manifestation of the myth. Recurrent dreams and recurrent myths express a leitmotif, or a significant main theme—the former in one's life and the latter in the collective life of the culture.[2]

To understand the myth life of our television culture, we must first consider the construction of the television message and the social, political, and economic nature of the processes of construction as they are reflected in the powerful visual and verbal symbols produced and perpetuated by the "diversified entertainment companies" of advanced capitalism—financial institutions masquerading as culture producers. We must then consider the status of the message receiver—the well-trained viewer—in this process.

Most of us are unaware of the highly politicized nature of the process by which our electronic information is conceived, produced, and disseminated before it directly engages our personal worlds. Yet the acts that constitute this process are a powerful, although largely unnoticed presence in the imagery given us. To understand the process, we must focus not only on content and technology—the visible manifestations of messages; we must also understand the institutional apparatuses that both structure content and establish parameters for the admission or exclusion of producers. These institutional apparatuses function according to the imperatives of (1) an economics of information manifested in the complex financial practices of entertainment conglomerates as they circumscribe the social boundaries of electronic discourse according to the bottom lines of profit formulas; and of (2) a politics of information manifested in battles over content, as government sanctions particular economic postures and social stances taken by dominant media organizations, while public-interest advocates on the fringes of the cultural debate put up a comparatively weak challenge to those sanctions they deem inequitable. Central to this ongoing process of cultural negotiation is the continuous reproduction of visual, verbal, and gestural language that constitutes a system of deep cultural meaning that is advanced, from a position of economic and political power, by our dominant communications institutions and is intended to control the nature of the social relations within our society.

How is television's language organized? Television, first of all, organizes the sale of a product—its audience—to advertisers, or, in the case of public television, to program underwriters. The audience is therefore implicit in the characters presented on the small screen.

Television's imagery is appropriated from other public arts, including the cinema, still photography, music, fashion, the speech, the novel, and drama. At the same time, television's imagery appears more real or lifelike than the imagery in other public media because of its heavy reliance on human conversation in restricted naturalistic settings and on the conditions of its reception on small screens in private spaces. Television is thus ideally suited to the needs of mercantile interests because it is able to convincingly relate products—decor—to pedestrian characters in a believable context. However, television's realism camouflages its clever appropriation of a dreamlike symbolic language to suggest to us that the path to everlasting happiness is the unending competitive expansion of our already highly charged acquisitiveness. By a continual transforming of complex inner experiences, desires, and feelings into unidimensional sensory experiences in the outer world, viewers are coaxed into believing they must, at any cost, be au courant. Lifestyle packages are quickly adopted and just as quickly discarded (in an era of technophilia, being is equated with belonging through the purchase of decor). Clothing, jewelry fashions, cosmetics, and luxury automobiles (e.g., *Dallas* and the urban-cowboy look); interior-design schemes (of all daytime soaps); and vacation spots (*Fantasy Island, The Love Boat, Hawaii Five-O,* and *Wide World of Sports*) are the totems of status, power, and respect created by an ecology of competitive consumption. The television programs themselves become ads for the commercials, highlighting "contemporary lifestyles" and reinforcing, through the artificially accelerated flow of action, editing, and incessant program interruptions, the frenetic pace necessary to reinforce the notion of turnover, a concept crucial to today's world of product and human-relationship impermanence.

Television, through its use of a powerful language comprising images, words, gestures, clothing, settings, music, and sounds, has become one of our society's principal repositories of ideology. Ideology is a constructed belief system that explains economic, political, and social reality to people and establishes collective goals of a class, group, or, in the case of a dominant ideology, the entire society. In short, ideology is an "image society gives itself in order to perpetuate itself."[3] Dominant ideology is normative—it succeeds in persuading us that the way things are now is the way they should remain; and that the way things are is a product of the actions of the dominant class— in an advanced capitalist system such as that of the United States, that dominant class is the finance-capitalist class with transnational ties and little personal loyalty. The members of that class have a responsibility to gain profits. They respond to people as "markets," not as people, despite their attempts to describe markets in anthropomorphic terms such as "audience."[4] Notions of efficiency, rather than morality, tend to define such a responsibility and response.

The constructed meanings of our dominant ideology operate as givens. The way things are appears commonsensical. Myth transforms the temporal common sense of ideology into the sacred realm of cultural prehistory and thus of eternal truth. Myth thereby serves an important political or organizational function. It defuses at the outset any oppositional ideology that attempts to emerge to show the world of social relations as it really is. Myth's work results in oppositional ideology appearing merely disruptive and counterproductive in a stable world.

At this point, it is necessary to clarify my narrow use of the term "myth"—a term which has, over centuries of scholarship, taken many meanings. The term has been most widely applied in the disciplines of anthropology and literature. In an anthropological sense, myths are derived from a potentially infinite series of historical, or supposedly historical, events from which a society draws a few relevant incidents that provide a broad outline of its cultural heritage. Myths are generally expressed through the narrative form of storytelling. They contain recurrent themes, references to and parallels with other myths.[5] Myths are objectified in works of literature and in representational visual art; they are also actualized in ritual performances.

Myths are man's oldest creation, comprising a key element in the development of oral culture. When myths were made respectable as part of religion (e.g., the various myths of creation), they were acknowledged as representative of a venerable tradition. However, when they lacked this traditional authority (e.g., in dramatic presentations such as Sophocles' Oedipus trilogy), they were relegated to the category of prescientific fantasy. In the latter case, while the aesthetic merits of the work embodying the myth might be acknowledged, the power of the myth to orient us to certain economic, political, or social realms of experience was largely discounted or ignored. Many contemporary Western commentaries continue to labor under the misconception of myth as outside the world of real experience. Even the highly regarded *Oxford English Dictionary* falls victim to such a tendency when it defines myth as "a purely fictitious narrative usually involving supernatural persons, actions, or events, and embodying some popular idea concerning natural or historical phenomena."[6] The OED proceeds to distinguish myth from legend, the latter implying a "nucleus of fact." This narrow positivist definition of myth holds that what is not true is that which cannot be empirically verified.

In traditional societies, myth played a central role in socialization. In many patriarchal societies, during secret initiation ceremonies, young boys would be told of the group's sacred myths describing the origins of the cosmos, the earth, man, and his tribe. According to philosopher Mircea Eliade, myth

> narrates a sacred history; it related an event that took place in primordial Time, the fabled time of the "beginnings"; . . . myth tells how, through the deeds of Supernatural Beings, a reality came into existence, be it the whole of reality, the Cosmos, or only a fragment of reality—an island, . . . a particular kind of human behavior, an institution. Myth, then, is always an account of a "creation"; . . . the myth is . . . a "true history," because it always deals with *realities*.[7]

For commentators such as Eliade, the distinction of facticity is moot in myth's case, for myth is always here, always alive; its very existence as communication between people within a culture demonstrates its essential "truth."

In traditional societies, myth was sacred social discourse. When one knew the sacred myth, one knew the origin of things and people and had the potential to control them. The knowledge of origins was traditionally experienced by enacting the myth in a ritual or ceremony which involved the active participation of tribal members in an extraordinary space set apart from everyday lived space, and within a carefully structured time frame (often commencing as night fell). The enactment of the myth was framed by singing or chanting; intense, often trancelike movement; and the wearing of sacred masks and/or elaborate costumes. The reciter of the myth and the listeners were forbidden to fall asleep or sit down.

The ritual in which the myth was enacted both engaged the individual's emotions and intellect and directed the individual toward the group, its past and its future. Myth thus became a "living tradition," supplying a model for human behavior and giving meaning and value to life. Myths are human phenomena (creations of the human mind and spirit); at the same time they are cultural phenomena (they effectively organize the way we, as a group, view portions of our world). Myths "live" in the sense that they enter what Eliade termed "sacred time"—a time which is both "primordial" and "indefinitely recoverable."

Contemporary Marxist social analysis, such as that of French critic Roland Barthes, clearly situates myth in the realm of the political by demonstrating the ways in which myth works to depoliticize ideology and intentionally camouflage social inequities existing within a culture. According to Barthes, "Myth has a double function: it points out and it notifies, it makes us understand something and it imposes it on us."[8] To Barthes, myth has an intentionality. Myth does not hide anything from us; rather, it distorts its subject and deceives us. Myth's meaning is grounded in history. It postulates "a kind of knowledge, a past, a memory, a comparative order of facts, ideas, decisions."[9] But, according to Barthes, myth "distances" this history by converting historical reality into an illusory image of the world as "nature." The natural order is produced by myth's making historical reality "pure" or "innocent" and thus unchallengeable (e.g., espousing the eternal character of empire, its sanctity, to counteract signs of its present visible internal decay). According to Barthes, myth "organizes a world which is without contradictions because it is without depth."[10] Myth is thus employed in the service of ideology—the process of transforming history into nature for the sake of the constant renewal of the dominant class.

Myth is not "action," as is revolution; rather, according to Marxist perspectives, it is "gesture" that seeks to camouflage, among other things, the human inequities evident in the history of the relationship of labor to capital. Myth, wrote Barthes, is essential on the political "right," especially as it legitimizes the value of order. The ultimate goal of myths "is to immobilize the world: they must suggest and mimic a universal order which has fixated once and for all the hierarchy of possessions. . . . Myths are . . . this insidious and inflexible demand that all men recognize themselves in this image, eternal yet bearing a date, which was built of them one day as if for all time."[11] I have adopted this latter use of the term "myth" as most relevant to the study of television.

While much "value-neutral" anthropological investigation of traditional cultures has attempted to elucidate the ways in which the individual is clearly linked to the culture through symbolic exchange, the main goal of which is to maintain the entire ecosystem rather than the individuals who constitute it, contemporary Marxist culture criticism has instead focused on basic values inherent in capitalist institutions that constitute an industrial or postindustrial culture whose "idealistic absolutes," as expressed through the culture's dominant media, obscure basic material facts of inequitable social relations in everyday experience.[12] Of particular interest to this analysis of television myth are such absolutes as progress in unproductive leisure and the ever-increasing commodification of life, facts in journalism, and truth and beauty in art.

In spite of their important differences, we do find a common thread which links the traditional sacred myths with their function of keeping alive and carrying to the future certain cultural traditions, and the secular myths that Barthes described as insidious vehicles employed to consolidate the power of the dominant capitalist class: their conservative social function as powerful cultural binding agents. They speak to us, openly or not, of tradition—of the proper order of institutions and people, and in the case of bourgeois myths, of hegemonic domination—of control of entire ways of thinking and being according to a capitalist imperative presented as commonsensical.

When we examine television texts in the chapters which follow, we will use myth analysis as the central critical strategy, in an attempt to locate the constructed meanings television produces for us. Central to this analysis will be an attempt to relate several contemporary myths through their "reciprocal intelligibility." By looking at their interrelationships, we will thus be able to reconstruct a more comprehensive system of ideological meaning. Our goal is the demythologization of ideology that will reveal the constructed nature of the representations of reality given to us by television, as well as highlight their suppressed ideological functions.[13] In the process, an outcome of this demythologization will be the opening up of alternative realities --representations rejected outright or coopted by the dominant television apparatus.

NOTES

1. Erich Fromm, comments from an interview included in *CBS Reports: You and the Commercial*, CBS Television Network, April 26, 1973.

2. Erich Fromm, *The Forgotten Language: An Introduction to the Understanding of Dreams, Fairy Tales and Myths* (New York: Rinehart & Co., 1951), pp. 156, 192ff.

3. Bill Nichols, *Ideology and the Image* (Bloomington: Indiana University Press, 1981), p. 1ff.

4. Richard J. Barnet and Ronald E. Muller, *Global Reach* (New York: Simon and Schuster, 1974)—A fascinating, detailed account of the role of the transnational corporation in contemporary world society.

5. Claude Levi-Strauss, *The Raw and the Cooked*, trans. by John and Doreen Weightman (New York: Harper & Row, 1969), pp. 16-17.

6. *Oxford English Dictionary*, 1933 ed.

7. Mircea Eliade, *Myth and Reality* (New York: Harper & Row, 1963), pp. 5-6.

8. Roland Barthes, "Myth Today," in *Mythologies* (New York: Hill and Wang, 1972), p. 117.

9. Ibid.

10. Ibid., p. 143.

11. Ibid., p. 155.

12. Nichols, *Ideology*, pp. 34-35.

13. For a lucid discussion of the important role of demythologization in formal television education, see Len Masterman, *Teaching About Television* (London: The Macmillan Press Ltd., 1980), pp. 1-20.

2

THE BIZ

Caution! Mythmakers at Work

In traditional societies, men, women, and children formed a collectivity in which the behavior of those who constituted the collectivity was regulated to conform to rigid cultural tradition. Physical survival was the paramount goal of such societies. The collectivity was responsible for the physical well-being of its members. To insure a collective future, populations were regulated by a variety of cultural ecological mechanisms, ranging from various ceremonies for the redistribution of wealth from tribal chieftains to tribal members, to infanticide. Spirituality was inexorably linked to the physicality of the surrounding environment: the unknown, the mysterious occupied much of the thinking and guided the acts of the group; over the next ridge, late at night at full moon, lies a new sensory experience, the unanticipated. The immediacy of life and death could not be ignored. The "art" of the time, reflected in ceremonial masks, rhythmic chants, totems, cave paintings, and other forms described the anxieties of the age as well as offered a common symbology through which the social unit might cohere and make it to the future. Nature was to be feared, to be marvelled at, and, above all, to be respected, for in nature was the key to understanding the origins of the group itself, and to understanding the necessary and proper relations among group members and between the clans that constituted the larger groups. Those charged with interpreting and transmitting the sacred stories of the group to future generations through their formulaic art were more like cultural historians than artists in any contemporary sense of the term.

As societies settled onto fixed territories and took up husbandry, increasingly hierarchical social, political, geographic, and economic constraints were placed on the group by ruling elites, both secular and religious; at certain levels of the society, semiautonomous "free" relations between individuals existed. Such relationships, however, were generally class-bound. An interesting relationship developed in feudal society between the artist and the art patron, whether king, pope, or wealthy landlord. In return for the enhancement of his dynastic prestige, the patron would employ and give nearly total creative freedom to an artist who provided him with the totems of power—works of art. The artist received ongoing financial support and a guaranteed audience for his or her works. Many artists thus became celebrities in their own right. The artist, however, was no longer making works for the collectivity. Rather, the works were intended for an elite community, whether that was the church, or the secular governors. The artist created visions of "the beautiful" that simultaneously displayed the material and incorporeal wealth of the owner of the vision and put all others in their class-bound places. The artist as culture worker in this less-than-symbiotic relationship was continually shortchanged by a relinquishing of equity in his or her work to the patron. As the mercantile class emerged from feudal society, a new system of patronage developed with its bourgeois element of the artwork as a commodity, linked to individual profit. This relationship continues today in a modified form in the artist/gallery owner/collector system. Its basic premise is the notion that spirituality—culture, refinement, or the cultivated mind—can be vested in the powerful, wealthy individual who rises above the mediocrity of the collectivity through the possession of art. The artist often becomes an ideological vehicle or tool to be bought in the quest for prestige and profits.

Today, in a corporate society fueled by the drives of advanced capitalism, art increasingly becomes a function of management. When corporations become art patrons, supplying the capital by which art is produced and distributed, prestige is measured less in terms of elitist art-circle membership than in bottom lines. Art is plugged in institutional advertisements as a sign of a corporation's sensitivity to such ideal absolutes as truth and beauty linked to the guiding spirit of the age. Corporate art patronage is equated with such values as trust and sincerity. The bottom line, however, speaks of investment in the company's future as it associates itself, through the sanctity of art, with the "good life" of culture and success. This association has come to include the underwriting and sponsorship of the more significant works of narrative art broadcast or cablecast on dominant television.

Beyond such visible displays of corporate culture, the contemporary art/business relationship is clearly manifested in the institutional world of television, where media entrepreneurs and the creative community—the latter comprised of both the fictional-entertainment creators and the news/documentary/public-affairs-entertainment creators, who produce, direct, write, and star in the unending flow of programs that fuel the television apparatus—co-exist in an uneasy but generally stable atmosphere of conflict and compromise. We easily recognize the archetypal corporate executives from both personal experience and contemporary lore. Clad in their three-piece black pinstripe suits, most of the men clean shaven and both the men and women with hair meticulously coiffed, they look confident, speak with a glib self-assurance, and yet remain intentionally unobtrusive. At the highest ranks in the communications-business hierarchy, they are extremely powerful, yet publicly invisible. These are the broadcast-network and local-broadcast-television and radio-station executives; the telefilm production-company executives; the program packagers or syndicators; the management of large cable-television corporations, both the distributors of packaged program services such as Home Box Office, and the multiple-system operators (MSOs) of cable-television franchises; the advertising executives; and the bankers who loan the whole system the necessary capital to keep it afloat. These are the men and women whose ultimate confirmation of being and hopes of becoming important rest on their ability to demonstrate to shareholders and investment analysts an ever-increasing corporate return on investment. We may not as clearly recognize the other group of businesspersons, many of whom seldom wear a tie or a three-piece suit, but instead wear work shirts and jeans to their offices—spaces strewn with papers, videotapes, film cans, beat-up old typewriters, and good reviews. These are the producers, writers, directors, and talent who must reconcile their art and their mercenary interests; these are the members of the so-called Hollywood creative community. With the help and the hype of their agents—"flesh peddlers," in the vernacular of the gossip columnists—these creative men and women operate in a commercial zeitgeist in which they try to sell their talents and ideas, but not their artistic souls, to the highest bidder in the popular-arts marketplace. When members of these groups get together or "have a meet," in the lingo of *Variety*'s showbiz reportage, or when they grant interviews to journalists anxious to cover the behind-the-scenes machinations of Hollywood, they describe their profession as "the entertainment business" rather than as "the television arts" and their creative output as "product" rather than as "works of art." Their terminology reveals the fundamental core of the world in which they have chosen to operate, a world in which the benchmarks of success are all too often monetary.

While business is common to both groups, so too is a consideration of art, at least as it joins the two major electronic-communications themes of content and profits. At the broadcast networks, broadcast-standards-and-practices departments, frequently denounced as censors by hostile program producers, review program ideas, story treatments, and series scripts for material they consider potentially questionable (i.e., ideas, visual representations, or aural statements that might upset some viewers and thereby scare away advertisers who have already committed to their program schedule). At local television stations, managers in charge of continuity acceptance will perform similar functions for programs and advertisements submitted for local airing. At cable MSOs, an executive at the headquarters level or, in some instances, a regional manager will make decisions regarding the advisability of carrying such cable-program services as the soft-core pornographic channels on their systems.

The program producers, who develop and oversee the execution of program ideas, are often ideologically at odds with those at the distribution end who rule on the acceptability of the material submitted. Questions of First Amendment rights of free speech are raised with great frequency. The distributor-businesspersons argue it is their right of free speech that is deserving of constitutional protection. The producer-business-persons argue it is the right of the viewer to have access to the widest range of ideas, which, above all else, must be ensured by the First Amendment.[1] But the reality behind this endless posturing over whose freedom should be protected is that the distributors exercise considerable freedom (especially under the current atmosphere of unregulation that motivates both the Federal Trade Commission, whose responsibility it has been since 1938 to protect consumers by policing "unfair or deceptive acts or practices in commerce," and the Federal Communications Commission (FCC), whose responsibility it has been since 1934 to ensure that broadcasters operated in "the public interest, convenience, and necessity"), while the television spectator is consulted only indirectly and cursorily through

A. C. Nielsen and Arbitron ratings systems that, wrote television critic Les Brown, "have neither point of view nor soul: they are merely static data dispassionately presented."[2] The "they" to which Brown referred are both the audience and the data by which the audience is described. Data and people merge in bottom lines as markets. The ratings deal in content givens and the past rather than in audience needs and desires for program materials that directly engage their everyday life activities and the future. Viewers suffer under the illusion of choice. Their program-selection decisions are tabulated and fed back into the production apparatus as justification for the continuation of a currently dominant program formula. Dominant television operates according to principles of audience familiarity and reassurance. It works overtime to maintain the loyalty of its markets.

In the daily commerce of electronic entertainment and information, there is little if any contemplation regarding impacts of these media on individuals, their culture, or their society. Yet, the mythmakers are at work, in both the business and the creative communities, the former using survey data and the results of content analyses, as well as the charted peaks and valleys produced by visceral response meters, and the latter employing intuition and proven aesthetic formulas to construct the endless flow of program material we see and hear. These mythmakers are bound to our culture's mythologies, reciting our myths to us, in television time and space, throughout the night and day. It is here, then, where we begin our quest to unravel the tightly woven core of myth that envelopes us. Since the reciters of the myths have achieved a special status in the society by virtue of some valued quality or skill, it seems only proper to focus first on the nature of that quality or skill.

THE MYTH OF ETERNAL PROGRESS AND THE GREAT AMERICAN DREAM

From downtown Burbank to midtown Manhattan, television is the work of extremely competitive, very clever urbanized men and women whose careers are made or broken in a highly volatile atmosphere involving, in the words of social scientist George Comstock, "the assembly of ideas and capital in pursuit of public adoration."[3] It can be convincingly argued that these television people, both business executives and program creators, become what they behold. Television work is done in New York City and in the Los Angeles area; the images, sounds, and pacing of television tend to reflect the distinctive auras of both ecologies, which are subsequently embedded in our collective consciousness, and which promise excitement, financial success, mobility, visibility, and emotional fulfillment—in short, the Great American Dream—the "good life" as described in the myth of eternal progress and characterized by the perpetual economic expansion of the society and the growth of personal material compensations. George Comstock astutely described what he termed the "tales of two cities":

> New York is a convergence of elites—fashion, finance, communications, the great corporations, and embodies . . . traditions of achievement and excellence. Los Angeles, is filled with as competitive, ruthless, hard-working a citizenry as any modern city in the world, nevertheless stands for the belief that there must be more to life. . . . Los Angeles is the capital of the conversion of personal vision to commerce.[4]

Like Comstock, critic Ben Stein sees the Los Angeles creative television community as comprising "a highly articulate, well-healed, highly motivated class on the move."[5]

Yet the myth of eternal progress has another, more human side, which is characterized by the desire for personal fulfillment that transcends material possessions. Both Stein and Comstock are quick to note, in this regard, the gulf separating the L.A. creative type and the New York corporate broadcast executive. According to Stein, "All of them [i.e., producers and writers], even those with millions of dollars, believed themselves to be part of a working class distinctly at odds with the exploiting classes—who, if the subject came up, were identified as the Rockefellers and multinational corporations."[6] It can be assumed from those comments that the producers and writers in Los Angeles count broadcast executives among the exploitative denizens of multinational corporate conglomerates. Stein's assessments are overgeneralized and simplistic, yet not without some merit. Comstock, in a more lucid assessment of the creative/business relationship in television, pinpoints the differences between the two groups as they relate to perceptions of art:

> The atmosphere exacerbated the dissension between network broadcasters and the Hollywood "hyphenates"—so-called because their jobs so frequently combine some portion of being a producer-director-writer—over the quality of programming. The Hollywood community,

already beset by restrictions on violence, fiercely deplored the confinement of serious drama to luxury display, such as in *Holocaust*....

The 1970s were new in the intensity of competition, but the values and interests of those who broadcast and those who create what is broadcast have never been in perfect congruence. The broadcasters are businessmen in the end even if they do not begin that way; anything else, given the way television is organized in America, would be gratuitous schizophrenia. The Hollywood people, however, bring to their jobs a residue of literary and journalistic intentions that have nothing to do with profits. They would like a system that provides opportunities to exercise originality, social concern—in short, a chance to parade themselves in the manner of poets or novelists. Whether rightly or wrongly, they believe that such opportunities have declined sharply over the past years. Of course, television does not encourage poor or clumsy work; the point at which these camps divide is whether what it does encourage is respectable, however skillfully executed. By the end of the 1970s, the Hollywood community, although turning out shows as steadily as ever, was bitterly saying so.[7]

Abby Mann is one of the highly acclaimed members of the Hollywood creative community who is outspoken in his denunciation of the business/creative relationship. Mann, who won both the Academy Award and the New York Film Critics Award for his first film script, *Judgment at Nuremberg*, developed the concept and the first three hours of script for the critically acclaimed 1980 Lorimar/NBC ratings-dud *Skag*. He also created *Medical Story*, won a national Emmy Award in 1973 for "The Marcus Nelson Murders," from which the series *Kojak* emerged, and directed the mini-series *King*, about the life of the Reverend Martin Luther King, which, like *Skag*, failed in the ratings wars. Mann, obviously a person with an abundance of talent by commercial standards, seems drawn to television's potential power as a medium of significant social statement, yet worries about its correlative power to promote blandness. He discussed his motivation for working in television:

I suppose I'm one of the very few writers that write both in motion pictures and in television. I get paid about five times as much for writing a motion picture script than for writing a television script. Now why do I do it? I do it because overnight something can become part of our culture. And I think . . . that television is crowded from morning to night with so much pap, I think it's a national disgrace. I think of my own experiences, and I can understand why people leave television.[8]

Mann has been sharply critical of NBC's treatment of *Medical Story*. In an interview with columnist Dan Lewis, Mann said, "I wanted it to be a hard-hitting, uncompromising series about the medical profession, but it wound up watered down."[9] In another interview, Mann talked at great length about his experiences with *Medical Story*:

> *Medical Story* became a cop-out and stilted and a bore. And it's very curious to me because the series did not only differ from the intention that I had. Somehow, in this inexorable stream of our society, it became the antithesis of the reasons I wrote them for. I was first approached by Columbia to do a medical anthology and call it *Medical Story*. Usually I shy away from those things, but a personal experience that had happened to myself and my wife made me want to do a story about doctors as they really are. You know, we've never really seen them as they really are. . . . This show is supposed to tell the truth. If you have an audience turning on a show, and it's not going to be that comforting father figure or Marcus Welby or the guy in *Medical Center*, then you need to have the truth. Nor do you have a show that gives them the comfort they need or the panacea that they're looking for. And perhaps one of the worst things that I saw was a piece done on malpractice which was fudged. . . . I felt I had an unknown collaborator in the AMA.[10]

Here is an excerpt from the show Mann referred to:

DOCTOR: In a way I'm kind of glad that you're here. It gives me a chance to say something about what happened.

MOTHER: We don't have anything against you, Doctor. That's why we're here: to say that we think you're a good doctor, a very good doctor. We don't have anything against you at all.

GIRL (22): I want to be independent. I want to get a dog. I want to go it on my own. I learned braille, but things being what they are, what kind of job do you think I could get?

MOTHER: Good worker, doctor. She really is.

GIRL: But you know what? For a blind person to get a good education, unless you have money. . . . Only thing I've got going for me is I'm blind. But it's the wrong minority. If you're a lousy WASP, you're last in line.

DOCTOR: O.K. I understand. You've got to do what you think is right. And you should be compensated. I don't argue that. But to say that it was malpractice when it wasn't—I've got to stand up and argue that.

GIRL: You think I don't know that. You saved my life. But this lawyer, he said we should go ahead and sue anyway. He said that the hospital is going to pay your insurance; you won't get hurt none really.

DOCTOR: No. He's all wet. It's more than just money that's at stake here.
    GIRL: But it's a way for me to get ahead.
MOTHER: He made it sound very . . . , he made it sound very attractive.

Mann commented on this excerpt from *Medical Story*:

Instead of a hard-hitting, searing thing, there emerged a middle-of-the road, bland, muddled, confused piece. Now when people talk to me and they say, 'Isn't it a pity that *Medical Story* has gone off?' I say I'm surprised it didn't go off before this. And I don't want it to be used as a whipping boy against other anthologies. It wasn't what it should have been. It deserved to go off.

While Mann may have felt this particular show was "confused" or "muddled," there is in fact a clarity of ideological purpose in the segment described above, a purpose not unlike that of the television apparatus itself. The segment described the truth behind the Great American Dream: The doctor makes big dollars, even if a few people are blinded in the process. The victims make money, even if the doctor is not at fault. The system, with its pecuniary mechanisms, frames the transaction. There is no individual responsibility, no individual accountability. This is especially true at the nexus of institutions and people who best represent success, including physicians, lawyers, and even television producers themselves.

Mann was also unhappy with the treatment of *Kojak* by Universal Television, the series producer. Universal, he argued, produced the police melodrama as a formulaic cops-and-robbers potboiler, whereas he had intended it "originally to show that cops should be watched." Elaborating on this theme, Mann said:

I wrote [the *Kojak* pilot] "The Marcus Nelson Murders" because I wanted people to understand how vulnerable we all are and that cops are human beings like everybody else. Now it's very interesting that *Kojak*, which is a show that I enjoy watching, has become exactly the reverse of what I intended. *Kojak* has become a series of programs, very entertaining, very professionally done, which I love to watch, but in which Kojak is imperturbable. He's always right, he's constantly disenfranchising blacks and minorities of their rights. . . . I just wonder . . . : If we presented the real life of cops in their many sides, would it be any less successful?[11]

Faced with the facts of his own work in television, Mann would unfortunately be forced to answer his own question in the affirmative. The facts include both his mini-series *King* and his ill-fated series *Skag*.

About his mini-series *King*, Mann noted with sadness: "It bothered me that for so many years, I couldn't get financing for a movie based on the life of King, and I had to tell him no one was willing to spend money to film his life. My great regret was that it finally materialized, but not before his death."[12] With *Skag*, Mann was given "complete freedom" by then NBC President Fred Silverman. Starring Karl Malden, *Skag* became the depressing but honest portrait of a middle-aged steelworker who, stricken by illness, can no longer take care of his family. The family begins to disintegrate as it struggles to survive. Mann was attempting to draw attention to a class of Americans who are grossly underrepresented on the home screen, and who, when they are allowed entry into television's dominant world of white, white-collar, middle-aged male protagonists, are seen either as bumbling bigots filled with malapropisms, or as the unintelligent but crafty inhabitants of smoke-filled bowling alleys.

It is noteworthy that one television work Mann condemned as being compromised by network/production-company subterfuges, *Kojak*, was a big ratings success, while the television projects he held most dear, and over which he had substantial creative control and could exercise and maintain artistic integrity, *King* and *Skag*, were ratings flops. Godlike physicians and macho law-and-order police live on in the mythic world of television's Great American Dream, where the dying are heroically brought back to life and wrongs are simplistically and quickly righted, while black leaders and blue-collar workers struggling in a realistic, untidy world of social injustice die quick video deaths, no matter the poignancy of the story or the skill of the storyteller.

It is ironic that this writer-director of "reality programming" dictates his scripts to three secretaries in a hilltop retreat, in the Hollywood Hills area of Los Angeles, where his meals are prepared by a personal chef and his drinks are served by a butler. One can thus live the American Dream while tangentially questioning its underlying structure. Television somehow easily accommodates such contradictions.

David Rintels, past president of the Writers Guild of America, West, has frequently written courtroom and political dramas. His television credits include the critically acclaimed 1975 television movie *Fear on Trial*, recounting the blacklisting of John Henry Faulk; episodes of *The Senator* on *The Bold Ones* series, for one of which he won the Writers Guild 1971 award for the best dramatic television script; and co-writer credits for the 1977 miniseries *Washington: Behind Closed Doors*. Rintels coordinated the successful campaign, led by the Writers Guild and producer Norman Lear, to have the courts overturn the FCC's "family-viewing-hour" rules.

Since the early 1970s, Rintels has been a very vocal critic of television networks' timidity in their prime-time programming. In 1972 he condemned commercial-television executives for rejecting scripts dealing with such topical, sensitive subjects as venereal disease, possible amnesty for Vietnam draft evaders, the U.S. Army's storing deadly nerve gas near large cities, antitrust issues, and drug companies' manufacture of drugs intended for the illegal drug market.[13] In 1977, in the midst of his family-hour battle, Rintels did not see any great improvement in prime-time entertainment television: "That's the television most of the people watch most of the time—seventy-five to eighty million people a night. And it is for many people a source of information about the real world. But the message they are getting is, I think, not an honest message."[14]

Rintels could point to numerous examples of this dishonesty from personal experiences. He described one such experience, at once both poignant and laughable:

Five or six years ago, while we were still in the Vietnam War, my collaborator and I wanted to do a show about a photographer, a Robert Capra type, a war photographer, one of those fellows who so loves to be at the scene of the action that you wonder what makes him tick. We went to a production company and to a network with the idea of doing a show about a photographer who follows some young soldiers, eighteen or nineteen years old, into their first combat. To boil a very long story down, a uniquely cocky kid—the photographer keeps a close track on him, and this young man gets separated from the rest of the platoon—he's a couple hundred yards away—and they run into a little trouble, and the photographer's taking pictures of him with a long lens. When they get back to camp—nobody was wounded or killed—the photographer develops the pictures, and the pictures show that the soldier was in fact behaving very bravely. The pictures were real, but he looks terrified. So the next day when they go out into combat and they get in more trouble, this time the guy was doing his job. He turns around to see where the photographer is, whether he is taking more pictures, and he turns once too often and gets killed. I'm boiling a more complicated story down. We sent that in to the network, which liked the story and wanted to do it as a ninety-minute show, but they said that Vietnam was terribly controversial, and we couldn't set the show in Vietnam. We didn't think there was anything controversial about the show—it was just a character study. They realized that it had to be a contemporary story, so "just relocate it in Spain." We weren't aware that there was a war being fought in Spain that week. We asked them what they had in mind and they said, "Well, very simple—we just change the soldier into a matador and when the bull charges, he'll look to see where the photographer is, and he'll do it once too often and get gored." That was television's way of dealing with the Vietnam War.[15]

Perhaps it is inevitable that in advanced capitalist America, the concept of struggle is thus divorced from political reality and from history. Rintels's proposed work is more than what he himself termed a "character study," for the background in which the drama was to have been enacted—a background called Vietnam—could never be politically or ideologically neutral. The seemingly unmessy, distancing metaphor of the bullfight could only barely camouflage the true meaning of the piece at a deeper cultural level—that of vanity, conquest, and the consequences of the confluence of the two. The political context of Rintels's story idea has much greater ideological significance than does the obscured network version of the same story idea, for the Rintels idea situates the individual's actions in a social history in which a particular set of value priorities is ascendant. Neither the soldier nor the cameraperson who documents the soldier's acts can escape history. Politically, the myth of eternal progress—of the successful conduct of a war of containment, of the civilized overcoming the savage in the steamy jungles of Southeast Asia—must not be exposed and thereby subverted by the watchful, objective eye of the journalist's camera. Technically, one can see the collusion of the photographic apparatus and the war it covers, as images of intense action and death are abstracted from their social contexts and used to sell newspapers and news magazines; with video, technique and the myth of eternal progress merge as instant transmission of scenes from the battlefront is presented to us via communications satellite for our instant edification. "Live" emphasizes the visceral at the expense of the cognitive. The myth, through images and sounds in the natural, seemingly unmediated context, is thereby enhanced through the apparatus of contemporary electronic communication.

Television lags behind the general culture. Teleplay writers and producers, who draw their story ideas from the well of contemporary culture, are deeply affected by television's retrograde posture. Gene important social issues in its dramatic-program fare, it should come as no surprise to anyone that it abhors the thought of addressing its own problems in any meaningful fashion.

The producer-writer team of Richard Levinson and William Link—whose credits include the highly successful *Columbo* detective series as well as the critically well-received television films *My Sweet Charlie, That Certain Summer*, and *The Execution of Private Slovik* —conceived, wrote, and produced an important 1977 television movie titled *The Storyteller*, which addressed the basic value system of Hollywood entertainment fiction, particularly those programs that employ violence—the so-called action shows. The central character of *The Storyteller*, television writer Ira Davidson (played superbly by veteran actor Martin Balsam), writes a world-premiere movie in which a series of fires is set. Immediately after watching the movie, a 12-year-old Seattle boy sets fire to his school building, is trapped in the flames, and burns to death. The press pursues the story and Davidson, who came from a poor family, who never went to college, and who began his career as a writer of radio drama, is forced to deal with the issue of televised violence, his role and responsibilities as a television writer, and his own personal value system as a wealthy but hard-working creative type, with a $200,000 house and a $10,000 swimming pool, who has come to perceive art as a job.

On one level, this telefilm unfolds as a highly articulate video essay examining the role of televised violence in our culture. On another level, it questions the entire structure of the civil society. Levinson and Link intercut Davidson's attempts to cope with his responsibilities as a television worker with a series of staged interviews in which a variety of persons, from academicians to the police, to electronic journalists, to housewives, share with us their personal, idiosyncratic perspectives on the impact of televised violence on society. Davidson, after lengthy soul searching, is forced to concede that his television work may indeed have deleterious effects on some people. His moral awakening is a painful, slow process. Immediately following the boy's death, when asked, by a reporter at a news conference, where he thought his responsibilities lie, Davidson replied, "To write as well as I can [about anything] within the bounds of good taste." Later, however, he was not so certain about the social implications of his creative freedom. Could his "little ideas," his stories that seemed so harmless to him, of good guys always winning and bad guys always losing, really kill people, that is, trigger violent responses in disturbed viewers?

Roddenberry, writer-producer of *Star Trek*, expressed
tration with television's reluctance to face the world in \
ates with such potential impact:

> Drama, of all the forms of communication, is the one tl
> reaches out and . . . makes you . . . feel, identify, hurt. Had
> able to write a drama of that type about what was happer
> Vietnamese peasant, or an American boy over there, and for
> audience] to become that dirt, that mud, that earth, I think
> in Vietnam probably could have been shortened.[16]

Roddenberry made the inevitable connections between r
cess, and "artistic freedom" that frame the television trans

> Most of the improvements [in network acceptance of content
> been in sexual areas. . . . But really, on basic things like the ind
> military complex, morality of the United States, the selling of
> ons to countries all over the world—the things that writers w
> talk about—you really can't get that on television, . . . at le
> drama. Of course, if you get what [Norman] Lear had and you
> show [that's] number one in the ratings, you can push the net
> around, because you've got a threat. . . . God help you, thou
> you've got a show that's just hanging on the edge.[17]

Alan Alda, actor, writer, and director of *M*A*S*H*, pui
a bit more philosophically: "A very big problem for us as a
a nation, as a culture, has been the idea that success in li
monetary success; that aggression is always at someone's
that you only succeed through someone else's loss."[18] In
vision microcosm of advanced capitalism, profundity is cc
with profitability. "Intellectuals" are the supreme marketin
tives. Financial gain at the three networks is inversely proport
our loss of authentic portrayals of our common lived experien
Safety is the key word in all this. Through observation o
wood story conferences—from which television scripts emer
blinding frequency as codes are converted to formulas to fe
nonstop demand for programming—critical scholar Paul Espin
duced a number of rules or "text-building practices" related
ways producers perceived their audiences. Rule four in Espi
scheme is particularly instructive: "Don't divide the audience
don't debate issues in the work. Espinosa observed, "Any issue
is likely to divide, and thus diminish the audience is viewed as a
to be avoided."[19] Since television has been so reluctant to e

The recurring theme of responsibility is raised in a poignant scene later in the drama as Davidson visits the home of the dead boy's mother, Mrs. Eberhardt. Ira refuses to shoulder the blame, arguing that television is a corporate art involving writer, director, actor, studio, and network. If responsibility must be accepted, it should be shared. But Mrs. Eberhardt will not accept this rationale. She frames the problem succinctly. The show *begins* with the writer, she points out. It is *his* show.

In the sanguine environment of corporate entertainment, where progress springs eternal, the problematic is attributed to a temporary failure of the *system*. Questions of individual responsibility are easily deflected—no one person is to blame.

The Storyteller, aired on NBC, was inspired by the controversy surrounding a 1974 NBC television movie, *Born Innocent*, in which a teenage girl in a detention center was gang raped with a broom handle by other inmates. Four days after the TV rape, a nine-year-old girl was sexually assaulted with a beer bottle by four children. The victim's parents brought suit against NBC, charging that the assault was a direct result of the airing of *Born Innocent*.[20]

The Storyteller was a highly unusual instance of television's questioning itself in public. Ira Davidson, a fictional embodiment of the Great American Dream, represented the sell out. In the end, having come to grips with his own personal values, Davidson was forced to recognize the emptiness of the Dream, and acted to salvage what was left of his own self-respect.

How did this film ever make it to the small screen in the first place? According to *New York Times* television critic John J. O'Connor, "They [Levinson and Link] simply hung around network corridors long enough to wear down program executives into giving them exasperated approval."[21] In fact, NBC was the second network to be offered the project. When Levinson and Link brought the idea to another network, "they were told that perhaps the program could open on a raging fire instead of an interview about violence, or failing that, perhaps the boy could simply shoot someone and, then, there could be a terrific scene with Ira visiting him in jail."[22] Levinson and Link stood their ground and provided viewers with a rare, honestly self-reflexive examination of the operation of the system.

The system operates in a constant tension as viewers' needs for basic information, which helps ground us in a comprehensible social world, collides with the economic constraints of profitability. No more clearly is this manifested than in the electronic news-gathering process. In many ways the Hollywood entertainment producer and the New York news producer face the same battles of access to the dominant channels of distribution. Both must constantly face the inevitable compromises between communication ideals and pecuniary realities. While the news-gathering-and-reporting process is hypothetically sacrosanct by virtue of its First Amendment free-press protection, and while the television networks provide insulation for their news operations by appointing a corporate officer, at the presidential level, to oversee the news division, there can be little doubt that entertainment values constantly creep into both the determination of what is newsworthy and the actual presentation itself. Not so rare is the electronic journalist who lambasts his or her own corporate organization for its sacrificing of the high principles of journalistic practice in favor of profits. Fred Friendly's story is a provocative case in point.

From 1964 to 1966, Friendly (a pioneer, with Edward R. Murrow, in TV-news documentaries) was president of CBS News. He resigned on February 15, 1966, in a dispute with CBS management, when it decided to broadcast a rerun of *I Love Lucy*, instead of carrying, live, former Ambassador to the Soviet Union George Kennan's testimony before the U.S. Senate Foreign Relations Committee, during its hearings on the Vietnam War. The background of this incident, recounted at length in Friendly's book *Due To Circumstances Beyond Our Control*, is itself worthy of documentary reportage.

Friendly called the Kennan testimony "an event of overriding national importance."[23] Although CBS President Frank Stanton believed CBS reporters were doing too much editorializing about the Vietnam War, he did sanction four CBS *Vietnam Perspective* broadcasts in August 1965. In a major CBS reorganization in 1966, the president of CBS News was informed he would no longer report directly to corporate President Stanton or to Board Chairman William Paley, but, rather, would answer to John Schneider, group vice president in charge of broadcast operations, in essence a midlevel manager. News judgment, traditionally made at the news-division level or at the highest corporate-management echelons, would now be made at CBS by people with entertainment or sales backgrounds. Friendly was understandably concerned with this switch in internal corporate policy. Schneider refused to carry the Kennan testimony live due, according to Friendly, to the probable loss of about $175,000 in ad revenues and to Schneider's assessment that housewives wished to see their soap operas and game shows. NBC did carry the Kennan testimony (ironically covered by CBS's pool cameras) live at ten o'clock on the morning of February 10, 1966. CBS carried reruns of *I Love Lucy, The Real McCoys,* and *Andy of Mayberry.* Friendly asked for a 90-minute prime-time special on the hearings, but received no reply from Schneider.

Friendly noted with bitterness, "Of course, the truth was that if we'd had a sponsor willing to pick up the bill for the Vietnam hearings or if the soap operas' sponsors had agreed to stay with us, there would have been no problem."[24] Friendly quoted from a 1958 speech by his old friend and journalistic coworker, Murrow, delivered to the Radio-Television News Directors' Association:

> One of the basic troubles with radio and television news is that both instruments have grown up as an incompatible combination of show business, advertising, and news. . . . The top management of the networks, with a few notable exceptions, has been trained in advertising, research, sales, or show business. But, by the nature of the corporate structure, they also make the final and crucial decisions having to do with news and public affairs.
>
> Frequently, they have neither the time nor the competence to do this.[25]

Ultimately, Friendly was to lay the blame on something larger than Jack Schneider: "The system," Friendly wrote, "had made the decision; Schneider was merely in charge of the stoplight."[26] He added, "Given their choice as responsible citizens, Paley, Stanton, Schneider and every member of the board . . . would have elected to broadcast the hearings. But a system designed to produce profits to respond to the stock market, which in turn responds to ratings, was governed more by concern for growth and earnings than for news responsibility."[27]

Business judgment has triumphed over news judgment, as it has over dramatic judgment. As Friendly noted, "The yield from the detergent, deodorant, bleach or food advertisers who possess the daytime schedule . . . is the principal reason why no serious programming can be sustained for any length of time during those hours."[28] This proposition is even more evident in 1984 than it was in 1966. An examination of ABC's daytime profitability is instructive: ABC controls more than 50 percent of the total daytime network advertising dollars, with its commanding 1982 ratings lead for the early morning (*Good Morning America*) and the entire afternoon, and with its soap lineup of *Ryan's Hope, All My Children, One Life to Live,* and the blockbuster *General Hospital*; *Hospital* rakes in a whopping $27,800 per 30-second commercial. According to *Forbes* magazine: "An average 30-second prime-time commercial fetches $75,000, compared with $16,000 for daytime. But more of that revenue is clear profit because daytime programming is so much cheaper to produce. A half-hour prime-time show can cost $350,000. For the same money, ABC can produce a full week of hour-long episodes of a soap opera."[29] A major crisis, national or international, such as an assassination of a political leader, will cause the network to break away from their profitable daytime schedules. But the critical, if often rambling public debates, such as that regarding the Kennan testimony, are rarely given the national exposure they deserve. A new definition of the informed citizenry, it appears, is emerging from the mythic world of television—a citizenry who will wildly scramble to a neighborhood shopping mall, to swoon over a macho soap-opera hero whose amorous exploits they have memorized from *Soap Opera Digest*, but who won't walk around the corner to participate in a political debate on issues of local importance. Network and local broadcasters perceive this and program accordingly.

In the Great American Dream, the notion of personal freedom transcends the notion of social responsibility, even when that freedom is really the unfreedom to be blithely entertained while being simultaneously ill- or misinformed. Ironically, what emerges as the Great American Dream is freedom from responsibility—either as a voter, as an assembly-line worker, as a media manager, or even today as an electronic journalist. We may register a vote, but do not comprehend the ideological ramifications of that vote. We crank out, through an advanced industrial system of multiple-serial production, vast amounts of inferior goods. We make great profits from popular art, much of which has the very real potential to create lasting negative social effects. And we offer up entertainment and call it news. Barthes called this general state of affairs "the quantification of quality." Qualitative elements of a life give way to quantity; substance, to technique and effect. Barthes wrote, "Bourgeois dramatic art rests on a pure quantification of effects: a whole circuit of computer appearances establishes a quantitative equality between the cost of a ticket and the tears of an actor or the luxuriousness of a set: what is currently meant by the 'naturalness' of an actor, for instance, is above all a conspicuous quantity of effects."[30]

CBS News correspondent Charles Kuralt, who has achieved great critical acclaim for his "On The Road" segments on the CBS evening news and who has so successfully anchored *CBS Sunday Morning*, is certainly no Marxist, yet he would nevertheless agree with Barthes's assessment, at least as it applies to contemporary television-news gathering and reporting. Kuralt recently wrote:

> The "quick news" idea has been preached for years by the shabby news consultants who have gone about peddling their bad advice to small television stations. They have never given a thought to the needs of the viewer, or to the reason the news is on the air in the first place—namely, that this kind of country cannot work without an informed citizenry. The ninety-second news story does not serve the people; neither do the thirty- and twenty-second stories, and that's where we're headed. Fast. With bells and graphics.
>
> In this sort of journalism there is something insulting to the viewer. . . . We are saying to this person, "You are a simpleton with a very short attention span," or "You are too much in a hurry to care about the news anyway. . . ." The networks are in the news ratings race. . . .
>
> The best minds in television news are thinking more about packaging and promotion and pace and image and blinking electronics than about thoughtful coverage of the news. I have worked in the field for twenty-five years and every year I thought we were getting better. Suddenly, I think we're getting worse.[31]

So far we have documented the thoughts of a few highly respected, serious workers in both the Hollywood creative-dramatic community and the New York electronic-news community. These people, through personal experience, have witnessed the inexorable movement of television away from serious drama and provocative news reporting and toward frivolous entertainment programming characterized by simplified story ideas and news reports, in which the attention grabbers are no longer engaging human dramas, of either the fictional or the real-life documentary kind, but, rather, car chases, sophisticated special effects, and strategically exposed flesh.

We now turn to the men and women, the network representatives with whom the Hollywood creative people seem to have the greatest contact, and with whom they seem to engage in a never-ending conflict—these are the West Coast directors of standards and practices, whose work it is to rule on the acceptability of the taped program material submitted to the network by the creative community. One such network executive was NBC's Jack Petry, who held his post from 1970 to 1981. Admittedly working for traditionally the most morally conservative of the networks, Mr. Petry, in an interview for the *New York Times*, noted that "there's no subject that the industry should avoid, as long as it is handled tastefully."[32] What is "tasteful"? To Mr. Petry, "hell" and "damn" are acceptable, while other four-letter expletives, such as those in George Carlin's "Dirty Words" monologue, are not; and showing "two people in bed in an adulterous situation who have obviously just finished or are just starting to make love," while against his personal moral standards, is acceptable if tastefully done—that is, "two people in a double bed can embrace and we'll fade out and go to a sunset."[33] Like Chauncey Gardiner, the protagonist of Jerzy Kosinski's novel *Being There*, we are excluded from the full range of human emotions and passions in our little televised dramas as we dissolve to a hackneyed visual metaphor or cut to a commercial where a similar drama, using the same structural techniques with an abbreviated time signature, is played out with the same results.

Petry took an early retirement from NBC because, in his words, "I was not enjoying what I was doing any longer. . . . I was being second-guessed from all quarters—from the New York management to people outside the network."[34] Petry was the network official who gave the go-ahead for *Born Innocent*, and many observers feel that television movie's airing and its subsequent impact, including the lawsuit discussed above, led to Petry's withdrawal from the NBC family. In the pressure cooker of corporate life, the men and women who must guard their country's morals and politics from the whims and liberal values of many of Hollywood's producers and writers often find themselves caught in the middle. Significant art is never safe; and while their allegiance is to their corporation, they cannot help being influenced by their role as mediators between business and art.

In spite of the philosophical differences between those who make the programs and those who distribute and promote them, the fact remains that members of both communities engaged in the lucrative television enterprise serve quite well as examples of the Great American Dream of acquisition of material goods, power, and status. CBS President Thomas Wyman reportedly earns $920,000 a year in salary plus a $1 million bonus he received for joining the company.[35] Gene Jankowski, president of the CBS Broadcast Group since 1977, earns an annual salary in excess of a half-million dollars. The presidents of successful independent Hollywood telefilm-production companies are multimillionaires. A television-series producer makes up to

$10,000 a week for a half-hour comedy series, and up to $25,000 a week for a one-hour television-adventure series. Writers under contract to production companies earn well over $100,000 a year. A television writer may make $25,000 or more for a one-hour television-adventure-series script. These people, who may think of themselves as hard-working "regular" people, are by no means members of the proletariat. Their attitudes and values, reflected in their everyday lives and in their television work, are reflections of the dream they help to define—a dream evidenced in their Rolls Royces cruising Malibu and in their Fleetwood limos parked on the Avenue of the Americas.

Is it any wonder then that the central myth that reveals the traditions and guides the destiny of the television community is the myth of eternal progress? According to this myth, anything is possible. Opportunities for success are available for the taking; all that's needed is a little talent, a little intuition, a lot of hard work, and a dash or two of chutzpah. But the myth deflects the questions of personal responsibility alluded to above; it allows for the acknowledgment of poor judgment in an occasional instance, but immediately offers a return to "business as usual." This is a form of what Barthes termed "the inoculation," i.e., "admitting the accidental evil of a class-bound institution the better to conceal its principal evil."[36] In the case of *Born Innocent*, the evil is portrayed as an errant "programming decision." In reality, *Born Innocent*, although itself critically acclaimed, signalled a trend in television to garner large profits through a depiction of titillating violence. As it is manifested in contemporary television and other popular entertainments, the myth offers us " a demented carnival of topping acts [and] hustling hype"[37] under the rubric of progress.

The Great American Dream of material quantity is promised to all, but achieved by few (whose ranks, incidentally, include the television elite who reproduce the dream). According to Larry Gelbart, the highly successful former writer and co-producer of CBS's *M*A*S*H*, the creative community cannot be held blameless, as much as it would like to, if television falls far below its creative potential, for television's creative community, "year in and year out, for its own reasons, plays ball. They do not—and I don't know how they could—insist on diversity in programming, on quality in programming. I think we all have our narrow interests, and we find ourselves doing things we don't necessarily like for wages which we very much do like."[38]

The creators play ball in a game in which the rules are devised and enforced by the owners and managers of large corporate conglomerates, who specialize in the distribution of entertainment for profit. And the profitable view is the prevailing view.

BUSINESS, SCIENCE, AND ART—THE FORMULA

On July 17, 1982, *New York Times* correspondent Sally Bedell revealed that CBS programming executives had for five years been using an audience-research technique, devised by a British research group, called TAPE (television audience program evaluation).[39] The TAPE formula uses a detailed list of factors to evaluate one-paragraph descriptions of ideas for television movies submitted to the network. These factors include the race, sex, and occupation of the protagonist, the setting, and the program genre, and were developed by a firm, TAPE, Ltd., over a long period through an analysis of telefilms that achieved high ratings. Three trained TAPE analysts in London translate their evaluations of television-movie ideas into success scores, with a score of 100 as a median. CBS dropped the TAPE research following reports that Hollywood telefilm producers complained to CBS executives that such a formulaic determination of content would stifle creativity. Although ABC and NBC do not buy the TAPE service, they both conduct audience surveys, using random-sampling techniques, by telephone and at shopping malls, to elicit viewer response to film ideas. All three networks test series pilots among selected audiences in theater settings such as Preview House in Los Angeles. CBS tests its programs among subjects in its New York City headquarters; its tests are conducted by in-house researchers.

While CBS executives played down the use of the TAPE formula, they did admit to Bedell that "it had been a generally reliable guide to the success of films made for television."[40] What, exactly, did the TAPE formula tell CBS about the most and the least desirable central characters, settings, and genres of movies made for television? Bedell gleaned the following description from a 12-page CBS memorandum distributed to management regarding the use of the service: The most desirable/successful central characters in the made-for-television film are white Anglo-Saxon Protestant males, followed by ethnic types such as American blacks, Mexicans, Jews, and Italians. Blue-collar workers and the "little guys" fighting the system are seen as desirable character types (tell that to Abby Mann). Orientals are undesirable central characters (i.e., viewers won't watch them). Another undesirable character type is the person of superior intellect who is portrayed as cunning and able to manipulate others without "getting his hands dirty." A somewhat curious representative of this character type is the "serious" composer. Desirable settings include islands where fantasies can be fulfilled (you might have guessed), and settings related to World War II, while England is among the settings seen as undesirable (although might England in World War II somehow be seen as moderately desirable?). A highly desirable genre is reportedly the "action-adventure" based on some thrilling tale that often involves revenge as a motive for murder. Undesirable genres include the musical and the science-fiction tale.

While it is disturbing that this research regime is used to judge program ideas in the first place, what is more depressing is the encouragement of closure—its delimitation of the creative space in the medium. It can be argued that such research activity produces a "chilling effect" in the creative community. If you know which ideas have very little chance of passing the initial network-screening procedure, which is predetermined, you will bury those story ideas, often subconsciously, before they ever find their way onto a piece of paper.

Conversely, the ideas that do make it are likely to be those rather vacuous, formulaic story lines, with the requisite action or sexual innuendo, that have registered strong among an audience. That audience is frequently a sample audience that previews a pilot episode of a network series in a screening theater such as ASI (Audience Survey Institute) Market Research's Preview House on Sunset Boulevard in Los Angeles.

ASI's executive vice president, Roger Seltzer, described the consumer-research organization's conception of the testing apparatus: "In the television industry, the consumer product is a television program. And what we're doing is providing for members of the industry some response from the consumers, and allowing consumers to have an input, allowing [a response by] television viewers who always complain that they have no say as to what goes on and what goes off the air."[41]

Writer David Rintels argued that the previewing process does not admit a cognitive response: "Preview House institutionalizes popularity at the expense of quality. Four-hundred people a night are given tickets to come there, and they sit with dials in their hands. The dials go from 'very dull' to 'very good' as if dull is the opposite of good, and they twist the dials as the show comes on. Their visceral responses are channeled into a computer which then gives a rating, and the higher the rating, the more likely it is that the show will get on the air."[42]

The dial provides quantitative information, on a second-by-second basis, as to how the sample audience is reacting to the image/sound combination flashed on the screen in front of them. It provides a measure of "flow," according to Seltzer, that allows the creative people to adjust the show's pacing if needed. Information about characterizations is provided by information from questionnaires administered following the screening and by monitoring the small-group discussions that ensue.

Danny Arnold, creator, writer, and producer of *Barney Miller*, scoffed at the purported aesthetic value of such testing, recounting an experience he had personally had at Preview House:

> We were testing a show, and on the chart that came out, the graph, the numbers showed the peaks where a laugh was present. Suddenly the needle took an enormous swing like an electrocardiogram that had reached a peak, and then after the laugh it would fall off and there would be some dialogue and then another laugh, and so forth. And he showed me this chart and he said, "You see all these peaks and valleys; . . . now if you could only take out the valleys, you'd have just one enormous peak." And I said, "But you don't seem to understand that in order to reach that peak, you must have the valley." The fundamental lesson of this is there is a straight line preceding a joke. They wanted to remove the straight lines. Now it's difficult for a writer or a creator to talk to somebody whose total orientation is numbers and peaks and valleys and lines and . . . you know, a thirty-five-year-old who's got turned-up toenails and this kind of economic area—he wants that; and here's a lady with a red hat who has three children, two of whom have left home! I can't deal with that. A creator has to write what he thinks is either funny or dramatic or whatever it happens to be, and then it's our job to convince the people at the networks that a show like that belongs on the air.[43]

Seltzer's answer to Arnold's complaint is a feeble, if expected one: "Whoever buys a television program, whether you consider it to be the network or a sponsor or whoever it is, they're using that program as a vehicle [to make money]. It may be unfortunate that television isn't totally an artistic medium; you have to consider it a commercial medium that makes use of art. The art that is successful on television has to be art that is acceptable to large numbers of the viewers."[44]

This entire question of art versus data is eloquently expressed in a scene from *The Storyteller*. Writer Ira Davidson and production company executive Arthur Houston are screening an action show at the fictional TV Sampling Center. They are standing in a darkened screening room overlooking the theater. A standard mystery-type sound track drones in the background. Closeups of hands turning dials, as suspense builds on the screen, are intercut with scenes in the pilot episode—an extreme closeup of a hand putting a silencer on a gun barrel, taking aim at a player on a tennis court below. Of the 400 people watching this pilot, 149 are actually hooked up to the data gathering system. Ira, noting that the network research people in the screening room are not watching the show, is informed by Arthur that they are only concerned with the data displayed on print-outs which register the sample audience's "like-dislike" responses. Ira finds this insulting. We cut to a point of view, Ira watching a typical car chase complete with the requisite loud screeching tires. We cut to a needle on a graph rising to the "very good" level. Ira is somber. He acknowledges that "people like it."

Arthur defends both the data-gathering "marketing tool" and the action sequence which turns the audience on. Neither, he argues, is immoral. They simply represent "legitimate dramatic conflict involving an audience."

Ira, his journey toward self-realization nearly completed, is not buying into Arthur's traditional Hollywood rationalization for profiteering. Instead, Ira offers the analogy that kids love candy, which is nevertheless bad for their teeth. But Arthur's retort, mired in democratic pluralism, is, for the moment, the last word: "Unless I run for King, I'm not sure I have a right to decide what's good for them."

Arthur's notion of quantitative democracy admits of no personal responsibility, no clearly articulated personal values. It is an impersonal vision ultimately lacking in compassion.

To use scientific tools in the service of art under the umbrella of big business is to determine future ideas from the limited ideas that proved commercially acceptable in the past, rather than to explore new creative directions. To accept the profitable past as the future is no doubt a safe stance from a businessperson's viewpoint, and an unimaginative one.

The TAPE formula and the Preview House experience reflect an even deeper symptom of our contemporary cultural malaise, namely, the reliance on technique to bring an artificial order to an otherwise

vital, disorderly world. As TAPE is a formula for evaluating television movies, so too are the movies themselves formulas—success breeds imitative success, while technique breeds more technique. The ultimate effect of technique in the service of entertainment is the legitimation of the existing relations of production in our society. Technique, a manifestation of the Great American Dream, is in the end intentionally stultifying and controling. In the eyes of the mythmakers, the viewer is not a spectator but a consumer, the transaction is not art but product, and the benefit is not enlightenment but profitability. Power is vested not in the art object but in the capitalist institution that profits from the sale of product.

The hard technical facts of our subservience to the stifling regime of profits and aesthetic dullness are camouflaged by mythical constructions of freedom as expressed in the notions of democracy and decentralization of decision making. While it may appear that we have an input into the programming decisions that determine the nature of our daily dose of television, the individual is in fact united with the collective television audience through the conscious planning of efficient corporations, including production companies, network program distributors, and audience-research firms. As social critic Jacques Ellul put it, the individual "is no longer a man in a group, but an element of the group."[45] We are data. We are incorporated into the formula. This is the enduring legacy of our electronic mythmakers.

NOTES

1. This categorization of producer and distributor is admittedly overly simplistic. Local stations, cable companies, and television networks do produce some of their own program material as well as distribute other program services, and many large independent program producers do syndicate their own programs to both domestic and overseas markets. Nevertheless, the philosophical tendencies toward one or the other basic position (large profits versus artistic integrity) can be distinguished according to one's perceived role in this process. In a commercial system such as that existing in the United States and in a large number of countries throughout the world, the boundaries become increasingly blurred. In a business environment such as that of the popular arts, in which an artist is allowed to work within certain confined creative parameters and, as the old showbiz saw goes, "is worth only as much as his last picture," if your work doesn't sell, you don't work.

2. Les Brown, *Television: The Business Behind the Box* (New York: Harcourt Brace Jovanovich, 1971), p. 58.

3. George Comstock, *Television in America* (Beverly Hills: Sage Publications, 1980), p. 71.

4. Ibid., p. 76.

5. Ben Stein, *The View from Sunset Boulevard* (New York: Anchor Press/Doubleday, 1980), p. 113.

6. Ibid., p. 10.

7. Comstock, *Television*, p. 24.

8. A conversation with Abby Mann on the program *You Should See What You're Missing*, produced by television station WTTW, Chicago, 1977.

9. Dan Lewis, "Abby Mann Ponders Fate," *Athens* (Ohio) *Messenger, Fun Magazine*, July 20-26, 1980.

10. Conversation with Abby Mann on *You Should See What You're Missing*.

11. Ibid.

12. Lewis, "Mann Ponders Fate."

13. David W. Rintels, "Not for Bread Alone," *Performance* 3 (July/August 1972):53.

14. Conversation with David Rintels on the program *You Should See What You're Missing*, produced by television station WTTW, Chicago, 1977.

15. Ibid.

16. Conversation with Gene Roddenberry on *TV For Better or Worse*, produced by WCVE-TV, Richmond, Va., 1976.

17. Ibid.

18. Conversation with Alan Alda on *TV For Better or Worse*.

19. Paul Espinosa, "The Audience in the Text: Ethnographic Observations of a Hollywood Story Conference," *Media, Culture and Society* 4 (1982):77-86.

20. NBC v. Niemi, 435 U.S. 1000 (1978). The U.S. Supreme Court refused to review a California court decision dismissing the suit brought by Niemi against NBC. However, the case and the movie, *Born Innocent* are credited with prompting the networks to establish family viewing time in 1975.

21. John J. O'Connor, "TV: Violence—'Storyteller' Asks 'What is a Writer's Responsibility?'" *New York Times*, December 5, 1977, p. 76.

22. Ibid.

23. Fred Friendly, *Due To Circumstances Beyond Our Control* (New York: Random House, 1967), p. 213.

24. Ibid., p. 239.

25. Quoted in ibid., p. 251.

26. Ibid., p. 243.

27. Ibid., p. 257.

28. Ibid., p. 263.

29. Steven Flax, "Staying Tuned to Tomorrow," *Forbes*, July 19, 1982, p. 69.

30. Roland Barthes, *Mythologies* (New York: Hill and Wang, 1972), p. 154.

31. Charles Kuralt, "The New Enemies of Journalism," *Channels*, April/May 1982, pp. 61-62.

32. Diane Wagner, "He's Kept Pace With America's Mores, Almost," *New York Times*, March 29, 1981, p. D31.

33. Ibid.

34. Ibid.

35. Stratford P. Sherman, "CBS Places Its Bets on the Future," *Fortune*, August 9, 1982, p. 72.

36. Barthes, *Mythologies*, p. 150.

37. Geoffrey Wolff, "Where the Action Was," *New York Times Book Review*, July 4, 1982, p. 72.

38. Conversation with Larry Gelbart on *You Should See What You're Missing*.

39. Sally Bedell, "CBS Drops a Formula Involving Race for Evaluating TV Film Ideas," *New York Times*, July 17, 1982, p. 44.

40. Ibid.

41. Conversation with Roger Seltzer on *You Should See What You're Missing*.

42. Conversation with David Rintels on *You Should See What You're Missing*.

43. Conversation with Danny Arnold on *You Should See What You're Missing*.

44. Conversation with Seltzer.

45. Jacques Ellul, *The Technological Society* (New York: Vantage Books, 1964), p. 335.

3

ADVERTISING

The Medium Is the Mirage

ADVERTISING'S ROLE IN CONTEMPORARY CULTURE

Nothing serves the cause of advanced capitalism more effectively and with more humility than does advertising. In print, on television and radio, and on billboards, sandwich boards and tee shirts, the mythic character of the combination of words, images, and sounds, and the various ideologies employed in these advertisements fuel the machines and stimulate the psyches of a highly acquisitive people. Ads cajole, boast, massage us, assault us with aesthetic projectiles, whisk us away through time and space on a magic-carpet ride to exotic cultures, offer us their approximations of eternal youth, and promise us "relief." Ads are selling us not only a product or service or politician—they are selling us a way of life. As such, they point explicitly and unambiguously to our culture; they do not apologize for either their presence or their behavior. They are self-assured and secure.

No clearer conception of the role of advertising in contemporary American culture has been presented than that of anthropologist Jules Henry in his seminal book *Culture Against Man.*[1] Henry, an authentic cultural observer, admitted his bias against our advanced capitalist society. He argued that "advertising is an expression of an irrational economy that has depended for survival on a fantastically high standard of living incorporated into the American mind as a moral imperative."[2] Henry ascribed a didactic intentionality to advertisers: "As a quasi-moral institution, advertising, like any other basic cultural

institution anywhere, must have a philosophy and a method of thinking. . . . I have dubbed this method of thought *pecuniary philosophy*."[3]

Henry proceeded to develop an entire lexicon to describe advertising as an institution and as an art form. We will briefly examine
that language and its rationale below.

Henry claimed that a new conception of truth emerges through
advertising—that of "pecuniary pseudotruth." This curious verity is
actually a false statement made to sound or look or read as if it were
true, but is not intended to be believed. It is true if it sells products
or services; it is false if it does not. For example, is it literally true
that "a woman in Distinction foundations is so beautiful that all other
women want to kill her"?

Henry dubbed one specific type of pecuniary pseudotruth "parapoetic hyperbole." Hyperbole is exaggeration. Parapoetic hyperbole
is an exaggerated claim employing high-flown figures of speech that
resemble, but are not, poetry. As a pecuniary pseudotruth, no reasonable person is expected to believe such a claim, but, rather, merely to
purchase the product or service. Revlon's 1960s campaign for Pango
Peach lipstick and nail polish provides a good example. This sensuous
color, said Revlon, comes from "east of the sun, . . . west of the moon,
where each tomorrow dawns." It is "succulent on your lips" and
"sizzling on your fingertips . . . and on your toes, goodness knows."
It promises to be a woman's "adventure in paradise." Pango, of course,
refers to Pango Pango, a town of about 1,250 people on the American
Samoan island of Tutuila.

A further "truth" brought to us by advertisers is that of pecuniary
logic. Here a person is asked to accept the value of a product on the
basis of questionable evidence. Examples abound. A quick search
through a popular magazine that happened to be on my kitchen table
revealed a particularly potent example of pecuniary logic. The hook
for this Merit cigarette ad read: "*Latest Research Results Conclusive*:
TASTE SPARKS SWITCH. Extensive smoker survey proves MERIT
taste key to switch from higher tar brands." Reading further in the
ad, we discover that a "nationwide survey reveals over 90% of MERIT
smokers who switched from higher tar are glad they did. In fact, 94%
don't even miss their former brands. Further evidence: Nine out of
ten former higher tar smokers report . . . that they *didn't give up taste
in switching*. . . ."[4]

We see powerful visual and verbal language operating here that
contributes to the visceral impact of the ad. Visually, we see a simple

still life, in limbo lighting, of two packs of Merit cigarettes, one a filter pack and the other a menthol. Nothing extravagant or ornate about this visualization—it is a cool, rational, and simple representation that reinforces the generally held conception of the objectivity of survey research. Verbally, we read a terse description of rational facts; articles are excised to highlight the clinical, no-nonsense report of the survey results. However, a look deeper into the ad's language is called for. Who conducted the survey? How many people were surveyed? What prompted the cigarette switch? These questions remain unanswered in the ad. We are asked to believe the claims on the basis of an "extensive smoker survey." This is not an isolated example. How many times have you tuned in to television and heard, "Four out of five doctors surveyed recommend. . . ."? How many doctors were surveyed? Were they enough to make the results statistically significant? How were the survey respondents selected, by a random sample of the universe of doctors in the United States, the world? Did the doctors who chose to respond exhibit different character traits than those who chose not to respond? Were the respondents friends of the ad agency's research director? We are not told. Yet we are urged to believe the results of the survey.

A survey, as we have come to understand its purpose, is not a haphazard technique for a rough guess at people's preferences for certain products or the lifestyles associated with them. Traditionally, survey research is supposed to employ a rigorous methodology that produces information that helps us better understand certain aspects of human behavior. Pecuniary logic asks us to be, in Jules Henry's words, "fuzzy-minded and impulsive." Henry added, "If we were all logicians the economy could not survive, and herein lies a terrifying paradox, for in order to exist economically as we are, we must try by might and main to remain stupid."[5]

Where is truth in the language of advertising? According to Henry, "The heart of truth in pecuniary philosophy is contained in the following three postulates: Truth is what sells. Truth is what you want people to believe. Truth is that which is not legally false."[6]

Herein lies a significant moral question raised by this convoluted conception of truth. When the gurus of Madison Avenue try to sell health or any other human services, where the issue is relief from human suffering—an inviolable value—there must be no deceit, no pseudotruth, no pecuniary logic. Likewise, when the "product" being marketed is a candidate for political office, whose judgments will directly impact our individual and social well-being, there is no room for deception. Especially in these instances must the institution of advertising be held accountable to the most stringent rules of responsible behavior.

Ultimately the issue is more than whether the ad folk intentionally attempt to hoodwink the public with specious imagery or spurious claims. (Advertisers have argued for years with genuine conviction that they do not engage in such practices.) The larger question is, in Henry's words, that of the "moral imperative" of acquisitiveness in American culture—a culture increasingly guided by a preoccupation with quantity rather than quality. Ask any child to show you his or her collection of broken, discarded toys and games collecting dust in an attic corner. Therein lies a compelling clue to the answer.

The moral imperative of acquisitiveness in contemporary advanced capitalist societies is manifested in such strongly held values as private property, security, competition, and achievement (often at the expense of others). This imperative is evident not only in adult life, but also in children's preparations for that adult life. Advertising provides children with pecuniary enculturation—teaching them how to grow up to be good consumers. This concept is actualized in the interminable parade of toys that are miniature versions of adult products, such as domesticated dolls with their dollhouse kitchens containing miniature brand-name appliances and products, and "swinging-singles" dolls (who are nevertheless going steady) that trigger the purchase of lifestyle accessories such as race cars, townhouses, swimming pools, and high-fashion wardrobes.

Advertising has radically affected the very structure of traditional adult-child relationships. The traditions of patriarchal and matriarchal cultures in which adults provided role models and moral direction for their children have been subverted and even reversed. According to Henry, "Advertising . . . has . . . forced its way into the family, an insolent usurper of parental function, degrading parents to mere intermediaries between their children and the market. This is indeed a social revolution in our time!"[7] Parents become "imps of fun," competing with one another to satisfy their children's insatiable appetites for products.

Henry's conception of the individual in contemporary society is not flattering. The responsibility for man's subservience to this pecuniary system rests entirely, in his view, with the institution of advertising:

Insatiably desiring, infinitely plastic, totally passive, and always a little bit sleepy; unpredictably labile and disloyal (to products); basically wooly-minded and non-obsessive about traditional truth; relaxed and undemanding with respect to the canons of traditional philosophy, indifferent to its values, and easily moved to buy whatever at the moment seems to help his underlying personal inadequacies—this is pecuniary philosophy's conception of man and woman in our culture. Since it is a very contemptuous one, it appears that Madison Avenue is not so much "the street of dreams" . . . but rather the Alley of Contempt, housing thousands who, through the manufacture of advertising, pour their scorn upon the population.[8]

While there is much of significance in Henry's conception of the role of advertising in our culture, there exists in his reasoning a questionable presupposition. Henry assumes, I think a bit simplistically, that the advertiser stands somehow outside the culture in which he is operating and is thus able to manipulate the rest of us—a hypodermic model of direct cause and effect that implicitly ascribes both an intellectual superiority and an evil intentionality to the efforts of the advertiser. A more reasonable approach to the question would view the advertiser, like the television executive, and the television producer as successfully immersed in the culture and guided, often unconsciously, by its dominant myths and ideology. The advertiser may be the dungeon master, but, like the rest of us, he is also one of its hapless inhabitants, himself driven by the rules of the dungeon.

Contemporary American culture seems to be guided in large measure by three interrelated concepts—fear, greed, and "the miracle" —that advertising, as part of that culture, draws upon and actively employs for its own purposes. Erich Fromm, discussing the role of advertising in our culture, highlighted the significance of these concepts. Fromm noted that fear was most apparent in the deodorant ads, which focused our collective attention on the stigma of body odor. (It is important to remember that we have always had body odor, and in many cultures that odor is a sexual stimulant. Personal-hygiene-product manufacturers launched a massive advertising campaign to transmute that naturally formed odor into an artificial, synthetically produced odor and to sell a product in the process. A side effect of this transmutation was the emission of fluorocarbons into our atmosphere.) Fromm added that fear operated "in a more subtle way through the general fear of not being loved."[9] This general fear operates primarily on an unconscious level.

In drastic ways employing paleosymbolic images stressing the fear of rejection, ads show us products that will make us loved (e.g., Ultra-Brite toothpaste and Certs breath deodorant). The solution to our rejection comes in the form of miracles. We are saved not by human power or human effort, but, rather, by the external power of the miraculous product. In Fromm's words, "love is dependent on a gadget." The ultimate symbolic relationship between fear and the miracle is the fountain of youth—a major guiding concept in contemporary television advertising, according to Fromm.

The miracle is both qualitative and quantitative. We come to believe that the "good life"—the secure life without fear—will be ours if we consume a wide variety of goods and services that cumulatively will resolve all our human weaknesses (most of which are related more to our appearance than to our essence). The irrational links between monetary accumulation and the purchase of release, in the guise of miracle products, from culture-bound anxiety are thereby solidified.

Are ads responsible for this general condition or do they reflect this condition? Erich Fromm provided a well-reasoned response:

> . . . it would be foolish to accuse the advertising people of poisoning the minds of the American public. They do what they *have* to do under the given rules and mechanisms of our mode of production and consumption. With our mode of consumption and production, especially [in the case of] big corporations, the taste of the public must be manipulated, must be made foreseeable. Otherwise the big, mammoth enterprise couldn't exist. And advertising is one of the means to do this.[10]

It becomes more apparent, as the analysis continues, that we must ultimately look to the ideological bases for the use of the system of advertising in promoting a particular way of life. Both Henry and Fromm have alluded to this. Henry's concept of the "moral imperative" of a "fantastically high standard of living," sought through the accumulation of products, and Fromm's concept of advertising's questionable coopting of basic human concerns and needs both point to the advanced state of acquisitiveness in which we exist. A third opinion, that of philosopher Bertrand Russell, sheds additional light on the ideology that guides this system. Russell wrote:

> Suppose that, at a given moment, a certain number of people are engaged in the manufacture of pins. They make as many pins as the world needs, working (say) eight hours a day. Someone makes an invention by which the same number of men can make twice as many

pins as before. But the world does not need twice as many pins. Pins are already so cheap that hardly any more will be bought at a lower price. In a sensible world, everybody concerned in the manufacture of pins would take to working four hours instead of eight, and everything else would go on as before. But in the actual world, this would be thought demoralizing. The men still work eight hours, there are too many pins, some employers go bankrupt, and half the men previously concerned in making pins are thrown out of work. There is, in the end, just as much leisure as on the other plan, but half the men are toally idle while half are still overworked. In this way it is insured that the unavoidable leisure shall cause misery all round instead of being a universal source of happiness. Can anything more insane be imagined.[11]

A defining characteristic of advanced capitalist society is a need to maintain order by preserving traditional relations between capital and labor, namely the competitive nature of labor—that the unemployed will gladly take work from the employed at lower wages. The increased leisure time produced by mechanization not only opens the possibility of individual cultural and intellectual enlightenment; it also encourages increased inquisitiveness potentially disruptive to the smoothly operating capitalist machinery as the enlightened workers begin to question the dominant culture's claims to authority. Therefore, an advanced industrial economy with a large middle and lower-middle economic class finds it in its best interests to channel the free time of its workers into areas of unproductive leisure, characterized by unbridled consumption of products linked to play, which does not threaten, but rather reinforces the given structure. The idle unemployed, not questioning their status in a politics of "acceptable levels" of unemployment, are held in reserve, supported at subsistence levels by government. And the advertiser helps the entire system achieve closure by stressing competition and by looking always toward the rosy future—the land of plenty—and the promise of "the good life," embodied in the product-purchase-to-come.

ADS: TV'S MOST SIGNIFICANT ART FORM

We've briefly examined some of the theoretical questions raised by the presence of the institution of advertising in contemporary society. On a more practical level, we can now discuss the process of ad making itself. How are ads made? Why are they made the way they are? What is their status as art?

The institution of advertising is not some abstract concept. It involves real people in real organizations making a living devising messages that are intended to reach certain types of real people on both the conscious and unconscious levels. Conceiving an idea for an advertising campaign; defining the lifestyles of people who would be most receptive to the messages in the advertisements; actualizing a number of spots of 30, 60, 90, or 120 seconds in duration; determining the best distribution channels, programs, and times of day in which to run the spots; and calculating the cost effectiveness of the campaign (in terms of dollars spent per thousand people of a certain type reached by the ad)—these are all salient components of the larger pecuniary mechanisms that fuel our advanced capitalist culture. The ad that we ultimately see on our television screens or hear through our radio or stereo speakers is a fascinating admixture of highly sophisticated market research and creative energies and intuitions. In this section we will briefly examine both the process of creating an ad campaign and the final works that comprise that campaign—the little works of art that reach more people in more direct confrontations than any other art of our time.

As art, the television commercial is an anomaly. Unlike the premiere of a Hollywood film or a gala opening of a one-person show at an uptown Manhattan art gallery, the premiere of a television commercial is a very quiet affair—it certainly couldn't be classified as an event. Yet that premiere may be viewed by as many as 100 million people. If you asked the relatively culturally literate person on the street, "Who directed the film *Apocalypse Now*?," the person would likely respond "Francis Ford Coppola." If you asked that same person, "Who directed AT&T's 'Tap-Dancing' television commercial?," the person would look at you as if you were quite crazy. Yet Coppola and Steve Horn both work very hard at their art, both have a style they feel marks their films, and both have presented images and sounds that have reached tens of millions of people (in Horn's case, hundreds of millions). Both work in a business in which the "bottom line" is the key to the next job (with a disastrous bottom line, there may not be a next job).

The making of a television commercial is an amazingly complex communal affair involving the client, the advertising agency, a director of commercials, performers, a film editor, and many other individuals and groups who work many long hours separately and together to create 30 seconds of "magic."[12] The budget for a 30-second spot may exceed $100,000 (the average national ad today costs between $20,000 and $60,000 to produce). The shooting ratio—the amount of film footage shot as compared to the amount of footage actually used in the spot—may run as high as 200-to-one. (Horn shot about 10,000 feet for the AT&T Long Lines "Tap-Dancing" spot, of which 45 feet were actually used in the 30-second spot.)[13] The period of gestation for a commercial—from its initial conception by a senior producer in an ad agency's creative group, to its ultimate emergence as a finished print—may be a year or two. These works are thus so big and yet so small. Perhaps they reflect the cultural and aesthetic sense of television as no other work possibly can.

How is a commercial born? What follows is an admittedly generic, although not uncommon sequence of events.

A corporation with a product, service, or general image to sell is contacted by an advertising agency that offers its professional services to help the corporation develop an advertising campaign—a series of advertisements with a common theme and a special selling strategy. (A politician running for public office will be contacted by, or will most often seek out, a media consultant offering to design the candidate's public persona, a task similar in concept to the ad agency's selling strategy.) If the ad agency convinces the corporation that the two organizations should work together, the corporation becomes the agency's client or account. At this point, the wheels begin to quickly turn and the campaign is fully developed.

The client will likely be represented by its advertising manager, who will oversee the progress of the campaign's development and will relay suggested campaign changes to the agency. The ad agency, meanwhile, will call upon an assortment of employees to work on the campaign. Among these employees are (1) account executives, who service the client—they are charged with holding onto old accounts and attracting new ones; they act as liaisons between the client and the ad agency, selling the agency's ideas to the client and conveying the client's suggestions for revisions in the campaign, or its complaints, to the agency's creative group; (2) the creative group (composed of senior producers, copywriters, art directors, etc.)—the artists at the agency who devise the campaign specifics, often naming the product as well as providing its theme line; (3) and the research department, which conducts studies, including psychographic or lifestyle research, to target the advertisements to specific groups of viewers or listeners (an important part of this work is determining how best to position the product, i.e., determine what is unique about it; this is done by pretesting ad copy on a target audience before the actual ad is shot).

These are the most basic client-agency relationships in the advertisement development process. Beyond these are perhaps the most
critical participants in the entire creative process—a number of independent artists who are selected by the agency's creative group, with
client approval, to work under contract in a variety of specialized
creative activities. (In many cases an independent production company will perform many of these activities under one roof.)

The most important of these specialized artists is the director of
commercials. Once the agency's creative group has outlined a theme
line for the campaign (e.g., McDonald's "You, You're the One" or
AT&T's "Reach Out and Touch Someone"), has developed a selling
strategy, and has created storyboards—scripts with dialogue written
by an agency copywriter, and sketches of major shots drawn by an
agency art director—a producer (the creative director in many agencies) will contract with a director of commercials, usually the head of
an independent film-production company. (If a commercial will be
run on a commercial television network, a storyboard is usually submitted to a network representative in the standards-and-practices department for approval before the agency hires a director. This is done
to ensure that the ad will comply with existing broadcast codes.) To
secure a director, the agency will send storyboards to a number of
directors and the directors will bid on the job; or the producer at the
agency will simply select a director who has worked with the agency
on past campaigns, and whose personal shooting style seems appropriate for the ad to be shot. The director will be responsible for a wide
variety of activities in the actual production process, including preparing a "shoot board"—an elaboration of the agency's storyboard—
shooting the film footage (most major national advertisements are
shot on 35mm film, although many regional and especially local ads
are now being shot on videotape for economic reasons), arranging
locations for the shooting, contracting with a wardrobe person (called
a "stylist"), and securing most of the properties that will be used in
the shooting. The director often has a number of assistants, including
an assistant director and an assistant cameraperson (the director blocks
the shots and most directors shoot the actual footage). The director
and the agency's creative group consult on casting, with the experienced director usually having the greatest input into this area. Actors,
called "talent," are found through talent agencies. Principals get paid
a flat fee per day plus residuals based on the number of spots and the
number of markets in which the ad is run. Extras get flat fees for their
work on the ad. Throughout the shooting process, the ad agency

approves the production details and the client has final approval. So the director is not operating on his own with total creative freedom. This process is most assuredly a collaborative one, and the collaboration is most evident at the so-called client meeting at which the final shooting arrangements are presented by the director and the agency for the client's approval. Present at this meeting are the director, his key staff members, the agency representatives (from both the creative and account groups), and the client representative (the advertising manager or someone with a similar function).

While visual shooting details are being finalized, other artists are focusing on the audio elements to be incorporated into the ad. The agency may contract with a composer who writes original music themes for campaigns (the jingles we subconsciously hum, and which refuse to disappear). The agency may then hire an arranger to adapt a music theme to a variety of moods and styles (e.g., jazzy, disco, rhythm and blues). Once the composing and arranging are completed, the agency will take the score to a sound studio to cut the jingles, using a variety of multitrack audio-recording techniques. The sound studio will prepare a "scratch track"—a rough audio cut used in shooting and later in editing the actual film footage.

Then it's out on location for the shoot. (Actually, not all ads are shot this way. Many local clients will bring their products, including an occasional automobile, into either a television station's studio or an independent producer's studio, where the ad will be shot, often with few frills and usually a lower budget.) The director, through his production company, hires union helpers such as grips—people who carry equipment around—for the shoot or for the entire project if needed. On location, the director may be renting people's homes or places of business as backgrounds for the action. Often the same homes are used in a variety of ad campaigns—they become significant archetypes for American lifestyles, which can be pretty heady stuff for their owners.

Once the location is prepared (which may involve moving or removing furniture, or creating artificial rain) and the camera, lights, and audio gear are in place, in most ads the talent is brought on. The talent may be people or even animals (who will ever forget Purina's dancing cats?). The people seem to be of two general types: actors and models. While on the one hand, actors may not be devastatingly beautiful or handsome, on the other hand, models, who frequently have only still-photographic "flat-work" experience, may not be able to deliver a line or move from one spot to the other with any conviction. Whether an actor or a model, the ad usually demands a certain "look" (e.g., a Boston/New England/Ivy League preppie look; a California look—Anglo-Saxon, blond, surferish; or a New York look—ethnic Jewish or Italian) that the client wishes to associate with his product. If the look works, the image is said to "read" well. Often the look demands what the creative people call "human touches," such as babies (for mothering) or cats or puppies (for cuddly friendliness). These can be very difficult to shoot since babies and cats don't always cooperate or follow directions very well. Even adults who are engaged in difficult physical tasks can try the director's patience. The Steve Mizerak ad for Miller Lite beer was shot 194 times before the trick pool shot he was attempting finally worked, according to Steve Horn, who directed that shoot.[14] One shot that lasts for perhaps no more than five seconds on the small screen might take two or three hours to set up and require scores of takes before the conscientious director feels it is right. When the format is 30 seconds, there is no room for sloppiness.

Once the shooting is completed, the director relinquishes artistic control of the work to an independent film editor, who will work with the ad agency's creative staff to cut the final version of the ad; there is no clearer example of the transference of creative energy from one media worker to another, reflecting, in Michael Arlen's words ". . . the piecework, communal nature of the business."[15] The film editor works with all the director's footage and, with the agency's creative representatives, makes the final choices as to which are the most effective takes. The director, of course, has already implied the editing structure by the way he shot the action. Once the editing is completed, the film is sent to an optical laboratory for color correction and the addition of any special effects such as fades or logos.

Finally, the work completed, it is taken by the agency representatives to the client for comments and for final approval for airing. A media buyer is hired—an independent negotiator who decides which program, on what day, would attract the most viewers or listeners who might be inclined to buy the product or service being advertised. The ads are placed.

Reviewing the terminology employed by the advertising professionals themselves, the process of ad making sounds more like a holy war than the practicing of an art. The terms rightly bespeak a battle: ad *campaign*, selling *strategy*, *target* audience, *positioning* the product, location *shoot*. Yet while the creation of ads is a business venture in a highly competitive marketplace, and while the production effort is highly fragmented and communal, who can deny the art that emerges in many of these spots?

Television spots have been an integral part of the commercial medium from its public inception in the 1940s. There is little doubt that many of our earliest television memories are of ads (especially of those with jingles). We can still recall the 1951 Muriel cigar campaign with that sexy voiceover cooing, in a blatant reference to Mae West, "Why don't you pick me up and smoke me sometime?" Remember the 1956 Pepsodent toothpaste campaign predicated on the bouncy selling theme "You'll wonder where the yellow went when you brush your teeth with Pepsodent"? Who can forget the 1955 "Marlboro Man" campaign—the rugged Western cowpuncher riding his noble steed to the beat of staccato bass rhythms? And the 1950 Old Gold cigarettes "Dancing-Packs" ad will live in the annals of commercial history—a long-legged beauty and a little girl, dressed in cigarette packs, tap dancing their way into your living rooms to the tune of "Bicycle Built for Two." The history of television spots is also a history of the technological advancement of the medium—from the rough-hewn live commercials in the late 1940s, to the more predictable and more slickly filmed black-and-white ads in the 1950s, to the colorful visual extravaganzas of the 1960s, to the more pragmatic, more compact ads of the 1970s, and to the high-tech, computer-graphic, New-Wave chic ads of the 1980s.

In its early years, dating from the late 1940s, television advertising was clearly derivative of radio's stylistic conventions, the most important of which was a stand-up announcer extolling a product's virtues. On television, of course, we could now see the product as well as listen to the description of the miracles it could perform. To build creditability, the advertisers used recognizable stars to hawk their items—Dennis James for Old Gold cigarettes, Bing Crosby for Philco refrigerators, and Red Skelton for J-wax. The ads were static, straightforward sales pitches. Most were done live, as were the television programs into which they were inserted.

Television soon became more tightly structured and more controlled as well as controlling. As the medium began using filmed programs much more extensively in the mid-1950s, so too did it encourage filmed advertisements. Some ad agencies set up film studios in their own offices, but production activity became chaotic. The agencies turned to industrial film makers to produce their commercials. These production companies were entire units like the Hollywood "majors," but on a much smaller scale. Many ads were done on location, and ads began to incorporate forms from theatrical-film genres such as dramas and musicals. The television ads were abbreviated versions, lasting no more than two minutes. They were generally balanced, resembling a traditional melodramatic structure—a problem was quickly set up and quickly solved in approximately equal amounts of time. Music signaled cuts and moved the action along. The talent in filmed ads consisted of people in naturalistic settings, or people dressed in surreal costumes consisting of giant models of the products being advertised, or, in many cases, animated characters (Speedy Alka-Seltzer, the Ajax dwarfs, Colgate's Mr. Tooth Decay).

The ads became more aesthetically complex with more concise structures and richer visual and aural textures. The agencies began drawing upon the talents of successful commercial still photographers who were intrigued with the potential of camera motion. Experimentation in new visual techniques began in about 1964. We began to see wide-angle close-ups with the resultant distorted faces that echoed sensations of discomfort. Directors began shooting into the sun, producing a bleached-out, overlit effect. Layers of gauze were placed in front of the camera lens to create a sense of the past—of remembering grandma (the "universal mother") and a saner, more peaceful life. The late 1960s were perhaps the golden age of the lyrical artistic ad. Stylistically, the lush arty ads and the frenetic visceral extravaganzas of the late 1960s became visual fantasies that cruised a very thin line between the serious and the absurd. They were undoubtedly influenced by contemporary art movements such as the Theater-of-the-Absurd writings of dramatists Eugene Ionesco and Samuel Beckett, by surrealism in painting, and by existential literature. According to art critic Bruce Kurtz, "It is not a large leap of the imagination from Beckett's absurdity to a dancing hamburger or a man dressed as a giant Clorox bottle."[16]

While this ad art was receiving rave reviews from critics, the agencies and clients were slow to question mounting evidence that while viewers may have loved the ads, they didn't necessarily flock to the stores to buy the goodies. Marshall McLuhan noted in the mid-1960s that "advertising is substituting for product, because the consumer today gets his satisfaction from the ad, not the product. This is only the beginning—more and more the satisfaction of all life will come from the ad and not the product."[17] While McLuhan may have made a conceptual leap of faith in concluding that we would all *become* the ad, his initial observation was borne out.

By 1970 recessions had become an unfortunate economic and social fact of life. Clients tightened their belts. Agencies began testing ads before they were produced. Many of the new campaigns consisted of brand-name product-oriented ads with a single selling theme extolling a single major benefit (research had demonstrated that viewers cannot remember ads that say two or more things). The soft-sell art commercial of the late 1960s gradually gave way to the return of the hard-sell ad.

As production costs skyrocketed, a truly significant aesthetic change occurred in ads. The standard length of the ad was reduced from 60 seconds to 30 seconds. In response to this came a change in the ad's time signature and its formal structure. The "vignette commercial" emerged in the 1970s as the artistic answer to ad economics. Instead of a generally coherent traditional narrative that takes longer to present, the vignette commercial is a "freestyle" sequence of associated scenes and situations. There is often no dialogue, but, rather, a jingle (theme line) that moves with the scenes. The vignette commercial tightly packs visual and aural information in a structure that heightens emotions through rapid visual cutting. Shots may average three seconds in length (some vignette ads, such as those for the McDonald's "You, You're The One" campaign, average one cut per second). Even when the traditional narrative structure of progressive action was used, in the 30-second spot there was absolutely no time for frills. Jonathan Price noted that ". . . by using a kind of ellipsis, . . . commercials have trained us to grasp what gets left out when we see someone open his front door, then—in a quick cut—get into his car; . . . you had to snap, shock and jolt."[18]

The progression described above is nothing more than a trend line tracing broad movements in the development of the art of the television commercial. Today's television commercial is marked by a number of aesthetic characteristics that, while certainly not applicable to all television ads, can be related to a substantial number of them.[19] Following are some general aesthetic characteristics of contemporary filmed television ads:

1. The frequent use of wide-angle camera lenses provides extra depth of field so that the interior backgrounds will recede while the main subject is thrust forward in the frame.

2. Lighting (especially backlight) is important and, like wide-angle lenses, serves to thrust the subject or object forward from its background so the viewer will "key" on that subject or object.

3. Because of time constraints on the length of the ad, attention is focused on general mood rather than on individual details (although individual details are meticulously constructed to enhance the mood).

4. Ads favor extreme close-ups that provide a greater sense of intimacy than do wide shots.

5. Action in the visualization must be clear and concise with no wasted motion.

6. The ad's concept must be simple and direct. It should draw from familiar cultural symbols and archetypes but should treat them with aesthetic individuality.

7. Since we view television "informally" as compared with theatrical film, the television ad must grab our immediate attention (its "hook") with dazzling visualizations or catchy audio. It must "resonate" with the viewer's life or moods.[20]

Just what kind of art is the television commercial? One television critic, Jonathan Price, observed:

> If commercials are artful, then the art is objective, not subjective; capitalist, not rebellious; part of a social activity rather than a personal search for expression; more like a Roman road than a lyric poem. Their beauty is economic.[21]

Price is correct is evaluating commercials as a mainstream art and "not rebellious." In their most basic sense the ads must be safe. They are artistic vehicles whose purpose is to move both people and merchandise. They must be popular. Therein lies one, but certainly not the only, measure of their artistic significance. According to art critic Bruce Kurtz, "Popularity is a condition of quality for popular art. . . . And today there is no art form more popular than television spots."[22] An important element of these works of so-called popular art is their conscious connection of formal conventions with certain motifs—themes or concepts drawn from our collective cultural experience (in the form of images, stories, or allegories). A good example of such a connection is the concept of the youthful, healthy, active American, reflected in the overlit visualization of the blond, aggressive, tanned California surfer bathed in blue seawater and golden sunshine. This motif has been employed in many television ads (from McDonald's "Hang Ten" to ads for Coca Cola, orange juice, milk, and many others). We want to believe these connections. Recall that Erich Fromm noted our preoccupation with seeking the "fountain of youth."

Price, however, is incorrect when he asserts that commercials do not represent a "personal search for expression," for beyond the standard motifs lies the domain of the commercial artists' personal touches —the techniques used to create a style that, for example, marks a commercial director's works. This personal style enables many commercials (especially the huge budgeted ad intended for national distribution) to transcend the domain of hackneyed, formulaic selling tools and become legitimate contemporary works of art.

Personal style, or aesthetic individuality, is taken very seriously by the advertising community. The Clio Awards, advertising's answer to the Academy Awards, are considered highly prestigious within the industry, especially among commercial directors who can proudly point to the Clio winners on their reels, and also among the agency creative groups. This is a mark of their personal achievements in their specialized world of art making. A Clio in a way separates the artist from the competitive business environment in which he works.

Every highly successful director of commercials is recognized by the agency creative people for using specific techniques that mark his personal style. The ads shot by these individualistic directors have a certain "look" or "feel" about them. The work of some of today's most influential commercial directors has been examined at length in recent books by critic Michael J. Arlen (*Thirty Seconds*, 1980), Bruce Kurtz (*Spots: The Popular Art of Television Commercials*, 1977), and Price (*The Best Thing on TV: Commercials*, 1978). What emerges from these examinations is a strong sense that the commercial director considers himself first an artist, then a member of the mercantile community. However, in trying to reconcile their dual roles as creative people in the service of a business institution, an undercurrent of uneasiness emerges in the commercial directors' deeper feelings regarding their cultural influence, social responsibility, and self-image.

Elbert Budin is a master of the cinematography of food. His reel includes Sunkist, Nabisco, and Breyer's Ice Cream. Budin uses precise lighting that he drags across his subjects, emphasizing their tactile or textural quality. He uses a "scanning" camera choreography that gently plays over the food. An 18mm, wide-angle lens bring the eyes closer to the food than they would be in real life and makes the food seem larger than life. Budin also occasionally manipulates the film speed, using slow motion to produce heightened emotion or tension (e.g., the explosion of bubbles from the opening of a bottle of beer or the seismic splash of a saltine impacting the surface of a bowl of soup). Budin emphasizes the lyricism of his work, comparing it with

Stanley Kubrick's film *Barry Lyndon*, in which beautifully articulated visuals dominate the story line. Budin also consciously works with the associations of eating and eroticism. On that subject he told Kurtz:

> The sexual part of eating, the erotic part of it has to be put on to film. You have to enhance it. You have to bring it further than reality, ... going past the reality of food, getting sexual, getting suggestive; ... it's stylized.[23]

Budin's description of the sexuality of the commodity fits well in an advanced capitalist system in which the sensual, with its connotations of joy, appreciation, love, and being, is reified. Food, like other material goods, becomes a possession. Budin sees the potential power of his transcendence of reality through art:

> ... it's a tremendous propaganda force ... and I guess I have to think about the moral issue of my ... influencing so many people. ... I've given myself certain taboos that I will not use my power for. When cigarettes were still advertised on television I refused to do cigarette commercials and I was really ostracized from a few agencies.[24]

Mike Cuesta is known for his warm human characterizations and his work in narrative structure. Many of his images take on the appearance of an informal documentary even though they are all carefully blocked and shot. His reel includes "The Hill" for Alka Seltzer, "Desk Sergeant" for Sanka coffee, and "Grandfather" for AT&T. Like Budin, Cuesta recognizes the power of the well-conceived and well-executed ad. As a pragmatist, Cuesta has built a self-defense mechanism into his concept of social responsibility. The commercial, Cuesta told Kurtz "does exploit. It can push things down people's throats that they don't want. ... We live and work within a system: we have to do things that rot out your gut. That's why you become an executer. You get involved on one level and you don't get involved on the higher levels of it."[25] The "higher levels" to which Cuesta alludes include questions of personal values and ethics, such as, "When can one abnegate responsibility for the effects of his work?" The ethical similarities between "executer" and "executioner" are too pointed to be so rationalized away.

Dan Nichols, a main driving force behind McDonald's "You, You're The One" campaign, specializes in creating an accelerated sense of time through rapid cutting, sweeping camera movements culminating in freeze frames; and by interrupting action with a series of cuts of related actions, with an eventual return to the original action. In his work, Nichols emphasizes upbeat, youthful lifestyles and the joys of family life. He sees ads as a potential uplifting force in our culture. He told Kurtz:

> There's so much pessimism; . . . all you have to do is flip on the news.
> . . . There's nothing that's going to lift you up before you go to sleep
> and make tomorrow seem like, "Hey! It's worthwhile getting up."
> That's the kind of thing I'd like to try to put in my own work—without
> forsaking the product. . . . When people are out [McDonald's] is
> like a treat, . . . a respite, . . . an oasis of sorts, and people are high
> just being together; . . . and the food almost becomes secondary to
> that.[26]

Nichols seems to live in his ads, and he may even bear out McLuhan's proposition mentioned earlier—that "the satisfaction of all life will come from the ad."

Steve Horn, the director of "Tap Dancing" for AT&T, Miller Lite beer spots, and spots for Coca-Cola, is a master of the vignette commercial. His personal style favors interiors and the telephoto, or narrow-angle, lens, which he believes is "less commercial and more real. Not really real, but more real than commercial."[27] Horn hints at the degrees of realism in the dream world of the ad. Unfortunately, "real" has become an illusive concept in his attempt at a definition.

A Case of Ad Magic

Advertising artistry's power to overwhelm some of our most deeply held values is evident in the following spot:

What appear to be moving-company employees load, into their moving van, the last remaining pieces of furniture and an area rug from the living room of an attractive two-story frame house, and drive off. Immediately, a couple drive up to the same house. Are they thinking of buying the vacant house? The man opens the front door, and we see him standing there, mute, vaguely surveying the interior. We cut to his point of view, and see a totally barren living room framed by a lonely fireplace in the background. The Warner Amex Security Systems logo comes on the screen as a voiceover warns, "Let opportunity knock on someone else's door." My immediate response to this little drama was laughter. The man's vacuous look and the absurdity of a couple of thieves making off with all possessions of a household overcame any cognitive response I might have had that I was laughing at someone else's misfortune. After a beat, I began to feel fear. What if this should happen to me? Then, standing back a little further from the ad, I realized the deeper structure operating. The competitiveness and self-centeredness of our culture was embodied in "let opportunity knock on someone else's door," which signified not that burglary was something to be condemned in the society, but, rather, was something to be personally avoided. "If it happens to the other guy, it's through his stupidity and it probably serves him right" is the message camouflaged in this drama, a message linked to the basic drivenness of our culture: The fittest survive, and the fittest can afford to buy the necessary protection. I realized that for the briefest moment, my defenses broke down. The commercial director, the agency copywriter and art director, and the film editor had worked their magic. Art and business were one once again.

TV ADS AS MYTHS

Nowhere is the "living tradition" of secular capitalist mythology more evident than in the advertisement, the imaginary exchange that frames the entire commercial-television transaction. On television, the sacred time is selling time (most visibly and powerfully during the sacred commercial break). The programs are in a deeper sense really ads for the commercials, depicting lifestyles for which the commercial has a product or service to plug in. They are prefatory statements that herald the ads; they become the everyday activities that surround but cannot intrude on the sacred time of the commercial break. In television culture, while the demands on the viewer are not nearly as great as those made on the participant in traditional rituals, there are nevertheless many interesting parallels with traditional myth recitation. The commercial jingles and background musical scores of television may substitute for traditional chanting. The jingles and chants are devices that aid our memory of the rhythm of the imagery with which they are associated. They produce a common memory of traditions within the culture and are temporally situated. The television icons—pictorial representations that, like traditional ritual masks and sacred religious icons, attempt to bring people into a relation with a world beyond everyday existence—are today's powerful public symbols. The space for the television receiver is very mobile yet personal and engaging. Prime time, as night falls, is our most powerful myth time, and commercial television's most lucrative advertising time. Television's internally structured visual and aural time signature is in many ways analogous to the rules for a traditional ritual—the segments, and particularly the commercials, "announce" themselves and demand our attention.

Within the commercial break itself, as many as four myths are presented, each of 30 seconds duration. By the advertiser's recitation of the myth (which recurs throughout the broadcast day and night) and the viewer's subsequent performance of the ritual of purchase (re-enactment of the creation of an acquisitive society), the audience is "steeped in the sacred atmosphere in which these miraculous events took place."[28]

All of this, of course, is too abstract to be believed in terms of its own logic without some verifiable evidence. What miraculous events are we witness to in the contemporary televised world? Critic Price has provided perhaps the most cogent statement about the "sacred atmosphere" of the television ad:

> This mythic world is magic. Voices in the air, not attached to bodies, regularly order us around in commercials, take care of us, and give us advice, just like spirits. In this realm we can change the shape of people who have indigestion, make a package of gum as big as a tree, or slice apart a car in an instant. We can fly over golf courses, ... we can drive on water, ... we can make a wild deer eat Oreos and go where we want. ... Commercials resemble the dreams of a primitive hunter or child in their faith in magic.[29]

These "dreams" of the mythic world of television advertising may indeed be less profound or sacred and more profane than traditional mythology, with its emphasis on cosmogony (the origin or creation of the world or the universe), but they are no less real. In some cases, advertisers have even called upon their own versions of the creation to sell products. The 1980-81 campaign for Japanese-manufactured Datsun automobiles bears the theme "Datsun Saves." While the ads explicitly talk about saving gasoline and therefore money, on a deeper, more spiritual level we see the euphoric smiles of consumers who have been "saved" through their wise purchase. Datsun is the miracle product. In this case, the bonds of capitalism are stronger than the metaphysical distinctions in Eastern and Western cultures.

Other ad campaigns that draw upon the creation myth include those for Michelob beer ("Weekends Were Made for Michelob") and AMF ("AMF—We Make Weekends"). The equivalencies of "make" and create are obvious. These are mercenary concepts or origins—profane uses of myths in a contemporary context. Reading these campaigns on a deeper level, we discover that weekends are vacant unless they are filled by corporations with leisure sporting activities that require sporting equipment and alcohol (and, in the old days on television, cigarettes). The AMF campaign uses highly effective animation featuring a lifeless replica of Rodin's "The Thinker" who miraculously comes to life as the weekend rolls around, and becomes a spirited athlete (the ideal fusion of mind and body on the ancient Greek model). The new spiritualism centers on the process of recreation. The day off becomes a context for play rather than for introspection.

Popular-culture theorist Arthur Asa Berger adds a famous Levi's jeans campaign to the list of commercials employing the origin myth.[30] "The Stranger" (with obvious reference to Camus) is the name of one of the Levi's spots. The Stranger enters a town where the inhabitants are colorless, listless blobs. He brings them Levi's, which add color and style to the dullards. He then wanders off. The spot has obvious forebears in the Western film and the Western television series—the lonesome cowboy/gunfighter who cleans up the town. It operates on a deeper level as a parable of the redemption of the fallen modern man—the isolated automaton of the advanced technological system redeemed by a supernatural power and made whole once again. In this case we are redeemed by a rather stiff garment.

In addition to these universal questions of creation and origin, ads have employed more secular myths in the service of consumption.[31] These myths are not necessarily nation-specific, but most do apply principally to advanced capitalist societies, and some seem especially American.

The myth of manifest destiny is a myth employed in one form or another by societies bent on expansion and empire building. The phrase literally means that "it is clear that our destiny is to take over the world," or "protect the world from communism," etc. The British used a form of the myth to build their worldwide sea empire. The attractive phrase "manifest destiny" made its debut in 1845 and quickly became a doctrine used by American politicians to take over the West. The myth was revived in the 1890s as the United States went to war against Spain in Cuba and the Philippine Islands. Today, while the phrase is no longer common currency, the notion is very much alive in the sense that America is the most powerful nation in the world. Advertisers appeal to our belief in the myth by focusing on the theme of "buy this to keep America strong" or of "support us to keep America strong." The former selling theme is being used (in desperation, some say) by U.S. automobile manufacturers, who are discouraging the purchase of imported (especially Japanese) automobiles. The latter selling theme is most evident in institutional ads from our leading oil companies, who try to justify the astronomical rise in costs of petroleum products by telling us that we must drill into the ocean floor at great expense to find our own crude and thereby break our dependence on third-world oil. This myth is driven by fear of weakness and compromise.

Another potent secular myth operating in our ad culture is a bizarre amalgam of a compulsion to be clean and a deeply embedded racism. Somehow linked to the pure spirituality of "whiteness" and virginity, this sexist myth plays on a woman's guilt. Wisk will assuage the woman's guilt caused by the "ring around the collar" on her husband's or child's formerly white shirt. A Massengill douche will cover up natural vaginal odors (the "clean" women in the ads wear white or pastel flowing dresses). Ultra-Brite will make one's breath fresh and white. The "Man From Glad" and "the Ajax White Knight," with his phallic lance, arrive in their white costumes to help keep food fresh and floors sparkling clean. In all these cases, the woman is satisfied by the "superhero sexuality" of the white male if she participates in the product-purchase ritual. And in all these instances on a deeper level, the good guy/bad guy, white hat/black hat stereotype is insidiously reinforced. The comedic genius of Jonathan Winters was used with intentionally wonderful aesthetic results and unintentionally provocative ideological results in the Hefty garbage-bag campaign. Winters, bumbling and frumpy in his white garbage man's suit, spoofs and thereby demystifies both the "Man From Glad" campaign and the entire myth. At the same time, he extols the functional virtues of the strength of the Hefty bags.

The myth of the frontier seems peculiarly American and has its roots in the Hollywood-cinema genre of the Western and in innumerable 1950s and 1960s Western series on television. This is the myth of freedom, virility, and ruggedness associated with the West. The frontier mentality continues to thrive in the 1970s and 1980s in the "urban frontiers" of crime melodramas (police and private-eye series). This myth is male dominated; men become comrades in their quest to conquer the harsh frontier elements. Women, where they exist in the myth at all, are relegated to the status of objects: the prostitute with the heart of gold; or the "nice lady" who wants the free male to settle down, marry, raise a family, and give up killing (the woman is seen as castrater or confiner). According to John Cashill, the frontier man becomes "the American Adam"—the archetypal hero whose "absolute rootlessness and his essential innocence, his lack of moral dilemma" suggest a purity of spirit in the context of the surrounding evil.[32] Ads frequently employ this myth to sell automobiles, beer, cigars, blue jeans and other western wear, tires, gasoline, and, in print, cigarettes. The frontier is associated with automobiles and pickup trucks aimed mostly at downscale blue-collar workers (Mustang, Pinto, Maverick, Duster). Ford has been the main auto manufacturer to employ the myth. Among the beer ads, Schlitz and Miller associate the man-to-man camaraderie in the frontier work environment (and, after work, in the leisure environment) with their "full-bodied" beers. According to one critic, these beer ads are beautiful, lyrical tributes to the romance of the working class and to the dignity of the work ethic.[33] However, while theirs is a rugged world, the heroes never get dirty or exhibit any frustration with the conditions of their work. Women enter the frame as barmaids or as fawning hero-worshipers. Television cigarette ads of the 1950s and 1960s were major purveyors of the myth. Especially prominent was the "Marlboro Man" campaign (which still exists in print). Clearly this myth has played a significant role in American television hucksterism.

The taming of the frontier brings civilization and, with it, sanity and compromise. Nowhere is this more evident than in the myth of the "country" or "rural middle landscape." This mythic locale takes the space between the frontier and the urban megalopolis. People who exist there are not isolates, as in the frontier, but are members of families in which companionship, human warmth, and happiness are central defining characteristics of human relationships. Nostalgia and nonurban purity are central feelings evoked by the presentation of this environment on television. The central characters of this myth are usually childlike innocents. The myth is evident in many comedic and melodramatic series (*The Beverly Hillbillies, Green Acres, The Andy Griffith Show, Little House on the Prairie,* and *The Waltons* are good examples). In ads we find the myth operating in the Hush Puppies "Henry and Pa" and Country Time Lemonade ads, in certain AT&T long-distance campaigns, and the Chevrolet campaign with the "baseball, apple pie, and Chevrolet" theme.

A variation of the rural middle-landscape myth can be found in many corporate ad campaigns (those which are intended to boost the corporation's image rather than to directly sell products or services). IBM is not a giant transnational conglomerate, according to a recent campaign. Rather, it is "people [plain folks] helping to put information to work for people." Ramada Inns and Holiday Inns are not multiple-serial-produced motel chains, but "nice people taking care of nice people" and "people pleasin' people." And General Motors is no corporate behemoth. No, it is merely "people building transportation to serve people."[34]

The rural middle landscape has become a favorite myth with our politicians. No better example can be found than Jimmy Carter, a man whose roots were in the rural middle landscape. Carter exploited the myth fully in his 1976 campaign and caught the imagination of a country, following the debacle of the Nixon/Watergate era, still skeptical of urban politicians. We see Carter in one ad kneeling down to pick up Georgia dirt at his peanut farm; the blue jeans and the cultivated land speak of farming and associated values. People wanted a return to purity and warm values of family and friendships. Within four years, however, the childlike innocence of the media hype proved incapable of dealing with the harsh international realities of Iran. It was inevitable that the gunslinger riding tall in the saddle would come to town to clear up the confusing mess. The rural middle landscape had quickly regressed to the frontier. Ronald Reagan promised to lead the "fight for survival." More bombs were built and the "waste" of social programs was cut to pay for them. It is interesting to note that both the rural middle landscape and the frontier myth as used by politicians imply a certain resentment of the intellectual or at least a skepticism that abstract thought can resolve social problems. This attitude was made most visible in contemporary politics by right-wing populists such as George Wallace.

The myth perhaps closest to the meaning engendered by the entire advertising system itself is that of the Puritan ethic. At its heart is the cliche "God helps those who help themselves." This myth powers our drive for success and the acquisition of ever-greater quantities of goods. We can hide behind the false religiosity that encourages personal financial gain while ignoring the traditional ethic of working for others (redistributing the wealth gained through one's labors to others less fortunate). This myth is applied to a social strategy that isolates the individual as a consumer from his or her role as a producer of the common store of goods and services that involves the society. The most devastating use of the myth can be found in certain luxury-automobile ads. Perhaps none is so powerful as the Cadillac campaign targeted at upscale men during prestigious golf tournaments. Here we find combined the myths of the Puritan ethic, the middle landscape, racism, and manifest destiny. The Cadillac slowly drives up to the country club, the suburban version of the middle landscape whose pioneers have worked hard to build well-manicured, lush greens and traps filled with desert sand from the scruffy terrain in the midst of the megalopolis. Since they worked so hard to build their paradise, it is only fair to exclude others who are unable to afford, or who are socially unworthy of, membership in the private society; the Cadillac represents this exclusion. Behind the purity of the images, in the locker room, sit black men who hand out towels to the members and scrape the mud from their golf spikes. They have their own dreams, which may also include Cadillacs.

A myth which is universal, but which is particularly potent in American television advertising, is the myth of eternal youth. Psychologist Erich Fromm analyzed this myth:

> ... there's really no limit to what a gadget can do. The product promises us the fountain of youth—eternal youth. There's a great deal of narcissism involved; the self-image of the beautiful person— good looking, strong, attractive—who never changes, who lives in a kind of sacred land in which this image of the beautiful, successful, energetic young man is never touched; the pretension must be that he never changes.[35]

The myth also applies, of course, to a woman. Oil of Olay promises youth (if not "eternal," certainly long lasting) to the woman who uses the skin cream with regularity. Geritol, which once was the antidote to "tired blood," now is intended for young marrieds and even college students, to keep them feeling young. Youth becomes enmeshed in a confusing advertising web of admiration, love, and sex appeal.

Beyond the mythic order of signification lies an ideology that infuses all of these secular myths. Ideology, according to Roland Barthes, explains how a mythical schema "corresponds to the interests of a definite society" and thus becomes a matter of "general history."[36] According to Jonathan Price, "Commercials show us the whole mythology of upper-middle-class existence but they don't help us pay for it. If we are poor, we may 'buy' that way of thinking without being able to buy the products."[37] To "buy" into the notion of a lifestyle is critical to the maintenance of the industrial mechanisms that fuel our economy. For if we cannot buy the products of the upper middle class at Bloomingdale's or Sak's, we can buy the relatively inexpensive imitations at K-Mart.

PSYCHOGRAPHICS AND VALS—THE GROUP IS THE MESSAGE

Erich Fromm noted that advertising tends to make people "want more and more" rather than "be more and more." Actually, advertising, more accurately, works hard at making people believe they need more and more merchandise and more esoteric personal services to enhance their preexisting modes of being, modes in part created by the ads in the first place. Underlying all of this, of course, is the ideology of unending acquisitiveness that leads to "the good life." Yet the concept of the good life in itself is too abstract to be the bearer of much concrete meaning. There are many variations on this particular theme, which today seems to connote, more than ever before, a dream world inhabited by beautiful people and luxurious things. These variations are the focus of advertising research.

According to Stanford Research Institute (SRI) senior economist Richard Carlson: "The whole concept of one general ad and one general audience is already dead, and advertisers are just starting to figure that out."[38] The fact is that advertisers "figured that out" some time ago and consequently developed relatively sophisticated audience-testing procedures that have been used for at least a decade. Critics often assail these procedures as voyeuristic and manipulative while advertising executives defend them as tools that provide important information about human needs in a rapidly evolving society. The procedures and their ideological implications warrant our closer scrutiny.

On the most basic audience-research level, the advertising agency will test for audience recall—the determination of whether people remember an ad they have recently seen. One method of testing recall is "copy pretesting." On location for a shoot, a member of the production team will shoot still pictures that highlight the progression of the action in the spot. These stills are then transferred onto videotape with some zooms and dissolves used as transitional devices (a "still-in-motion" technique also frequently used in the historical documentary). This videotape is called a "photomatic." The agency then contracts with an outside supplier to test the photomatic against a target audience. A spot will be bought on a particular show for the photomatic to be aired (usually on UHF television stations in a small number of selected test markets). On the day prior to the show, research people make telephone calls and get a sample of viewers to agree to watch the show. The researchers call back after the show and ask the viewers whether they remembered the ad (a test of unaided recall). If they can't respond yes, the researcher will prod them a bit, asking, "Do you remember the ad for. . . ?" (aided recall). There is another approach, referred to as related recall—the viewer's being able to remember specifically what he or she saw in the ad. If at least 22 to 24 percent of the interviewees have related recall, the ad is considered a success. Obviously this method of analysis is subject to some researcher distortion, for the very nature of the questions asked implies that the researcher must prompt the interviewee to obtain an answer.

A more direct and diagnostic research approach often used by agencies is the mobile-van interview. A van will be driven to a shopping center. People will be asked to enter the van to watch an ad, a screening of the photomatic. Afterward, a researcher will ask them diagnostic questions about the ad, such as, "Was the ad humorous? Rate on a scale of zero to five."

Three powerful, if somewhat exotic, research approaches used in advertising research are motivational research (MR), psychographics, and Values-and Lifestyles (VALS) research. While each has its advocates, psychographics and, more recently, VALS are the dominant approaches in effect today.

In the 1960s Ernest Dichter, who pioneered in motivational research in advertising, counseled corporations on the Freudian meanings of products. Dichter and his associates relied on in-depth interviews with individuals or small groups. They administered word-association tests to their interviewees to elicit these deeper psychic meanings. Examples of MR results include people's association of prunes with old maids and of drinking tea with sickness.

Some ad agencies do their own MR by using "focus groups." A therapist/researcher talks to "regular people" around a table, trying to determine their deeper feelings about a product.

These methods have some significant drawbacks for the advertiser. First, they are primarily intuitive; they are not predictive of audience behavior in regard to the actual product being marketed. Second, the sample is so small that it is hardly predictive of the behavior of the population.

In the 1970s another research approach was applied to advertising. Called psychographics (sometimes also termed segmentation research), this approach recognizes that the television audience has split into many disparate segments and tries to identify a particular market segment—members of a specific group of consumers—according to a lifestyle common to, or a psychological makeup of, that market segment. The ultimate goal of this research approach is to develop a group's so-called psychographic portrait, consisting of generally applicable personal values, attitudes, and emotions. Psychographics moves beyond such often unreliable demographic information as income, age, sex, and place of residence, all of which are incomplete descriptive data rather than interpretive information.

Psychographics employs personal interviews or mail questionnaires as research tools. These are administered to a large sample of the population, which allows a statistical analysis of the responses and which ostensibly results in a more objective assessment than does MR.

The results of this research can be presented in a form similar to the following example of the toothpaste market supplied by Daniel Henninger.[39] According to Henninger, the toothpaste buyers can be separated into four distinct psychographic segments: worriers, sociables, sensory people, and independents. Worriers are usually families with children and are concerned about cavities. Crest toothpaste has traditionally positioned its campaigns to reach this group. Crest campaigns are serious, stressing Crest's cavity-prevention record (it's difficult to know how many cavities are prevented; thus, this claim is extremely dubious, although the appeal seems reasonable). Sociables are generally young marrieds or singles who are very active and who often are smokers. Ads appealing to this segment are upbeat, light, often use fast cutting, and stress the sex appeal of the active young person with white teeth. Ultra-Brite campaigns are good examples of this approach. Sensory people are generally children who want a pleasing flavor and appearance. Ad campaigns aimed at this segment may be animated and will likely stress tingly taste or colorful stripes or specks in the toothpaste itself. Ipana, with its hero, Bucky Beaver, is a good example of a 1950s and 1960s toothpaste campaign appealing to this market segment. Currently, Stripe toothpaste appeals to the sensory among us. Finally, there are the independents who foul up the ad person's dreams and schemes. These are price-conscious adults who will listen only to rational arguments and who will buy the least expensive brand of paste that they believe will do the job. That means these individualists will likely buy "house brands" that cost less because their manufacturers and distributors don't spend a great amount of money on ad campaigns.

Once the advertiser has this psychographic data, he can position his product in the market by "targeting" a particular type of consumer. Anyone aware of lifestyle changes in the past decade-and-a-half will certainly recognize the shift from the baby-boom adolescent singles (the "Pepsi Generation," as coined by the Batten, Barton, Durstine & Osborn agency in 1964) to the dual-income family, the working single parent, and active single lifestyle of the 1970s and early 1980s. Products for discriminating people who demand quality, but are in a big hurry, have positioned themselves to capture this market segment and are doing very well. These products include food processors (pioneered in the consumer market by Cuisinart), microwave ovens, and freeze-dried, boil-in-a-bag luxury dinners (expanded from the bourgeois campsite to the butcher-block dining table).

The Stanford Research Institute, after many years of in-depth interviews with consumers, created VALS, a psychographic-type emotional-, social-, and economic-profiling approach to the analysis of American society. Based on extensive SRI interviews, VALS attempts to understand the consumer's general attitude toward life. VALS segments adults into eight groups, each with a special character-typing. These groups include (1) belongers, who tend to be patriotic, traditional, and stable, are of all ages, and who are generally quite happy with their lives; (2) achievers—prosperous, middle-aged materialists; (3) emulators—ambitious young adults; (4) impulsive, narcissistic young adults—the psychographic sociables; (5) experiential, generally young, people-oriented, inner-directed adults; (6) societally conscious, mission-oriented people who have chosen to live simply; (7) survivors—old poor people with little optimism; and (8) sustainers—resentful poor people.[40]

Ad agencies use these categories to develop campaign strategies that will appeal to a combination of these groups. For example, Young & Rubicam, today's most exhaustive user of VALS, prepared a campaign for its personal-computer client, Atari, that would address both the needs of achievers, who want the computers for their children to learn faster, and of the intelligent and committed societally conscious, who have entered the market with the idea of trying to establish computerized cottage industries, and who might get turned off if they perceived the machines as taking over from people.

Is psychographic and Values-and-Lifestyles research a gimmick? Does it tell the ad people anything more than they could have intuited? Is it an invasion of our collective privacy?

On its grossest level, psychographics and VALS are attempts to predict changes in the scope and direction of our culture's "moral imperative of acquisitiveness," described by Henry and cited earlier in this chapter. According to Henninger, ". . . psychographics is the product of statisticians, sociologists, and psychologists trying to figure out how a shifting market of finite consumption capacity can absorb an endless proliferation of goods and services. For them, computers have replaced the couch."[41]

On a more insidious level, psychographics and VALS appear to be a high-stakes game played by people whose dual objectives are accumulating wealth and possessing others' psyches. Henninger reported a conversation he had had with Shirley Young, director of research for Grey Advertising, in which Young candidly told him "the personality and lifestyle data. . . allow us to become voyeurs into the psyche of the consumer."[42]

Do these researchers need to pry into our very souls? Price argues no:

> For all the research that corporations have done to find out who buys their products and why, . . . for all the sociological jargon that has been Xeroxed, the resulting advertising strategies are often little more than what a good salesman would suggest after a year on the road. Market research prospers simply because people like the obvious to be confirmed before okaying a $3 million ad strategy.[43]

Price's statement should not tempt us to discount the deeper meanings of the very act of conducting this type of research in our society. For the act itself indicates the existence of highly skilled individuals, with advanced degrees from respected educational institutions, who are using sophisticated measurement techniques against the general population so as to promote a way of life that many of our most respected scholars have argued is ultimately suicidal, as it rapidly depletes natural resources and turns family member against family member and neighbor against neighbor in the struggle to consume and enjoy the elusive good life. At the very least, the researchers know as much and perhaps more about us than we do about ourselves, which, of course, calls into question our personal control over our own destinies.

VIEWERS: THE PERSUADEES

The National Association of Broadcasters (NAB) has a Television Code that limits the amount of commercial time permitted on television to nine-and-a-half minutes per hour during prime time (8:00-11:00 P.M., EST) and to 16 minutes per hour at all other times, except in children's programming, during which the time limits are generally more restrictive (nine-and-a-half minutes per hour on Saturday and Sunday and 12 minutes per hour from Monday through Friday). The NAB code defines children as under 12 years of age. Since today the length of most television ads is 30 seconds, the number of ads the viewer might be exposed to each hour ranges from 19 to 32. The average television viewer today watches a little more than four hours a day; that viewer may see as many as 130 video ads a day and over 900 ads each week, or about seven-and-a-half hours of ads a week. That figure is awesome in quantity alone, discounting for the moment the impact of the emotional assault on our psyches.

How is the viewer to deal with this ad onslaught? Henninger discusses what he terms a viewer's "perceptual screen," which simply means that viewers are capable of watching ads without letting them register. On the surface this is obvious from our earlier discussion of related recall—as many as 78 percent of the viewers may not recall the specifics of an ad and yet the ad will still be considered successful. On a deeper level, the individual ad may not be the issue at all. Rather, we may talk about the cumulative impact on the viewer of the presentation of a dominant culture's vision of life.

Fromm perceived such cumulative impacts as intensely negative.[44] He believed ads molded one's personality, just as do the institutions of school, church, and family. Ads do this, according to Fromm, through an insidious process of "semihypnotic" suggestion that is "demagogic"—it attempts to break down a person's rationality and critical sensibilities and then to in essence force the person to accept anything. This is the direct opposite of the act of convincing—providing rational arguments as to the value of something.

Can't viewers or listeners resist this semihypnotic suggestion? Do people really believe what the ads say? Fromm answered yes and no. People know the claims "are all nonsense," but at the same time, "they would like to hope that there might be something to [them], and so we have an experience which is not clearly that of differentiating between reality and fantasy, but reality and fantasy become mixed up."[45]

This semihypnotic magic land located on the edge of the real is brilliantly revealed by Marshall McLuhan in his significant 1951 treatise on print media, *The Mechanical Bride*:

> ... the ad agencies function in relation to the commercial world much as Hollywood does in respect to the world of entertainment. In his cogent study, *The Hollywood Hallucination*, Parker Tyler summed it up in a sentence: "The movie theater is the psychoanalytic clinic of the average worker's daylight dream." That is, the spectator dreams in the darkened theater. He dreams the dreams that money can buy but which he can neither afford nor earn in the daylight world. ...
>
> So Hollywood is like the ad agencies in constantly striving to enter and control the unconscious minds of a vast public, not in order to understand or to present these minds, as the serious novelist does, but in order to exploit them for profit. The novelist tries to get inside his characters in order to tell you what is happening on the invisible stage of their minds. The ad agencies and Hollywood, in their different ways, are always trying to get inside the public mind in order to impose their collective dreams on that inner stage. ... The ad agencies flood the daytime world of conscious purpose and control

with erotic imagery from the night world in order to drown, by suggestion, all sales resistance. Hollywood floods the night world with
daytime imagery in which synthetic gods and goddesses (stars) appear to assume the roles of our wakeaday existence in order to flatter
and console us for the failures of our daily lives. . . .

 . . . the ad agencies and Hollywood turn themselves unwittingly
into a sort of collective novelist, whose characters, imagery, and situations are an intimate revelation of the passions of the age. But this
huge collective novel can be read only by someone trained to use his
eyes and ears, and in detachment from the visceral riot that this sensational fare tends to produce. The reader has to be a second Ulysses
in order to withstand the siren onslaught. . . . Without the mirror of
the mind, nobody can live a human life in the face of our present
mechanized dream.[46]

McLuhan, as did Henry and Fromm, appealed to our rationality
as adults in the effort to stem the tide of increasing fantasy invading
our wakeaday world. Unfortunately one must begin to resist in child-
hood, not an easy task.

Price summarized social science findings regarding children's
cognitive development and its relation to advertising. When the child
is five or six years old, he has difficulty distinguishing fantasy and
reality, make-believe and lying. He does not doubt adults. He often
confuses the programs with the ads, but does not seem to be particularly harmed by the ads. Between seven and ten years of age, the
child is most vulnerable to televised manipulation; by age seven he
can usually distinguish reality and fantasy; by age nine he has asked
for many products, received them, was disappointed in their performance, but still had high hopes; he might suspect deception in the
ads, based on his personal experience with the product, but cannot
articulate the exact nature of that deception; by age ten many children decide that ads always lie. Thus, ads become very harmful because they turn the child into a cynic. By ages 11 and 12, the child
develops more balanced views; he begins to understand the purpose
of ads, and he seems more willing to tolerate adults' lies in ads. This
is the real birth of the adolescent's enculturation into a system of
social hypocrisy.[47]

The NAB, facing increasing pressure from citizens' groups, especially Action for Children's Television (ACT), issued a five-point bulletin on children's advertising in 1970. The bulletin placed restrictions
on the fantasy elements allowed in these ads and prohibited special
video or audio effects that had been previously used to distort the
size, value, or performance of the product. However, with the limited

cleanup of commercials on television shows aired during "children's hours," many toymakers pulled their ads from these time slots and moved them to early prime-time hours where these restrictions did not apply. Studies have repeatedly demonstrated that children watch more hours of adult television than programs aimed specifically at children.

Not only must we protect our children; it now seems as though responsible members of our adult population are being made to look like mindless children themselves in ads. Ron Rosenbaum terms this personal affront the "humiliation sell"—a return to the "real-people" ads of the late 1960s, with the average viewer becoming an actor in a product testimonial. In these suburban vérité testimonials from consumers extolling the virtues of detergents, aspirin, and beers, we find people who, according to Rosenbaum, "are so malleable, so willing to say whatever the ad people want them to, they might as well be ventriloquists' dummies as far as the ad people are concerned."[48]

The viewer seeking a respite from the advertising barrage has traditionally turned to commercial-free public television for help. But in 1982 that sanctuary, under pressure from the government to find private funding to take the burden of support off public tax dollars, began an 18-month "advertising experiment" in ten public television stations, including WNET in New York and stations in Chicago, Philadelphia, and Miami.[49] While each station devised its own approach to commercials, Congress set two guidelines for all stations: The ads must be clustered and must not exceed two minutes an hour; and they must not interrupt programs. This commercial experiment is an extension of the 1981 expansion of the PBS corporate-underwriting policy that allowed the display of a corporate logo accompanied by a very brief description of the product or service provided.

According to WNET-TV President John Jay Iselin, "Enhanced corporate identity might well serve as an inducement to a strengthened [public-TV] partnership with the private sector."[50] Iselin is absolutely correct. Unfortunately, the "strengthened partnership" is exactly what is not needed. While Iselin believes that clear commercial guidelines will distinguish program content from institutional messages, our study of secular myths and ideology has revealed that the belief in the possibility of such a distinction is naive.

According to social theorist Jacques Ellul, a human environment is good or natural when it satisfies man's basic material needs if it also leaves him free to use the environment as a means to fulfill his individual spiritual needs.[51] We have noted in this chapter how the institution of advertising in our advanced capitalist society appears to be continually usurping those individual spiritual needs through a substitutional process that equates human worth with material goods.

Advertising has become one of our culture's primary educational tools, and, according to Henry, "The function of education has never been to free the mind and the spirit of man, but to bind them, ... for where every man is unique there is no society; ... for originality, by definition, is different from what is given, and what is given is the culture itself."[52]

The genres of television programs discussed in succeeding chapters will reveal themselves to spring from the culture, as does advertising, using a particular language to develop a secular mythology guided, often unconsciously, by our culture's dominant ideology. And programs, like the ads they frame, reveal much more about our own lives than we are normally willing to admit.

NOTES

1. Jules Henry, *Culture Against Man* (New York: Random House, 1963); see especially chap. 3—"Advertising as a Philosophical System," pp. 45-99.

2. Ibid., p. 45.

3. Ibid.

4. *Time*, February 1, 1982, p. 11.

5. Henry, *Culture Against Man*, p. 48.

6. Ibid., p. 50.

7. Ibid., p. 76.

8. Ibid., p. 79.

9. Erich Fromm's comments were taken from an interview included in *CBS Reports: You and the Commercial*, aired on the CBS television network, April 26, 1973.

10. Ibid.

11. Bertrand Russell, *In Praise of Idleness and Other Essays* (New York: Simon and Schuster, 1972), pp. 16-17.

12. For a fascinating inside look at the making of one television commercial, see Michael J. Arlen, *Thirty Seconds* (New York: Farrar, Straus & Giroux, 1979).

13. Ibid.

14. Ibid.

15. Ibid., p. 173.

16. Bruce Kurtz, *Spots: The Popular Art of American Television Commercials* (New York: Arts Communications, 1977), p. 10.

17. Marshall McLuhan, "Television in a New Light," in *The Meaning of Commercial Television*, ed. Stanley T. Donner (Austin, Texas: University of Texas Press, 1967), p. 104.

18. Jonathan Price, *The Best Thing on TV: Commercials* (New York: Penguin Books, 1978), p. 6.

19. See Kurtz, *Spots*.

20. Tony Schwartz, *The Responsive Chord* (New York: Anchor Press/Doubleday, 1973), p. 22.

21. Price, *Commercials*, p. 2.

22. Kurtz, *Spots*, p. 30.

23. Ibid., p. 27.

24. Ibid., p. 28.

25. Ibid., p. 55.

26. Ibid., p. 108.

27. Arlen, *Thirty Seconds*, p. 158.

28. Mircea Eliade, *Myth and Reality* (New York: Harper & Row, 1963), p. 18.

29. Price, *Commercials*, p. 161.

30. Arthur Asa Berger, "Brainwashing through the Boob Tube," in *The TV-Guided American* (New York: Walker and Co., 1976), pp. 58-61.

31. John R. Cashill has skillfully described many of these secular myths operating in television advertisements in an informative essay, "Packaging Pop Mythology," in *The New Languages*, ed. by Thomas H. Olgren and Lynn M. Berk (Englewood Cliffs, N.J.: Prentice-Hall, 1977), pp. 79-88.

32. Ibid., p. 84.

33. Ron Rosenbaum, "The Hardsell: How TV Ads Talk Tough In the New Troubled Times," *Mother Jones*, December 1981, p. 30.

34. Ibid.

35. Fromm, from *You and the Commercial*.

36. Roland Barthes, "Myth Today," in *Mythologies* (New York: Hill and Wang, 1972), p. 128.

37. Price, *Commercials*, p. 156.

38. John S. DeMott, "Going After the Mightiest Market," *Time*, September 14, 1981, p. 56.

39. Daniel Henninger, "Worriers, Swingers, Shoppers, 'Psychographics' Can Tell Who'll Buy Crest, Who'll Buy Ultra-Brite," in *The New Languages*, ed. by Thomas H. Olgren and Lynn M. Berk (Englewood Cliffs, N.J.: Prentice-Hall, 1977), pp. 70-77.

40. William Meyers, "Of Belongers, Achievers, Survivors et al.," *New York Times*, December 5, 1982, p. F29.

41. Henninger, "Worriers," p. 73.

42. Ibid., p. 72.

43. Price, *Commercials*, p. 62.

44. Fromm, from *You and the Commercial*.

45. Ibid.

46. Marshall McLuhan, *The Mechanical Bride* (New York: Vanguard, 1951), p. 97.

47. Price, *Commercials*, pp. 144-45.

48. Rosenbaum, "Hardsell," p. 32.

49. John Jay Iselin, "Commercials On Public TV? Don't Despair Quite Yet," *New York Times*, February 14, 1982, sec. 2, p. D31.

50. Ibid.

51. Jacques Ellul, *The Technological Society* (New York: Alfred A. Knopf, 1964).

52. Henry, *Culture Against Man*, p. 286.

4

TV COMEDY
AND
CONTEMPORARY LIFE

Mayfield, Mayberry, Minneapolis, and Manhattan

Critic Joseph Campbell defined comedy as "the wild and careless, inexhaustible joy of life invincible."[1] Philosopher James K. Feibleman wrote of comedy that it "is one kind of exemplification of the proposition that nothing actual is wholly logical."[2] Life—often joyous, not entirely logical, sometimes confusing, with an infinite variety of complicated predicaments resulting from the unpredictability of human interaction—is the proper subject of comedy.

Comedy, both in its traditional literary and theatrical modes and in its contemporary cinematic, radio, and televisual modes, is grounded in both time and place—it addresses the immediate life conditions of the society in which it is produced. It may do this through lovable, if often absurd individual characters who prompt us to ask, "How will this impossible misfit react to a situation with which we are all familiar?" The viewer, in this instance, is allowed a superior position vis-a-vis the performer in that the viewer knows the situation and the accepted codes of behavior. Or comedy may confront us, through satire or irony, as it addresses our collective fears and concerns regarding the constraints placed on the human spirit by impersonal institutions or outmoded customs.

The term "comedy" presumably originated with the Greek *komos*—a village revel—and was associated with an ode sung at a feast in honor of Dionysus, god of fertility. These revels were crudely phallic and involved a *gamos*, or sexual union.[3] By the time of the Greek Aristophanes (fourth century B.C.), the gross lyrics, jokes, and rustic satire had given way to an almost lyrical comedy with a chorus criticizing contemporary events, and, in the end, celebrating the unity achieved among the characters upon the successful resolution of their conflicts.

The Aristophanic comedies were in turn replaced by a form of comedy that flourished in the Roman era and that was more realistic; the dramatic plots usually involved young lovers being deceived by their parents, guardians, or other worldly-wise antagonists. The society's absurdities were ridiculed as they interfered with the natural order of things, namely, mating and procreation.

While medieval comedy, like medieval visual arts, often strived to present a high moral religious tone, this was offset by the tendency to poke fun at man's earthy weaknesses; the buffoon became a central comedic character in the later comedies of the period. The Italian *commedia dell'arte* of the sixteenth and seventeenth centuries, cited by many critics and artists as an important model for television comedy, was a racy mixture of rapid-fire satirical dialogue, slapstick, buffoonery, music, and sometimes dancing. There was little coherent drama, but, rather, a sequence of sideshows, not unlike the British-music-hall and American-vaudeville traditions.[4]

In the sixteenth- and early-seventeenth-century Renaissance comedy, and especially that of the Elizabethan master William Shakespeare, humanism predominated. These comedies often focused on man's complexities and contradictions. Themes ranged from escape from actuality to bitter satire. The comedy of Ben Jonson dealt with the ridiculousness of the emerging middle class's preoccupation with acquisitiveness. The seventeenth-century dramatic comedy of the French master Moliere focused even more critically on contemporary social abuses—the excesses of the pretentious manners of the middle class, religious hypocrisy, and the general lack of moral scruples in the society.

Victorian comedy of the late nineteenth century employed nonsense to emphasize the confusion of the conventional modern world, bound by artificial class distinctions and stultifying manners. Twentieth-century dramatic comedy, especially that of the modern comedic genius Bernard Shaw, pinpointed the growing conflicts between the individual and the dominant capitalist/industrial social order. Shaw realized that while man was not perfectible, man's societies were capable of reform. Shaw, like other great writers of comedy, was able to transcend the unidimensional limitations of farce to produce comedy that became a powerful instrument of social criticism.

It should be apparent from even such a brief and limited historical survey of the types of comedy which have developed in Western cultures that the art form has served and today still serves a very important social function. According to Feibleman, "Comedy is always . . . realistic; . . . it gets to handle . . . the traditional and ever-present irritations which people know as evils but which they also find themselves powerless to eradicate."[5] The feeling person finds it difficult to cope with actuality's defects and needs a sense of order superimposed on the chaos of daily life. Such order emerges as we recognize and admit to the limitations of actuality itself. Comedy, which reveals to us ludicrous and ridiculous aspects of our existence, represents the logical order of the ideal. Comedy "in its broadest sense is the appeal away from things as they are and toward things as they ought to be."[6]

Comedy, especially dramatic comedy, is a crying out for human improvement; it thrives during troubled times, when it is possible for both the artist and the spectator to note the contradictions and value conflicts of society. In the twentieth century it has flourished, most notably in the cinematic artistry of Charlie Chaplin; in the provocative comedy-dramas of Samuel Beckett; in the biting satire of Bernard Shaw; the cutting wit and irony of George Carlin; and the often powerful television comedies of Norman Lear, especially *All in the Family*, *Mary Hartman, Mary Hartman*, and Robert Altman's and Larry Gelbart's *M*A*S*H*.

STRUCTURAL AND INSTITUTIONAL CHARACTERISTICS OF THE TELEVISION COMEDY APPARATUS

While television comedy is grounded in the forms of theatrical comedy, it exhibits unique formal-structural characteristics. The situation or domestic comedy, television's staple comedic vehicle, is simply a 23-minute, two-act playlet with an epilogue. Episodes are generally self-contained. They revolve around a single "umbrella" plot or situation. There is a regular cast of core characters who are generally stereotypical ones and who engage in ritualistic humor through the repetition of action and "running gags"—physical comedy of gestures and one-liners. The main characters' stance toward the world of social relations is generally illogical or irrational. A situation or domestic comedy is today frequently shot before a live studio audience (e.g., *All in the Family*), although more traditional techniques, such as shooting film style on a soundstage, persist (e.g., *M*A*S*H*). As a rule, a single director is employed to direct all or most of the episodes of a comedy series, and therefore stylistic consistency in production elements is achieved (e.g., in the choice of shots, style of lighting, and method of blocking the action). In 1980 dollars, a comedy director earned about $6,000 for a single episode and about $18,000 for a comedy pilot. And they indeed earn their money. Their workweek includes three days of rehearsal, including actor improvisations and setting of stage business, one day of blocking out camera angles, and one day of shooting. The atmosphere is charged and the deadlines must be met. Long-form comedy/sketch formats, such as that for NBC's *Saturday Night Live*, are generally more elaborate. NBC's Studio 8H in New York, in which *Saturday Night Live* was produced before an audience (20 original shows with repeats were done per year) often has 11 sets on the studio floor. Five video cameras move from set to set during the course of the production, with no greater than three cameras used in a single sketch. All sketches are written in two days, blocked out in two more days, and a run-through rehearsal and a dress rehearsal are done the same day as the airing of the program. The chaotic pace of the work process, tempered by the professionalism of the writers, directors, actresses and actors, and crew, provides the controlled aesthetic edge so necessary for good comedy. The live character of the production allows for a topicality that is critical to television satire, given our expectations of instant analysis.

An analysis of the production apparatus of television comedy reveals much about the look of this work—lifelike characters are seen in enclosed spaces, are revealed in tight two- or three-shots and close-ups, acting out the mundane everyday world manifested in incongruous if not bizarre configurations. Situation and characterization are crucial to the success of this work. But beyond the aesthetics of television comedy lies its relationship to the real world of social relations.

Scholars who have attempted to elucidate the range of television comedy have developed a variety of analytical schemes ranging from a breakdown of types of television comedy, according to genre characteristics, to a typology of the social roles of the central characters in comedy series. While the carefully constructed models are useful in analyses, all have some weaknesses that bear close scrutiny.

James W. Chesebro's scheme of narrative television "communication strategies" includes, but is not limited to, comedy.[7] This scheme, which owes an acknowledged debt to the work of critic Northrop Frye, is based on the relationship between a central character and the viewing audience, with intelligence and ability to control one's circumstances seen as the key variables determining that relationship.

Chesebro isolated five strategies: (1) the "ironic," in which the central character is intellectually inferior and less able to control circumstances than is the audience—"the rhetoric of the loser"; (2) the "mimetic," in which the central character is as intelligent and in control as is the audience—the character is "one of us"; (3) the "leader-centered," in which the central character possesses superior intelligence because of some specialized training, but deals with events similar to those in which the audience is involved; (4) the "romantic," in which the central character remains "human" but superior to the audience in both intelligence and control over circumstances and (5) the "mythical," in which the central character transcends the mundane world of the audience and is confronted with a mystical experience.[8]

According to Chesebro, television comedy most frequently employs the mimetic strategy, with a few notable comedies employing irony and an occasional comedy using a leader-centered strategy. The mimetic strategy, "used to create the *impression* that typical behaviors and values are being reflected,"[9] becomes an agent for reinforcing traditional dominant value orientations and thus becomes a primary mechanism for socialization. Problems which arise in this comedy are treated as the result of "misunderstood intentions"—a principal ingredient of traditional television situation comedy. The basic underlying questions of the relationship of intentionality to social control remain, on the surface of the comedic text at least, unexplored. Among the more aesthetically and financially successful of the contemporary mimetic television comedies are *The Mary Tyler Moore Show, The Bob Newhart Show, Happy Days, Laverne and Shirley, One Day At A Time,* and *Barney Miller*.

The ironic strategy has two distinct sides: what Chesebro terms "Socratic irony," in which the central character pretends to be ignorant so that his or her adversaries will be forced to reveal their false ideas as they try to explain them to the central character (the melodrama *Columbo* used this strategy quite effectively); and "unknowing irony," in which the central character reveals his or her own ignorance and social powerlessness to the audience. Certainly a clear example of the latter character type in comedy is Archie Bunker of *All In The Family*. His malapropisms and inability to clearly and accurately interpret his world frame the comedy, which has frequent pathos. Archie, according to this strategy, is the eternal loser. By inference, so too are those in the audience who share his value priorities.

The leader-centered strategy, which produces central characters who exhibit moral courage and strength, who are articulate, and who face easily identifiable situations, is not a strategy often used in television comedy, according to Chesebro. There are, however, occasional exceptions to the rule. Chesebro cites both *M*A*S*H* and *Maude* as clear examples. Maude and many of the members of the 4,077th flaunt conventions; they are authentic in that they thoughtfully consider and actively attempt to change their less-than-perfect world.

The romantic strategy, in which legendary central characters exhibit tremendous courage and endurance, and the mythical strategy (at least as Chesebro defines it, which, I believe, is too limited) of ritual, dreams, and universal struggling to achieve a new social order are the proper domains of heroic/epic adventure melodramas rather than of television comedy.

What Chesebro's analytical scheme lacks is a clear theory of the material and ideational conditions of the world of social relations outside the world of the works themselves. While value priorities frame considerations of this world on one level, they do not clearly reveal the locus of ideological control of the society. Mimetic comedy reinforces; but reinforces what? "Unknowing irony," as defined by Chesebro, turns our attention away from social conditions and inward toward the fictional character's personality; away from the symbolic —the essential questions of the survival of the entire system of meaningful human exchange—and toward the imaginary, egocentric world of the foolish character. (Clearly *All In The Family* is much more than that.) Even the authenticity of the leader as described above is tempered by the leader's entrapment in a system that may occasionally give and bend to a degree, but that is ultimately characterized by stasis rather than perpetual, if subtle change.

We need more concrete conceptual guideposts to help us come to grips with both comedy's joyous illogic and its confrontational character. Many essays point to thematic statements about social relations that, their authors claim, cut across the subgenres of television comedy. Here, the analysis attempts to relate television characters to broad social movements, and to temporalize that relationship.

According to Sylvia Moss, the comedy of "ingroup-outgroup" emerged in the mid-1960s.[10] Pioneered, in her view, by *The Beverly Hillbillies*, and including *Bewitched, The Munsters, The Addams Family*, and *My Favorite Martian*, this comedy scheme relied for its laughs on the "clash of social conventions" that clearly differentiated the two groups. Each group adhered to its own code of conduct. As the "small, alien culture," the ingroup was enclosed by the "modern society" of the outgroup, according to Moss's definitions, and thus the accepted societal norms were reinforced. The ingroup never affected the outgroup's basic value system, and the audience, which is "apprehensive of healthy, happy, uninhibited rustics," was never threatened or challenged.

The ingroup/outgroup scheme, while certainly overgeneralized and of limited application across comedic subgenres, is useful in framing dominant cultural/subcultural group relations. However, I take issue with Moss's basic categorization. She has her terms confused. The outgroup, by definition, is "small" and "alien." Today, it signifies the quaint, childish segments of our society not in step with our predominating myth of eternal progress. These outgroup members are laughable because their actions are illogical (i.e., antitechnical), given the dominant ideology of perpetual growth through conspicuous acquisitiveness.

A variation on this ingroup/outgroup scheme was advanced by *Newsweek* critic Harry F. Waters in 1979.[11] Describing the post-*All In The Family* world of television comedies as "escapist, feel-good *Zeitgeist*," Waters developed a series of polar social statements he found reflected in these comedies. These statements included: "The adult is a dolt"/"Children know best"; "Dumb is cool"/"Smart is square"; "The working class is the classiest"/"The well-to-do are ethically and morally inferior"; and "L.A. is the way we are"/"Slums, panhandlers, subways, and traffic jams do not exist." The ingroup in this scheme analyzing late 1970s television comedy comprises wisecracking children who live in Los Angeles and lecture their parents on sexual matters and personal values, and working-class or ethnic people who are dumb. The outgroup comprises mature, intelligent parents and financially well-healed urbanites. Waters concluded that when the television entrepreneurs decide to court what he termed an "adolescent" audience, "the small screen is bound to reflect a distorted image of the culture as a whole."[12]

One difficulty with this analytical scheme is its apparent confusion as to what is fictional and what is real—the traditional fantasy/reality conundrum. Maybe Los Angeles *is* the way we are *becoming*, due in no small measure to television's presence in our culture. Maybe the well-to-do *are*, in many cases, ethically suspect if not inferior. Maybe the adult has become an egocentric child, perhaps from seeing too many televised ads for Seiko watches, hot tubs, and sparkling burgundy. This scheme does, in fairness, at least acknowledge a world "out there" of which both the television apparatus and the viewers are a part.

Arthur Haugh proposes a more meaningful analytical scheme in which television comedy is separated into "domestic situation comedy" and "nondomestic situation comedy."[13] Each of these genres is further subdivided into subgenres. The domestic sitcom encompasses the traditional family (*I Love Lucy*), the nuclear family (*Leave It To Beaver*), the eccentric family (*The Beverly Hillbillies*), and the social and ethnic family (*All In The Family*). The nondomestic sitcom encompasses the military sitcom (*Gomer Pyle USMC*), the business sitcom (*Petticoat Junction*), the fantasy sitcom (*The Addams Family*), the rural sitcom (*The Dukes of Hazzard*), the adventure sitcom (*Get Smart*), and the working-group sitcom (*The Mary Tyler Moore Show*).

Haugh defined a sitcom as

> normally an open-ended series of thirty-minute, self-contained television episodes which revolve around a single umbrella plot or situation and a regular cast of core characters; . . . it generally involves stereotypical characters and ritualistic humor (repetition and "running gags"); and it frequently incorporates an irrational approach to reality leaning strongly on blindness and concealment.[14]

The critical feature distinguishing Haugh's two sitcom genres is the presence of a family in the domestic situation comedy. The family, a traditionally stable social unit that has, since the birth of television itself, undergone rapid and major change in its composition and role in advanced capitalist society, takes on a variety of new forms, many of them makeshift as compared with the traditional forms, and thus is ideally suited to the illogic of comedy. The more unstable the basic family unit, the more potential there is for a variety of disruptive human interactions; at the same time, the idea of family, with its traditional values of sharing and mutual support, tethers the characters to a human reality.

In the early days of television, nondomestic situation comedy often served as a backdrop for a "showbiz act"—a series of sketches tied together by the presence of a star—a type of television vaudeville. *The Jack Benny Show* was a highly successful example of this hybrid form. However, the nondomestic sitcom developed into a more purely television form in the mid-1950s. Although Haugh does not acknowledge it as such, an important feature of this entire genre is the presence of working groups. (Haugh isolates the working group as one of many subgenres of the nondomestic comedy.) These working groups have ranged from the shrewd military noncoms on *The Phil Silvers Show* to the bumbling secret agents of *Get Smart*, a spy adventure spoof, to the almost folksy news team on *The Mary Tyler Moore Show*.

According to Haugh, "the old cliche of the struggle between the boss and the employee began to be replaced in the 1970s with a happier scene, the 'cooperative working group.' "[15] Laughs were generated less from awkward situations and confusion and more from the interactions of human beings. In this way, the nondomestic working group began to assume the characteristics of a family, characterized not only by normal internecine tension, but also ultimately by cooperation and understanding. Running gags and physical comedy, timeless comedic devices, were not totally rejected, but were, in many series, subordinated to a comedy of warmth and character.

Haugh also did quantitative research on the historical development of the television situation comedy. By counting and typing characters, settings, types of family units portrayed, and class membership, Haugh was able to provide a rough profile of television's comedic ambience. Of the 400 sitcom series aired between 1948 and 1978, only 17 percent took place in apartments; over half (211) of the casts lived in metropolitan settings; and nearly a fourth (93) of the sitcoms were set in New York City. Until the 1970s, about three-fourths of all domestic sitcoms featured upper-middle-class or middle-class settings and central characters. In the 1970s, the social and ethnic domestic and nondomestic comedy of the lower middle class emerged and prospered. While widowhood was the principal explanation provided for the single-parent television family until the early 1970s (examples include *The Real McCoys, The Beverly Hillbillies,* and *My Three Sons*), by the late 1970s, 23 divorced characters inhabited the prime-time world of the situation comedy. And while blacks and Hispanics gained limited access to starring roles in sitcoms in the 1970s, Asians and Native Americans were, and still are, almost nonexistent on the small-screen sitcom. The demographic inequities in the presentations within these genres are obvious to even the most casual observer. Their social significance will be discussed in detail in the analyses that follow.

Haugh's discussion of comedy provides a useful, if limited survey of television's comedy genres. Notably absent from his scheme is the satiric comedy/variety genre (ranging from *That Was The Week That Was* [1964] to *Saturday Night Live* [1975-] —a highly significant television-comedy vehicle. While Haugh's breakdown of the family types in his domestic-situation-comedy genre is a good starting point for analysis, as social types the families are not clearly located in any contemporary social reality. Even in his own analysis, Haugh has obvious difficulty distinguishing between interactions within the biological family and those within the working group, and between the working group and his other nondomestic-situation-comedy subgenres. A Marine Corps platoon is a working group and a surrogate family. The Clampetts of Beverly Hills are a rural family, traditional in many ways (e.g., in their standards for courting behavior, and elders), yet eccentric in relation to the bourgeoisie that constitutes the dominant social structure of Beverly Hills.

If we are to come to terms with television comedy's relationship to an extant social reality, perhaps the most honest approach begins with an acknowledging of television for what it is—an extremely powerful vehicle for storytelling, a medium whose intimate presence in our lives (it has become a part of most of our bedrooms and dens) lends its stories a sense of truthfulness that tends to obscure their status as fiction. Comedy series and serials, like other television forms, with their repetition of setting, situation, and character, are well suited to myth analysis as this author has previously defined it. Figure 1 includes those television comedies that I believe are particularly significant examples of the comedy types they represent. In this chapter and in Chapter 5, I will examine each of the mythic constructs in television comedy, using selected episodes from various series in each category as examples of the myths at work. The examination will point to both an aesthetic reality—why these works make us laugh— and a material historical reality—what these works reveal about the nature of social relations in a contemporary society.

THE SUBURBAN-MIDDLE-LANDSCAPE COMEDY

Americans are proud of their heritage as a nation that reveres the "common man." This heritage is related to a variety of ambiguous political, social, and economic constructs, including plebiscitary democracy, in which the vote of each citizen is presumed to have equal status in the policy-making arena; majority rule, with its inherent notion of a compromise of principles in the name of consensus; and marketplace economics, in which even the relatively undereducated, unskilled worker, through personal determination, luck, and perhaps a little guile (i.e., callous disregard for the sanctity of authentic communication between human beings), can become a

Suburban Middle Landscape

The Adventures of Ozzie and Harriet, 52 66

Father Knows Best,
54 . . . . 60 . . . . 63 Reruns,

Leave It To Beaver,
57 63

My Three Sons, 60 72

Rural Middle Landscape

The Real McCoys, 57-63

The Andy Griffith Show, 60 . . 68

The Beverly Hillbillies, 62 71

Petticoat Junction, 63 70

Green Acres, 65 71

Sanford and Son,
72 77

Urban Comedy

I Love Lucy,
51 57

Make Room For Daddy/
The Danny Thomas Show,
53 64

The Honeymooners,
55—56

The Dick Van Dyke Show,
61 66

The Mary Tyler Moore Show,
70 77

The Bob Newhart Show,
72 78

Barney Miller, 75 82

The Jeffersons, 75 . . . .

Taxi, 78 . . . .

highly successful entrepreneur—a case of the highly valued rags-to-riches dream that incorporates the myths of the Puritan ethic and eternal progress. Success, however, often exacts a high personal price unless it is tempered with humility, for the American must never forget his/her roots in the common people. We are constantly reminded of this through our highly developed folklore, which includes, as central characters, George Washington and Thomas Jefferson, farmer-presidents; Benjamin Franklin, thrifty, level-headed publisher/statesman; Abe Lincoln, woodcutter and small-town lawyer/president; and Dwight D. "Ike" Eisenhower, midwestern country boy/general/president.

It is this highly intriguing mixture of the drive for personal gain through hard work and the need to acknowledge the humble roots of the common man that represents the archetypal American character. This character is reinforced through the way Americans perceive and use space. The United States has a geography characterized by vast, empty space, and a history characterized by expansion and conquest—the myth of manifest destiny has operated for the past century, in particular, to legitimize that expansion. In our language, we tend to refer to those who established settlements in the western territories as "pioneers," from the French word for foot soldier, rather than as "settlers," a term with more peaceful connotations.

Nineteenth-century American expansionist strategies that incorporated the vast western wilderness were pursued because of a need to expropriate the natural resources of those areas to fuel a furiously expanding industrial economy. Railroads were built, often at great human expense, to transport raw materials and people over great distances in the name of progress and commerce. Native Americans who got in the way of this progress were expendable. Once an advanced industrial economy was firmly established in the early twentieth century in the United States, another form of geographic dispersion was inevitable. Advanced industrialization required internal mobility within the work sector, both within an organization and between organizations, and within a geographical area and between geographical areas, and encouraged new-home building and the concomitant strategy of increasing consumption of identical durable goods for the single-family home. Predictability became an increasingly crucial element in expansion and dispersion, leading to the ultimate observation that all McDonald's hamburgers everywhere taste the same—not great, but predictably acceptable. People were encouraged to "move up" in their home and durable-goods purchases; as they were promoted within their companies, more spacious and elegant accommodations, deluxe consumer durables, and more luxurious leisure pursuits requiring sophisticated equipment and specialized training became the mark of the upscale. Aided by advances in automotive technology, President Eisenhower's interstate highway program (a primary intention of which was to facilitate the rapid transport of military equipment in a national emergency), the widespread availability of television as a means for decentralized entertainment and outside information, and the development of efficient air-conditioning systems, workers found it desirable (and in fact were constantly encouraged by the hegemonic demands of an advanced industrial economy reflected in corporate behavioral norms) to fan out from overcrowded, polluted urban industrial ghettos into the suburban developments that sprang up to accommodate the post-World War II environment (characterized by rapid family formation).

In the suburb, space, while personal in the sense of separating one family from other families, was not necessarily individualized. The spaces and the dwellings occupying those spaces were often equivalent, with houses of essentially the same design with minor structural variations on identical quarter-acre parcels of land. The repetition of suburban-tract homes was both an acknowledgment of the myth of eternal progress (through the glorification of technique), and a personal acquiescence to America's heritage of the common man.

The era of what social critic Raymond Williams termed "mobile privatization" had arrived. Mobile privatization, according to Williams, is characterized by the confluence of "two apparently paradoxical yet deeply connected tendencies of modern urban industrial living: on the one hand mobility, on the other the more apparently self-sufficient family home."[16] The American suburb was clearly a new social form, signifying increased middle-class geographical and social mobility; but its roots could be clearly traced to American ideological traditions and material history.

Television's version of suburban life was most clearly presented in the situation comedy. An idealized vision of surburban living, the myth of the suburban middle landscape reinforced basic American notions of progress tempered by humility. The suburb was the mythical space between the untamed rugged frontier—the wilderness—and the chaotic, dangerous inner city. It was a place where sanity prevailed, a place of full employment; conventional white, white-collar corporate families; clean streets, well-kept, weedless lawns, neatly trimmed hedges, and, in the older suburbs, an occasional freshly painted white picket fence. People there were not rugged isolates, as in the myth of the frontier, but neither were they exactly oriented to the world of the close neighborly bonds in the traditional rural community. There were so-called neighborhood associations, but their activities seemed to focus mainly on pressuring homeowners delinquent in their yard-care activities to beautify their properties to meet neighborhood aesthetic standards. The puritan ethic dominated the mental landscape of the suburban dweller. Success was measured by its visible material manifestations. Since neighbors generally minded their own business, with occasional limited interaction occurring when some problem arose (usually a case of parents trying to sort out their children's misbehavior or social crises), conformity to community values was signified more through these material possessions and less through the more traditional moral and ethical codes of conduct. In fact, the ultimate moral imperative in the myth of the suburban middle landscape was acquisitiveness; the inhabitants were comfortable, having built a world of material objects within which they found security. While a feeling of humanity surfaced in the interactions of the central characters within the nuclear family in the suburban-middle-landscape comedies of the 1950s and 1960s, underlying the entire genre were notions of complacency and exclusion. This was a surface world cut off from the larger social environment with its racial tensions, its decaying urban industrial centers (most suburbanites, it could be presumed, worked in the inner-city business centers), and its Cold War between the United States and the Soviet Union, with the constant threat of nuclear annihilation. Television's myth of the suburban middle landscape became an idealized representation of the quality of life of upwardly mobile white Americans divorced from the social infrastructure that allowed that mobility (we are inevitably upwardly mobile at another's expense). We see the results of progress limited to the privileged, but we are denied access to the broader social reality in which that progress occurs.

The suburban-middle-landscape television comedy was a comedy of reassurance. Beneath its funny situations, involving the often inexplicable, illogical actions of cute kids who refused to become adults, was a very nearly uniform world view that television executive Sprague Vonier once termed the "urban outlook."[17] The urban outlook framed a world in which principles of fair play prevailed; judges were sober; lawyers were intelligent and honest; police were calm, understanding, brave, and, above all, incorruptible; everyone had a right to freedom of speech; everyone was entitled to the best possible education; the able, hard-working person would, with a bit of luck, do well financially; everyone should be kind to children and animals; and society will come to the aid of an individual in a personal crisis.[18]

This was the comedy of the true nuclear family. Sons and daughters struggled to grow up while their parents, who tended to smother them in piety and sociological wisdom, were constantly faced with their children's fantasies and nonsense, which, while illogical from an adult's point of view, were nevertheless refreshing and adventurous in a world of conformity and of fear of deviation from norms. We all know that when Beaver Cleaver says "sure, dad," what he really is saying is, "I'll do what you want me to do because you're a grown-up, but I really would rather have fun." This universal generational difference defines the basic comedic structure of the genre while it simultaneously points, albeit indirectly, to a social reality in which the archetypal adult says to us, all children at heart, "When you grow up, you too will find it necessary to conform to the dominant ideology so that you may be successful like us." Our laugh is a knowing one—we apprehend the irritations of our own constraints and admire the idealized freedom of Beaver, a little boy with buckteeth and an explorer's psyche.

Of all the suburban-middle-landscape television comedies of the 1950s and 1960s, four stand out as significant examples of the genre: *The Adventures of Ozzie and Harriet* (1952-66), *Father Knows Best* (1954-60, with reruns in 1960-63), *Leave It To Beaver* (1957-63), and *My Three Sons* (1960-72).

Of these four comedy series, only *Ozzie and Harriet* featured a real-life family as central characters. Ozzie, Harriet, David, and Ricky Nelson resided in a television house modeled on their real Hollywood home. On television, Ozzie was never acknowledged to have a job. He just seemed to hang around the house all the time, although we all knew he was an actor. Harriet was a housewife. Ricky sang pop songs on the series and soon became a real-life rock-and-roll star. Both David and Ricky grew up on the show. When they married in real life, their wives joined the cast of the show as regulars, becoming part of the entire enterprise. The medium of television became our kitchen window as we curiously peeked at the goings-on of our next-door neighbors, the Nelsons. Success abounded: The Nelsons were successful television stars, acting out their successful suburban lifestyle, the Hollywood dream of eternal progress, on the small screen before millions of viewers.

The other three series assembled adult and child actors and actresses to play families. *Father Knows Best*, which launched Robert

Young's highly successful television-acting career, featured Jim and Margaret Anderson (Young and Jane Wyatt) and their three children —Betty, 17 when the series began; Bud, 14; and Kathy, nine—who lived in the comfort of Springfield (in the Midwest). Jim, an agent for the General Insurance Company, and Margaret, a housewife, played the roles of thoughtful, responsible parents. As in all suburban-middle-landscape comedy, family members never raised their voices to one another. Problems were resolved quietly and sensibly, according to the wisdom of the parents and the dominant ideology of the day, to everyone's satisfaction. The children, while generally towing the line, occasionally successfully asserted their independence. The Andersons so epitomized the middle-American character of their time that the U.S. Department of the Treasury commissioned the series's producers to film a special episode to promote the 1959 U.S. Savings Bond Drive. Called "24 Hours in Tyrant Land," this episode showed the Anderson children trying to live for a day under a fictional dictatorship. This was late-1950s-television comedy's contribution to the Cold War. Other television personalities, most notably *Dragnet*'s Jack Webb, had made similar anti-Communist propaganda statements on celluloid. While the "24 Hours" episode was distributed to schools, churches, and meetings of civic organizations to promote the maintenance of democracy, American style, it was never aired on television.[19]

My Three Sons began its long run (five years on ABC, followed by seven on CBS) in 1960. The family was guided by widowed patriarch Steve Douglas, a consulting aviation engineer. Played by Fred MacMurray, Steve was strictly upscale, white collar. An avid golfer, he personified the pace of the myth of the suburban middle landscape —slow, deliberate, quiet, and, above all, even tempered. Steve's office was cramped, signifying either he was not at the top executive echelon, or he was not given to posturing or ostentation. The limited space of his office was in marked contrast to the spaciousness of the Douglas home—a two-story abode elegant by today's standards, yet a standard-issue upper-middle-class home in the mid-1960s. Its early-American furnishings and leather chairs bespoke tradition and success. In 1960 the Douglas brood included 18-year-old Mike, 14-year-old Robbie, and seven-year-old Chip—Steve's three sons. After five years on the show, Mike married and left the series, and Steve adopted Chip's next-door pal Ernie, an orphan. "Bub" O'Casey, Steve's father-in-law and surrogate housewife for the first four years of the series, was replaced by his brother, "Uncle Charlie," a crusty old sailor. "Bub" and "Uncle Charlie" provided perspective on the roots of the upscale Douglas family. They were gruff, undereducated, yet decent men. They were both taken in by the highly successful yet humble son-in-law. Their social position, however, was confounded as they functioned in the household as tireless, if willing, servants and as the boys' grandfathers.

The Douglases began their television life in "a medium-sized midwestern city" but moved to North Hollywood in 1967 because of Steve's job. Robbie had married Katie Miller in 1967 and they had triplets, all boys of course. In 1969 Steve married the widow Barbara Harper, one of Ernie's teachers, and in 1970 Chip eloped with his college-girlfriend Polly. By this point in the series run, all the men except O'Casey and Ernie had married and the premise of bachelorhood that had sparked much of the series comedy was gone. The series was fading fast in the ratings and a new era in television comedy, marked by the premiere of *All In The Family*, was beginning.

Like its predecessors, *My Three Sons* posited a clear view of the authority of the adult, especially the male, and stressed the sanctity of traditional American values such as the nuclear family, with its bonds of trust and concern, the importance of hard work, and the drive for success tempered with humility. This comedy also very clearly represented the myths of eternal progress and manifest destiny that were exemplified by the 1960s "space race" initiated by President John Kennedy at the beginning of the decade. When the scene shifted to Steve, the aviation engineer, at work at his desk, we see, in a medium-shot, on the wall immediately behind him, neatly framed photographs of powerful guided missiles exploding from their launch pads. These missiles, with their phallic signification, subtly reinforce notions of competition, a drive toward conquest (of space via the moon and of the Soviet Union), and, ultimately, patriarchal control of both the nuclear family and the larger world family. Their presence in the suburban middle landscape of the 1960s reveals the true colors behind the myth's camouflage.

Perhaps the most enduring example of the myth of the suburban middle landscape can be found in *Leave It To Beaver*. While the series's first run lasted six years, an average run for a successful television comedy, it seems destined for immortality, at least in television terms, in syndication. In 1982, 25 years after its premiere, *Leave It To Beaver* was being seen daily in 35 of the 50 largest U.S. cities, on virtually every cable system in the country via Ted Turner's Atlanta superstation WTBS, and in Japan and Africa. Its 234 episodes, all shot in black and white, provide us with a glimpse of a deceptively simple era in our recent history that ironically has reemerged, as proven by the TV rerun—a time immediately preceding the social upheavals of the Vietnam era, the free-speech movement, the revolt against the traditional authority of the family and state ideological apparatuses, and the ascendence of women toward equal partnership in the work experience. The quiet, idealized, insulated life of the suburban middle landscape would soon be confronted with a harsher reality outside our television screens. But the myth, though shaken, would live on.

The show's creators and principal writers, Joe Connelly and Bob Moser, had 12 children between them and were, by virtue of that statistic, qualified to write on the subject. Many of the rather mundane incidents and crises on the series were drawn from their own life experience. The ensemble acting of Hugh Beaumont, Barbara Billingsley, Tony Dow, and Jerry Mathers was of high quality for television comedy. Unlike *My Three Sons, Father Knows Best,* and even *Ozzie and Harriet*, in which the actors seemed to be acting and thus lacked artistic probability, *Leave It To Beaver* rang true as a work of realist fiction. As the embodiment of the suburban-middle-landscape myth, it speaks to us of an attitude, a world view with which we are now quite familiar.

The premiere of *Leave It To Beaver*, titled "Captain Jack," provides us with a clear example of this world view: In 1957, in the suburban town of Mayfield, lived a nice couple—a handsome, rugged looking, but gentle accountant in his late thirties or early forties, and a beautiful, pert, almost sexy housewife with blond hair and a marvelous wardrobe—and their two sons—one, 12 years old and entering puberty, was showing the initial signs of interest in girls and dating, while the other, five years his junior, hated girls and was interested in pet frogs as any kid would be. This was the quiet world of the Cleavers: Ward, June, Wally, and Theodore, the Beaver.

We fade in from black to a close-up of a pair of black shoes resting on a curb, then slowly tilt up to reveal a policeman in a black uniform. He is twirling a nightstick and, from this low-angle shot, he looks somber and threatening. Throughout this opening shot, we hear Ward Cleaver delivering his opening lecture in a voiceover; Ward, you'll remember, lectured a lot. He told the viewers: "Children and adults look at the world through different eyes. When you're young, a policeman stands ten feet tall. And if you see it in print, it's supposed to be true." Thus is established the series's basic premise—that in this world, the authority of adults and societal institutions is sacrosanct; skepticism has no space reserved for it in this psychic, mythic geography.

The scene shifts to Beaver and Wally sending away for a "genuine Florida alligator" advertised for $2.50 in the *Robot Men of Mars* comic. Ward and June of course know nothing about this, nor is it at all clear where the young boys got the money, a tidy sum in 1957, to purchase the animal. An illustration in the comic book shows a handsome man in a pith helmet, wrestling an alligator. From the relative sizes of the man and the alligator in the illustration, the scaly creature appears to be eight feet long. The boys trust the ad, but when their gator arrives at the Mayfield Post Office, they are chagrined to discover it is a baby alligator no more than six or seven inches long. There is no discussion of suing the company for false representation or of demanding their money back. Rather, accepting the deception, they visit their local "alligator farm" (every city of repute has one) to learn more about their new pet. A crusty old soul named Captain Jack operates the farm. He is every boy's dream of adventure—unshaven, wearing a soiled helmet and a striped boat-neck shirt, his gruff voice exhibiting his many years of experience in the jungle air. His demeanor, however, belies a periodic nip or two from the bottle— something adults would understand, but not little boys. He is exotic but unthreatening. Captain Jack gives the boys a regime for caring for their alligator, including feeding the little bugger a bizarre mixture of brandy and milk and raw eggs and massaging it with beauty cream. The boys swear fealty to the captain and appropriately name their baby gator after him. They return home elated.

To hide their alligator from their parents, yet keep it in or near water, Wally and Beaver place the gator on a sponge and float it in the toilet tank. (The producers had to fight for this scene with CBS censors, who had to that point prohibited the showing of toilets on the air. The producers won their battle.)

In the second act, we fade in to the Cleavers' substantial two-story home in what was an older suburban neighborhood; its white picket fence spoke of tradition, of an almost rustic serenity. (Later in the series, the fence disappeared and the house seemed more urban than rural.) We cut to Ward sitting calmly at the breakfast table while June serves him breakfast; she was seemingly chained to her toaster and skillet, although in 1957 the bondage appeared natural. Minerva, the Irish maid, enters the kitchen. In late middle age, white, and frumpy, if not dumpy, Minerva signifies suburban affluence—a Cleaver possession—yet avoids the racism attached to having a black maid working for whites. June turns to Ward and matter-of-factly states "I told Minerva to come three times a week now to help with the cleaning and the laundry." Ward says to June: "That's fine with me." June's statement implies Minerva has worked for the Cleavers before, but her duties, and, one assumes, the Cleavers' income, are presently increasing. Following this verbal confirmation of the Cleavers' bourgeois status, Ward notices that certain items are disappearing from around the house, most notably his brandy (no beer drinker is Ward). June confirms that her eggs and beauty cream, items associated with women/wifehood, are also rapidly disappearing. Ward suspects Minerva of sipping his brandy, when we know Wally and Beaver are mixing it with milk and feeding it to their pet, who has grown ever larger. The comedy here is generated in a traditional manner, by the withholding of important information from some of the core characters. In an incredible class-bound statement, Ward condemns Minerva by saying to June: "Maybe after a few nips, she begins to feel romantic." Here middle-aged, unattractive Minerva, representing the drabness of proletarian life, is portrayed as incapable of love or romance in her real conditions of existence; only when inebriated can she begin to understand the mysteries of romance withheld from her. This is reminiscent of many video and print ads from the peiod for such items as lipstick and hairspray, which, when used, transport the drab, lifeless woman to exotic lands to share her newly found sexuality with some muscular nut-brown lover who lives in a grass hut on stilts. Today, these housewifely fantasies are pandered to by Harlequin romances. The Cleavers, exemplifying the suburban middle landscape, can, of course, transcend the need for fantasy and escapism and find romance in their luxurious surroundings. The Cleavers are on the inside track, disdainfully looking out, the haves scorning the have-nots. Their status, and, by implication, their control over their own lives, admits the sensual under normal material conditions of existence.

The materialistic bias built into this episode is further revealed in a strange scene in which Wally and the Beaver play the role of youthful entrepreneurs, charging their school chums ten cents apiece to see the alligator as the boys regurgitate Captain Jack's inflated, circuslike discourse on the lives of alligators in the wild. As we watch a line of satisfied young customers filing out the Cleavers' front door, we know that Wally and Beaver have made a high rate of return on what began as a pet and has subtly changed into an investment.

Later, when Minerva goes down to the Cleavers' basement to get the laundry, she discovers the alligator, which the boys have moved from the toilet tank to the basement sink because it outgrew its initial habitat. Minerva, extremely agitated, informs Ward and June of the pet's presence. However, Ward, thinking Minerva is once again drinking, commands her to go home and dry out before returning to the Cleaver household. June goes to the basement, discovers the alligator, and so informs Ward, who, still unbelieving, takes a skeptical look for himself. The alligator bites Ward on the finger, thus providing his punishment for his treatment of Minerva while, at the same time, deflecting the more basic issue of Ward's distrust of blue-collar workers.

Naturally, the gator must go. Ward, the rational, gentle family patriarch explains to Wally and Beaver that he is proud of them for raising the alligator, an act which implied responsibility, an adult quality stressed throughout the series. He adds, "Someday you boys are going to grow up, leave your mother and me, get married, and have a family of your own." Such a cycle was of course inevitable in 1957. Captain Jack, the alligator, would certainly want the same opportunity. So the understanding mother and father, and the acquiescent boys return Captain Jack to Captain Jack's alligator farm. Even this scene stresses the Cleavers' bourgeois status, for while all the other tourists at the alligator farm wore only shirts or plain dresses, Ward, Wally, and Beaver all wore coats and ties and June wore an expensive, well-tailored dress that could have been purchased in Beverly Hills.

The inferior role of women and the status of adults as the agents of social control in this mythic world were continually represented in the series. In a 1962 episode, near the end of its run, *Leave It To Beaver* tackled the evils of slothfulness, a character trait out of sync with the myths of eternal progress and the puritan ethic. Ward entrusts Wally and Beaver, who are now 17 and 12, respectively, with the job of cleaning up the front yard and the garage. It is a beautiful Saturday morning (it never rains on the suburban middle landscape) and the boys' fancies turn to lighter matters than raking leaves. They end up doing goofy things like taking target practice with Beaver's old bow and arrow, which are due to be discarded with the other trash, and playing catch. Time passes fast when you're having so much fun, and the boys finally finish their yard work later in the afternoon, too late to have Mr. Peck, the local trash hauler, take the refuse to the Mayfield city dump. Wally's friends, Clarence "Lumpy" Rutherford and Eddie Haskell (the latter the prototypical con man), happen to be driving through the neighborhood in Lumpy's jalopy. They agree to haul the trash for half of what Peck would charge. Lumpy and Eddie drive off with the trash, but, being lazy, dump it on a vacant lot in the middle of town instead of at the dump. The lot owner, a

Mr. Hill, finds a magazine with Ward's name on it among the rubble and lambastes Ward for being a litterbug. Ward, irate that his reputation has been tarnished, commands all four boys to clean up Hill's vacant lot the following morning. In an interchange following the incident, Wally admits, "If we hadn't goofed around all day, then this whole mess wouldn't have happened." Ward, angry but reserved as always, replies: "That's exactly what it means Wally. So the next time you fellows just do what you're told when you're told, and we'll all avoid a lot of trouble." This episode, like most other episodes, represents an event that helps initiate the boys into the adult society as defined in the dominant ideology. The woman in this society, while not lazy, as are the children, is represented instead as vacuous. In the same episode, Ward makes small talk with June, a device often used as a bridge between the two scenes that involve the boys. Ward says to June: "How is the news today?" June responds, "Well, I started to read the paper. I found that sewing was much more restful." The woman does not think in this milieu, and is not a part of the events that frame the world outside the house; in other words, in a world in which the woman's place is in the kitchen or at the beauty parlor, the woman is not a socially relevant being.

The signs of the material existence of the suburban middle land-scape are manifold in *Leave It To Beaver*, as in the other comedies of the genre—June wears white cotton gloves to go shopping; Ward eats breakfast in a tie and a buttoned sports jacket; the Cleavers' two-story brick home has carriage lamps outside; and Ward's study resembles a library in a mansion, with hard-wood, floor-to-ceiling bookcases containing innumerable leather-bound books (the "Great Books" series and encyclopedias were big door-to-door sales items at the time). The Cleavers, as were the other television suburban-middle-landscape families, were upscale, socially conservative, politically inactive, essentially kind to one another, and generally dull.

The P.T.A. Magazine praised *Leave It To Beaver* as showing children and adults how "to value each other more truly and to set up worthy standards for their life together."[20] With its emphasis on everyday things and on learning lessons, *Beaver* was a product of the times, which were changing even as *Leave It To Beaver* was being produced. The suburban middle landscape is the epitome of comfort, where the values of family support are portrayed amidst the reassurance of modest wealth. It is here that an entire generation of the middle class grew up and purchased its happiness. Yet the material wealth rested on a thin base of pretension and inauthentic human interaction. The wealth was accumulated at another's expense, a matter left untouched in these suburban-middle-landscape television comedies. We were slow to realize this, but many finally awoke to it. We rarely see our television protagonists even remotely acknowledge these social facts or question their own social status outside their nuclear-family existence. The outside world is a vague abstraction providing the background for a didactic morality play, with comedic elements inserted to hold the viewers' attention.

THE RURAL-MIDDLE-LANDSCAPE COMEDY

A certain sanctity existed in the suburban-middle-landscape comedies of the 1950s and early 1960s; it was characterized by the gentle authority of the patriarch and the strength of warm family re- lations exemplified by the loving, if often vacuous mothering activ- ities of the homemaker that overcame such personal character defects as the slothfulness, lying, and unbridled greed hidden just beneath the surface of respectability. At the same time, a barely detectable undercurrent of class separation and tension framed the human trans- action in this mythic milieu. In contrast, in the rural-middle-landscape comedies of the late 1950s and throughout the 1960s, and especially in such immensely popular comedies as *The Beverly Hillbillies* and *Green Acres*, we find class separation and tension surfacing; however, expressed through the often bizarre acts of some very odd central characters, these class tensions are thus concealed, rendered both comedic and sterile. Unlike the suburban-middle-landscape comedies, in which the children were ridiculously illogical by adult standards (to which they were always expected to adhere), in the rural-middle- landscape comedies, that character trait shifts to the naive yet noble adults who inhabit a world filled with urban con men and pretentious middle-class boors reminiscent of Moliere's characters.

In the suburban-middle-landscape comedies, the adult central characters are motivated by drives for success and material acquisition tempered with humility—tacitly acknowledging the humble roots of the common man. This traditional rags-to-riches dream incorporating the myths of the puritan ethic and of eternal progrsss surfaced throughout the entire subgenre. In this mythic world, conformity to community values was signified through the reification of traditional moral and ethical codes of conduct (e.g., clean living—a clean front yard free of dirty old leaves, dandelions, and scraggly bushes; em- ployed in this project was a battery of bourgeois implements such as electric hedge trimmers, weed eaters, mulchers, and fertilizer wagons; or, if one wished to flaunt his bourgeois status, he would simply hire a lawn-care service to do the work for him). In contrast, in the rural-middle-landscape comedies, the central characters either have inadvertently achieved wealth and simply have no interest in the status related to possession of money (e.g., Jed Clampett, through hunting for some food, struck oil); have worked hard for wealth and subsequently rejected it for a purer, more spiritual existence (Oliver Wendell Douglas giving up Park Avenue for the serenity of Hooterville); or have transcended the very notion of material wealth through upbringing and staunchly held traditional values (Amos McCoy and Andy Taylor). In all cases, the central characters of the rural middle landscape, rooted to their humane ecosystems by the warmth of their biological families, safe from the perils of the isolation of the frontier and from the deception in the city, speak to us of basic human values. Yet, their portrayal as children outside the mainstream of contemporary technicized culture condemns their actions to the status of antitechnical responses to a society they do not understand and cannot keep up with. The rustic, in questioning the entire milieu of advanced capitalism and its principal bourgeois and petit bourgeois actors, is rendered both quaint and unthreatening because one operates outside the guiding myth of eternal progress. We can therefore laugh at the hillbilly without heeding his or her warnings dealing with questions of morality and ethics in advanced capitalism.

The Real McCoys, the pioneer rural-middle-landscape comedy, began its six-year run on ABC and CBS in 1957. Financed by Danny Thomas Productions, the series barely made it to the small screen: NBC turned it down, but ABC, then with a very weak schedule, was finally convinced of its potential. ABC would not be sorry for its decision. Production began. Writers Irving and Norman Pincus created an ensemble of simple, folksy characters who were nothing short of stereotypical. The patriarch of the McCoy clan, Grampa Amos, played by three-time Academy Award-winning actor Walter Brennan, walked with a gimp, and spoke in a high-pitched, broken voice verging on a hoarse shout. Amos, a repository of country wisdom and a constant meddler, was a wily old codger, careful with what little money he had, and ready to stand up for his rights—the wisdom of experience had taught Amos to be wary of strangers, especially city slickers. Amos's grandson Luke, played by Richard (then known as Dick) Crenna, was the prototypical young male hillbilly—strong, angularly handsome, naive, gullible, kindhearted, and a bit slow to catch on. His devoted wife Kate was a simple country girl who was comfortable in the kitchen and had few material wants. Luke's 11-year-old brother Little Luke, a relatively docile youngster, understood the meaning of respect for adult authority. Pepino, the guitar-playing Latino, referred to in the show's theme song as "the Hired Hand," was happy-go-lucky, always smiling, and complacent in his position of subservience.

The McCoys, referring to the origins of their namesakes, Hatfield and McCoy, were a West Virginia mountain family that moved to a ranch in California's San Fernando Valley in search of the American Dream. While they had yet to realize that dream of prosperity, the family bonds—"together they share all the sorrows and joy" (again from the theme song)—were very powerful, and compensated for their material wants. It is true that the family bonds of the suburban-middle-landscape comedies were also strong. Yet, in *The Real McCoys,* as in the other rural-middle-landscape comedies, the bonds, exemplified in both the geographical and psychic space of the rural environment, were constantly threatened by the encroachment of the city—a common motif in this comedic subgenre. The city indeed became a psychic threat. Its residents exhibited such character traits as greed, deception, and vanity—the traits of the bourgeois and petit bourgeois classes in an advanced capitalist economy. The rural residents, who held to their more traditional agrarian/populist values, honesty and a sense of sharing, at first seemed no match for their cunning urban counterparts. But, in the end, the purity of the peasants won the day. Of course, the characterizations of both classes were so exaggerated that it became difficult to accept the results of the conflict of values as meaningful.

A 1962 episode of *The Real McCoys* provides striking evidence of the use of this class conflict to garner laughs. By this point in the series, Luke is a widower and Amos is trying to find him a wife. Amos and neighbor George MacMichael take off in George's car for a convention, leaving Luke to mind the house. An old ranch-style home, well kept but sparsely furnished, it signifies a basic "dignified" poverty, reflected in the kitchen cabinets covered with curtains instead of cabinet doors. Before he left, Amos had asked Luke to fix the leaky roof while he was away. We cut to a sign on the side of a modern, shiny automobile that reads "New Age Building Materials." In the car sit Jack Masters and Sally Burton, both sharply dressed and neatly coiffed, but exuding the veneer that clearly belies their status as city-type traveling salespersons. The stage is set for the con. Masters sends the beautiful, well-proportioned Miss Burton ahead to the McCoy

ranch in an effort to sell Luke some roof coating. Luke, the shy, gullible adult-child, is easily taken in by Sally's appearance and tight
sweater. Sally describes her product to Luke—a "new miracle plastic
spray" that gives "100 years of worry-free roofing." Luke responds,
"Imagine that! You can still have a roof after the house is gone."
Sally grimaces. She continues, "Our company has developed this material for weatherproofing of missiles." While Luke buys this obvious
nonsense, he is still reluctant to commit himself to the project because
of its cost. Masters, the fast-talking con man, must use pressure to
make the sale. He appeals to Luke's "manliness," his need to take
charge, to fix his house, to make an adult decision, and, at the same
time, cites the need to help Sally keep her job, which will be lost if
she doesn't make some sales in the neighborhood. Luke, unsure of
his status as man or child, wavers. Sally begins to cry. Luke empa-
thizes, "Now don't go gittin' yourself all onionized." Moved by this
display of womanly frailty and feeling guilty for her plight, Luke
agrees to buy the roofing treatment and to help sell the product to
his neighbors, for 2 percent of the gross.

Act two finds Luke conducting a meeting on his front porch. In
the foreground is an old beaten-up pickup truck, its tailgate lowered,
and a hay bale in the truck bed, signifying the poverty of the area and
framing the entire scam in progress. Luke, totally caught up in the
headiness of the role of entrepreneur, is the proverbial "snake-oil
salesman." He's now a "man," in charge of a meetin', and moving his
neighbors through his oratorical powers. Luke shouts to the assembled
crowd: "As you all know, us McCoys is just poor dirt farmers like all
you. Why, to us, money is practically just a word in the dictionary.
So when we spend it, we got to get double value. . . . I'm going to give
you a demonstration that's going to open your eyes to the wonders
of science." Luke preceeds to demonstrate a sample of a shingle supposedly treated in the miracle plastic spray, which he describes as
"treated with all them chemical goodies" and "satchumerated with
all them chemicals." The neighbors are impressed and they all buy. By
now, Luke is feeling very proud of his efforts. Sally turns to Masters
and comments, "His head's starting to swell up like our shingles in
the rain."

When Amos returns from the convention, Luke tells him of all
the activity. Amos is quickly skeptical. Luke demonstrates their newly
coated roof by turning the garden hose on the shingles. Amos, sitting
in his living-room rocking chair, is drenched. Luke, despondent and
admitting he was "the Judas goat" leading the lambs to slaughter for

a payoff, helps Amos bait a trap. They call Masters and Burton back on the pretense that George MacMichael wants to have his roof coated. They all meet at the McCoys'. Amos pretends to get his painful "weather knee," which signals rain. Masters and Burton become visibly nervous. Amos describes other "swindlers" who have come to the valley, especially the "magic-fertilizer swindlers."

AMOS: Remember them?
GEORGE: I bet they haven't forgotten us either.
MASTERS: What happened to them?
LUKE: They recovered . . . eventually.
AMOS: They was young and healthy to start with. They recovered quickly. But the crooks with the miracle stock feed.
GEORGE: That was pitiful. Just pitiful.

Luke sprays the roof with the hose. Masters, sitting in Amos's chair, is drenched. The neighbors, who have been waiting outside, angrily converge on the two city salesperson-con artists. Masters reluctantly returns all their deposits. Luke turns to Sally and notes, "Miss Burton, you have just set the cause of the American business woman back 50 years." Masters says to Amos, "You tricked me. And I trusted you."

In this last scene, we find a key story element that has often been employed in the rural context, although generally in melodrama—the city dweller's fear of the evil that lurks just beyond the bend in the country road. For while the rural middle landscape in its comedic form is full of rather gentle, charming, if dull-witted characters—misfits with pure values—beneath this idyllic surface lives a seething rage that emerges when the fast-talking city slicker stumbles into the town, bringing his contemptible values.

The adult masculine icons that represent the materialization of this basic value conflict are clearly established—the muddy or dusty jalopy, the floppy hat, and rumpled clothing and unshaven face representing the purity of the country, the earth, and the common heritage; and the highly polished, chrome-plated sedan with whitewall tires, the fedora (or, absent a hat, the shiny, slicked-back hair), and the neatly pressed suit and clean-shaven face representing the jaded wealth of the bourgeoisie. The adult female icons follow the same general patterns—the honorable rural woman's neatly pressed but very simple, loose-fitting cotton print dress, and a minimum of makeup; and the urban woman's snug-fitting business suit or sweater and skirt, and her heaviness of makeup and hair spray.

The Real McCoys broke television ground. The series's high ratings—number eight in the 1958-59 season, and number five in the

1960-61 season—opened the door for the other rural comedies that were to rule the airwaves in the 1960s as the suburban-middle-landscape comedies faded away.

One of the most successful television comedies of the 1960s, *The Andy Griffith Show*, would bring to the rural-middle-landscape comedy a true human warmth exemplified in the character of Sheriff Andy Taylor of the small town of Mayberry, North Carolina. Andy, a widower with a young son, Opie, played by Ronny Howard, later of *Happy Days* fame, lived with his Aunt Bee. At work, Andy was faced less with the problems of preserving law and order than with the difficult task of preserving his own sanity in the presence of his incredible, bumbling deputy, Barney Fife, played to perfection by Don Knotts, who won five Emmy Awards as best supporting actor in the role. (He left the series in 1965 to pursue his own series.) Andy was philosophical, a kind father to Opie and to the denizens of Mayberry. The show's opening reflects this relationship between father and son as we see a two-shot of Andy and Opie quietly strolling along a lake, fishing poles on their shoulders, Opie barefooted, and Andy with his comforting hand resting on Opie's shoulder. Andy's gentle masculinity was in sharp contrast to the skinny, nervous, pip-squeakish Barney—a man without an original thought but with plenty of opinions; a man who constantly tried to imitate Andy, but who simultaneously was possessed with an overwhelming drive to be macho. His totally laughable attempts at masculinity through constant posturing and bravado provided many of television comedy's finest moments. Aunt Bee provided the womanly warmth in the series. The epitome of the countrified "mother hen," Bee, who always wore her hair in a bun, was eternally good-natured, jovial, and generally very slow until she got excited, at which point she would scurry around in total confusion "like a chicken with her head cut off." However, Aunt Bee broke the stereotypicalness of the countrywoman character in one way—she was a lousy cook.

Mayberry was generally unthreatened and unthreatening. There was hardly any crime in this peaceful setting. The jail's occasional occupants were mostly town drunks like Otis, who seemed to be a permanent resident. Once in a while, a city criminal would pass through town and cause a momentary uproar. The conflicts which arose in Mayberry were motivated not so much by greed or jealousy or vanity as they were by individuals' needs to maintain their sense of self-esteem, to demonstrate that they were of some value to the community. Pride was based not on a neighbor's defeat or on assuring someone else's lower social status, but, rather, on one's own sense of accomplishment or contribution to the goals of the community. An early-1961 episode provides a clear example of the human warmth and sense of caring that define this version of the rural-middle-landscape comedy.

Each year for the past 11 years, Aunt Bee and Clara Johnson had entered the pickle contest at the county fair. Clara had won the contest every year. She feigns humility, but we can tell she is very proud of her success. She is the town "pickle expert," as is reflected in her confident explications of the proper combination of ingredients and the techniques of pickling necessary for the successful pickle-making endeavor. Her success in pickle making compensates for her shortcomings in other areas. Aunt Bee, on the other hand, makes terrible pickles, as Andy, Barney, and Opie will quickly attest to. Act one begins with Clara tasting Aunt Bee's latest batch of pickles and offering Aunt Bee expert advice on possible modifications in Bee's approach. Bee, while at first graciously admitting Clara's pickling accomplishments, soon becomes tired of Clara's barely hidden condescension. In this "little world," success, while limited in its larger social impact, is nevertheless important in an interpersonal context.

Aunt Bee brings a jar of her new pickles to the sheriff's office for Andy and Barney to sample. Their faces drop in despair. To please Aunt Bee, they bite into the pickles and pretend satisfaction. Meanwhile, a fly lands on a pickle on Andy's desk and promptly expires. After Aunt Bee's exit, Barney turns to Andy and declares, "I don't know how I can face the future when I know there's eight quarts of these pickles in it." Thus is the stage set for the complication and confusion that frame so much action in the situation comedy. Andy and Barney decide to replace the "bad old home pickles" in Aunt Bee's jars with "good old store pickles." Andy explains this deception to Opie as father, son, and deputy Fife carry out the deed in Aunt Bee's kitchen: "Opie, I want you to understand. Ordinarily I don't approve of doin' things behind folks' backs. Now you know why we're doin' this?" Opie answers "Yeah, 'cause we don't want to hurt Aunt Bee's feelings." Opie has learned his values well. Having pulled the switcheroo, the boys must dispose of Aunt Bee's pickles. Barney takes them to the highway, and begins to stop cars with out-of-state license plates, giving their drivers a "safe-driving award"—a jar of Aunt Bee's deadly pickles. At dinner, everyone can comment on the deliciousness of the (store-bought) pickles. But the deception backfires, as it must. Aunt Bee had decided that the pickles were to be her last batch and she would not enter the contest. But since the boys seemed to like them so much, she decided to enter them in the fair. The joke was beginning to go as sour as her pickles. What if Clara got beat by a store pickle?

We cut to a scene in which Clara shows Andy her pickle scrapbook with its 11 blue ribbons. Clara confides in Andy: "Whenever I get lonely or discouraged, I take out my book and look at my ribbons." Her eyes light up as music swells in the background: "I don't know how to explain it, but it's a great comfort to know that there's something I can do. Well, I suppose I'm just a foolish old lady." Andy, obviously moved, responds, "Oh well, now, I wouldn't believe that for a minute." Clara answers, "You probably think I'm just putting on airs. But I do try to make my pickles better every year. It means so much to me." Here we have a clear clue to the true meaning of the rural middle landscape. Clara, the traditional artisan, is not alienated from her work; she has direct control over it, and it thus reflects and in fact is a part of her being—Clara and her pickles are inseparable. Andy relates the encounter to Barney: "What's small potatoes to some folks can be mighty important to others. Barney, that poor soul just lives for that contest, and if she got nosed out by a store pickle, I'd never forgive myself."

Barney and Andy are forced to eat all eight quarts of store pickles in a hurry so that Aunt Bee will make a new batch of homemade pickles and enter those in the contest. This she does, and we cut to the judging at the fair. The judges, barely able to continue their work after tasting one of Aunt Bee's homemade pickles, suspect that the pickles were dipped in kerosene. Clara wins again. Aunt Bee is a very gracious loser: "As long as my family likes what I make, that's blue-ribbon enough for me." Because the boys liked the pickles so much, she made 16 more quarts.

In the epilogue, Barney comes over to Aunt Bee's to pick up Andy, who is eating breakfast. He sits down to eat a piece of toast, opens the jelly jar. They both sniff. Barney says to Andy: "You been doin' some paintin' in here?" Andy: "No. Probably just some glue Opie's usin' on model airplanes." Barney: "Don't smell like glue to me. Smells more like ammonia." Andy: "You don't think that gas stove's leakin', do ya?" Barney starts to eat his toast with the jelly on it, but nearly passes out; it's Aunt Bee's homemade marmalade. They just can't win.

Aunt Bee's "family" and Clara's blue ribbons are their respective "small potatoes," very personal concerns related not to larger questions of social relations, but, rather, to the immediate everyday experience of the insulated environment of the rural middle landscape.

The problem of self-esteem is raised throughout this series. In a 1966 episode, Andy and Goober, who runs the local gas station, go to an evening continuing-education class to study American history. The men of Mayberry all wear suits and ties to class—reflecting the importance they have placed on this activity. Goober feels inadequate because of a self-perceived limited cognitive capacity, which is in truth a lack of educational background. He lags far behind the class, although he has studied hard. With no confidence and with a vocabulary inadequate for the discussion of the history of political thought, Goober drops out of school, goes on a three-week hunting trip, something he is very skilled at doing, and returns to Mayberry sporting a beard (he forgot to take his razor). The people of Mayberry think Goober, with his new facial hair, looks like a scholar. They refer to Goober as a "deep thinker," a "scientist," an "ambassador," or a "philosopher." Goober wastes little time taking these compliments to heart, grows a full beard, and with confidence, or a swell head—the line between the two is often a fine one—returns to class toting a briefcase and an unstoppable mouth. A veritable fount of knowledge, Goober develops a country analogy for every political event involving U.S. domestic and international policy making. His grammar and syntax are still pure rural middle landscape, but his ideas are generally sound. As he stands to discourse in the foreground of the frame, a picture of Abe Lincoln on the back wall of the classroom is shown over his left shoulder. The link is obvious.

Soon Goober becomes the town boor. He is not really engaging anyone in authentic human conversation, but, rather, is merely demonstrating his newfound knowledge. Pumped up with pride like a country rooster, he's talking to himself, but he can't hear the echo. People begin avoiding him in the street. His wisdom is carried to the level of absurdity. One day he stops at a fruitstand, picks up a red apple, and addresses it: "One time you was a seed." He visits his chum Floyd, the barber, and states with authority, "A man's best friend is not his dog. It's people." Andy, who can stand no more, ultimately takes responsibility for ending both Goober's pontifications and his isolation, which is now almost complete. Andy says to his old friend, "Confidence is something that's on the inside. . . . It doesn't hurt to listen once in a while." Goober subsequently regains his humility, shaves his beard, and with renewed confidence, returns to the evening class as himself.

The Andy Griffith Show, which ran from 1960 through 1968, was immensely popular. It was never lower than seventh in the ratings, and in its final year it was the highest-rated series on television in the

1967-68 season. By then the Vietnam conflict was well along; the free-speech movement at Berkeley had signaled a new student awareness of political and social inequity; we were about to come to grips with Tet and napalm in a rural context halfway around the earth; and our urban slums were about to burn; but we took refuge in the television security of Sheriff Andy Taylor of Mayberry, North Carolina, deeply embedded in the rural middle landscape, where there was no war, no crime, and no deep division in our social fabric.

If *The Andy Griffith Show* stressed warm human values within the generally isolated cognitive and geographical space of rural America, *The Beverly Hillbillies* and *Green Acres*, each in a distinct way, brought the rural middle landscape face to face with the greed and vanity of the city. In this dialectic of rural purity and urban seaminess, we find positive values of the rural area, such as familial love and support, honesty, and humility emerging victorious, although the victory is a hollow one, for the human manifestations of rural purity—the charming, oddball central characters—in all their naiveté, manage to deflect and thereby subvert the very significance of the confrontation.

The Beverly Hillbillies was one of those rare television phenomena—an immediate smash hit. Created and produced by Paul Henning, it was the highest-rated program in its first two television seasons (1962-64). However, its charm began to wear thin by its third season as it fell to twelfth in the ratings and stabilized between the eighth and twelfth spots for the next four years. Featuring actor-dancer Buddy Ebsen in the title role of Jed Clampett, the Clampett clan included Granny (Irene Ryan), Elly May (Donna Douglas), and Jethro Bodine (Max Baer, Jr.)—a motley group of kind, nature-loving Ozark Mountain hill people who struck oil in their front yard, instantly became enormously wealthy, and moved to a Beverly Hills mansion on the advice of their relatives. Jed, the clan's patriarch, is a widower. Full of native intelligence if not book learning, Jed is the voice of compromise and restraint, who must constantly arbitrate between the quick-tempered ancient countrywoman, Granny—a feisty hellcat whose character was the exact opposite to that of Aunt Bee of *The Andy Griffith Show*—and Mrs. Drysdale, the Clampetts' next-door neighbor, and wife of Milburn Drysdale, president of the Commerce Bank of Beverly Hills, an institution deeply indebted to the Clampetts for their business. The two young ones, the beautiful blond-haired virgin Elly May and the large-framed, bone-headed country oaf Jethro, provide innumerable causes for guffawing as their seemingly total ignorance of urban customs and lack of formal education get them into awkward situations. Both have been educated in the woods, and commune much better with "critters" than with city folk. Jed must constantly rescue Granny, Elly, and Jethro by humbly apologizing to the city folk who have been "wronged" by the naive Clampetts' actions. It seems as if the Clampetts are always begging forgiveness for their status as outsiders. This, of course, makes their superior values easy to write off.

As with *The Real McCoys*, California seemed to hold the key to the American Dream for the Clampett clan. However, Jed et al. did not go to California in search of a living wage, as did the McCoys, but, rather, because, as the theme song tells us, it "is the place ya oughta be"—a beckoning mecca complete with movie stars and swimming pools. The Clampetts are more the observers of than participants in the American Dream. They, as are many viewers, are fascinated with status that seems to come naturally to the wealthy in advanced capitalist America. However, the Clampetts, while millionaires, are indeed on the periphery because of their unkempt appearance and country ways, and they intend to remain there. They maintain their heritage of self-sufficiency, for while they could easily afford a mansion full of servants, they have none, preferring to perform all house duties themselves. It is, of course, possible that had they desired servants, none would agree to live and work in such an eccentric, low-status atmosphere and to cook possum bellies for Granny.

The Beverly Hillbillies is highly dependent on physical comedy and gestures. Jethro's herculean strength, Elly's awkward shyness, Jed's country amble and bowlegs, and Granny's militant duck walk give the characters distinctive movement qualities, and dictate much of the "business" in which they engage. This ranges from Jethro's lifting automobiles and airplanes off the ground and moving them around, to Granny's charging after the Drysdales, shotgun thrust forward, as she prepares, as she says, to "feud 'em." The objects of civilized society become properties used in this physical comedy. For example, in one episode the Clampetts confuse a beautiful old billiard table that came with their new mansion with what Granny called an "eatin' table." The pool cues became "pot passers"—the table was so large that four people could not conveniently pass food around it without inserting the pool cues through the pot handles and gently easing the suspended pots across the green expanse. Jed sharpened a few of the pool cues and they were used to pass whole parts of a turkey from serving platter to hungry Clampetts. The table rail was a bit unusual for an eating table, but Granny surmised its function as preventing plates from slipping off onto the floor. The green felt was a sign that the previous owners were indeed bad housekeepers; Granny, thinking the tablecloth was stuck to the table underneath, tried in vain to peel it off, but finally gave up in frustration and disgust. While we must really suspend our disbelief when faced with such ridiculously illogical situations—after all, what rural county doesn't sport at least one bar, or, if dry, a meeting hall with a pool table in it—the Clampetts' total isolation from the modern world becomes the series's consistent comedic premise; and as physical comedy it works very well, although after a while, such comedy grows stale if not accompanied by complex characters who develop as the series progresses.

Beyond the physical comedy of *The Hillbillies*, the dialectic of rural and urban values is a frequent theme in the plot lines. These values are directly tied to socioeconomic class differences. The Clampetts are an amalgam of the rural hick and the nouveau riche, with their rural values controlling the use of their wealth. Milburn Drysdale is a callous bourgeois banker, putting capital to work for the Clampetts; he is conservative to the point of being overly cautious as the Clampetts try to give money away or help finance their rural friends' rather odd entrepreneurial ventures. Drysdale is portrayed as an angry, shameless, and ruthless parasite. He underpays and verbally abuses his employees, most notably Miss Jane Hathaway, his personal assistant. Yet he always looks the fool as he must humble himself before his main depositors, the Clampetts, whom he can barely tolerate. Drysdale's wife, a fat, lazy woman with no wit, represents the decadent blue blood. Her family having fallen on financially hard times, she married the commoner Milburn to regain the pride that comes with material wealth. Her voice, rising in a cracking falsetto, reveals her unbearable pretensions. The Clampetts, especially Granny, while finding her insufferable, nevertheless are willing to accept her character defects if only because she is their neighbor.

In one particularly revealing episode very early in the series, Drysdale's 35-year-old stepson Sonny (played by Louie Nye), comes home to visit from Harvard, where he has been an undergraduate student for 17 years. Effeminate, immature, vain, and slothful, Sonny is a fop—the archetypal "blue blood-on-the-skids." Sonny hates his stepfather's low caste. His mother consoles him: "I know it was wrong of me to marry a common bank president, but I wanted you to have everything, and all I could give you was the heritage of a fine old family. But it takes money too, darling." Sonny would have none of this: "Money. I hate that word. It makes the rich the social equal of us." "Oh, no, dear," responds Mrs. Drysdale, "it would never do that."

Milburn, who constantly seeks ways to please the Clampetts, has decided that Sonny should date Elly May. Having never seen Elly, Sonny is reluctant to participate. He informs his stepfather, "I refuse to date a strange girl just to benefit your economic situation." Mrs. Drysdale chimes in: "I've heard the most disturbing reports about the Clampetts. I understand they're no better than peasants." Sonny, appalled at the thought of dating a peasant, is quickly won over, however, when he spots Elly lounging by her back-yard swimming pool. Sonny, the fallen aristocrat, lacks any sense of principles, and has no commitment save to the pursuit of ephemeral sensual pleasure. He is a 35-year-old child, as much outside the world of meaningful adult social relationships as are the Clampetts.

In Act Two, Jed and Granny prepare Elly for her date with Sonny. Totally unaware of her own sexuality and knowing nothing about the customs of dating or of the phrase "the birds and the bees" (which both Elly and Jed believe refers to critters in the woods), Elly is about to begin her initiation. Jed describes "courtin' and sparkin'" to her, and it seems as though she gets the general drift of that activity. Sonny, meanwhile, prepares for his date, admiring himself in the mirror. We cut to Sonny's arrival at the Clampett mansion: Dressed to kill in a double-breasted blazer, he arrives in his Mercedes-Benz 190 convertible, parks next to Jed's dilapidated truck, gets out, and saunters to the Clampetts' front door. Jethro enters the frame; dressed in a coat too small, his pants held up by a rope and falling a little below midcalf, his black socks and gigantic brogan shoes calling attention to his status as country clown, Jethro is mistaken for an eccentric servant. Referring to Jed's truck, Sonny asks Jethro to move that "weird thing." Jethro of course thinks Sonny is talking about the Mercedes, and after Sonny is admitted to the mansion by Granny, Jethro and Jed (who has arrived on the scene) store the Mercedes behind some bushes, safely out of sight. Elly comes down the stairs to meet Sonny. She is dressed in a pretty, promish party dress, but she is not wearing shoes. After some preliminary niceties, including Sonny's gift to her—a framed picture of himself—he tries to kiss Elly's hand. Thinking Sonny is trying to bite her, Elly flips Sonny. He lands on his back and, dazed, picks himself up and flees the house. Jethro, having hidden Sonny's automobile, has returned to the front of the house. Upon learning that his Mercedes has been so disposed of, the irate and feeble Sonny begins pummeling Jethro in the chest with karate chops. Jethro, feeling no pain, stands immobile as Sonny hurts his hand.

Following this incident, we cut to the Clampetts arriving at the Drysdales to apologize for their actions. Sonny's car is returned, Elly is sorry she misunderstood Sonny's intentions, and Jed regrets not greeting Sonny at the front door, "as a proper pa should." Granny, who has nothing for which to apologize, and wouldn't have apologized if she had, reluctantly invites the Drysdales over for Thanksgiving dinner. In the final scene, following Jed's saying grace, we see the pot passers in action and we note the looks of consternation on the faces of the Drysdales, who are "slumming" so that they can continue to benefit from the Clampetts' wealth.

Throughout this episode and the entire series, the humor is produced both by the Clampetts' ignorance of urban customs and language, which generates much of the physical comedy, and by Drysdale's constant groveling at the feet of these humble millionaires, who would seemingly not even consider withdrawing their money from his bank. The folksy Clampetts seem firmly tied to tradition, to the family as an institution, and warm human values such as sharing one's good fortune with the less fortunate; at the same time, as outsiders, their acts seem anachronistic, gestures to be laughed at rather than emulated. The Drysdales, on the other hand, seem lost. Mrs. Drysdale deludes herself about maintaining her aristocratic heritage; and Milburn has no tradition, living from day to day, fearing the loss of his wealth, which could occur by virtue of a single act—the Clampetts' removal of their assets from his vault.

In retrospect, this rural-middle-landscape comedy appears quite cynical, admiring but ultimately discounting basic human values associated with the pure spirit of rural life, and condemning yet tacitly accepting the life of Beverly Hills, a jaded version of the American Dream.

One additional version of the rural-middle-landscape comedy gets brief mention here, if only because of its basic premise and the fact that *The Beverly Hillbillies* creator, Paul Henning, created it, too. *Green Acres*, an exact reversal of the situation in *The Beverly Hillbillies*, had a successful six-year run on CBS (1965-71). It featured Eddie Albert in the role of Oliver Wendell Douglas, a highly successful Manhattan lawyer who wanted to "get back to nature"; his urban-chic wife Lisa was played by Eva Gabor. Oliver bought a 160-acre farm, sight unseen, just outside Hooterville, the setting for yet another rural comedy, *Petticoat Junction*. The Douglases got conned, this time by a rural wheeler-dealer, Mr. Haney. They bought an old shack on a rock pile, but at least Oliver was determined to make a go of the rural life. While Lisa was never able to adjust to being a rustic, she did become quite fond of their farm animals, naming each of the chickens and cows. There was frequent interaction between the characters of *Green Acres* and of *Petticoat Junction* because of the common Hooterville setting. The old-timers, skeptical of Oliver's motives, constantly laughed at his farming ineptness; he was outside the outsiders, yet he persevered. Lisa constantly lobbied for their return to Park Avenue, but he would have none of it. Instead, he felt at home with his neighbors, who included pig farmer Fred Ziffel and his highly intelligent pet pig Arnold, who watched television and did tricks; handyman Ed Dawson, who helped fix up the run-down property; and country-store owner Sam Drucker. What one remembers most clearly about this series was its portrayal of rural people as generally plain, unattractive, and not above an occasional deception if it meant making money off a city slicker. Rather than the purity of rural values transcending the evil influence of civilization and city ways, a basic characteristic of the myth of the rural middle landscape, here we see a transparent version of the myth in which many of the town's inhabitants are wily, shrewd entrepreneurs hiding behind the guise of the country bumpkin. We are reminded here of the fear, in real life, of having our automobile break down in some small town in the middle of nowhere and of being charged an exorbitant price for what should have been a minor repair. Clearly much of this fear is generated by the Hollywood cultural production machine itself.

Rural-middle-landscape comedy introduced America to black protagonists on a television series in 1972. Norman Lear's *Sanford and Son* (immediately following his success with *All in the Family*), brought America's deep south to life on the small screen—the setting was actually transplanted to the black Los Angeles ghetto, the site of an urban seaminess different in character from the Clampetts' Beverly Hills environs, but seamy nonetheless.

Junk dealer Fred Sanford and his son Lamont represented positive rural values—deep familial love and support, and an underlying honesty (Fred's shrewd, rural-entrepreneurial character traits were effectively counterbalanced by Lamont's guilt and moral suasion). A panoply of charming rustic eccentries inhabited this urban version of Appalachia—Fred; Aunt Esther—the Bible-toting southern-Baptist proprietor of the dilapidated Sanford Arms boarding house; and Fred's dear old buddies, the slow-moving, gentle Bubba, and the kind-but-confused Grady Wilson.

While Lear's social satire would, on occasion, emerge as Fred, the black racist, derided Julio Fuertes, his Puerto Rican neighbor and Lamont's friend, this was a minor subtext to the comedy's essentially rural aesthetic. Fred's constant verbal assaults against Rollo Larson, another of Lamont's friends and clearly a cynical, streetwise urban con artist, placed Fred squarely in his rural milieu, in which shrewdness exuded a peculiar charm—a charm unknown to the likes of Rollo.

As in most rural comedy, in which business is conducted at home or within walking distance of it, Fred and Lamont's junk business was carried on in the living room, in the yard, and in the kitchen.

Perhaps most significantly, the main character, Fred, was a cantankerous old geezer reminiscent of Amos McCoy of *The Real McCoys*. Like Amos, Fred was a widower with a grown son living at home. And like Amos, Fred's gruffness obscured, but not completely, an underlying naivete and compassion. *Sanford and Son* demonstrated that, according to the myth of the rural-middle-landscape comedy, blacks, like their rural hillbilly counterparts, were not to be taken seriously in our culture.

This brief journey through the comedic rural middle landscape has attempted to expose the mythic realm of seemingly pure traditional values that paradigmatically reveals the ways in which those values are rendered meaningless through the characterization of those who hold those values as quaint childlike actors in a contemporary situation they can neither truly comprehend nor change. These comedies, while often hilarious by virtue of their physical comedy, their use of malapropism, and their absurd characterizations, ultimately reinforce dominant notions of the American Dream. While we, like the rustics in these comedies, can escape to a less complicated, less threatening physical and psychic landscape, we will always be subjected to the visions of eternal progress being projected just beyond the boundaries of the rural middle landscape. After all, Andy Taylor did eventually move to the city.

URBAN COMEDY—ETERNAL PROGRESS

If there is a genre that develops most naturally from the life experience of those creative television workers who represent the New York-Hollywood connection, that genre is the urban comedy. According to critic Arthur Haugh, who has done an extensive traditional-content analysis of the television comedy, of the 400-plus situation comedies that appeared on television from 1948 to 1978, 211 casts lived in a metropolitan setting, 93 series were set in New York City alone, and 67 of the couples involved lived in apartments.[21] These data don't reveal much about the character of the urbanity of these series, but they do at least indicate quantitatively the pervasive presence of this comedic type on our prime-time screens.

Work plays an increasingly significant role in the social relations depicted in urban comedy. Whereas to the protagonists of the suburban-middle-landscape comedies, work was but an occasional digression from the main business of raising a family; and whereas to the protagonists of the rural-middle-landscape comedies, work was occasional and done somewhere else (e.g., Oliver Wendell Douglas, the gentleman-farmer of *Green Acres*), not done at all (e.g., Jed Clampett, the multimillionaire patriarch of *The Beverly Hillbillies*), or simply a way of leisurely passing the day (Sheriff Andy Taylor of Mayberry), work in the urban comedy is truly a way of life, albeit a televisual one, around which other activities revolve.

Some of the urban comedies are mildly cynical. *Barney Miller*'s 12th Precinct in New York City's Greenwich Village employed a broken-down old cop named Fish, who always seemed to have one foot in the grave and who constantly griped about everything–the classic case of urban burnout. *Taxi*'s characters, mostly part-time moonlighters, consisted of a frustrated actor waiting for a big break, a boxer who never won a fight, and a lost student searching for meaning, all of whom are dominated by a tyrannical dispatcher. *The Honeymooners* unfolded in a sparsely furnished, depressing, claustrophobic kitchen/living-room setting, with a window looking out on the brick facade of another tenement building. The main characters, blue-collar workers, seemed trapped but nevertheless dignified. *The Bob Newhart Show* featured a variety of wealthy, urbane professionals who, in spite of their material comfort, were lonely and insecure.

The other urban comedies, for the most part, border on the euphoric. *I Love Lucy, Make Room for Daddy, The Dick Van Dyke Show,* and *The Mary Tyler Moore Show* all celebrate the excitement and glamour of show-business lifestyles. Lucy's plight as a frustrated actress, whose husband wanted her to remain a housewife in their Manhattan apartment, was vaguely, if at all, understood by an audience locked in the context of social relations of the 1950s. Only in the final episode of *The Mary Tyler Moore Show* did the euphoria collapse as the television station, which framed the action of the series, was sold and the entire news team fired, except, ironically, the incompetent news anchor Ted Baxter.

Whether mildly cynical or bordering on euphoria, at the core of all these comedic works is the myth of eternal progress. From the New York City bus driver Ralph Kramden and his sewer-worker sidekick Ed Norton of *The Honeymooners*, to the Ph.D.-psychologist Bob Hartley of *The Bob Newhart Show*, and the dry-cleaning entrepreneur and social climber George Jefferson of *The Jeffersons*, the social construct of the good life is manifest in these works—an urban American vision framed by the achievements of commerce and of the new pluralist pseudoenlightenment of equal opportunity. The protagonists, even those in the mildly cynical urban comedies, are not fatalists; they are always searching for the way forward, whether by opening one's own business and thereby shifting one's status from worker to entrepreneur (e.g., Ricky Ricardo's opening his own nightclub, the Ricky Ricardo Babaloo Club, on *I Love Lucy*); or by searching for the foolproof get-rich-quick scheme (Ralph Kramden of *The Honeymooners* was constantly on the lookout for the fast buck, but his efforts were always thwarted by his inept neighbor and lifetime buddy Norton); or by working hard and being pliant in order to win a promotion within the group (e.g., Mary Richards's promotion from her initial position as assistant producer to associate producer and finally to producer, and Lou Grant's concurrent promotion to news director at Minneapolis's WJM-TV). From show business to news and police business—from Ricky Ricardo, Danny Williams, and Rob Petrie whose lives in show biz continually interfered with their lives at home, to Mary Richards who had little home life as a single career woman and apartment dweller, and to Captain Barney Miller, whose family was written out of his world not long after the series debuted—the quest for personal status outside the traditional confines of the nuclear family became increasingly important. The protagonists' human frailties and their frustrations with the various pressures of everyday urban life have provided the context for both laughter and empathy. The outcomes, however, were never in doubt; in the words of Mary's theme song, "You're gonna make it after all." Or would she? Bob Hartley, week after week, ministered to the emotional castoffs of an ungrounded urban social milieu. Ted Baxter would have been a perfect candidate for Bob's therapy. It was inevitable that urban comedy in the age of television would achieve many of its finest moments on the couch of a wealthy Chicago psychologist.

The biological families of the suburban- and rural-middle landscape comedies are either supplemented or replaced in the urban comedy by the nonbiological work family that provides the protagonists with the support needed to survive and progress in a chaotic, constantly reforming world. The need for community, in these comedies and seemingly in our own everyday lives as well, is increasingly satisfied through office or workplace relationships.

According to critic Janet Maslin, writing in the *New York Times*: "The workplace has grown especially popular with television writers at a time when family life is particularly hard to explain. Besides, as it is presented on television, the shared experience of a group of people working together can be as important as family life—in some ways even more so."[22] Maslin is correct, as far as her argument goes, in her assessment of the social importance of the new work family as a group of people cooperating to resolve common difficulties and offer mutual support in a familylike setting in times of personal crisis. The relationships of these television characters, especially the archetypal boss/worker relationship, provide the viewers with a comprehensible social context so that they can laugh at the limitations of power in the persona of the boss/father-figure, while recognizing the basic humanness that frames the television version of work life. In *The Dick Van Dyke Show*, Melvin Cooley, the balding, pompous producer of the fictional *Alan Brady Show* (and the brother-in-law of the show's star) was made the constant fool by Rob Petrie and coworkers Sally Rogers and Buddy Sorrell. Lou Grant, Mary Richards' newsroom boss on *The Mary Tyler Moore Show*, possessed a gruff exterior, underneath which was a heart of gold; he was never the fool but would, on occasion, be forced to retract some epithet or rash judgment made at a moment of hotheadedness as we laughed at his discomfort while still admiring his basic humility. On *The Bob Newhart Show*, Bob Hartley's understated manner and the constant frustrations of his work were the source of amusement, as his bizarre patients and his sassy receptionist Carol seemed always to have the upper hand in the social transactions around the office; at the same time, sanity prevailed, due in large measure to the maturity of Bob's wife Emily and to Carol's underlying respect for Bob's professionalism.

The increasing difficulty in explaining family life as seen in the contemporary biological family, and the presentation of the work family as a significant social institution often functioning as a surrogate nuclear family providing comfort and security, in many ways reflect an actual confusion regarding the social importance of the nuclear family in the everyday activities of today's advanced capitalist/ consumer economy—is the family becoming an institution whose raison d'etre is the provision of leisure commodities for its anomic individual members, a group wherein parents, in the words of cultural anthropologist Jules Henry, have become "imps of fun," struggling to please their children by providing unlimited opportunities for material gratification at the expense of human contact? Over the past two centuries, as work was separated from the range of activities in which the nuclear family engaged as a unit, it was inevitable that the power of the family as a socially binding institution would wane. Yet, the essentially conservative television apparatus cannot let the family appear to be dying or relinquishing its larger social role. The medium's constant pull toward the center, through its espousal of the dominant ideology (which stresses individual opportunity within the context of benevolent social control), predetermines certain motifs, among them the power of the "family" group to enforce social norms through "education." The naive Mary Richards is educated to the ways and rituals of the newsroom by her surrogate father Lou. The naive Rob Petrie is educated to the sometimes sordid ways of the production of television comedy by his worldly-wise "older brother and sister," Sally Rogers and Buddy Sorrell.

In these comedies, success outside the world of nuclear-family relationships seems assured, if temporary, and in most cases it comes very easily. Success in the biological-family unit is often more difficult to achieve. Lou Grant was separated from his wife Edie in the 1973-74 season. Mary's news work began following the breakup of a four-year relationship. Critic John Phelan argues that the difficulty in achieving stable family relationships is in part due to a lack of "moral clarity from enduring values" in both the television world itself and the real world upon which the television world comments.[23] In the primary world of our everyday lives, which television appropriates in its series of realistic plays in settings that convey the appearance of authenticity through their intimacy of a small enclosed space, the fragmentary and the temporary have become the rule. Contemporary television narrative, especially evident in urban comedy, often reveals a world of "multiple real alternatives, . . . the plurality of self-worlds [and] the fragments of unconfident sub-cultures."[24] We are offered a world of "plurality without purpose," according to Phelan. Bob Hartley's patients would surely agree. Urban comedy offers us transient togetherness disguised as humanity in a highly competitive white-collar work context best described as professional-entrepreneurial. Meaning floats on the surface of this milieu. As Phelan notes about modern narrative, it neither promises nor delivers transcendent meaning. It does afford companionship, the universalism of vulnerability, the venting of vicarious rage or lust, however banal in motive and meaning. In modern narrative, one is offered a peek into another room of the enormous modern mansion where there are others, in different clothes, with different jobs, just like oneself in age, or values, or expectations. Everyone can observe a media counterpart, . . . command an episode. There are no . . . ideals or models for inner emulation. Rather, there are representative figures which attract universal attention and thus give meaning to various self-worlds.[25]

Familiarity and reflexivity are hallmarks of television and, generally of the popular arts. In a half-hour episode, one simply does not have the latitude to probe the human character in any depth, to reveal anything new. Admittedly, over many years, a series can develop characters who do exhibit inner growth, but that series, especially in comedy, is rare. Transcendent meaning is not something most members of the Hollywood creative telefilm community and few if any members of the business world of television entertainment feel very comfortable with. While such meaning may emerge through insightful critical analysis of a television work, in no way is transcendent meaning intended as part of urban comedy's meaning-bearing systems. This is certainly true if we consider the absence of any truly alternative or oppositional strategies in these comedies. One of the more respected writer-producers in television comedy today, *The Mary Tyler Moore Show*'s James Brooks, stated the case clearly and honestly: "We try not to get into right and wrong. I don't know what's right or wrong. I'm personally distrustful of anything political. We don't get into much conservative-liberal argument. It's never an issue with our show."[26] Brooks's statement may well serve as the credo for urban comedy on television. Brooks pointed to an episode of *The Mary Tyler Moore Show* in which Mary was faced with the very difficult decision of claiming a journalist's privilege—i.e., the right to protect the identity of her news source, which would likely lead to her being tossed in jail for contempt of court, or perhaps to her revealing the source and breaking the trust established in the journalist-source relationship. This dilemma is currently of major importance in the journalistic community. Viewing the treatment of this very volatile issue regarding the freedom to gather news, Brooks termed it "a very human" show about "someone who didn't want to get caught up in issues."[27] Mary, pure of spirit, didn't want to be thrown in the slammer with prostitutes—an understandable reaction, but one that negated the possibility of a meaningful personal and professional commitment. Of course, the comedy emerges as Mary reverts to the persona the audience has learned to love—the beautiful associate news producer whose veneer of professionalism is stripped back to reveal her true vulnerability. This dilemma is revealed to us as, in a two-shot, we see Lou Grant, dressed in a rumpled white shirt, his tie loosened, sitting behing his plain, uncluttered desk; and Mary, in her neatly tailored beige business suit with a white turtleneck and fashionable pumps, sitting in an office chair facing Lou:

LOU (*in a close-up*): The whole concept of freedom of the press will be destroyed, and, with it, democracy as you and I know it and cherish it.
       Cut to:
MARY (*reaction shot, looking very sad*).
       Cut to:
LOU and MARY (*two-shot*).
       LOU: But don't let that influence you. (Laugh track.)
       Cut to:
   MARY (*close-up*): Well, I'll just have to go to jail. That's the right thing, it's the honorable thing, it's the only thing.
       Cut to:
LOU (*reaction shot, approving*).
       Cut to:
   MARY (*close-up*): There's just one problem . . . (*Tears well up in her eyes as she cried out.*) I don't wanna go to jail. (Laugh track.)[28]

The audience track laughs at Lou's encomium on the "sacred trusts" of press freedom and democracy as he tries to make Mary feel the slightest bit of guilt about her ambivalence regarding her professional journalistic commitment. This is in keeping with the series, which stresses the social life of the television newsroom against the hazy backdrop of issues that cross the news desk. This was a comedy of character rather than of issues, a "joyous" comedy rather than a comedy of irony, satire, or sarcasm.[29]

A particularly poignant example of this type of character comedy is the "Chuckles the Clown" episode. The circus comes to Minneapolis. Ted Baxter is chosen to be its grand marshall. Lou refuses to let Ted compromise the dignity of the newsroom by participating. Ted is crushed and threatens to resign. Ted, the child in all of us, is replaced as grand marshal by WJM's own TV clown, Chuckles. We dissolve to Lou, distraught, entering the newsroom; Chuckles, it seems, went to the circus parade dressed as "Peter Peanut" and was crushed by a rogue elephant. The hilarity begins as Ted improvises, in his inimitably inept way, an absurd eulogy for Chuckles on the evening news. No one knew Chuckles, whose real name was George, very well, although he worked for the station for 20 years. Murray begins to make Chuckles jokes; Lou and Sue Ann join in the merriment. Mary berates everyone for their callousness. Lou defends humor, in times of tragedy, as a "release." We cut to the funeral parlor as the priest delivers a panegyric on Chuckles. All in attendance are somber except Mary, who finally needs her release. As the priest recounts all the ridiculous characters Chuckles played in his television program, Mary bursts out laughing. The priest asks her to stand. Extremely embarrassed, Mary is, however exonerated as the priest finds her behavior admirable, saying "nothing would have made [Chuckles] happier. He loved to make people laugh." In the epilogue, at Mary's apartment, the news people talk about the type of funerals each would prefer. With great empathy, we fade to black.

The Mary Tyler Moore Show clearly represents the ambience of most of television's urban comedy. It is an intermediate step between the self-deceptive naivete of the suburban- and rural-middle-landscape comedies that represent cultures cut off from the real world of social relations and the self-reflexive comedy-drama that grounds both character and family firmly in that world with all its ambiguity and disconnectedness.

NOTES

1. Joseph Campbell, *The Hero With a Thousand Faces* (New York: Pantheon Books, 1949), p. 28.

2. James K. Feibleman, *In Praise of Comedy* (New York: Horizon Press, 1970), p. 178.

3. Henry Ten Eyck Perry, "Comedy," in *Collier's Encyclopedia*, vol. 7 (New York: Macmillan, 1980), p. 44.

4. Elton Hocking, "Commedia Dell'Arte," in *Collier's Encyclopedia*, vol. 7, p. 59.

5. Feibleman, *Comedy*, p. 272.

6. Ibid., pp. 134-5.

7. James W. Chesebro, "Communication, Values, and Popular Television Series—A Four Year Assessment," in *Television: The Critical View*, 2d ed., ed. Horace Newcomb (New York: Oxford University Press, 1979), pp. 16-54.

8. Ibid., pp. 21-22.

9. Ibid., p. 31.

10. Sylvia Moss, "The New Comedy," *Television Quarterly* 4 (Winter 1965): 42-45.

11. Harry F. Waters, "TV Comedy: What It's Teaching The Kids," *Newsweek*, May 7, 1979, pp. 64-72.

12. Ibid., p. 68.

13. Arthur Hough, "Trials and Tribulations—Thirty Years of Sitcom," in *Understanding Television*, ed. Richard P. Adler (New York: Praeger, Inc., 1981), pp. 201-23.

14. Ibid., p. 204.

15. Ibid., p. 221.

16. Raymond Williams, *Television: Technology and Cultural Form* (New York: Schocken Books, 1975), p. 26.

17. Sprague Vonier, "Television—The Urban Outlook," *Television Quarterly* 3 (Winter 1964):24-29.

18. Ibid., p. 25.

19. Tim Brooks and Earl Marsh, eds., *The Complete Directory to Prime-Time Network TV Shows: 1946-Present* (New York: Ballantine Books, 1979), pp. 196-97.

20. Quoted in Jack Behar, "On TV Criticism," *Television Quarterly* 4 (Summer 1965):60.

21. Hough, "Trials and Tribulations," pp. 201-23.

22. Janet Maslin, "In Prime Time, the Workplace Is Where the Heart Is," *New York Times*, February 10, 1980, sec. 2, p. 1.

23. John M. Phelan, *Disenchantment: Meaning and Morality in the Media* (New York: Hastings House, 1980), p. 35.

24. Ibid.

25. Ibid., pp. 35-36.

26. Conversation with James Brooks on *TV For Better or Worse*, produced by WCVE-TV, Richmond, Va., 1976.

27. Ibid.

28. Excerpt from *The Mary Tyler Moore Show*, shown on *TV For Better or Worse*.

29. Feibleman, *Comedy*, p. 205.

5

TELEVISION'S
SOCIAL COMEDIES

THE SELF-REFLEXIVE COMEDY-DRAMA: TELEVISION TOPICALITY AND THE CLASS STRUGGLE

As we enter the "real world" of social relations depicted in television comedy, we do so with our eyes open wide, recognizing television's peculiar ability to present us ostensibly significant social commentary that, in its deeper layers, reinforces traditional values, and thereby makes the threatening unthreatening and incorporates potentially emergent oppositional social strategies into the social fabric as demanded by the dominant values of the culture.

Such is the case with television comedy's most substantial "dramatic" form, the self-reflexive comedy-drama. Significant examples of this form as well as the satiric comedy-variety form are represented in Figure 2. Here the thin line between laughter and despair is crossed again and again, but finally, the ambiguity of everyday experience is resolved—usually, although, thankfully, not always—with predictably sanguine results. In this comedy we see the emergence of clearly drawn class distinctions. The false consciousness of the working class clearly emerges in *All in the Family* through the principal character of Archie Bunker. The pathos of the helpless working-class rural "children" completely narcotized by the television dream life reveals itself through Mary and Tom Hartman of *Mary Hartman, Mary Hartman*—this American Dream is a composite television commercial. Socioeconomic-class confrontation is represented, albeit often crudely, in *Soap* as the anomic bourgeois characters, Jessica and Chester Tate,

1946 47 48 49 50 51 52 53 54 55 56 57 58 59 60 61 62 63 64 65 66 67 68 69 70 71 72 73 74 75 76 77 78 79 80 81 82 83

Self-Reflexive Comedy-Drama
(television topicality and the class struggle)

Satiric Comedy-Variety

TW3,
64—65

The Smothers Brothers
Comedy Hour,
67 69

Rowan and Martin's
Laugh-In,
68 73

Dream Machine,
71—72

All in the Family, 71 79

Maude, 72 78

M*A*S*H*, 72 83

Mary Hartman[2],
76—77

Soap, 77 81

Saturday Night Live, 75 . . . .

The Richard Pryor Show,
77

collide with Jessica's sister Mary and her foolish, macho, working-class husband Burt Campbell. The Tates' black servant, Benson, takes great joy in Jessica's and Chester's miserable marriage and their constant bickering—the archetypal fall from grace. In the most enigmatic of all television series, the late, lamented *M*A*S*H*, we find the ultimate sardonic working-class comedy—highly skilled draftee-surgeons working in the assembly-line atmosphere of the wartime operating room. The "products" are not engine parts but people, processed through techniques of multiple serial production; the goods in this body shop are patched up and returned to the fray or sent home maimed. This is the ultimate black humor, associated with the eternal progress of an ever-increasing sophisticated technology that can find more efficient ways to kill. Doctors become the "white-collar proletariat." War is ultimately the equalizer of all men as well as the ultimate metaphor for advanced capitalism.

These self-reflexive comedy-dramas give us room to examine the human foibles that constitute our contemporary milieu, with its vestiges of ethnocentrism, warlike posturing and war making, and subservience to cultural production in our media that trades on the most blatant symbolic language encouraging self-centeredness, fear, and envy. Through these works we can see, in ourselves as a people, the human results of our most careless thoughts and actions. Yet, curiously, these same works tell us that in spite of our foibles, the strength of family bonds will help us endure our darkest moments—television's traditional answer to the bewildering complexity of contemporary social relations. Further, the mythic geography of the comedy-drama is not the real world, as we might at first glance believe, but, rather, the geography of the television screen itself.

All in the Family, which premiered in January 1971, brought millions of American viewers face to face with the television version of the harsh realities of urban working-class existence in the culturally isolated, multiethnic and racially mixed Corona section of Queens, New York. At 704 Houser Street, the Bunkers—Archie and Edith—and their son-in-law Michael (Meathead) and daughter Gloria, Archie's "little girl," grappled with all the social and personal issues television had ignored during the 1960s—issues which had polarized an entire nation, dividing what was once naively considered a country united into a society of warring subcultures. *All in the Family*'s structure employed the grossest oppositions to make its social comments. In the Archie/Michael pair, for example, we find value conflicts organized as conservative/liberal, WASP/ethnic, prejudiced/open-minded, undereducated-worker/overeducated-student-professor, and pseudo-religious/atheist-humanist dichotomies. In the Archie/Edith pair, dichotomies include dominant employed male/subservient, unemployed woman-housewife, and rational, boisterous male/irrational, quietly emotional female. In the Edith/Gloria pair, we find the naive-mother/worldly-wise daughter, and the traditional husband-centered woman/new-liberated-woman oppositions. True, the roles shifted when the occasion and dramatic license warranted—Michael would become an irrational, babbling idiot, just like his father-in-law, when provoked by the latter's enormous prejudice and hatred, although Michael did so in the best of the bleeding-liberal tradition. Edith could overcome her guilt and embarrassment regarding the discussion of sexual matters when Gloria and Michael needed the warm family counseling of a mother. Gloria could break down and cry, just like daddy's little girl, when accosted on the subway. Of all the characters, Archie maintained his dominant role as family patriarch and tyrant, the defender of the flag and the traditional values for which he believed that flag stood—values such as the use of religion in the service of jingoism; the sanctity of the police state over the rights of individuals, except of course himself, when he felt personally wronged; and the state sanction of ethnocentric, exclusionist social practices. Archie Bunker, television representative of the contemporary American working-class "stiff," was a living, breathing anachronism. And the audience loved him.

Why was this put-down of the American working-class lifestyle-and-value system the incredibly popular number-one television series from 1971 until 1976, with ratings exceeding 30.0 for the entire period? Was it because in the end, Archie was damned to eternal torment, could not escape from the ethnically and racially "inferior" people he so despised? Was it because viewers subscribed to the same value priorities as he did? Was it because *All in the Family* was a superb comedy of gestures, relying on the extremely powerful small-screen aesthetic device of the reaction shot, so sensitively executed by all of the cast members, but especially Carroll O'Connor? Or was it because the Bunkers were survivors, weathering the social storms of the times, secure in their tiny piece of the American landscape, marked out as "private property"? Each viewer brought a personal perspective to *All In The Family*, and the series allowed for a multiplicity of readings. Therein lies its significance as an artistic vehicle—its openness to a variety of readings.

Those readings were quick to emerge. Two months following its premiere, *All in the Family* was both soundly condemned and fervently defended by certain of our popular television critics. *Life*'s John Leonard wrote of the premiere of the series: *All in the Family* is a wretched program. . . . [It] is not merely insulting to minorities: it is insulting to Mr. O'Connor, Miss Stapleton, Miss Struthers, Mr. Reiner, the American workingman, CBS and everybody who watches the program. Bigotry becomes a form of dirty joke."[1] Leonard looked into the series's ideological signification and discovered "a double-edged lie . . . [that] tells us that workingmen are mindless buffoons: their opinions, unlike ours, are unrelated to social, psychological or political conditions; . . . [and] that . . . Archie is, anyway, charming. Forgivable."[2] Thus, Lear, CBS, and the audience are pandered to; all are better than Archie, who is ridiculous and not to be taken seriously. In this way, our antihero comes to represent a vision of America not unlike the adult-child of the rural middle landscape; the main difference between the two character types is, of course, that Archie's blue-collar workingman is naively bigoted while Jed Clampett's kind rural folk hero is simply ignorant.

Saturday Review's Robert Lewis Shayon took a decidedly different view of the series, although his endorsement was not without an important qualification. Writing in the same month as Leonard, Shayon found the novelty of the series in view of the 1971 television milieu, "exhilarating, . . . a unique experience in television viewing."[3] Shayon believed the value of the series was located in its ostensible power to reinforce the values of those who came to the series already convinced of the evils of prejudice and ethnocentrism. As to the argument that *All in the Family* would reinforce bigotry, Shayon concluded that bigots would feel threatened by the series and would tune out. The major flaw in the series, Shayon perceptively noted, was Archie's utter inability to recognize his own sinful ethnocentrism. Shayon added, "If Archie did know—if he were, even in the smallest degree, self-critical and willing to engage in dialogue about his hostility to all groups but his own— . . . he would be . . . a powerful vehicle toward the remedying of prejudice."[4] Maybe so, but then the comedy-drama would sacrifice its "unknowing irony" and become not a biting artistic revelation of bigotry in a contemporary social milieu, but, rather, a popularized group-therapy session thrown in the audience's face. If Lear had followed Shayon's advice, chances are that the series would have quickly faded from public attention.

Writing some four years after the premiere of *All in the Family*, *The New Yorker*'s television critic, Michael Arlen, noted that the series was not primarily focused on its central character's prejudice, but, rather, as in Lear's other television comedies, it revealed "a curious, modern, undifferentiated anger."[5] While Arlen gave Lear credit for introducing viewers to television comedies that deal with serious contemporary social problems such as racism (*All in the Family*), alcoholism (*Maude*), the inferior social status and immense personal struggles of lower-class blacks (*Good Times*), and sexual taboos (*Hot L Baltimore*), he also pointed out the tendency in Lear's work for this "angry" humor to be transformed into "an accepted form of stage business" and thereby to relinquish its social and political meaning as it deflected its focus from the outside world to the narrow world of the central characters. Insult and vituperation have no place in the comedy of the ideal future, but are instead static and socially meaningless. What is meaningful in these works, according to Arlen, is their status as "our first true 'media' dramas," which are more like television talk shows than traditional narratives—they provide viewers with "a commonality, . . . created largely by television itself, . . . of casual worldliness and [of television's] ability to propel . . . vast, undifferentiated quantities of topical information, problem discussions, psychiatric terminology, and surface political and social involvement through the national bloodstream."[6]

All in the Family is "mainstream"—it makes us feel connected to "social change" while simultaneously defusing any truly emergent oppositional ideology that could clearly posit strategies for such change. As Arlen so perceptively discerns, beneath its surface tension, *All in the Family* is all talk.

There are, despite this basic mainstream character of the series, moments of ironic brilliance that the critic would be remiss to ignore and that highlight the major value conflicts inherent in the social relations of this Queens family and their neighbors—conflicts which frequently involve the sanctity of institutions versus human dignity and individual autonomy. Two particularly memorable scenes from *All in the Family* demonstrate the sensitivity with which the series's creators could treat human problems in drama tempered with comedic overtones. One scene explored the obligation of the individual to submit to the demands of his government regardless of the perceived injustices of the state's cause. The other focused on the son's unquestioned acceptance of his father's teachings and actions despite the son's vague doubts as to their ultimate wisdom.

"The Draft Dodger" episode of *All in the Family*, written by Jay Moriarty and Mike Milligan, was aired on December 15, 1976. The scene was the Bunkers' dining room, Christmas Eve, 1976. Mike's friend David, a draft dodger living in Canada, has come to dinner. Archie has invited his good friend Pinky, whose son Steve had been killed in Vietnam. David's presence was too much for Archie to handle. Mike and David are dressed in coats and neat but casual trousers; Archie is bedecked in his usual open-necked white shirt; Pinky has on traditional Christmas colors of red and green. The scene follows:

ARCHIE: How do you like that, Pinky, huh? We got a draft dodger here who writes a snotty letter to the Commander in Chief. I mean, what the hell do you do with that?
(*Wide shot—all around the table, we see*
ARCHIE, EDITH, GLORIA, MIKE, PINKY.)

DAVID: Look, Mr. Bunker. I don't want to spoil your Christmas dinner, so maybe I should go.

EDITH and GLORIA: Oh, no! Don't make him go.

ARCHIE: Certainly he's got to go! What are you talkin' about. (*A beat.*) If the FBI was to find him here, we could all be havin' Christmas dinner in the hoosegow.

GLORIA: Daddy, it's Christmas Eve. Now don't go making a big crisis out of this.

MIKE: (*Slams his napkin on the table and bolts out of his chair*) Arch. What David did took a lot of guts.

ARCHIE: What do ya mean, a lot of guts?

DAVID: My own father doesn't understand. Why should he?

MIKE: (*extreme close-up shot, screaming*)
When the hell are you going to admit that the war was wrong?

ARCHIE: (*in a three-shot with* MIKE *and* DAVID *looking on; he is shouting*)
I ain't talkin' about the war. I don't wanna talk about that rotten damn war no more.[7] I'm talkin' about somethin' else. And what he done was wrong. Sayin' he won't go. (*To* DAVID.) What do ya think, that all the people in this country can say whether or not they wanna go to war? (*Beat.*) You couldn't get a decent war off the ground that way. All the young people would say no. Sure they would. Cause they don't wanna get killed. (*Beat.*) And that's why we leave it to the Congress, 'cause them old crocks ain't gonna get killed. (*Beat.*) And they're gonna do the right thing and get behind the president and vote yes.

PINKY: (*stands*) Arch. If my opinion is of any importance, . . .

ARCHIE: (*calming down*) Certainly your opinion is important. (*Beat.*) A Gold Star Father. Your opinion is more important than anyone else's in this room, and I wanna hear that opinion. You tell 'em Pinky, you tell 'em.

PINKY: (*in a two-shot, over* ARCHIE'S *shoulder, speaks calmly but with obvious pain as the camera slowly zooms in to a close-up*)
I understand how you feel, Arch. My kid hated the war, too. But he did what he thought he had to do. (*Beat.*) And David here did what he thought he had to do. But David's alive to share Christmas dinner with us. And if Steve were here, he'd wanna sit down with him. And that's what I wanna do.

(*PINKY reaches out to shake hands with* DAVID. DAVID *holds back the tears.*)

PINKY: Merry Christmas, David.

(PINKY, *still shaking hands, places his left hand on* DAVID's *shoulder*)

DAVID: Merry Christmas, sir.

(*Wide shot of dinner table.* DAVID, PINKY, MIKE *sit down.* ARCHIE *remains standing, shocked. He walks away, alone.* EDITH, *faithful as always, gets up to attempt to console him.*)

EDITH: Archie, please. Sit down and eat.

ARCHIE: Aw, no, no, no.

EDITH: But Archie, it's Christmas.

ARCHIE: I can't. I gotta work this out, Edith. I can't think about that.

EDITH: But Archie, you asked Pinky what to do and you see what he's doing. You oughta do the same. Come on.

(*Silently,* EDITH *and* ARCHIE *move back to the table.*)

EDITH: There's a drumstick for ya.

ARCHIE: Oh Edith, I ain't thinkin' about eatin'.

MIKE: I'll take it, Ma.

ARCHIE: (*immediately snaps back*) Leave it on the plate. (*Beat.* ARCHIE *is sweating profusely.*) Well, I don't wanna stop none of youse from eatin' Edith's nice Christmas dinner here. So you might as well eat it. But I'll tell you one thing: When dinner's over, I still gotta work this out. (*Beat.*) You better remind me to do that, Edith.

EDITH: I will. (*She kisses* ARCHIE *on the cheek.*)

Of course, Archie was never able to "work it out," nor did he really seem to want to. His pride was hurt, but his dogmatic view of militarism was essentially unshaken, as the audience would expect and as the comedic aesthetic would demand if his character was to remain the wellspring from which irony would continue to flow.

Also unshaken was Archie's belief in the correctness of his upbringing, which included his father's severe disciplinary measures and bigotry. Archie was not in the habit of reading child-development texts or of attempting to deal with questions of the relationship of a child's later aggressive and belligerent behavior to his parents' child-rearing techniques. Instead, the curiously "romantic" Archie chose to remember only the vague distanced scenes of his father's love for him. And above all, he respected his father's manly power. This is revealed in a touching scene from the February 8, 1978, episode "Two's A Crowd," written by Phil Sharp. Archie and Mike accidentally lock themselves in the storeroom in Archie's bar; it's getting cold outside, there is plenty to drink to keep warm. The two men crawl under a piece of an old awning they find in the storeroom and proceed to get drunk. The conversation leads to Archie's lack of trust in Mike and slowly the scene takes on a melancholy air. Archie describes his school days during the Great Depression and reveals his incredible cynicism:

ARCHIE: The hell with the world! The world out there, kid, ain't up to no good. You don't trust nobody out there except for your own kind, and you remember that, Meathead.

MIKE: (*A beat.*) There's another thing. Meathead. Why must you always call me Meathead?

ARCHIE: What the hell? Why does that bother you so much? I bet I wasn't the first one to call you Meathead.

MIKE: You were the only one to call me Meathead. They never called me Meathead in school. In school they always called me Michael.

ARCHIE: That's all they called you?

MIKE: Well, Mike, or Mikey.

ARCHIE: What a sweet little school you went to. No wonder you grew up thinkin' the world was beautiful.

MIKE: Why? What did they call you in school?

ARCHIE: (*ad lib resistance*) Oh . . . different things.

MIKE: What? Tell me. What'd they call you in school. Tell me what they called you.

ARCHIE: (*takes a drink*) Well, I remember one winter during the depression, we didn't have no money 'cause the old man lost a job, and we was all busted . . . and I couldn't go to school with only one shoe; but my mother, she found a boot, so . . . I had a shoe on one foot there and a boot on the other. A shoe and a boot; shoe, boot. So the kids called me Shoebootie.

MIKE: Kids all made fun of you, huh?

ARCHIE: (*his voice becoming increasingly slurred*) Yeah, they all made fun, well, . . . all except one little black kid by the name of Winston.

MIKE: (*incredulous*) A black kid liked you?

ARCHIE: Oh, no. The black kid beat the hell outta me.

MIKE: Why?

ARCHIE: (*mumbles*) I don't know. Nothin'.

MIKE: He musta had a reason.

ARCHIE: Well, he said that I said he was a nigger.

MIKE: Well, did you?

ARCHIE: Yeah.

MIKE: Well then, that's the reason.

ARCHIE: What the hell reason was that? That's what all them people was called in them days there. I mean everybody we knew called 'em people niggers. That's all my old man ever called 'em there.

MIKE: Did you ever think that possibly your father just might be wrong?

ARCHIE: Wrong, my old man? Don't be stupid. My old man, let me tell you about him. He was never wrong about nothin'.

MIKE: Yes he was, Arch.

ARCHIE: (*barely able to articulate*) Huh? Your father who made ya? Wrong? The breadwinner of the house there, the man who goes out and busts his butt to keep a roof over your head and clothes on your back; you call your father wrong? Your father, the man who comes home bringin' candy. Your father's first guy to throw a baseball to you and take you for walks in the park, holdin' you by the hand. (*Holds up his hand.*) I'll tell you. He busted that hand once, and he busted it on me to teach me to do good. My father. He shoved me in a closet for seven hours to teach me to do good 'cause he loved me. (*Beat.*) Don't be lookin' at me. (ARCHIE *gets up, moves away, leaving* MIKE, *seen in a close-up, looking sad and bewildered.*) Let me tell you somethin', you're supposed to love your father. 'Cause your father loves you. (*Beat.*) Now, how can any man who loves you tell you anything that's wrong? What's the use in talking to you?

(*Beat.* ARCHIE *lies down on a tablecloth that is on the floor. He falls asleep. After a few beats,* MIKE *rises, crosses to* ARCHIE, *carefully covers him with the awning, and looks down at him.*)

MIKE: Good night, Shoebootie.

Archie, drunk and uncomprehending, has fallen into the existential void. His physical awakening will not correspond to any cognitive or moral awakening. Mike's sad, bewildered look brilliantly reveals Archie's permanent state of unfreedom; Archie is helpless against the world.

These scenes, brilliantly acted and carefully scripted and shot, transcend the general comedic level of *All in the Family*, a series with high-pitched insults that Archie continuously and indiscriminately flings at outsiders and insiders alike. There were, of course, other poignant scenes, including that showing Archie's despair at losing his job, Archie's genuine display of love for his grandson, and the family's tender good-byes as Mike and Gloria left Queens for a new life in California. This last scene was particularly revealing as Archie, wanting to express his love for his son-in-law, could not utter the words. The power of Archie's closed cultural tradition dominated one final time. Archie, a "real man," was not permitted to express his softness in public.

While many television critics continued to praise the series for its effort at "breaking down old taboos," the cultural climate, of which television was but one part, had in fact already sanctioned that breaking-down. Television, as always, through its most persuasive creators, followed. "The Draft Dodger," taped in late 1976, merely confirmed the growing sentiment that Vietnam was a colossal mistake. Only Archie and those diehard jingoists whom he represented were blind to that fact. "Two's a Crowd," shot in 1978, alluded to the pressures that signaled the breakdown of patriarchal authority long underway, as the changing nature of family relations had manifested itself in postindustrial social systems. Blue-collar children such as Mike had come to know the advanced education their fathers (represented by Archie) could never achieve. The fathers encouraged this education so that their children could improve their relative material status in the dominant social and economic structures, not so that they would become enlightened about the social inequities inherent in advanced capitalism or about misguided ethnocentrism. The American Dream, as lived by second- and third-generation blue-collar immigrants, cut both ways, and the changes brought about by opening higher education spoke to both. *All in the Family* uses this value conflict as a major focus of its action and characterization.

We should not expect anything revolutionary from entertainment television. As social critic Todd Gitlin noted about the difficulty, if not impossibility, in having truly controversial material enter our public electronic arts, "Alternative material is routinely *incorporated*: brought into the body of cultural production. Occasionally oppositional material may succeed in being indigestible; that material is excluded from the media discourse and returned to the cultural margins from which it came, while *elements* of it are incorporated into the dominant forms."[8] The "casual worldliness" and "topicality" Michael Arlen attributed to the series provides us with an outline of our contemporary world of social relations. The substance inside that outline, however, is still without sufficient elaboration.

While *All in the Family* used Vietnam as a vehicle to discuss larger political and social conflicts in America, another comedy-drama used a different, though not dissimilar, war of containment to reveal the personal tragedy brought about by the abstractions of politics. *M*A*S*H* took on nothing less than the human condition in the age of mechanization and its ultimate manifestation in efficient warfare. Such material is an appropriate subject for the logic of the ridiculous as best expressed through black comedy.

On September 17, 1972, America was still mired "waist deep in the Big Muddy" of Vietnam, as the Pete Seeger song went; we were searching for a way out. The bombing of Cambodia had precipitated a national outcry for disengagement. The outcry, most visibly manifested on our nation's university campuses, triggered confrontations between authority—the National Guard protecting what was fast becoming a police state, the goal of which was the securing of bourgeois property and the prolonging of a war that had brought an economic recovery and material prosperity—and the student rebels who were seriously and continually deconstructing this country's dominant cultural value priorities. When the smoke from the tear gas cleared from the battleground at Kent State, students—some innocent bystanders— lay dead. The war had at last come home. The small screen, on which the actual footage of this distant war had been shown to a packed house for nearly a decade, now trembled with scenes from northern Ohio, scenes far more difficult to explain and much harder to swallow.

The setting for a new television comedy series (and for the Robert Altman theatrical film, based on a novel by Richard Hooker, from which the series was derived) was Korea. The time was the early 1950s. The protagonists were U.S. Army surgeons, nurses, and corpsmen assigned to the 4,077th Mobile Army Surgical Hospital—a frantic tent city five miles from the battlefront. All the doctors at the series's beginning were draftees (later, an army lifer would assume command of the unit). We knew that this was more than just Korea—it was all war, and, more immediately, it was Vietnam.

M*A*S*H's main contribution to television comedy-drama was the sincerity with which it tackled the more existential questions of man's quest for personal meaning in an anomic culture. Throughout the series's 11-year run, there was revealed a nagging sense of futility and insanity about war. Humor was a key ingredient for survival—it highlighted despair and provided a temporary respite from the hopelessness of war by ridiculing war's basic modus operandi.

The doctors—Captain Benjamin Franklin "Hawkeye" Pierce; Captain "Trapper John" McIntyre; company commander, Lieutenant Colonel Henry Blake; and, later, Captain B. J. Hunnicut—were always breaking regulations, asserting, in whatever feeble attempts they could mount, their independence from an inhumane, unforgiving system that inexorably ground forward, using up young men in the quest for highly questionable political ends. The central protagonist, Hawkeye, offered the most consistent voice that questioned the moral validity of war. His role was that of the philosopher who always seemed to be burdened with the understanding of the conflict's ultimate meaninglessness. His understanding carried with it a rage, a frustration, and a cynicism contained just below the mask of calm professionalism. Hawkeye's character, as it developed over the life of the series, is one of the most complex in television comedy—that of a "bitter idealist,"[9] whose ultimate optimism is continually challenged by the realities of the wartime operating room. The role was brilliantly revealed to us by actor, writer, and director Alan Alda, surely a contemporary television folk hero.

M*A*S*H was accessible to a television audience searching desperately, although perhaps unknowingly, for a framework to help explain the meaning of the Vietnam War and of the domestic social confrontations of the 1960s. How could a sensitive observer reconcile an enlightened domestic policy that was making serious attempts to correct the sordid environments of racial, ethnic, and economic subcultural groups—conditions exacerbated by decades of governmental neglect—with the fact that the sons of these groups were being urged to enlist or were drafted as cannon fodder for a jingoistic war? The irony of this policy confusion was all too apparent to the upper-middle-class child who was demonstrating on his or her college campus; however, it was not so apparent to the inner-city youth who had not been provided with the proper education with which to see the sham. The American Dream had soured. Some people recognized the fact and grieved. Others used the occasion to question the basic tenets of that dream.

M*A*S*H provided clear-cut characterizations that defined much larger cultural issues framing contemporary value conflicts. The war was the backdrop for the definition. We find, on its most basic level, the confrontation clearly presented in the oppositional characterizations of Hawkeye and Major Frank Burns. Hawkeye represented individualism, the right to rebel, peace, and skilled professionalism in the service of life. His was the existential voice crying out in the wilderness of social control, ultimately manifested in the hierarchical social relations of the military apparatus. Frank, Hawkeye's opposite force, represented the authority, bureaucracy, war, and butchery that easily accepted death as a given. His character struggled to uphold the sanctity of institutions and their ostensibly legitimate claims to power.

The classic confrontations of *M*A*S*H* were acted out in the naturalistic theater of the operating room, the one place where life, both the physical and emotional, constantly hangs in the balance.

Characters were allowed to grow throughout the life of the series. Maxwell Klinger, hairy-chested son of a Lebanese immigrant family from Toledo, was constantly seeking a discharge for a mental disability. He was laughable in an assortment of dresses used as he played a transvestite to no avail. In 1979, following the departure of Corporal Radar O'Reilly, Klinger was appointed company clerk and was subsequently promoted to sergeant. His new responsibilities overshadowed his strong desire to exit from the war; in one sense, his promotion within the hierarchy also represented his cooptation. This theme in *M*A*S*H*, of the conflict between the deep feelings of responsibility for the welfare of the 4,077th "family" and the desire to escape the horror, was a constantly recurring motif. In the end, Klinger became a team player, as we expected he would; the renegade was enculturated into the family atmosphere of the unit. Ironically, Klinger married a Korean girl at the war's conclusion and stayed in Korea to search for his new bride's parents. He would be the last of the unit to leave.

Margaret "Hot Lips" Houlihan gradually transcends her initial stereotypical role as an army brat-sexpot with shady morals who loves to have affairs with superior officer-doctors. Through inner development brought about by her marriage, subsequent divorce, and the painful process of reconciling her strong passions with an understanding of the authentic human communication of love, she matures as the series unfolds through the years. The series writers increasingly shift our attention to Margaret's function as a paraprofessional, highly skilled nurse and generally effective administrator as the drive in the United States for the passage of the Equal Rights Amendment intensifies. Thus, the two times are intertwined—1970s values are successfully implanted in the social relations of the 1950s.

The company-commander role changed during the series as well. Lieutenant Colonel Henry Blake, the kind but bumbling and weak-willed commanding officer of the unit, who just wanted to get by until the conflict faded away, was "killed" in a plane crash on his way home following his discharge (another ironic twist). In his place came Army lifer Colonel Sherman Potter, a veteran of World Wars I and II —a compassionate man, as was Henry, but also a strong-willed soldier who believed in at least a modicum of discipline, although he knew the value of good surgeons even when they were as wacky as Hawkeye and B.J.

Hawkeye changed in more subtle ways than the others and in more profound ways throughout the series. Early in the series we saw Hawkeye following the model established in the Altman film. Dressed in a Hawaiian floral-print shirt, the swinging bachelor wooed the nurses and used his quick wit, ribald humor, and imitations of Groucho Marx to provide the people of the 4,077th, except for Frank Burns and Margaret Houlihan, with the needed release and a sense of optimism. Gradually, however, the optimism gave way to Hawkeye's bitter cynicism. He tried to maintain his comic demeanor, but the audience felt the substantive emptiness the jokes unintentionally revealed. We, of course, see and hear hints of the tenuous nature of the relationship between sanity and insanity as expressed through dark humor even in the series pilot. Hawkeye and his tent mate at the time, Trapper John McIntyre, are walking slowly through the camp reflecting on their roles as doctors in war:

HAWKEYE: I keep telling you: We gotta give up this preoccupation with keeping people alive or we'll never get outta here.
 TRAPPER: It's no use. We're doomed.
HAWKEYE: Maybe we should start using rusty instruments.
 TRAPPER: Or not washing our hands.
HAWKEYE: Or raising our prices.

Hawkeye's bitterness clearly surfaced in a 1978 hour-long episode modeled on the Edward R. Murrow (CBS/TV) *See It Now* documentary episode titled "Christmas in Korea" (1953). Correspondent Clete Roberts interviews the members of the 4,077th in the fictional early winter of 1952. His questions, as did those questions posed in the Murrow documentary, probe the soldiers' feelings about their "work," attempting to reveal the war in human terms. The war is more than a series of scenes revealed in the newsreel footage shipped back to the United States—it is people with expressions, voices, and reflections. At the beginning of the interview, Hawkeye still manages to maintain his basic optimism as he responds to Roberts: "I'm very impressed now with the . . . terrible fragility of the human body, and the unbelievable resiliency of the human spirit." However, later in the episode, Hawkeye reveals his inner torment in a voiceover accompanying a scene of choppers descending from the heavens, bringing in more wounded, and of ambulances hurtling down the dusty road into the camp: "The wounded keep coming and coming. The common denominator is blood. It's all red. And there's an awful lot of it leaking out around here." We cut to a scene in the operating room. Shells are exploding all around the camp. Lights are flickering on and off as the surgeons attempt to continue their work. Hawkeye looks beyond the war to the social relations that encourage such activities. His soliloquy is among the most direct ever offered on commercial entertainment television: "I just don't know why they're shooting at us. All we want to do is bring them democracy and white bread, transplant the American Dream—freedom, achievement, hyperacidity, affluence, flatulence, technology, tension. The inalienable right to an early coronary sitting at your desk while plotting to stab your boss in the back." Later, Hawkeye comes to a clear and incredibly simple understanding of the meaning of all this—the powerlessness of the individual worker to affect the apparatus of production—as he notes with sadness, "They keep coming whether I'm here or not."

Hawkeye is a philosopher whose real milieu is the 1960s and early 1970s. Indeed, Korea, as recognized in a graphic overlay in the pilot episode, was "1950: a hundred years ago." The war issues, in their human terms, were the central focus of the series. The war came home to the central protagonist in *M*A*S*H*'s final episode: Hawkeye is locked in a mental ward of an army hospital. He has finally cracked. He had tried to operate on a patient without using an anesthetic because he believed the anesthesiologist was trying to smother the patient with the mask. Hawkeye relates a story to his psychiatrist, Sidney Finkelstein, of a dark journey on a bus returning members of the 4,077th to camp following a day of rest and relaxation at a beach. The bus had stopped along the way to pick up some refugees and wounded soldiers (one could never really escape the war). The bus was forced to stop that night before reaching camp because it was feared that there were Chinese soldiers in the area who would be attracted by the engine noise and the headlights. A Korean refugee woman with an infant was riding at the back of the bus. The infant began to cry and would not stop. Hawkeye made his way to the woman and yelled at her to keep the child quiet. The situation was desperate. The woman, looking fearfully at Hawkeye, responded by smothering her baby to death. Hawkeye went mad. The gin mill to which he and B.J. and Trapper and Henry and Sherman had so often turned for solace would do him no good here, for he was in uncharted territory. His recovery was painful as he had to move beyond his guilt. In a way, his recovery was more rapid and the questions less resolved than artistic probability will allow, given the years of inner turbulence and soul-searching suffered by this sensitive surgeon. He is, quite visibly, emotionally scarred for life, although he continues to work upon his return to the unit. A very highly skilled surgeon, he has chosen to shun the rat race of big-city surgical practice and possible millionaire status in order to return to the small town from which he came and start a quiet practice in family medicine, à la Marcus Welby. Yet the enigmatic Hawkeye will bring his emotional scars to this rural middle landscape. We sense he will live out his life in character, always on or near the edge, filled with compassion yet haunted by the bitterness and guilt engendered by "his" war. The motif of the personalness of the war experience is *M*A*S*H*'s primary artistic strength as well as its primary ideological shortcoming, although the latter is not, on balance, a fatal flaw. The profundity of war lies in the inevitable fact that a great many individuals die, are maimed, or survive physically unscathed yet emotionally scarred, having fought in a relatively limited geographical space in a short period of time. The intensity of that experience makes it an ideal subject for art, especially allegory. On the other hand, the personalness of war is framed, in reality, by the ideology of war. Wars are conducted by generals and presidents and emperors in response to disagreements in basic social, political, and economic principles neatly abstracted from the daily fighting and the daily deaths. Wars are conducted in rooms, often below ground. The ultimate victory or defeat or stalemate resulting from the successful or unsuccessful or marginally successful conduct of war produces some shift in ideology and in the system of material and social relations in those states who were engaged in that war. The men in the trenches and the civilians on whose ground the war is fought are impacted by these shifts but do not control them—they simply live or die in defense of one or another position that they are led to believe is "sacred" or natural. *M*A*S*H* offers a pointed critique, on an allegorical level, of all war. This critique stresses the impact of war on the individual—the impact of war's utter barbarity, its lack of discrimination between soldier and civilian, and its seeming unendingness. Yet the conflicts, Korea and, by implication, Vietnam, that provide the specific social context for the series become mere settings—backdrops for the personal struggles which unfold. Ideology, as it directly impacts on the modern question of the justifiability of wars of national liberation as opposed to wars of foreign intervention, is conspicuous by its absence. This led critic Roger Hofeldt to suggest that within the structure of comedy, *M*A*S*H* presented controversy without change, reinforcing traditional institutions and values and acting as "a bulwark against change and social criticism."[10]

And while it is true that *M*A*S*H* suffers when put to the test of such social-realist criteria, its 250 episodes move beyond this critique. Artistically, *M*A*S*H* pioneered a new approach to television comedy. Many episodes were singular attempts to structurally revise the television-comedy form. One episode was shot as a black-and-white documentary; another hour-long episode, mentioned above, drew upon the Murrow documentary style of the *See It Now* series; another episode featured a "subjective camera" that became a character; many episodes were aired without a laugh track (including the final, two-and-a-half hour "Goodbye, Farewell, and Amen"); and a real-time episode was aired in which the doctors had 20 minutes to successfully treat a soldier before he became paralyzed for life—a clock in the frame ticked inexorably onward, showing the viewer how much time was left.

The comedy in this comedy-drama often, though fortunately not too often, lapses into rather stale army jokes most of us have heard a hundred times. Perhaps those who have served in the military justifiably take some small pleasure in reminiscing about the seemingly pointless little events that distanced them from the more immediate gravity of the larger situation in which they suffered and many of their friends died. Such events include the constant revulsion at the thought of eating the same soggy meals day after day—overcooked liver, runny mashed potatoes, coffee that tastes like iodine; and the incredibly frustrating military bureaucracy. One scene in *M*A*S*H* features an ignorant officer in the Quartermaster Corps who is authorizing the 4,077th's request for a jukebox and a pizza oven, but withholding the incubator the unit had requested, while another scene features Henry Blake signing redundant forms for a requisition. In the same scene, Henry asks Radar, "Tell me, Radar. Do you understand any of this?" Radar responds, "I try not to, sir. It slows up the war."

Likewise, the series sometimes slips into self-indulgent melodrama, as in the final episode, in which Major Charles Winchester, the New England blue-blooded thoracic surgeon inadvertently "captures" five Chinese musicians who are trying to surrender. He teaches them a favorite Mozart piece they slowly master during the course of their detainment in the camp. Here we are presented with the simplistic old saw that calls music the "universal language" that transcends the differences of war. The musicians are taken away, despite Winchester's protestations, to another holding area, but en route their truck is shelled and they all die. Winchester, grief-stricken, smashes a recording of the Mozart piece he kept in his tent. Music, said Winchester, would no longer be "a refuge from this miserable experience, but now it will always be a reminder." The naive notion of music's transcending the sordidness of everyday experience is played out through Charles's hyperbolic romantic character. While the acting makes the scene indeed touching, the underlying cliche points awkwardly to itself, and to standard television-melodrama convention.

The general level of comedy, however, transcends the one-liners and physical comedy that often keep the individual episodes moving; and the drama generally reveals complex characterization in which the protagonists must search for deeper meanings as they face their eventual return to civilian life, realizing their experiences in Korea will have measurably changed them.

As Joseph Campbell wrote, ". . . the divine comedies of redemption . . . in the ancient world were regarded as of a higher rank than tragedy, of a deeper truth, of a more difficult realization, of a sounder structure, and of a revelation more complete."[11] *M*A*S*H*'s portrayal of the strength of family bonds as a "transcendence of the universal tragedy of man," in which "enduring being is made manifest,"[12] ultimately reveals the comedy's indifference to the contention of life and death—it is focusing instead beyond that immediate struggle to the larger question of the value of a life itself in a desensitized world in which bureaucracy, with its charts, data, and strategies, controls man's basic human actions, a world in which control is vested in unapproachable, powerful institutions. The battle was waged and concluded; the results were recited over the radio playing in the operating room as the surgeons of the 4,077th operated as a team for the last time:

> . . . the cost of the war to the United States has been placed at $22 billion. [The camera tilts down to reveal pools of blood on the operating-room floor.][13] . . . . In human terms the cost was much greater. The UN forces have suffered the following casualties: killed in combat, 71,500; missing and captured, 82,263; wounded, 250,000. . . . On the Communist side, 1,347,000 people were killed or wounded; . . . also killed [were] 400,000 Korean civilians. If you add it all up, it comes to more than 2,000,000 people killed or wounded.

In the era of the "bottom line," the money spent on this war of containment became the headline, followed by the tally of bodies.

The atmosphere of the assembly line was revealed everywhere. War was surely nothing more and nothing less than work. As Hawkeye had once bitterly noted, "You just do your job and try to forget there's a war going on outside the window." In another scene, he told Sherman Potter, "Maybe we should charge them piecework."

M*A*S*H brought to an audience of 125 million viewers (60 percent of all homes with television) in its final episode a sense not so much of closure, of a merciful end to a terribly depressing condition, but of openness to a future where reasonably sane and sensitive people could see through the camouflage of myth to ideology manifested in such absurd myths as those of manifest destiny (assuming the role of the world's policeman) and of eternal progress (the glorification of technique and its deployment in the service of foolish military escapades). *M*A*S*H*, to the credit of its creators, writers, directors, and actors, of whom Larry Gelbart, Alan Alda, and Burt Metcalfe stand out, had at least on occasion the courage to be oppositional—a rare act in contemporary commercial television.[14]

Perhaps the most clearly oppositional work in television comedy, and perhaps in all of television, was *Mary Hartman, Mary Hartman*. While its television life was short (January 1976 to July 1977), and its audience small by network standards (it was turned down by all three networks, although CBS had financed the pilot, and instead it ran in syndication in about 100 markets), this work made a significant impact on the critical community and established a cult following; it continues to run extensively in syndication. The part legitimate soap opera and part spoof (no one was ever quite certain which part was which since the serial had the wonderful ability to easily slide between sardonic humor and pathos via the hesitancy of its incredibly ambivalent characters) was produced by Lear and T.A.T. Productions and aired for a half hour Monday through Friday, on most stations either in late afternoon or late night. The program was losing about $50,000 a week because its initial 26-week "charter contracts" negotiated with station groups had a minimal try-out fee—a necessity for oppositional work that could not secure immediate network financing. The serial was so popular in some markets that two major station groups, Kaiser and Metromedia, offered to renegotiate their contracts at higher fees to keep the serial alive. This was a fascinating commentary on the willingness of business interests to ignore the oppositional nature of material when it is highly profitable. Its popularity seemed to operate on two levels: One audience, in all likelihood, took the serial as pure entertainment—a soap-opera spoof—while another audience reveled in its biting social satire.

Part of the serial's popularity was undoubtedly due to its very frank treatment of contemporary problems of sexuality, including impotence, extramarital affairs, and lechery. Unlike the prime-time soaps featuring wealthy anomic meanies such as *Dallas*'s Ewings, the Hartmans—Tom and Mary—and their friends Charlie and Loretta Haggers, were essentially honest blue-collar, middle-American working folks from Fernwood, Ohio, with good intentions and a strong underlying sense of morality. But Tom's and Mary's total dependency on the television world, their low self-esteem brought about by their sense of inferior socioeconomic status, and their increasing inability to communicate with one another led to the breakdown of their marriage, their desperate search for human interaction in extramarital affairs (Mary with handsome police-sergeant Dennis Foley, with whom she makes love in his hospital bed; and Tom with Annie, an upper-middle-class cultural snob), and their eventual separation.

The odd assortment of characters lends the serial a surreal quality while, at the same time, the marks of the rural blue-collar proletariat force the viewer to acknowledge the realism of the scenes played out in Mary's kitchen, her true domain, and in the lunchroom of the Fernwood Assembly Plant, Tom's workplace. This dichotomy provides *Mary Hartman, Mary Hartman* with unusual artistic power.

The characters in the serial are among the most memorable on television. Mary Hartman, played by Louise Lasser, is the prototypical blue-collar housewife—unfulfilled, constantly dreaming of the glamorous life she has seen enacted far too often on television, and especially in television advertising. Her inability to achieve the American Dream is a constant source of frustration and leads to ultimate confusion and an eventual mental collapse. This confusion is not of the mindless variety so often seen in the glorious domestic situation comedies of *I Love Lucy* et al.; it is a gnawing substantive inner confusion—a confusion of values. Mary's braids and bangs, her buck teeth, and her little-girl clothes reveal her basic innocence and lack of emotional development. Her personality is "unintegrated."[15] Mary's 13-year-old daughter Heather is a miniature version of her mother. We can see the sad inevitability of her future, a potentially capable child burdened with circumstances beyond her control. Mary's husband Tom is a pure rural blue-collar proletarian with all the marks of small-town insularity. He has never really grown up, as evidenced by his ever-present blue-and-white Fernwood High School jacket and base-ball cap. His lunch pail is filled with Twinkies. He drinks too much, although he is miraculously cured during the course of the series. His personal problems lead to his impotency; and when Mary offers her-self, body and soul, to him, he angrily proclaims that the male deter-mines when to have sex with his wife. Mary's and Tom's best friends, Charlie and Loretta, represent the naive optimism of rural workers. Charlie and Loretta are sexually active and presumably very happy with one another as the serial opens, in marked contrast to Tom and Mary. Charlie is much older than Loretta, balding, physically unattrac-tive, yet a powerhouse in bed, or so Loretta says. Loretta is young, pretty, vivacious, and a talented country-western singer. She believes in her Bible-belt religion and displays a strong moral character in pub-lic. Other, less prominent characters in the serial are even more bizarre than Mary. These include Chester Markham, who plans to blow up the entire state of Ohio; Mary's 80-year-old lecherous Grandpa Larkin, out of jail on probation, who is dating his young woman social worker; Mary's ignorant parents, George and Martha Shumway; and eight-year-old Reverend Jimmy Joe Jeeter, a Marjoe Gortner type, and his con-man father, Merle. With all of these characters, and their glaring human weaknesses, levels of frustration pile on top of one another and in the end become oppressive. This is television's true theater of the absurd.

The worker is presented as generally inarticulate, with low self-esteem, and as unable to hold a job (Tom lost his at the assembly plant, which hastened his emotional decline). The protagonists seem out of control. This is ingeniously reflected aesthetically in the serial's structure as the rotating and periodically suspended plot-line structure of the traditional soap opera is convoluted—*Mary Hartman, Mary Hartman* (even the redundancy of the title evokes this) gives the viewer a strange sense of the "haphazard, without a conspicuous overall plan or consistent development."[16] The viewer is engaged in the "ordinary" disjointed world of the residents of Fernwood, a world of shallow topicality framed by the god of topicality itself, television.

Our heroine, Mary, seems the character most taken in by the televised American Dream. In values-and-lifestyles-research terms, by which so many advertisers live and breathe, Mary is a cross between the patriotic and sentimental "belonger" and the "sustainer," who has a hard time making ends meet and is resentful of her condition.[17] Such an anomaly is appropriate as it propels this artistic vehicle for-ward. Mary wants desperately to be a "belonger," but does not have

the necessary educational background or social status and has a difficult time coming to grips with this sad fact. Critics Tamm, Hanson,
and Gordon described Mary's unenviable state perhaps best:

> . . . in all her glory [Mary is] one of the most pathetic figures of our
> era: the modern housewife—who really believes what advertisers and
> media simplifiers have told her, because she *wants* to believe them.
> Eventually this fiction disclosed its premise: a reverse analogy of
> Ibsen's *Doll House*: Mary, outside the house, wanted to get *in*. The
> delusion annihilates Mary—or drives her mad—because she has been
> so cruelly victimized by the shallow cultural ideals she worships.[18]

Almost everything in Mary's world has a pointed relationship to
television; here the emphasis is on commodities and surface appearance at the expense of authentic human communication. In Mary's
world, household items indeed take precedence over human relationships. While a police detective questions Mary in her kitchen about
Heather's possible sighting of a mass murderer in their neighborhood,
Mary is more concerned with whether her kitchen floor has a "yellow
wax buildup." In another scene, Mary engages in a serious debate with
a neighbor regarding the pros and cons of freeze-dried versus perked
coffee, rather than worrying about her physical safety, which is indirectly threatened by the presence of the mass murderer in the
vicinity. When a reporter for the *Fernwood Courier* comes to the
Hartmans' house to take a photo of Heather, who is becoming an instant celebrity due to her sighting of the mass murderer, Mary says
no, not because of considerations regarding Heather's privacy, but,
rather, because Heather's hair is out of place and covers the "beautiful bone structure" of her face—the normal reaction of an ideal
"media mother."

All of Mary's food has an advertising jingle attached to it, which
she dutifully recites when the opportunity arises: "Want some sausage,
brown and serve?," or, "I usually buy mountain grown."

Television has intimate, if incredible, ties to both death and insanity in this self-reflexive serial. The child reverend, Jimmy Joe
Jeeter, was electrocuted while watching TV in the bathtub. Zoning
Commissioner Rittenhouse was strangled to death on a television-talk
show. Mary herself mentally collapsed under questioning from three
so-called experts—a women's liberationist, a sociologist, and a sexol-
ogist—on the David Susskind Show. Ironically, the television audience
thought her breakdown was part of the entertainment (a reminder of
Paddy Chayefsky's *Network*). Mary's relationship to television did

not end here. She was admitted to the mental ward of the Fernwood Receiving Hospital, whose chief administrator wanted to keep her locked up, despite her doctor's recommendation issued for her release, because of her celebrity status and the attention it was bringing the hospital. When Mary wanted out, she was told to "sit and look at television to show them that you are normal."[19]

Perhaps no bit of dialogue better sums up the underlying ambience of *Mary Hartman, Mary Hartman* than Charlie's last words to Mary and Tom as he and Loretta leave for Nashville to cut Loretta's first country-and-western album: "We'll send you a pecan log from Stuckies." The mundane then merges with the bizarre to produce a disquieting tableau of America—scenes from a poorly printed, out-of-focus four-color postcard showing a roadside restaurant by a four-lane interstate.

Mary Hartman, Mary Hartman went voluntarily silent in July 1977 "because of the strain of producing five shows a week," according to critic Les Brown.[20] It was succeeded by *Fernwood 2-Night*, a short-lived fictional talk show involving many of the *Mary Hartman, Mary Hartman* characters. The serial had provided television viewers with a rare glimpse of blue-collar life permeated by doubt, low self-esteem, the trivial topicality of television itself, and the harsh reality that the American Dream, manifested in the myth of eternal progress, was more fantasy than substance. This mythic rural middle landscape was not at all like the one we witnessed in *The Beverly Hillbillies, The Andy Griffith Show,* or *Green Acres.* It was, instead, a rural middle landscape that we fear, not cherish—a psychic landscape that reveals the darker side of human nature and holds it up to careful, critical self-evaluation. *Mary Hartman, Mary Hartman*'s creators had the insight to provide their audience with an amalgam of two forms—soap opera and comedy—that brilliantly revealed the uneasy relationship between the emptiness of ordinary workers' lives and their desperate need for fantasy, which is so cleverly provided by our most accessible communications medium.

THE SATIRIC COMEDY-VARIETY SERIES

Another hybrid televisual form that has provided a dominant cultural arena for the occasional expression of emergent oppositional ideology is the comedy-variety series. Over the 35-year public history of television in America, a few series in this genre stand out as exemplary—*That Was the Week That Was* (*TW3*, 1964-65), *The Smothers Brothers Comedy Hour* (1967-69), *Rowan and Martin's Laugh-In*

(1968-73), *The Great American Dream Machine* (1971-72), *Saturday Night Live* (1975-present), and *The Richard Prior Show* (1977). These shows combined satirical sketches often lambasting the spokespersons for the dominant ideology, occasional protest songs, and acerbic commentaries on such sacred cows as television commercials and network television-news programs. The programs were uneven, ranging from the devastatingly political protest ballads of Pete Seeger on the *Smothers Brothers* series at the height of the war in Vietnam to the nonsensical mugging in John Belushi's "Samurai Warrior" sketches and the perverse if intriguing "Mr. Bill" films on *Saturday Night Live*. Like all good satire, the strongest of the shows dealt directly with topical issues and social irritations produced by inequities in the extant system of social relations. They did so, however, within a larger structure—the eclectic variety-show format—that tended to diminish the potential overall impact of the satiric and even sardonic work that emerged, work that frequently provoked public controversy. Television would always find a way to make the potentially unpalatable somehow palatable, or if it could not do so, it would simply cancel the offenders; that is, unless the said offenders are gaining substantial ratings. Comedian George Carlin, whose "Dirty Words" monologue sparked the WBAI/Pacifica case, put it this way: "If truth and candor are proved to be hot items in the rating game, the networks will jump all over them."[21] Steve Allen, who directed his satire against the television medium itself, noted, "You can get away with anything on television if you have a big enough rating. Network executives may wince, but . . . they would much rather have a vulgar or politically offensive show with a 30 Nielsen than a tasteful, inoffensive program with a 15."[22] Both Allen and Carlin tend to exaggerate the networks' willingness to accede to any content if it is profitable, as we shall shortly see.

Contemporary American satire, especially in its television form, traces its heritage to the coffeehouse worlds of Lenny Bruce and Mort Sahl in the mid-to-late 1950s. Bruce's ribald humor and acerbic wit were reminiscent of the formal comedy in the theater of classical Greece in which risqué "religious" exercises celebrated Dionysus—a comedy of rebellion and revolution against constraining social systems. Bruce and Sahl were "creator-comics," as Carlin terms them, who, unlike traditional stand-up comics, wrote their own material and brought with them a sense of strong personal social commitment. They cut through the camouflage of the dominant ideology to reveal the harsh realities of American politics in an era which witnessed the emergence of the powerful corporate state. Their comedy was ultimately more about freedom, however, than about politics.[23] The coffeehouse satirists created a psychic geography that appealed to the rapidly growing number of American college-educated youths who were becoming increasingly skeptical about the dominant institutions of corporate America. They opened the creaky, conservative doors of our dominant electronic communications medium to the satiric comedy-variety series of the 1960s and 1970s. Bruce and Sahl were experts in using their characters, voices, gestural attitudes, and informal modes of dress to cloak their biting satire in personality and make it acceptable not only to those seeking an emergent counter-culture, but also to those on the fringes of the social debate who were curious but not yet committed. Bruce and Sahl chose a carefully orchestrated performance stance to make their points; they represented the universal motif of the angry young man. The time for this stance was right. Civil rights confrontation and, soon, a highly questionable war would merge with the feelings of anomie and alienation that had come to characterize the corporate 1950s—a bland era in which white people were consumed with the idea of "belonging." Sahl and Bruce led the walk away from the suburban middle landscape and into an urban world in which social revolution would seem a meaningful response.

Television itself would intensify this atmosphere through the power of its incessant imaging. Carlin himself perceptively summed up the atmosphere in which television satire emerged:

> The extended coverage of recent assassinations and their aftermaths, the daily Viet Nam battle film, campus rebellion, the extraordinary political year 1968, including Chicago's police riots— . . . all of these events documented nightly on the home screen have served to convince the viewer that the little box is more than a vehicle for escape.[24]

Carlin added that the audience "can accept social satire as a logical extension of the absurd reality viewed on news and information programs. The frame of reference . . . (the very medium which provides our yardstick of the norm) is perfect."[25] In fact, as Carlin noted, "The very use of the satiric form supposes respect for audience awareness."[26] The audience watched the two wars at home—the Freedom Riders and the famous 1963 civil rights march on Washington highlighted a domestic war, while the Tet offensive brought a foreign war into clearer perspective. After Walter Cronkite's reassuring image faded from view for that evening, the debate would often rage on among those who remained gathered around the screen as scenes were recalled; the screen would light up again, in prime time, for the satiric follow-up—a forum for a continued questioning of our nation's basic value priorities.

That Was the Week That Was enlivened our television screens from January 10, 1964, to May 4, 1965. It would serve as a model for subsequent television-news satires. The previous week's top news items were subjected to pointed, and often brutal satire through comedy sketches, blackouts, musical-production numbers, and news reports. The series introduced David Frost to an American audience. Frost had hosted a British series upon which *TW3* was modeled, and he hosted the second and final season of the American series as well. The most memorable participant in the series was writer-composer Tom Lehrer, whose scathing songs condemned racism, political cronyism, chemical pollution, and a variety of other social irritations. These songs included "National Brotherhood Week," "Whatever Became of Hubert?," and the infamous "Vatican Rag" and "Pollution." The latter song was appropriate in a period following the publication of Rachel Carson's book *Silent Spring* and a subsequent CBS television documentary that chronicled the controversy involving Carson's basic challenge to the corporate chemical giants and the U.S. Department of Agriculture. The series, with moments of true oppositional ideological expression, never broke into the top 25 Nielsen shows. According to Steve Allen, the series failed because it came five years too early for the American audience, and many of its actors, who included Henry Morgan and Phyllis Newman, weren't very engaging.

While *TW3* never achieved popularity with America's mass audiences, a comedy-variety series that was aired two years later was able to find that large audience, and particularly the younger demographic group. In the interim, America had been exposed, via television news, to the possibility of a cruel hoax 10,000 miles from home. Vietnam had entered the national debate; young men were being drafted and were dying there. The emotional fires ignited in August 1965 in Los Angeles by the Watts riots were still smoldering and would soon be rekindled in urban ghettos throughout the United States. It was February 5, 1967, and an important milestone in television was achieved as *The Smothers Brothers Comedy Hour* premiered on CBS. For the next two-and-a-half years, the series, with its many artistic ups and downs, its constant battles with network standards-and-practices managers and its status as legitimizer of the counter-culture, would highlight the social and political crises that seemed to hit this country almost daily. The series was hosted by Tom and Dick

Smothers and featured comedian Pat Paulsen. Tom, the "dull brother," played the guitar; his older and much wiser brother Dick played the bass violin. Tom's famous line, "Mom liked you best," provided the series with a distinctive personality—the codes of sibling rivalry were a comic dodge used to keep the audience open to the more serious fare that emerged in the series. The two brothers would open each show with a song that never quite went right. Keeping in character, Tom would always mess the song up by forgetting either the lyrics or tune or he would become recalcitrant and childish and want to change the entire routine. But beyond the internecine quarrels, *The Smothers Brothers Comedy Hour* satirized almost every hallowed American institution, and especially political institutions. Tom and Dick, it seems fair to say, did not themselves often "do political or social satire. It is more correct to say that political and social satire are presented on their show."[27] They had, however, a strong social consciousness—a personal commitment to exposing social ills—and that was the crucial element which carried the series through its roughest moments in CBS corporate boardrooms. Sketches on the series included a highly controversial antireligion polemic aired early in 1969; and antiwar ballad titled "Waist Deep in the Big Muddy," sung by Pete Seeger, a frequent guest on the program, who had long been blacklisted on television; and a bizarre campaign for the presidency of the United States, waged by Pat Paulsen. In the summer of 1968, Paulsen attempted to take his campaign on the airwaves via the *Comedy Hour*, but CBS, fearing demands for equal time from other political candidates under Section 315 of the Communications Act, kept Paulsen's campaign off the air until after the November elections. Paulsen's campaign slogan became a rallying point for dissatisfied college students throughout the country who had lost faith in our national leadership (Lyndon Johnson, himself buried waist deep in regard to Vietnam, had declined to seek reelection, and the specter of Richard Nixon loomed ominously on the national political horizon). Paulsen, in his droll deadpan manner, asserted with confidence: "If nominated I will not run, and if elected I will not serve."

Tom and Dick engaged not only the dominant political institutions, but also the powerful media institutions they depended on for survival. They often failed to deliver their completed programs early enough for editing. This helped them sneak their oppositional material past wary network officials and traditionally conservative affiliate-station managers, but it also so angered CBS executives that the series was replaced in June 1969 with *Hee Haw*, a rural-hillbilly takeoff on the highly successful NBC series *Laugh-In. The Smothers Brothers Comedy Hour* managed to achieve relatively high ratings for both its 1967 and 1968 seasons (it ranked sixteenth and eighteenth of all rated series aired in those respective years), but it slid in the ratings in the 1968-69 season, perhaps the real reason CBS canceled it. Its oppositional material was no longer achieving a significant payback. The series received an Emmy Award in 1968-69 for "outstanding writing in comedy, variety or music." For those who struggled through this volatile period in American cultural and social history, *The Smothers Brothers Comedy Hour* provided a needed satiric perspective on the incredible events unfolding daily. The series would continue to evoke strong memories of the important questions regarding personal commitment in a society characterized by anomie.

Another comedy-variety series of the time, *Rowan and Martin's Laugh-In*, which ran on NBC from January 22, 1968, to May 14, 1973, while not as overtly political as either *TW3* or *The Smothers Brothers Comedy Hour*, nevertheless poked fun at many of America's bourgeois social codes while at the same time, seeming to revel in the social milieu. The series format was anchored by the individual performer's sketch, which became a personal trademark. The series's roots were in the fast-paced, seemingly unstructured action comedy of such early film comedians as the Keystone Cops, and in the news satire of *TW3*. With *Laugh-In*'s huge cast of 40 or more regular players delivering rapid-fire catch phrases such as "sock it to me," "velly intellestink," and "look that up in your Funk and Wagnalls," and with the frenetic pacing of the regular features—the go-go-dancer-filled cocktail-party scene, the "Flying Fickle Finger of Fate Award," "Laugh-In Looks at the News," and the show's concluding segment, the "Joke Wall"—the program became a frenzied hour of tomfoolery that reflected the confusing mosaic of everyday experience of the late 1960s and early 1970s, a period in which events and personal relationships seemed far from the ordered state of things as reflected in the suburban middle landscape of the 1950s and early 1960s.

Laugh-In was a smash hit. It was the top-rated television series in both the 1968 and 1969 seasons. One reason for such success may have been the series's ability to get even the most famous national figures to do guest appearances on the show. Who can forget a perplexed Richard Nixon, in close-up, saying to the camera, "Sock it to *me*?"

Laugh-In's cohost, Dan Rowan, is firmly convinced that comedy is, above all, "visual," and the series reflects that philosophy—it is a visual three-ring circus without magicians, bears, or acrobats, more the province of traditional variety shows, which were so successful in television's early period (e.g., *The Ed Sullivan Show*). Rowan saw his series as distinct from *The Smothers Brothers Comedy Hour*, about which he noted, "[They] have a definite direction and philosophy and are simply using comedy as a platform for a doctrine. Whether or not we agree with the Smothers (and we generally do), we aren't doing *that thing*."[28] The dirty-old-man sketches and other sexual innuendos that pervaded *Laugh-In* were allowable in a period in which the youth audience was becoming increasingly important to the networks; demographics had become a relevant analytical tool employed by advertisers to help them target their audience. In 1970, CBS performed a major housecleaning, removing its rural-middle-landscape comedies and middle-aged variety stars—its staples for decades—in favor of what it called relevant urban-oriented works it felt would appeal to younger city audiences comprised of recent college graduates who would soon be decidedly upscale, once the social protest subsided. It was clear, at least to Rowan, that the mainstream audience, to which *Laugh-In* appealed, would accept a raucous mixture of topicality, slapstick, sex, violence, and the portrayal of the human idiot. Rowan disclaimed any comedic "revolution" here, asking, "What's new?"

Indeed, *Laugh-In* was not as polemical as were the Smothers Brothers or as consistently acerbic as *TW3*. But it did at least expose the outlines of irreverent comedy to a larger audience. The much smaller audience that in 1971 could tune through the UHF snow to find the local Public Broadcasting Service outlet might have been treated to one of our finest, yet most short-lived, satiric comedies—*The Great American Dream Machine*. Produced at WNET/13 in New York, this series of one-hour episodes was aired from January 1971 to January 1972 and featured some memorable television moments as satire, serious documentaries, drama, and music segments were blended into a coherent and often scathing attack on American values. It seemed the Great American Dream had run amok, at least with many people. The "machine," whether political, economic, or cultural, kept cranking out products—public symbols behind which cowered questionable value priorities. Etched in memory is the mustachioed, plump, frumpy, and brilliant Marshall Efron, who, with the precision of a neurosurgeon or a highly skilled criminal lawyer, would in his consumer segments, meticulously demystify the apparatus that actualized our pecuniary philosophy, psychology, and biology. Of all the great moments, none stands out more to me than Efron's incredible revelation that the trash compacter, seen lurking lifelessly in the background, ready to grind away on call, and which sold for a mere $400, could "turn 25 pounds of trash [he holds up unwieldy trash bag] into 25 pounds of trash [he holds up compacted bag of trash]." The *Dream Machine* ran into serious political trouble late in its run as it aired a documentary accusing the Federal Bureau of Investigation of planting its agents as "terrorists" whose job it was to convince college-student radicals to sabotage public facilities, to help them build bombs for that purpose, and then to arrest them. The series was disbanded after one year for lack of funding, according to television critic Les Brown.

In 1975 a new series emerged, modeling itself in many ways on both *Laugh-In* and *TW3*. The series, *Saturday Night Live*, was to serve as a late-night NBC showcase for young comedians, and it did precisely that. Live, 90 minutes in duration, and transmitted from New York originally three Saturdays each month (the fourth Saturday was devoted to Lloyd Dobbins's excellent documentary magazine *Weekend*), *Saturday Night Live* premiered October 11, 1975. Its first guest host was George Carlin. The resident cast included Chevy Chase, Dan Ackroyd, John Belushi, Jane Curtin, Garrett Morris, Laraine Newman, and Gilda Radner, all of whom became household names among America's youths. Each comedian, as was the case with *Laugh-In*, developed his or her own trademark character. Chase became famous for his satirical newscast and impressions of President Gerald Ford stumbling around. He left the series in 1976 to pursue a successful film career. Ackroyd and Belushi remained with the series for four years before leaving for Hollywood to make films as a comedy team. Belushi's samurai-warrior routines lent a classic touch of the absurd to the show.

Highlights from the series are difficult to cite in a limited space, but the most imaginative work often emerged in the commercial spoofs that were ingeniously built into the program's flow so that the audience was never immediately certain whether the real thing or a takeoff was unfolding. This aesthetic device pointed clearly and self-reflexively to the perceptual stance ingrained in television viewers over time—we had unconsciously become part of the flow of television. *Saturday Night Live*, at its best, jerked us out of that flow. Who can forget the incredible Jerry Rubin doing a pitch for "Yippie Wallpaper," something to help the now-upscale, former radical-revolutionaries of the 1960s remember the glorious "good old days." Rubin, himself a revolutionary turned stockbroker, was the ideal pitchman in the new era of the "me generation."

Saturday Night Live has been extremely uneven throughout its run. Some sketches bordered on the ridiculous, such as "The Killer Bees," but other recurring sketches, notably the "Cone Heads," did insightfully address contemporary social issues such as parochialism and prejudice in suburbia. Segments such as the "Mr. Bill" filmed narratives simultaneously appealed to our odd cultural sense of morbidity and titillated us, creating an uneasy ambiguity. These sketches often stretched the bounds of acceptability, which in itself tests the fiber of the dominant ideology.

One cannot leave the genre without at least a brief discussion of the shortest-lived program in the group, *The Richard Pryor Show*, which premiered September 13, 1977, and died a quiet death October 20 of the same year. It was the black comedian's first regular television series. He had originally committed himself to a minimum of ten shows with NBC, but censorship problems with the network reduced his quota to five. Pryor got off on the wrong foot with the network brass; in what was to be the opening segment of his first program in the series, he appeared on camera nude from the waist up. As the camera slowly tilted down revealing what appeared to be a nude Pryor (he was really wearing a body stocking), he was delivering a monologue on his relationship with NBC, stating he had lost nothing in his censorship battles. The segment was cut from the show. Another memorable sketch was a bitter and poignant attack on guns, especially handguns that seemed to kill a disproportionate number of urban blacks. The impassioned attack and plea for sanity was, of course, directed by implication at the National Rifle Association, and at its blind adherence to the myth of individual freedom, as expressed in its libertarian/conservative politics. This was strong stuff for prime-time network "entertainment" television. But ultimately there was little for NBC to worry about. The network had conveniently counter-programmed *The Richard Pryor Show* against ABC's smash hit *Happy Days*, which drew an audience twice as large as did Pryor.

While it is impossible to adequately sum up the discussion of the wide variety of comedic presentations described and interpreted in this chapter, a few common threads are worth noting. Works of television comedy are contemporary; i.e., they are culturally relevant because of their temporality. Television comedies reflect, and occasionally call into question, the predominant operational myths of the culture. Television comedies tend to lag slightly behind the broad social movements that produce subtle yet large-scale cultural shifts; as such, the comedies, while seemingly oppositional, are in fact more like cautionary tales whose confrontational quality is at best mildly provocative. There can be little doubt that those who produce, write, perform, and direct television comedy are among the best talents working in the medium today. And of all the genres of television, comedy, especially satiric comedy and comedy-drama, provides us with the clearest opportunity to express emergent oppositional ideology. At the same time, the institutional apparatus that might permit such occasional forays into the deep waters of social criticism can easily pull the plug on the maverick producer through counter-programming, prior censorship, or outright cancellation. And, although the networks will stay with a controversial comedy series that sells very well, it is apparent that the more truly oppositional series, with the notable exception of *M*A*S*H* and, to a lesser degree, *The Smothers Brothers Comedy Hour*, are never great audience successes. In the end, the television networks and their corporate shareholders have the last laugh.

NOTES

1. John Leonard, "Bigotry as a Dirty Joke," *Life*, March 18, 1971
2. Ibid.
3. Robert Lewis Shayon, "Love That Hate," *Saturday Review*, March 27, 1971.
4. Ibid.
5. Michael Arlen, "The Media Dramas of Norman Lear, *The New Yorker*, March 10, 1975.
6. Ibid.
7. Archie's voice was dubbed over the video. The actual line Archie delivered in the scene was, "I don't wanna talk about that goddam war no more." The producers and/or the networks decided that the language, even for *All in the Family*, was too much. It is one of those rare cases where the actor, totally involved in his part and improvising, given the nature of the action, transcends the controls of the television apparatus and makes a clear statement about his personal feelings, revealing at the same time the potential power of performance.
8. Todd Gitlin, "Prime Time Ideology: The Hegemonic Process in Television Entertainment," in *Television: The Critical View*, 3d. ed., ed. Horace Newcomb (New York: Oxford University Press, 1982), p. 451.
9. Roger L. Hofeldt, "Cultural Bias in M*A*S*H," in *Television: The Critical View*, 3d. ed., p. 161.
10. Ibid., p. 164.
11. Campbell, *Hero*, p. 28.
12. Ibid.

13. The amount of blood shown during the course of the series increased dramatically in sync with the overall increasing levels of cynicism and anger expressed by the protagonists. Looking back on the series, the shift seems to have been subtle.

14. It should be noted that, as was the case with *All in the Family*, one can take risks if one is profitable. The final episode of *M*A*S*H*, while costing more than $1 million to produce, earned CBS in excess of $10 million, according to published news reports. Thirty-second spots sold for about $450,000.

15. Robert Craft, "Elegy for Mary Hartman," in *Television: The Critical View*, 3d. ed., p. 153.

16. Ibid., p. 149.

17. William Meyers, "Of Belongers, Achievers, Survivors et al.," *New York Times*, December 5, 1982, p. F29.

18. Goran Tamm, Hans Ingvar Hanson, and George N. Gordon, *Man In Focus: New Approaches to Commercial Communications* (New York: Hastings House, 1980), p. 26.

19. Craft, "Elegy," p. 151.

20. Les Brown, *Encyclopedia of Television* (New York: Zoetrope, 1982), p. 267.

21. George Carlin, "Made For Each Other: TV and Satire," *Television Quarterly* 8 (Winter 1969):25.

22. Steve Allen, "The Revolution in Humor," *Television Quarterly* 8 (Winter 1969):11.

23. Ibid., p. 12.

24. Carlin, "Made for Each Other," pp. 25-26.

25. Ibid., p. 26.

26. Ibid., p. 24.

27. Allen, "Revolution," p. 8.

28. Dan Rowan, "What Revolution in Comedy?" *Television Quarterly* 8 (Winter 1969):24.

6

TELEVISION MELODRAMA

The intentional ironic comedy of *Mary Hartman, Mary Hartman*, one of the very few instances of emergent oppositional ideology in the history of commercial television, played off the journalistic realism of television soap opera, one of television's most significant traditional melodramatic forms. The realism of the television soaps constitutes one pole of the melodramatic continuum. At the other extreme are the romantic epics of loner-heroes and wanderers whose mystical experiences reveal a mythic dream world of fear and conquest. Like melodrama generally, both the soap opera and the romantic epic take a centrist position. In the former instance, the protagonists and antagonists operate within a highly constrained code of conduct in which erratic/anarchistic behavior is punished; in the latter instance, the loner-hero, while suffering numerous tests of physical and moral strength along the journey, prevails and is incorporated back into society.

Television melodrama has its roots in the early-nineteenth-century stage play in which romantic, sensational plots and incidents were mixed with songs and orchestral music. The word melodrama evolved from the Greek *melos*, meaning song or music, and from *drama*, a deed, action, or play, especially a tragedy. However, unlike tragedy—in which the hero is isolated from his society so that he may understand his own and the society's moral weakness, but, once enlightened, he cannot stave off the disaster embedded in the social structure beyond his control—melodrama finds the hero's acts constantly reinforcing the dominant ideology. The melodramatic hero, whether wanderer or a sedentary voice of authority, represents incorporation into his society. Critic Northrop Frye described a central theme in melodrama as "the truimph of moral virtue over villainy, and the consequent idealizing of the moral views assumed to be held by the audience."[1] Since melodrama, according to Frye's viewpoint, exists squarely within a mass-cultural framework, it could easily become "advance propaganda for the police state" if it were taken seriously.[2] Frye sidesteps this fear by positing that the audience does not take such work seriously. Such a conclusion is simplistic, and discounts the power of melodrama.

Peter Brooks, in contrast to Frye, finds melodrama acting powerfully in society, reflecting the socialization of the deeply personal. Brooks finds the heightened dramatization and excess enactment of melodrama reflected in psychoanalysis: "Psychoanalysis can be read as a systematic realization of the melodramatic aesthetic, applied to the structure and dynamics of the mind."[3] Brooks sees in the melodramatic aesthetic unremitting conflict, possibly disabling, excessive enactment, and clarification and cure. Brooks elaborates:

> Melodrama regularly stimulates the experience of nightmare, where virtue, representative of the ego, lies supine, helpless, while menace plays out its occult designs. The end of the nightmare is an awakening brought about by confrontation and expulsion of the villain, the person in whom the evil is seen to be concentrated, and a reaffirmation of the society of "decent people."[4]

Melodrama demands strong justice—"a perfect justice of punishment and reward, expulsion and recognition,"[5] while tragedy, in contrast, often includes the ambivalence of mercy in its code. Melodrama is highly significant in an age of surface complexity and contradiction (which we experience in our everyday lives), for it provides us with models of clear resolution for highly personalized, intensely enacted conflict. As Brooks notes, contemporary television melodrama substitutes for the traditional forms of social control—the rituals of organized religion and, before that, of "primitive mythologies"—that provided easily understandable models of "primal, intense, polarized forces."

Melodrama is thus powerfully conservative. Like the ceremonial ritual that bound tribesmen together, melodrama today, repositioned in politics and economics, draws us into the prescriptions of the dominant culture.

THE HERO AS A CULTURAL SYMBOL

Central to the melodrama is the hero. The dominant concept of the hero in Western culture dates from the heroic period of Grecian history that preceded the return of Greek soldiers from their conquest of Troy in Asia Minor (early twelfth century B.C.). Hero was the name given to a man of superhuman strength, courage, or ability who was favored by the gods. In antiquity, the hero was regarded as an immortal intermediate between the gods and men—a demigod who was the offspring of a god or goddess and a human being.

Later, the heroic class came to include mortal men of renown who were deified because of great and noble deeds, or for firmness or greatness of soul in any course of action they undertook. These men became national or local heroes. They included men distinguished by extraordinary bravery and martial achievement—the illustrious warriors; and men who wandered in quest of adventures—the hero-errants (called knight-errants in medieval culture). Many heroes were boldly experimental or resourceful in their actions. Heroic actions were not always pure, however; cunning became a characteristic of the hero as he used his wit to outsmart the enemy (as exemplified by Homer's epic hero Odysseus's invention of the wooden horse, his encounter with the sirens, and his beggar's disguise that tricked his wife's suitors). Punishment of those who disturbed the proper order of things was harsh. Odysseus slaughtered all 108 of his wife Penelope's suitors in order to restore decency to the court of Ithaca. Women as well as men possessed heroic qualities such as valor, resourcefulness, intelligence, and moral strength (although she had no knowledge of Odysseus's fate, as he was forced by the gods to wander the Mediterranean for ten years, Penelope nevertheless remained faithful and put off all her suitors with courage and moral conviction).

The world in which the classic hero operated was a world of heightened emotional intensity—a harsh world in which the norm included unending tests of both physical and moral strength, and the constant threat of death. The hero represented a carefully defined value system in which good triumphed over evil in the end, and in which the actions of the hero, with the assistance of the gods, produced order and stability out of chaos.

Stylistically, the classic Greek epic poem, composed in the oral, mnemonic form that favored recurrent themes and motifs and flexible rhythms, presented to the listener an accessible form in which to deal with the complex narrative development. Structurally, Homer's

Odyssey is the precursor of the modern television "backstory" or flashback—the narrative begins near the chronological conclusion of the story and Odysseus's ten years' wanderings are recounted later in the story.

Scholars date the creation of the *Odyssey* in the eighth century B.C. Almost 2,700 years later, the German composer Richard Wagner wrote a series of musical dramas that stand as modern epics. *Der Ring des Nibelungen*, four operas which address the relationships between humans and gods, was written between 1853 and 1874. The *Ring* presents in epic terms the destiny of man determined by supernatural agents—a common theme of most heroic epic poetry. However, at the *Ring*'s conclusion, Wagner posits a new condition in which the responsibility for the future is placed in the hands of mortals—heroic man must bravely explore and shape the future without the help of the gods. Wagner's *Ring* thus reflects a broad artistic concern of the late nineteenth and twentieth centuries, namely, a move from the primitive mythic realm toward social realism.

While Homer's *Odyssey* and Wagner's *Ring* deal in myth and legend, one cannot ignore their grounding in cultural tradition. The sociopolitical ramifications of the heroic epic are of consequence, for we create heroes, whether literary or real-life public personages, to fulfill the archetypal needs of social organization. Plato condemned Homer's poetry as morally corrupt, while Aristotle praised it as the height of brilliantly crafted lies. The ambiguity of Wagner's philosophy in the *Ring* opened the mammoth work to a variety of social interpretations. Bernard Shaw saw the heroism in the *Ring* as symbolic of a socialist struggle, with the gods representing the decadent bourgeois capitalists defiled by their greed. Supporters of Adolph Hitler used the *Ring* as a rationalization of their aggressive twentieth-century ambitions.

Heroes are ultimately "social types," which, according to sociologist Orrin Klapp, represent "roles which, though informal, have become rather well conceptualized and in which there is a comparatively high degree of consensus."[6] Social types are drawn from a cultural stock of images and symbols. They provide models people try to approximate, and perhaps more importantly, they act as "a kind of photograph" of the society's previous activities.[7] A close examination of the character traits of our heroes thus reveals much information about our cultural traditions. Distinguished from stereotypes—inaccurate popular concepts that are applied indiscriminately to individuals without regard for those individuals' actual characteristics—

social types are both accurate and revealing. Klapp posits, correctly I believe, that social types represent "basic dimensions of social control in any society."[8]

Heroes cannot exist without one or the other of two additional social types—villains and fools. Heroes are praised, followed, set up as models, and given a central part in our dramas (both fictional and real); they are ultimately better than societal norms. Villains are negative models of evil to be feared, hated, and ultimately eradicated or reformed by the actions of the hero; villains are dangerous to societal norms. Fools are negative models of absurdity, to be ridiculed; they fall far short of societal norms.[9]

Within the television melodrama, these social types operate as images or signs, constructed according to our society's dominant values, reinforcing commonly held concepts of the "proper order of things." The hero, villain, and fool are therefore ideological, representing an ensemble of social relationships and social constraints, an operational mythology—the images of a society presents to itself in order to perpetuate itself. A closer look at melodramatic heroes, villains, and fools—at their words, clothing, gestures, interactions, and institutional affiliations—reveals, through the basic transparency of their characterizations, the locus of social control in contemporary American society.

THE STRUCTURE OF TELEVISION MELODRAMA

The essential feature of orally composed, lengthy epic poems such as Homer's *Iliad* and *Odyssey* is the use of verbal formulas—groups of two or more poetic words that fit metrical positions in the poetic line, or extend over several lines. The key element is repetition. Homer employed alternating long and double-short syllables to build a rhythm and to help hold the listener's attention—to draw the listener into the poetry.

In grand opera, of which Wagner's *Ring* is the great example, a series of distinct acts, each generally signifying a change either in time or place, is linked by orchestral transitions. Superfluous exposition is eliminated. We see a series of intense highlights of the lives of the protagonists and antagonists. Orchestral music introduces action, provides a background for plot movement, and reinforces moments of heightened dramatic intensity. Opera is generally constructed to formula—as in literary melodrama, plot dominates, initiating excitement and suspense by raising for its protagonists questions of self-preservation. Characterization is secondary.

In nineteenth- and twentieth-century literature, melodrama came to signify "democratic drama." Harsher critics condemned the form as sensational, sentimental entertainment for the "masses." Rural-type melodrama—with its beautiful, virtuous, poor heroine, its pure hero, its despicable villain who ties the heroine to the railroad tracks, and the rustic clown who aids the hero (wonderfully satirized in the television cartoon "Dudley Doright of the Royal Canadian Mounties," a segment of *Rocky and Bullwinkle*)—gave way to city melodramas focusing on the seamy underworld, and to suspenseful crime-dramas such as those of Agatha Christie.

Television melodrama has drawn freely from all these precursors, both structurally and conceptually. Highly segmented plots—i.e., four 12-minute acts, each with a climax, and a happy ending—are carried along by background music and stress peaks of action and emotional involvement. Suspense and excitement are heightened by a sense of realism created through sophisticated, if formulaic visualizations (car chases being obvious examples). Characterizations are generally one-dimensional, employing eccentric protagonists and antagonists who are made credible by good acting. Ideologically, the plot elements reinforce conventional morality.

The rhythm of the commercial television melodrama depends on a predictable structure, as did the rhythm of the Homeric poems. In television melodrama, the structure is motivated by the flow of the program-segment-music-commercial sequence. A typical structure might be sketched as shown in Figure 3. This plot structure beautifully combines aesthetics and ideology. As suspense builds and the plot thickens, we are carried forward at various critical junctures by a combination of rapid visual cutting and an intense buildup of the background music and ambient sound that create the smooth transition to the frenetic, high-pitched ads. The rhythm produces a flow with which we have become quite comfortable. In fact, it can be argued, we have come to both understand and accept the genre conventions in the context of the production mechanisms that define the regime of commercial television.

Critic David Thorburn described the structure of television melodrama according to what he termed a "multiplicity principle," by which a particular television melodrama will

> ... draw ... many times upon the immense store of stories and situations created by the genre's brief but crowded history.... By minimizing the need for long establishing or expository sequences, the multiplicity principle allows the story to leave aside the question of

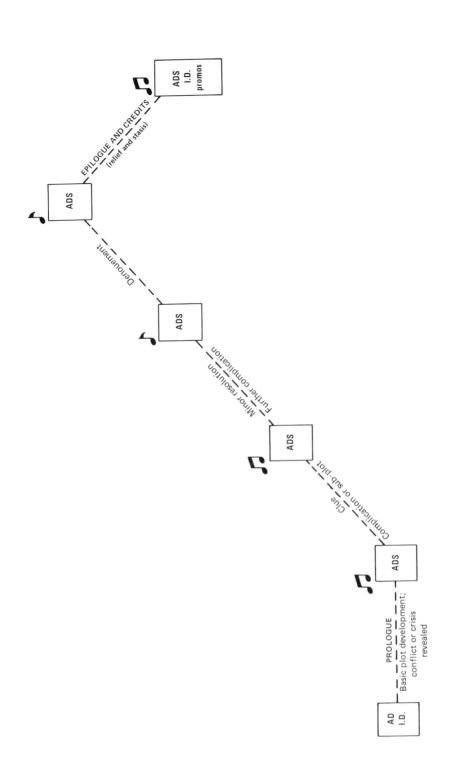

how these emotional entanglements were arrived at and to concentrate its energies on their credible and powerful present enactment.[10]

Thorburn is correct in locating the dramatic power of the television melodrama in a series of powerful if somewhat isolated scenes that highlight intense interpersonal confrontations. Taking this interpretation of melodramatic structure one step further, we discover that much more than dramatic power is involved. Pecuniary philosophy is also operating, for by cutting down on exposition or establishing sequences that tend toward lengthy, deliberate, and complex characterizations, 'the purveyors of melodrama are able to break their little tales into shortened, fast-paced, and often disconnected simple sequences that make commercial breaks feel natural to viewers.

Culture critic Raymond Williams, with characteristic insight, related the concept of what he called "planned flow" to both the medium and to the institutions which sustain it:

> What is being offered is not, in older terms, a programme of discrete units with particular insertions, but a planned flow, in which the true series is not the published sequence of programme items but this sequence transformed by the inclusion of another kind of sequence [incorporating advertisements], so that these sequences together compose the real flow, the real "broadcasting." Increasingly, in both commercial and public-service television, a further sequence was added: trailers of programmes . . . or more itemized programme news [program promos]. This was intensified in conditions of competition. . . .
>
> But this flow is planned: not only in itself, but at an early stage in all original television production for commercial systems. . . . There is a characteristic kind of opening sequence, meant to excite interest. . . . In American television, after two or three minutes, this is succeeded by commercials. . . . What follows is apparently quite unconnected material. It is then not surprising that so many of these opening moments are violent or bizarre: the interest aroused must be strong enough to initiate the expectations of (interruped but sustainable) sequence. . . . Some part of the flow offered is then directly traceable to conditions of controlled competition, just as some of its specific original elements are traceable to the financing of television by commercial advertising.[11]

Thus, we often describe our experience as "watching television," not as watching "the CBS News" or "the ballgame." The flow is always there, easily accessible—the central organizing principle of the medium.

The production imperatives of television-series melodrama reinforce Williams's concept of the commodification of flow. Producers Richard Levinson and William Link describe the production procedures as they existed in the early 1980s. The network commits itself to a new television series in mid-April. The series premieres in early September, leaving four-and-one-half months lead time for producers to hire staff, including writers and directors, prepare scripts, and begin shooting and editing. It takes four weeks, under the best conditions, to complete an episode of a melodrama; with luck, four shows will be "in the can" by the season's premiere, with others in varying stages of development (at any time during this process, many series episodes will be in development simultaneously, one being edited, another shot, and another scripted). By October, the initial four episodes will have been aired, and the fifth will be nearly ready. If the show is renewed at midseason, the producer will need 22 episodes for the entire season. By December, there will be but a matter of days between the final edit and the airing of an episode, as inevitable delays shorten the turnaround time. In addition to normal time problems, there are problems with staff. Levinson and Link cite the frequent problem of having a good free-lance writer in demand who agrees to write for one producer's shows as well as those of other producers. This craftsperson with a track record will be juggling an outline for one show, a first draft for another, and a "notion" for a third.[12]

In the frenzied world of the daytime soap opera, actors get the script the night before the taping, begin run-through rehearsals at 7:30 the next morning, do three rehearsals before taping, and tape between 3:30 and 6:00 that afternoon. This hectic ritual is repeated five days a week.

The prime-time-melodrama production process is ruled by shortcuts, scattered attention, and network interference in content, created by the fear of viewer response to controversial material that may range from questionable street language, however dramatically appropriate, to sexual taboos. Simplicity, predictability, and safety become the norm.

Planned flow, the melodrama's highly symbolic heroic ideal, its formal conventions, and its reinforcement of the society's dominant value systems render the genre highly significant as a centrist cultural mechanism stressing order and stasis.

Examples of television melodramas discussed in the following section are presented in Figure 4.

1946 47 48 49 50 51 52 53 54 55 56 57 58 59 60 61 62 63 64 65 66 67 68 69 70 71 72 73 74 75 76 77 78 79 80 81 82 83

The Frontier

The Lone Ranger, 49 57

Gunsmoke, 55 75

The Life and Legend of
Wyatt Earp,
55 61

Cheyenne, 55 63

Wagon Train, 57 65

Have Gun Will Travel,
57 63

Maverick, 57 62

Tales of Wells Fargo,
57 62

Zorro,
57 . . .59

The Rifleman, 58—63

Bonanza, 59 73

The Virginian, 62 71

The Big Valley,
65 69

Dallas, 78 . . . .

1946 47 48 49 50 51 52 53 54 55 56 57 58 59 60 61 62 63 64 65 66 67 68 69 70 71 72 73 74 75 76 77 78 79 80 81 82 83

The Adventurer - Hero

Route 66, 60—64

The Fugitive,
63 67

Star Trek,
66 69

The Prisoner,
68

Then Came Bronson,
69

1946 47 48 49 50 51 52 53 54 55 56 57 58 59 60 61 62 63 64 65 66 67 68 69 70 71 72 73 74 75 76 77 78 79 80 81 82 83

The Urban Frontier

Focused often on life in the urban frontier

Kraft Television Theater, 47 58

Studio One, 48 58

Goodyear TV Playhouse, 51 60

Playhouse 90,
56 60

Dragnet,
52 59

Medic,
54 . . . 56

Perry Mason, 57 66

M Squad,
57 60

77 Sunset Strip,
58 61

The Untouchables,
59 63

Ben Casey, 61 66

The Defenders,
61 65

East Side/West Side,
63

Dragnet,
67 70

Mission Impossible, 66 . . . 73

Hawaii Five-O, 68 80

The Mod Squad,
68 73

Columbo, 71 77

1946 47 48 49 50 51 52 53 54 55 56 57 58 59 60 61 62 63 64 65 66 67 68 69 70 71 72 73 74 75 76 77 78 79 80 81 82 83

The Urban Frontier (continued)

Barnaby Jones, 73 81

Kojak, 73 78

Police Story, 73 . . 78

The Rockford Files,
74 81

Baretta,
75 78

Quincey, M.E., 76 83

Lou Grant, 77–81

Hill Street Blues,
80 . . . .

Skag,
80

The Suburban Middle Landscape

Daytime Soaps

Peyton Place, 64 . . 69

Marcus Welby, M.D., 69 . . 76

Family, 76 . . . 80

Dallas, 78 . . . .

Knots Landing, 79 . .

Dynasty, 81 .

Falcon Crest,
81 . . . .

The Rural Middle Landscape

Waltons, 72 81

Little House on the Prairie, 74 . . . 83

TELEVISION MELODRAMA AND CONTEMPORARY SOCIAL RELATIONS: A HISTORICAL VIEW

C. Wright Mills observed that American society of the 1950s was increasingly controlled by the heads of large corporations, the warrior-chieftains in the Defense Department, and professional celebrities. Mills focused on our mythology's glorification of the chief executive as an individual who makes it to the top with "an element of luck."[13] Mills interpreted the myth to mean, rather, that the chief executive made it to the top with "an accumulation of corporate success," corporate executives choosing one another for promotion to ever-higher corporate positions within a closed system of entry and advancement. This was a world in which the rise to the top depended in large measure on the corporate achiever's "beginnings," especially educational tracking and gender.[14]

This was clearly not the world of the 1950s suburban-middle-landscape comedy in which the handsome professional father exhibited humility, individuality, and compassion for his coworkers, his domestic servants, and his family. Nor was it the world of the socially myopic kitchen dramas of the "Golden Age" of television—so called because of their limited interior settings and their personal, narrow focus, which kept out social and political issues. Presented in weekly anthology programs such as *Kraft Television Theatre* (1947-58), *Studio One* (1948-58), and *Playhouse 90* (1956-60), such television classics as *Marty, Requiem for a Heavyweight*, and *Twelve Angry Men* zoomed in on what teleplay writer Paddy Chayefsky labeled "the remarkable world of the ordinary"—the world of individual problems created by ethnicity, and reflected as the old-world social customs versus those of the brave new world of America; of family relations reflected in the children deserting their parents and in the loneliness of growing old without family support; and of the narrow-minded provincial attitudes of undereducated Americans toward race, religious differences, and progressive ideas. Reginald Rose's 1954 drama *Thunder on Sycamore Street*, for *Studio One*, sponsored by Westinghouse, was based on a real racial incident in Chicago in which a black family moved into an all-white housing project and the whites stoned them. Westinghouse refused to allow the family to be black. Rose converted the blacks to the family of a white ex-convict to satisfy the advertiser's demands. While many of these little dramas dealt with working-class life, such as Chayefsky's *Marty*, the story of a homely, lonely Italian butcher who has never been married, and Rod Serling's *Requiem For a Heavyweight*, the story of an over-the-hill fighter, they never really approached the important economic questions of working-class subservience in the capitalist social order. This is not unexpected, for the anthology drama grew up during the era of blacklisting of members of television's creative community. Hundreds of actors, writers, and producers in Hollywood and New York were marked as Communist sympathizers by groups such as Aware, Inc., which received encouragement from politicians such as Senator Joseph McCarthy of Wisconsin. Sponsors of anthology drama were pressured to disapprove certain actors and writers with alleged Communist connections. In such an atmosphere, the kitchen dramas were careful to avoid the potential stigma of controversy.

The nonanthological television melodrama of the 1950s, framed by the Western in the mid-1950s and by the private-detective/G-man series in the late 1950s, likewise refused to examine a contemporary social milieu in which the corporate capitalist establishment joined in a partnership with the huge postwar military apparatus in a Cold War against the Soviets. Melodrama would not acknowledge the impact of advanced capitalism on the personal lives of both those who were allowed to ascend the corporate hierarchy in exchange for their individuality, and those who, as unskilled laborers, semiskilled operatives, or intelligent-but-female clerks, powered the corporate profit centers but were relegated to second-class citizen status. Even after McCarthy's Communist witch-hunts were exposed, our distrust of the Soviet Union did not diminish. McCarthy's escapade was treated more as a fatal flaw in his individual character than as a general systemic overreaction. As Russia launched Sputnik in 1957, Americans were rudely awakened to their technological shortcomings and we needed reassurance—a sense of control and order and power—in an international atmosphere of nuclear tension and superpower mutual distrust. We were in no mood for a self-critique.

What television melodrama gave us during this period of global uncertainty was a predictably highly simplistic ideological frame in which petty criminals were quickly and easily apprehended by the authorities—law-and-order cops whose crime-solving methods, often excessively violent, went unquestioned. From the realistic routine of police work so effectively portrayed in *Dragnet* (1952-59), the melodrama of the urban frontier moved to the excesses of *M Squad* and to the ultraviolent *The Untouchables*, men who fought the violence of organized crime with a retribution unparalleled in television history and backed by the authority of our federal government. When the police establishment proved incapable of solving the crime, private detectives such as Peter Gunn and the boys from *77 Sunset Strip* would step in—they were often better police than the real police, and provided viewers with an interesting ideological perspective; that is, what was to be valued above all was the maintenance of order, whether that order was maintained by the duly constituted authorities or by private citizens in positions of power sanctioned through extralegal relations with civil authority—in effect, the condoning of a system of vigilante justice.

On the western frontier, the duly appointed authorities kept the peace at the fringes of civilization where the id bubbled over each weeknight. *Gunsmoke*'s Matt Dillon, the fictional sheriff of rugged Dodge City, Kansas, and Marshal Wyatt Earp of *The Life and Legend of Wyatt Earp*, the real-life marshal of Dodge, kept the frontier town safe for white pioneers to live out their lives and build a future for America's heartland. *Tales of Wells Fargo*'s hero-agent Jim Hardie made certain the money to finance this growth got through to the bankers. As was the case in the urban frontier, when the authorities in the wild West could not cope, justice was brought in by the vigilante-cowboys—ranging from the wanderers of *The Lone Ranger* and *Cheyenne* to the more sedentary characters of *The Rifleman* and *Zorro*. These archetypal loner-heroes in the myth of the frontier were pure, their motives clear and unassailable; and their relation to a real West in which the myth of manifest destiny fueled the Anglo conquest of the Native Americans was confused. To these pure heroes, Injuns merely got in trouble a lot through their inability to handle alcohol, burned log cabins, raped white women, and practiced queer religious ceremonies, while in actuality Native Americans got in the way of American expansion and occupied valuable land by declaring it sacred territory.

An unusually sophisticated Western wanderer was the hired gun-man Paladin, played superbly by Richard Boone in *Have Gun, Will Travel* (1957-63). Paladin was drawn from the Charlemagne romances in which one of the 12 famous warriors of Charlemagne's court, Count Palatine, was the foremost warrior, a knight-errant and renowned champion. Palatine's television counterpart Paladin was a college-educated (West Point) man of culture and ethics who lived at the Hotel Carlton in San Francisco and took on assignments, if the price was right, that led him from his opulent, courtlike surroundings into the uncivilized countryside. His business card featured a white chess knight, an emblem of his goodness, and contrasted with the sinister appearance of his black duds and black mustache. Paladin's character was certainly more complex than the traditional sheriff or cowpoke-errant. He would turn on those who hired him if they were guilty. He showed little mercy to the prey he was hired to get. The dialectic of culture/violence, white/black, and mercenary/defender of justice lent dramatic credibility to this modern Western hero. On the other hand, Paladin's pecuniary motives remained unquestioned.

The 1960s were ushered in by the optimism of John F. Kennedy's New Frontier. A mood of youthful exuberance, expansionism, and, however briefly, of compassion swept the nation. Kennedy offered the hope to minority cultures that they could achieve equal status with Anglos. The 1962 Cuban missile crisis had managed to blot out the sour taste of the 1961 Bay of Pigs debacle. Americans no longer as a nation seemed so preoccupied with Soviet domination of the world or with impending nuclear annihilation. Perhaps this significant change in attitude was a result of the dramatic catharsis that had occurred, with the Kennedy-Khruschev missile showdown, itself, interestingly, conjuring up images from the opening sequences of *Gunsmoke*. Feeling strong and just as a nation, America exported the Peace Corps and began to prop up an ailing South Vietnamese regime. Television melodrama meanwhile was reinforcing this decidedly upbeat mood.

In the urban frontier, the tough cop of *Dragnet* and the implacable government agent of *The Untouchables*—the unidimensional, self-righteous defenders of the dominant order—were waning in popularity. These superheroes were replaced by the socially concerned lawyers and physicians. In the courtroom, *Perry Mason* (1957-66) had become the most popular of the television barristers. Mason never lost his cool and never lost a case. His lawyering, however, was framed in the standard murder/private-investigation motif—he operated in a world of individual problems centering on mistaken identity and the setup, situations unrelated to the social conditions which so often surround violent crime. In 1961, teleplay writer Reginald Rose (*Twelve Angry Men* and *Thunder on Sycamore Street*) created the series *The Defenders*, which, for four years, provided, for its time, a rare fictional television discussion of controversial subject matter ranging from abortion to euthanasia, blacklisting, and capital punishment. In the urban frontier, two lawyers, Lawrence Preston and his son Kenneth, whose youthful exuberance and idealism were tempered by his father's experience and wisdom, sought a human-justice system that accounted for the underdog and acknowledged prevailing social conditions. Their compassion and total dedication to the causes of their clients attracted a viewership of liberal humanists whose criticisms of capitalist America were given voice as the justice system on television appeared to be working for the benefit of all, equally. Of course, life was nothing like that. The Cook County jail and Attica prison are testimonies to the realities of the justice system. While *The Defenders* was a significant departure from the melodrama's seemingly inherent fear of taking on the world of real social relations, the talkative legal atmosphere in which these problems were addressed tended to abstract the seamier side of life and to deflect consideration of the urban crises about to explode. Not only in the courtroom, but also in the operating room, melodramatic heroes were attempting, in their limited fashion, to address social issues. *Ben Casey* (1961-66) was a highly popular doctor melodrama highlighting life in the urban hospital. It was not the real hospital we were to shudder at a decade-and-a-half later during the provocative documentary series *Lifeline*, but it at least attempted to portray the system of hospital care in an essentially honest manner. Like *The Defenders, Ben Casey* featured a "father-son" relationship of youthful idealism and elder rationality. Casey's mentor, chief of surgery Dr. David Zorba, acted much as did Lawrence Preston, urging Ben's caution and patience. Ben, like Kenneth (and John Kennedy) boldly moved ahead. While dwelling excessively on its virile young doctor-hero's surgical exploits and love interests, *Ben Casey* did on occasion tackle the medical establishment, which was shown to be highly conservative and not always concerned with the rights of patients. Still, the profession was always finally vindicated by Casey's seemingly superhuman technical skills.

One bold attempt was made during this period to explore the urban social reality that would erupt in the mid-1960s riots in Watts, Newark, Detroit, and many other American cities: Premiering in 1963, *East Side/West Side* was a powerful study, both visually and dramatically, of the daily routine of a social worker in the New York City slums. Its visualization was rooted in the realist medical melodrama *Medic* and Jack Webb's *Dragnet*. The viewer was provided a view of urban life at once stark and gloomy. Social worker Neil Brock, played by George C. Scott, was faced day after day with unremitting grimness revealed in the individual disasters that were the cultural results of a system of gross social inequity. Stories focused on child abuse, welfare, drug addiction, aging in the ghetto, and included one particularly wrenching episode in which a black ghetto child died from a rat bite. Produced by Talent Associates/David Susskind, *East*

Side/West Side conjured up memories of Lincoln Steffens's long late-night walks through the streets of New York in the late nineteenth century. *East Side/West Side* lasted one year. It was not to disturb the mythic geography of television's generally sanitized urban frontier.

In television's mythic world of the frontier, the gunslingers of the 1950s gave way to the warm, compassionate father-figures of Ben Cartwright and Matt Dillon—the Western heroes of the early 1960s. These weather-beaten frontiersmen resembled Ward Cleaver, Steve Douglas, and Jim Anderson, of the suburban-middle-landscape comedy, more than they did the tough-as-nails pioneer of the traditional Western. By 1963, most of the television Westerns so successful in the 1950s had played themselves out. *Gunsmoke, Bonanza*, and *Wagon Train*, all very successful and all developing the family motif, remained.

Bonanza, with its powerful, wealthy, mature, and humane patriarch, Ben Cartwright, and his three sons, who formed a composite character at once witty (Adam), powerful but gentle (Hoss), and young and strapping (Little Joe), became an ideal reflection of the American spirit of the times. The Cartwrights, while they lived in baronial splendor, old-West style, nevertheless worked hard to acquire and maintain their possessions. They were far removed from the aristocratic snobs of Europe whom the Americans had always disdained even while trying to emulate their cultural gentility; but they did represent a peculiarly American aristocracy whose emblem was the accumulation of vast amounts of territory (the Ponderosa Ranch was about 100,000 square miles), but whose celebration of manifest destiny was tempered with humility. And they had a vision for the future —a vision of civilization, namely, the consolidation of their wealth and their continued status as respected patrons of Virginia City, Nevada. The Cartwrights would quarrel internally on occasion, for dramatic purposes, but they would rarely if ever clash over questions of ethics. They lived according to the democratic code of the West— each man could dare to be different (women in this world were conformists, almost always sedentary, and waited for their men to return; furthermore, women did not seem to live long due to the harsh environment and the difficulty of childbirth—Ben's three wives, each of whom had given birth to a single Cartwright son, had all died, leav-Ben a perpetual widower). Daring to be different was accepted so long as one's actions remained within the scope of the law (a law established to protect the interests of men of property like the Cartwrights). If a man chose to live alone in the wilderness as a vagabond, the Cartwrights respected that decision, so long as the vagabond didn't end up squatting on the Ponderosa. *Bonanza* was America as it once was, a nation in which the heirs of the aristocratic Tidewater society of Thomas Jefferson would coexist, however uneasily, with the heirs of Andy Jackson and the independent earthy men of the Piedmont. It was an America which held firmly to visions of expansion through space, the sanctity of privately held property, polite exclusion, and male domination. Drawing upon the success of *Bonanza* was *The Big Valley*, which premiered in 1965. While the characters were not as well developed as the Cartwrights, Victoria Barkley, the hard-nosed matriarch, her three handsome sons, and a beautiful daughter were all quite well off at the Barkley spread in the San Joaquin Valley of 1870s California. The series's premise was quite simple: Successful settlers continually fought off lawless elements to preserve their large landholdings. The Barkleys faced the standard set of Western antag-onists, including schemers, murderers, bank robbers, and even Mexican revolutionaries. The America of the Cartwrights and the Barkleys was also the America of modern-day sons of nouveau riche aristocrats, such as John F. Kennedy, and of middle-class self-made "country boys" such as Lyndon Johnson, Richard Nixon, Gerald Ford, Jimmy Carter and Ronald Reagan.

As the frontier and urban-frontier cycles played themselves out and America began to relax, a new public symbol of America's pre-occupation with space emerged. The romantic motif of "the journey" dominated television melodrama in the 1960s. Two parallel develop-ments in American culture encouraged this preoccupation—the de-velopment of the American suburb, and exurb, with its dependence on the personal automobile and the superhighway, and America's re-assertion of its technological leadership, as manifested in President Kennedy's challenge to land a man on the moon before the decade's end.

The Western adventurer-hero, a mystified historical and legend-ary type, à la Paladin, was locked in time. The new adventurer in tele-vision melodrama was our contemporary, "one of us." This new ad-venturer, searching for pleasurable experiences, was emblematic of the growth of the suburban "superkids" who Tom Wolfe so brilliantly described in *The Electric Kool Aid Acid Test*:

> But of course!—the *feeling*—out here at night, free, with the motor running and the adrenaline flowing, cruising in the neon glories of the new American night—it was very Heaven to be the first wave of the most extraordinary kids in the history of the world—only 15, 16,

17 years old, dressed [in] the *haute couture* of pink Oxford shirts, sharp pants, snaky half-inch belts, fast shoes—with all this Straight-6 and V-8 power underneath and all this neon glamour overhead, which somehow tied in with the technological superheroics of the jet, TV, atomic subs, ultrasonics—postwar American suburbs—glorious world! and the hell with the intellectual badmouthers of America's tailfin civilization. . . . They couldn't know what it was like or else they had it cultivated out of them—the feeling—to be very Superkids! the world's first generation of the little devils—feeling immune, beyond calamity. One's parents remembered the sloughing common order, War & Depression—but Superkids knew only the emotional surge of the great payoff, when nothing was common any longer—The Life! A glorious place, a glorious age, I tell you! A very Neon Renaissance. . . .[15]

Cut off from history, the superkids would come to reject their parents' struggles. The parents, happy to have escaped the "sloughing common order," would do everything in their power to insulate their children from such a state of existence.

While the family Western of the early 1960s, à la *Bonanza*, was providing viewers with a mythic psychic geography remarkably similar to that of the suburban-middle-landscape comedies of the period— what adults wanted to believe was the new order of pecuniary security and family love and warmth—the new adventurer, first seen in *Route 66* (1960-64) was providing viewer perhaps unintentionally with a more accurate version of that psychic landscape—a version in which the transcendent values were materialistic and in which our protagonists seemed to be traveling nowhere in particular at very high speeds.

Route 66's protagonists are Tod Stiles, born to wealth, but whose father squandered his money; and Buz Murdock, who grew up in New York City's Hell's Kitchen area and who had been employed by Tod's father prior to his death. The young men set off in Tod's Corvette in search of adventure and romance. *Route 66* played off two universal themes. Tod and Buz bear a striking resemblance to the priest-errants of Carl Orff's secular cantata *Carmina Burana*. The cantata is based on texts of 200 sacred and secular poems dating to the thirteenth century and discovered in 1903 in a Bavarian monastery, and written by earthy vagabonds called goliards—defrocked monks and minstrels who delighted in the pleasures of the flesh. Orff divided his work into three motifs: spring, the tavern, and love. There are poems of fortunes lost, of spring and youthful virility ("And over all the boyish god rules"), and of heavy drinking in the tavern ("On the broad road I move along as youth is wont to do. I am entangled in vice, and unmindful of virtue. Greedy more for lust than for welfare; dead in soul, I care only for my body"). Tod and Buz, as the new youthful television priest-errants of the 1960s, show only the vaguest hints of vice. They are not above fistfights and romantic encounters. Yet their wanderlust is tempered with a certain undirected compassion (how else could Chevrolet market its masculine Corvette to a general market?). While Tod and Buz had no particular destination in mind, they were drawn, like Odysseus, along a predetermined path, in their case Route 66—named by John Steinbeck "the Mother Road." In his *The Grapes of Wrath*, it becomes "the path of a people in flight." Stretching from Chicago to Los Angeles, established in 1926 by the National Highway Act, Route 66 has entered our folklore. It carried the Okies and the Arkies of the dust bowl on their escape to find a new life in California. It was a symbol of despair, but more so a symbol of hope. By the 1950s it had become a symbol of America's neon roadside culture—the emblem of a mobile society. In 1960 it still retained its mystique, although very soon it would be replaced by our superhighway system of monotonous four-lane interstates, Holiday Inns, and McDonalds—the new streamlined, high-tech America. Unfortunately, Route 66 became a meaningless backdrop for the adventures of our young melodrama protagonists—just another concrete slab in the open spaces that allowed the Corvette to move out. Like Wolfe's superkids, Tod and Buz were divorced from social history, as manifested in the road on which they traveled but did not really understand.

Another wanderer, Dr. Richard Kimble, was forced to give up his comfortable suburban environment for a life as *The Fugitive* (1963-67). In the traditions of the epic wanderer-hero Odysseus, Kimble was forced by fate to wander, enduring trials and tests to prove his inherent moral strength. The melodramatic premise is simple: Kimble, a physician, is wrongly accused and convicted of murdering his wife (shades of the Dr. Sam Sheppard murder case, a cause celebre at that time), is sentenced to death, but escapes while being taken to death row. For 120 episodes, Kimble is relentlessly pursued by Lieutenant Gerard, who was accompanying him when he escaped, while Kimble himself pursues a mysterious one-armed man who Kimble knows was the actual murderer. Throughout his ordeal, Kimble is reduced to a common man, taking odd jobs to support himself as he searches for the killer, and assuming new identities at each stop. He learns much about regular folks from these encounters and in turn impacts on those with whom he comes in contact. In the final episode, a two-parter, Kimble finds the one-armed man, is himself in great danger, but is saved by Lieutenant Gerard, who has come to admire Kimble's resourcefulness and resiliency and now even believes in Kimble's innocence. Gerard shoots and kills the one-armed man. Kimble is exonerated. And while Kimble, the good doctor, has grown from experience, we get the distinct feeling that he can now, like Odysseus, return to his home—in Kimble's case, the suburban middle landscape —and reclaim his material wealth and his medical practice.

The television adventure moved from the suburban middle landscape to outer space in 1966 as *Star Trek* premiered. The warts on America's self-complacent expansionist politics had barely begun to show in Vietnam. Journalists such as David Halberstam of the *New York Times*, Neil Sheehan of United Press International, Malcolm Browne of the Associated Press, and Morley Safer of CBS News had, since 1962, pointed out the political and moral quagmire that was Vietnam, but they were a small minority in the news community. America still saw the war in the just terms cited by the late President Kennedy—that "we will fight any foe" to protect the world for democracy. Gene Roddenberry's *Star Trek* offered the American television viewer a variety of subtle and relatively safe antiwar themes including the impersonal quantification of the results of war—the body counts —that had become a nagging fact of America's Vietnam involvement on the nightly news. One episode of *Star Trek* dealt with a society that fought war with a computer. Everyone who was listed as "killed" was forced to step into a disintegration machine. Unlike Vietnam, there was no property damage (this episode foreshadowed the absurdity of the neutron bomb). The *Enterprise*, a metaphor for the hard work of the myth of the puritan ethic, was piloted by all-American boy Captain Kirk; it was the ultimate cosmic policeman/meddler. Living with a pseudoreligious fervor, as befitted the myth of manifest destiny, Kirk and his crew spread truth, justice, and the American way of life, including a life of high technology and eternal progress. In one episode, "A Private Little War," Kirk was forced to introduce high-technology warfare into a planet where the evil klingons had interfered. There was now no turning back. Vietnam, and today Central America and the Middle East, are contemporary real-world analogues of such a condition.

While *Star Trek* framed the epic journey in contemporary terms, it failed to go far enough in its condemnation of militarism. Ultimately the goals of Kirk and the international crew of the *Enterprise* were

never seriously and consistently questioned; a certain sense of jingoism, tempered with liberal abhorrence of war deaths, remained.

Two other adventure series of the late 1960s seriously questioned
contemporary social relations although, like *Star Trek*, they ultimately
defused the issues they raised. In one, *The Prisoner*, created for British
television by Patrick McGoohan and aired in the United States in the
summer of 1968, the viewer is presented with a hero whose journey
is inward, into a mental landscape in which he is trapped by a materialistic, totalitarian state apparatus. In McGoohan's first television
series, *Secret Agent*, he played British intelligence agent John Drake,
a rather violent character. The premise of *The Prisoner* builds from
the backstory of *Secret Agent*: Drake comes to question the morality
of his work. He resigns from the intelligence service as *The Prisoner*
begins, an act which will lead him into the uncharted hell of technology and the repression of the corporate state. Over 17 episodes,
Drake, imprisoned by the state in a mental landscape known simply as
"the Village," becomes "Number Six." The Village appears harmon-
ious, but this is a bizarre illusion. "Number Two," the Village's main
authority figure, is clearly not the person at the top (the mysterious
"Number One"). This is a metaphor not only for the invisibility of
the corporate chieftains, as described by C. Wright Mills in *The Power
Elite*—the true leaders use their managers and professional celebrities
as fronts, choosing to run things from the background—but also, in
the case of the character Number Two, for the interchangeability of
the managers (Number Two is different in each episode). Number
Six, the representative of individual freedom, is subjugated to the will
of the state. He should think he is free, for the Village is idyllic and
all his material needs are easily satisfied; but he resists the initially
subtle but finally not-so-subtle attempts at brainwashing. He is euphe-
mistically described as a "guest" of the Village, not the prisoner that
he is. Number Six's dual desire to escape and to understand the forces
that have captured him frames the ongoing struggle. In the final episode of the allegory, Number One is revealed as the prisoner's alter
ego, the side of the repressive authoritarian. Like everyone else in the
Village the prisoner cannot be trusted. This cynical view of human
nature in the end deflects responsibility for social conditions into
the murky realm of psychologism, where all seems hopeless. As *The
Prisoner* concludes, we see Drake driving down the road in a sports
roadster, his hair blowing in the breeze; he is free from totalitarian-
ism and the corporate state, yet not free from his own nature. Nothing has changed, and although he now "understands" his condition,

he seems incapable of any action other than personal escape, the only solution to his alienation.

With *Then Came Bronson* in 1969, Americans had an adventurer-hero who clearly reflected the times. Jim Bronson was a newspaper reporter. His buddy, a Vietnam veteran, committed suicide. Bronson wanted to do a story on the suicide and its social meaning. His editor refused, saying it was not newsworthy. Outraged, Bronson quit the paper, with its drudgery and lack of autonomy, and headed out on his fallen friend's motorcycle to search for meaning in life. Scarcely seeming to understand his own motives for wandering, in a modern sense he is ineffective. He cannot resolve other people's dilemmas, as could Richard Kimble and Captain Kirk. He does not come to the self-realization Number Six came to. What *Then Came Bronson* reveals to viewers is its hero's sense of inner dissatisfaction, emptiness, lack of commitment, frustration, and lack of direction coupled with an underlying goodness and tolerance of those around him—in short, here is the archetypal flower child. Yet, while Jim Bronson seems awkward and powerless, his character is in the initial stages of a progressive transition from the low-mimetic to the traditionally mythological, in which outward deeds of the hero are less important than inner realization. As Joseph Campbell wrote of the traditional hero of mythology, "the passage of the mythological hero . . . fundamentally . . . is inward—into the depths where obscure resistances are overcome, and long lost, forgotten powers are revivified, to be made available for the transfiguration of the world."[16] Bronson has vanished into the American wilderness—has gone to the mountaintop—seeking a clearer understanding of the rhythms of nature and of people. He had not reemerged with any answers as the series was canceled after one year. The series's slow pacing, introspection, and antiacting did not lend itself to Williams's concept of commodified planned flow described earlier. While many young Americans—so-called cultural radicals who tuned in, turned on, and dropped out—empathized with Bronson's antipolitical response of noninvolvement, others were engaged in active political protest in the streets of Chicago and Berkeley, and on the campuses of Columbia and the University of Wisconsin. Television, with the occasional exception of the nightly news programs, was not the forum in which the heated political discourse of Vietnam and American interventionism generally was aired. In spite of the fact that his acts lacked overt political motivation, Jim Bronson was rare for series-television heroes—his ethics of nonpower spoke to larger issues of social control and personal states of unfreedom.

For a brief period at the end of the decade, commercial entertainment television made its acceptable response to Vietnam and the civil rights movement by airing so-called social-relevance melodrama, such as *The Mod Squad* (1968-73) and *Storefront Lawyers* (1970), which featured youthful hip protagonists fighting for justice and equality. A far remove from the artistic sensitivity of *The Defenders* and the social commitment and grit of *East Side/West Side*, these programs were blatant in their exploitation of the movement of the 1960s. Their hipper-than-thou attitude and handsome stars and starlets rang false.

In 1968, the year *The Mod Squad* was introduced, another new television entry signaled the true shift in direction of television melodrama from the adventurer to a return to the sedentary world of the suburban and rural middle landscapes. *Marcus Welby, M.D.* reintroduced the father figure to television melodrama. Welby, who practiced family medicine, was the community patriarch—kind, gentle, competent, and humble. For seven years, this wise physician diagnosed the most bizarre ailments known to medical science (his wisdom went far beyond his medical training), offered informal psychiatric advice to his patients, and made house calls. He was revered by millions of American viewers. Welby brought stability to an external world reeling from the horrors of Tet and the Robert Kennedy and Martin Luther King assassinations. The show was performing the true popular melodramatic function, acting as a force pulling the society toward its center—the peace, affluence, and optimism of the suburban middle landscape.

Another highly successful melodrama, premiering in 1972, served the same function. *The Waltons*, focusing on the rural middle landscape of Appalachia, was a humane celebration of the values of strong family bonds, and of the inherent goodness and seriousness of country folks. Fighting their way through the Great Depression, the Waltons were survivors. This message rang true to an America painfully working its way out of Southeast Asia, trying to forget Kent State, and shortly to be faced with an Arab oil embargo—another stark realization of the limits of American power in the world.

The conservatism of melodramatic television series on occasion admitted a made-for-television movie that might question, in a limited fashion, the dominant ideology. Levinson's and Link's 1969 telefilm *My Sweet Charlie*, a personalized story of race relations in the South, and their 1972 telefilm *That Certain Summer*, a story about the coming out of a homosexual father, both broke television taboos. As an

essentially two-shot play, a television movie can risk mildly controversial material without any long-term negative impact. The network
can choose to publicize a piece it believes will draw big numbers and
not be terribly offensive (as ABC did when it promoted the 1983
movie *The Day After*, whose conservative premise was that people
will survive an all-out nuclear conflagration and carry on—a clear
example of television melodrama's motif of the stiff upper lip). Or it
can take its more controversial work; air it during a traditionally light
viewing period such as late summer or during the Christmas period;
satisfy the more vocal among the Hollywood creative community
who call for artistic integrity; fend off a few irate telephone calls
from viewers; and continue on with its standard *Marcus Welby* fare.
The Levinson and Link teleplays, while opening doors to controversial contemporary social material in a melodramatic context, did,
however, manage to come down firmly on both sides of the debate
on both race and homosexuality, under pressure, they insist, from
network censors. Levinson and Link admit, in their own analysis of
That Certain Summer, that they would rewrite the speech of the
homosexual father in the final scene, in which, having come to terms
with his life as a gay, he reintroduces the guilt he has successfully
overcome by saying to his son, "If I had a choice it's not something
I'd pick for myself."

While a television movie now and then would brush up against a
difficult contemporary social problem in the early 1970s, and while
Norman Lear was turning out social comedy after social comedy,
American television melodrama was tame. *Gunsmoke* and *Bonanza*
neared the end of their runs, both having lost most of their artistic
drive. *Marcus Welby* was immensely popular. The proletarian cop in
Columbo entered on the scene in 1971. *Columbo* was steeped in the
classic murder-mystery tradition of Ellery Queen and Agatha Christie.
It was good entertainment, well written, and television's best adapta-
tion of the literary-murder-mystery form to date. Viewers were led
by Columbo through a world of elegant, wealthy criminality. We came
to envy the antagonist's surroundings while disapproving of his character and his acts. What on the surface seemed to many critics to be a
celebration of the working cop was really nothing more than a skillful
voyeuristic journey into the land of the wealthy and a reinforcing of
the moral superiority of the common viewer, a motif which emerges
again a few years later in *Dallas*.

In 1974 America almost came apart at the seams. Watergate had
bubbled away in the American conscience for two very visible years

as television slowly and painfully revealed the grimy underside of American politics. The facial contortions of Richard Nixon, the cold distance of John Dean, and the smug arrogance of John Erlichman and H. R. Haldeman were seen in public speeches and before the Senate's public hearings. This visceral display proved to Americans television's true potential as a recorder and transmitter of the feelings of those upon whom it turns its gaze. The unblinking lens of the camera sits in judgment—a neurosystem linked directly to almost every American; the soft red glow of the camera's tally light is an amazingly powerful force—it tells you that "you're on!" Watergate seemed to drain every last ounce of optimism from the American public. Kennedy's Camelot had turned first into Johnson's Oriental quagmire and now Nixon's last stand—like Custer, his ego and blindness to reality led to his end.

Television's response to this malaise was threefold. The relevant social comedies of Norman Lear continued as strongly as ever. Nixon became an acceptable, legitimate target. While questions remained as to the social impact of the Archie Bunker character on ultraconservative and liberal viewers, there is little doubt that the Lear comedies of the period, especially *Maude* and *All in the Family*, attempted to grapple with contemporary social problems. Television melodrama, on the other hand, chose its traditionally conservative response. This was manifested in two ways. One was a return to the frontier, but a frontier with decidedly rural-middle-landscape characteristics. *Little House on the Prairie*, which premiered in 1974, involved a loving family surviving hard times in the 1870s in Minnesota. The Ingalls family—the father, Charles; the wife and loving mother, Caroline; and daughters Laura, Mary, and Carrie—were good people. Charles was a pioneer farmer who had come from Kansas. The Ingalls struggled against natural disasters and the eventual collapse of their hometown, Walnut Grove. They were forced to move to a city in the Dakota territory, but hated city life and headed back to their Minnesota farm—a prototypical rural-middle-landscape journey, away from contemporary social problems, a return to the garden and to grace. A second melodramatic response was more insidious: the recognition of contemporary evil and its subsequent punishment via a system of summary justice. Such a typical melodramatic response had appeared in the late 1950s and early 1960s television melodrama, and now reappeared with some modifications.

As the 1960s stumbled to an end, America's technological superiority could not compensate for its untenable ideological position in

Vietnam. Television's creative community, contrary to Ben Stein's arguments in *The View From Sunset Boulevard*, was in touch with public opinion in America in the later years of the decade. Many, though certainly not all or even a numerical majority of Americans, were disillusioned with the militaristic exploits of a nation that continually found its way out of recessions by engaging in foreign military adventures, manifested in the formation, during and immediately after World War II, of a military-industrial complex. Yet the resistance to this politics was vocal, committed, and persuasive. Further, Americans had come to despise their highest public officials, who were corrupt or corruptible and who maintained ethically questionable connections with wealthy businessmen. This growing cynicism was at last reflected on our television screens in the police melodrama of the mid-1970s, which included an assortment of protagonists, from the private detectives of *The Rockford Files* and *Barnaby Jones*, to the undercover cop in *Baretta*, the detective in *Kojak*, and coroner *Quincy*. A central antagonist for all these law-enforcement types was the evil businessman. Writers and producers began to define this character as the "true criminal," whose criminality was directly reflected in murder, maiming, extortion, and drug smuggling—in short, in felonious activities which smacked of organized crime, but which, unlike the investigation of organized crime, would ultimately lead to the arrest and conviction of the criminal businessman; he never got away, unlike the president and his associates. The game of clear-cut avarice and subsequent punishment became a unidimensional ritual dance ignoring or bracketing the more relevant and prevalent contemporary business problems of white-collar crimes, committed against workers, that resulted not only in their physical deaths (when safety hazards went uncorrected), but, on a much larger scale, their psychic deaths.

As America did a sufficient number of public-media mea culpas following its defeat in Vietnam and the shock of Watergate, the public media—especially television—began to refocus its gaze on corporate life. Now, instead of the guilt that produced images of evil, of corrupt businessmen as felons and common thugs, we were given the conservative celebration of business success manifested in the myth of the individual. A hero type, the individual winner/smart operator, predominates in the current prime-time soap-opera cycle—a person who lives in a world of intense competition; a captain of finance who outsmarts other smart operators but who does not swindle innocent people. We have returned at last to a belief in the American system of laissez-faire capitalism that favors such a portrayal.

The frontier world of *Dallas*, like the frontier world of *Bonanza*, is framed by achievement. However, this achievement is manifested in different ways. Ben Cartwright represented, in his uniquely American-frontier way, the old values of the traditional aristocracy—a sense of civic responsibility, charity, and warm family relations. In an equally American vein, he succeeded through hard work and investments made after careful consideration combined with his superior intuition and mature judgment. His frontier wisdom substituted admirably for his lack of intellectualism. In contrast, Jock Ewing, the modern patriarch of South Fork, represented a more contemporary version of the American upper class. He succeeded through a cynical mixture of common sense, hard work, and often questionable business practices. In Jock's wife, Miss Ellie, the Ewing matriarch, we are presented with an aristocratic model of old values and standards. But these values are under constant assault as Jock's sons, J. R. and Bobby—the two sides of their father's ambivalent personality—constantly battle for supremacy. Sweet yet hard-nosed Bobby tries hard to win honestly, while J. R. employs every shady business tactic known to man, including bribery, duplicity, and spying to succeed. On a deeper level, Jock's two sons are warring at the ideological edge of the advanced capitalist system. To the question, "Is it worth winning at any cost?" J. R., representing the reality of advanced capitalist relations in contemporary America, answers an unqualified yes. Bobby, on the other hand, representing America as it once was before it lost its innocence, is not sure at what price is success.

The audience is given a backstory in which in the process of becoming rich, the Ewings are characterized as "smart operators," hardworking entrepreneurs who built a huge oil-and-cattle empire in Texas—the new land of opportunity. However, staying rich, in the world created by the Ewings, means the villainous rogue—a flouter—is in control, but just barely. This latter character type is ably represented by J. R. Ewing, the often hilarious antagonist who operates in the melodramatic tradition of the ambivalent evil buffoon, always on the edge of personal destruction, yet always making a comeback. Nonetheless, the viewers are led to sense J. R.'s ultimate doom. He almost gets killed, but recovers. There is, of course, a clear ideological rationale for this characterization in both contemporary American life and melodrama, which is by definition highly centrist.

Dallas's success on television throughout the world is a triumph of the symbolic world of the new upper class over that of the proud old upper class in America. The old American upper class, which acquired money through ancestors, has generally been defined as those families who, for at least five generations, have been accepted in the society of the Metropolitan 400 and other such elitist symbols of social status. Having turned their attention to other matters such as philanthropy (an excellent tax shelter), civic responsibility (through contributions to elitist arts institutions), and elegant play, they have been pushed aside in the status game by the nouveaux riches, who have little sense of community values, use social relations to accumulate ever-greater wealth, which they need to prove their status to the world, and thrive on cheap publicity (often gained not through their donations of works to the permanent collections of art museums, but, rather, through their purchase of professional sports teams, which instantly catapult them into the public spotlight). This is their only way to encroach upon the status relations established by the old upper class in America.

C. Wright Mills is provocative on this battle for status:

> "Conspicuous consumption," as [Thorstein] Veblen knew, is not confined to the upper classes. But today I should say that it prevails *especially* among one element of the new upper classes—the *nouveaux riches* of the new corporate privileges—the men on expense accounts, and those enjoying other corporate prerogatives—and with even more grievous effects on the standard and style of life of the professional celebrities. . . . And, of course, among recent crops of more old-fashioned *nouveaux riches* dramatized by the "Texas millionaires."[17]

These new upper-class groups—the high-level corporate managers, professional celebrities, and Texas cattle and oil barons—whom Mills labeled "the power elite," are now celebrated as our proper leaders. The Ewings are the ultimate public symbol of this power elite—the new upper-class "Texas millionaires" with a thirst for ostentation and cheap publicity (which provides them status they do not possess by virtue of manners or education), and a total lack of concern for the values of community. The Ewings operate in a Texas version of the cafe society, with its increasingly popularized motif of ostentation via, not the garden party, but the big Texas-style barbecue. The glamor of the Sunbelt, with its elaborately coiffed cowgirls and strangely un-Western-looking cowboy—entrepreneurs, provides the viewers with an atmosphere of the suburban middle landscape to which they can easily relate, while simultaneously offering viewers the dream life of the new frontier—of the rugged cowboy making his way alone in the corporate boardrooms of the latest office tower in the international style, doling out his personal, eccentric version of corporate justice.

The new frontier of *Dallas* is a reflection of our social conservatism and of the "me" generation of Americans—it is the current celebration of doing one's own thing, except that, rather than the 1960 anthem, which meant seeking personal experience, the 1980 anthem signals a search for personal wealth and status. It is a world in which a government energy-department representative reveals oil-lease secrets to the Ewings in exchange for family favors, including a trip to the annual Ewing barbecue. And no one flinches. Critic Michael Arlen saw in *Dallas* a revelation of the general breakdown of rules of conduct in American society generally (rules for so long framing and providing logical order to the chaotic, despicable social relations of daytime soap opera), and the resultant loss of any clear sense of ethical behavior or social responsibility. Arlen wrote:

> ... in the audience, our citizens reconstitute themselves ever more rapidly according to fashion "looks" (proletarian, Russian, Chinese, Navaho, cowboy, preppy). ... Meanwhile, our new television favorites float free above their glossy plots. ... In other words, ourselves aerodynamically advanced, we cheer the streamlined, destabilized characters we so resemble.[18]

This can be said of our upper-middle-class achievers who see the glow of the new suburban middle landscape and who find this selfish, anomic behavior acceptable and even desirable. But what of the others—the white- and blue-collar proletarians who are aliens to this world of celebrity, casual sex, and corruption, but who are negatively affected by such a system every day of their working and leisure lives as the surplus value of their labor is converted to the profits that support the ostentatious lifestyle of the protagonists represented in these melodramas? As Mills wrote:

> The idea that the millionaire finds nothing but a sad, empty place at the top of this society; the idea that the rich do not know what to do with their money; the idea that the successful are poor and little as well as rich—the idea, in short, of the disconsolateness of the rich—is, in the main, merely a way by which those who are not rich reconcile themselves to the fact. Wealth in America is directly gratifying and directly leads to many further gratifications.[19]

Workers are thus encouraged to take on an attitude of moral superiority while accepting their financial and general inferiority. This deception has its counterpart in the traditional argument of wealthy organized religion, that is, of "the righteousness of the poor." Beyond the realm of the personal relationship of the viewer and the melodrama character is a social realm of the melodrama in which he sees the central characters' personally and socially destabilizing actions as not met with external sanctions from the dominant social authority, but, rather, internalized as personal discomfort and unhappiness. *Dallas* and similar contemporary melodramas do not question institutions but instead focus on individual misconduct—on the corporate executive as duplicitous, not the corporate apparatus itself. The consequences of the Ewings' acts are not social but personal—turned inward on themselves. Further, because of the general atmosphere of individual destabilization, the consequences of their acts seem random—not clearly linked to behavioral proscriptions. Viewers can revel in both the Ewings' wealth (which creates the condition of desire in viewers) and their discomfort (which provides the viewer with a sense of moral superiority while he acknowledges his economic and social inferiority), and simultaneously not feel at all threatened by the Ewings' fictional power.

Another current melodrama, *Hill Street Blues*, which premiered in 1980, reflects the continuing social power of the "me" generation. The series was cocreated by Steven Bochco and Michael Kozoll (Bochco wrote many *Columbo* episodes, and *Hill Street* benefits from his emphasis on intelligent dialogue). Aesthetically, its structure is complex for television, although it still fits very comfortably into the commodified planned flow of commercial television. Scenes constantly shift; plot strands are left hanging in its open-ended, serial format. Contrasty lighting, reminiscent of *The Untouchables*, and hand-held, remote camera work lend it a sense of realism and immediacy. Overlapping conversations, as in Robert Altman films, enhance the feel of everyday experience. Its 13 major characters—led by inner-city precinct Captain Frank Furillo; his lover, and by 1983 his second wife, attorney Joyce Davenport; Sergeant Philip Esterhaus, Lieutenant Howard Hunter, and Officers Lucy Bates and Andy Renko—form a complex web of personal stories that move the series along. The characters are archetypes of the constantly shifting status positions in today's social system. Furillo, a divorced father, suffers from guilt because he is so happy in his torrid bathtub love affair with gorgeous Joyce while his plain-looking ex-wife Faye is decidedly not happy. The residual ideology of the nuclear family is still an ideal for Frank. He eventually marries Joyce, although he is resentful of Faye's happiness with another man.

On the job, Frank is tough but compassionate. Work at the precinct house centers around Philip, a working man's working man with a good heart—the model of the kind, understanding shop steward who has the interest of his men at heart. Lieutenant Hunter is intentionally one-dimensional—a cariacature of the SWAT mentality of the post-Vietnam era. Lucy Bates is liberated, but wants to be loved; however, her work is very important to her, and she does "a man's job" very well. Andy Renko is a white racist at heart, but his work with his black partner deflects the prejudice of his upbringing (blacks are O.K. if they save your life).

In *Hill Street Blues* we return once again to the urban frontier of violence and lawlessness. The lines are clearly drawn and the correspondences to the myth of the frontier, Western style, are evident. The cowboy-Indian confrontation translates into the white-black/Hispanic confrontation. Indians were nature oriented and had the advantage when the game was played on their field. Blacks and Hispanics (and, in *Hill Street*, Irishmen) are streetwise and, like Native Americans, have the home-court advantage. Whites (cowboys-cavalry and police) invade their territory to bring civilization, that is, to control the neighborhood and its social transactions. Whites use tactics and strategies, and eventually the power of education and law-and-order, to civilize the more body oriented ghetto residents. However, *Hill Street* astutely points out another parable that counters the traditional presentation of the confrontation of savagery and civilization, namely, the parable of Vietnam. The blacks and Hispanics may be seen as the Vietcong (certainly Howard sees them as such, as does Renko, although it is more difficult for him to admit it)—guerrillas in the urban frontier, hanging on despite all odds in a war of attrition. The ambiguity in *Hill Street Blues* is that while the social-worker mentality is obviously inappropriate, do we then resort to force after all? Unfortunately, *Hill Street*'s weakness, like that of *M*A*S*H*, lies in its failure to transcend personalness to reveal the ideological underpinnings of a system of social, political, and economic dominance and subordination. That this is true of television generally is borne out by the critically acclaimed melodrama series *Lou Grant* (1977-81), which attempted to expose institutional impropriety and social negligence but was unable to sustain such a focus as it, too, slipped back into the personal.

Lou Grant, Mary Richards, and crew were fired from the news staff of WJM-TV in Minneapolis on the final episode of *The Mary Tyler Moore Show*. Lou has moved to Los Angeles as *Lou Grant* opens. He has become city editor of the struggling *Los Angeles Tribune*, owned and published by the strong-willed aristocrat Margaret Pynchon, Lou's equal in stubbornness and underlying compassion (class differences melt away as common character traits transcend the tremendous differences in upbringing that ultimately define Lou and Margaret). Lou's staff included the hot-shot, hot-headed investigative reporter Joe Rossi; the sensitive, ambitious young WASP woman reporter Billie Newman; quietly efficient, professional assistant city editor Art Donovan, and Vietnam-veteran-turned-hippie staff photographer Animal. Lou's old buddy Charlie Hume, who helped Lou get the job, was managing editor of the *Trib*. Lou's new work-family members at the *Trib* frequently disagreed with one another over such issues as journalist-source relationships and other ethical questions regarding the nature of news-gathering practice itself, yet they invariably pulled together in the end to get the scoop. The *Lou Grant* stories were topical—a pastiche of the contemporary problems plaguing the urban frontier—focusing on prison conditions, terrorism, police corruption, senile judges, ghetto violence, the poor living conditions in nursing homes and the inadequacy of their regulation, the bad treatment of Vietnam veterans, the plight of illegal immigrants, and the safety violations at nuclear-power plants. And because the journalistic establishment has gained high visibility since the publication of *The Pentagon Papers* and the Watergate investigations, journalistic practice itself became a motif of *Lou Grant* topicality. Issues such as the gatekeeping function of the news process—why one story was selected and another rejected for publication—were often raised.

Yet, while *Lou Grant* traded on topicality, the mythic demands of contemporary television melodrama depoliticized the very ideology in the issues it raised. In an effort to engage feelings and bring in what its creative people termed the "human elements," highly charged political discourse such as that involving terrorism was rephrased to become the anger, frustration, and feelings of emasculation of the individual terrorist. The journalist of *Lou Grant* became the local welfare worker whose liberal solutions to the plights of individuals with problems tied to social inequities did not impact on the larger system itself. Like the cops of *Hill Street Blues*, the *Trib* protagonists tell us that the social problems they face daily are indeed real, serious, and painful, but are ultimately beyond their power to change. Underlying the empathy that oozes from these melodramatic humanists is the same cynicism that pervades the world of television's urban frontier. The protagonists are coping through the warmth of close personal-professional relationships, having realized that the system operates with a power far beyond that of their own power to intercede on behalf of its victims.

Television Melodrama and the Portrayal of Work

Hill Street Blues is one of a long line of police melodramas that show work. From *Dragnet* through *Police Story* (1973-77)—an anthology of psychological portraits created by Joseph Wambaugh and focusing on a variety of police officers engaging in mundane areas of police work and dealing with their personal lives outside the force—to *Hill Street*, the viewer gets a sense of the nature of police work, much of which is unglorious routine. These depictions hint at the status position of police in our everyday lives—they are not highly regarded, nor are the risks they take and the lack of substantial pecuniary rewards for their work clearly understood. But the depictions fail in one major sense; that is, they fail to examine the state of false consciousness in which police live and work. They may be totally committed to enforcing the law, but they don't seem to understand the social and political ramifications of their work. As Anthony Bouza, Bronx chief of police in the 1970s, noted in Alan and Susan Raymond's video-vérité documentary *The Police Tapes*, aired on both PBS and ABC in the late 1970s, "I'm very well paid to be a commander of an army of occupation in the ghetto." The rank and file are not as well paid, nor do they understand the context of their work as clearly as does Bouza. They don't seem to understand, for example, why the residents of the ghetto resent their presence there. All they see, in Bouza's words, is "a flowing river, and all the garbage is coming down *through* it."

Of the other serious television melodramas that use the urban ghetto as a backdrop, *East Side/West Side* was the only series to critically explore the nature of the social work that occurs there. Its cynical verdict is an accurate reflection of the context of that work as it is. The social worker understands his social role and the system of operating social relations. He does not care for what he sees. He is still locked within the system, a professional welfare worker, with centrist bureaucratic obligations. This realization must emerge before opposition can be properly placed in its social context.

The blue-collar worker, presented in television comedy in farcical characterizations, is nearly invisible in television melodrama, certainly as a central protagonist. And when workers are presented, unless they are in service occupations, they are presented in nonwork settings. Thus, they are divorced from their labor, and their predominant characterization is as commodity consumers. *Skag*, a gutsy short-lived series about a steel worker stricken by illness, no longer able to care for his family—his whole reason for being and the confirmation of his manhood—showed the collapse of the great American Dream in

America's heartland. No one was buying. *Skag's* exploration of the ramifications of false consciousness would have yielded a truly provocative television melodrama. It simply wasn't afforded the opportunity.

One gets the clearest conception of the secondary status of work in television melodrama from a survey of over three decades of daytime-television soap opera, for here we come to understand that which is concealed from us by the blatancy of its exclusion day after day, year after year. According to critic Dennis Porter, soap opera presents the viewer "a country without history, politics or religion, poverty, unemployment, recession or inflation, and with only minimal references to class and ethnicity." We are given instead problems of character, such as "sexual identity, family situation, . . . romantic love, or sexual dysfunctions." Work does not intervene to distract the hedonistic pursuit of soap opera's protagonists and antagonists. Instead, the soap opera, as does most melodrama, presents "decor in the absence of an historical or socio-economic frame of reference, commodities in space."[20]

While 1981 saw some major changes in assumptions about issues that could be safely presented in daytime soaps, including homosexuality, and the substitution of adventure and fantasies of escape from mundane daily experiences for the soaps' traditional motifs of domestic strife, the on-location shoots, like their studio predecessors, were all about voyeurism and commodification. The more things seemed to change, the more they remained the same. Specifically, what remained the same were the soaps' demographics: Soaps were, are now, and will likely continue to be populated by upper-middle-class WASPs, with very few rich, and fewer operatives, laborers, or clerical workers, whose lives are considered too mundane to sell the commodities of the suburban middle landscape even though in actuality these workers today constitute much of the population of that domain.

Bradley S. Greenberg and his associates at Michigan State University reported in 1982 the results of a large study on soap-opera occupations.[21] They found a much higher incidence of professional occupations of both men and women, but women were still generally not employed. Very few minorities were in evidence. Very few crafts persons or operatives appeared, and even fewer laborers. Very few clerical or sales persons were represented, compared to the 1975 census breakdown of occupations. The researchers also noted a decline in the amount of "business" talk on the soaps, and more "relational" talk. In short, soaps depict how those of the new bourgeoisie spend their unproductive leisure hours—namely, in infidelity, petty bickering, and consumption of commodities.

William Winpisinger heads the International Association of Machinists and Aerospace Workers (IAM). In 1980 and 1981 he organized television-monitoring campaigns aimed at a better understanding of the images of unions presented on newscasts and in entertainment television. Two-thousand monitors from the IAM, the International Union of Operating Engineers, and the Bakery, Confectionery, and Tobacco Workers International Union in 36 states watched ABC, NBC, and CBS in February 1980 and April and May 1981. The project—"Television: Corporate America's Game"—reported these results: Unions were almost invisible on television; when they were depicted, they were seen as "violent, degrading and obstructive"; and television scarcely shows factory occupations that produce goods, in contrast to showing service workers. The report concluded: "Television continues to portray workers in unionized occupations as clumsy, uneducated fools who drink, smoke and have no leadership ability. They may as well be robots. They are nameless, personality-less people who take orders, do their jobs and disappear."[22]

Labor's causes are clear and could make important subject material for melodramatic work. Plant closings, workers' health and safety problems, corporate crime, and diversion of pension funds into anti-labor investments are all provocative, highly relevant topics in an era of big-labor and big-business activities that often seemed linked at the higher level of decision making. Yet not only are these causes not addressed, but as we have seen, laborers generally are absent from television and, when present, are depicted as cut off from the power relationships that frame the material discourse of the work experience.

While the labor movement is somewhat more visible on television news, it is still packaged within a frame Ralph Nader described as "tailored to fit big business." Labor leaders are not sought out for their advice on the solution of national or international problems; the newscasters rarely explain why workers are on strike; and on the Sunday-morning public-affairs series, such as *Meet The Press, Face The Nation,* and *This Week With David Brinkley*, organized labor is not newsworthy unless associated with a major breaking story in which they are a major focus (e.g., the PATCO debacle or the United Mine Workers strike).

It seems to be a general condition of work in the United States that workers wish to escape when the whistle blows. That says much about both the quality of the work experience and the images of unproductive leisure with which television and other public media provide the worker. In the land of television melodrama, it's always "Miller Time."

TELEVISION DOCUDRAMA: TRUTH AT WHAT PRICE?

Roots, Washington Behind Closed Doors, and *Playing For Time*— stories of generations of slavery in America, of cynical high politics, and of the Nazi death camps—share a common bond. In television terminology, which is often obscure if not inaccurate, these programs are labeled "docudrama," a curious blend, so the definition goes, of melodramatic recreation of real historical events. Critics of television's banality want to applaud the more serious efforts of this program type as art, yet are stymied by their own insistence that the form be measured against television news and documentaries. When so done, it comes up somehow predictably short—as pseudorealism. These same critics ignore the inherent interpretive nature of newsgathering and of feature writing generally and of television news and documentaries in particular. Some critics have attempted to segment docudrama in order to better understand its relationship to reality. One scheme divides the form into "biographical" docudrama—actual historical characters are dominant—and "novelized" docudrama—invented characters dominate but events are real or historically situated, or the invented characters are based on historical persons and invented events (these of course correspond to the literary biography and to historical fiction). In either case, the argument between defenders of the form and detractors comes down to a debate between the importance of portrayal of character versus provision of journalistic or historical information. This argument can only be resolved, it would seem, by attribution of the artist's intentionality—a very tricky resolution. What claims does the docudramatist make in her work; i.e., how are the artist's claims to historical accuracy revealed in the rhetoric of the form?

Television producer-writers Richard Levinson and William Link, authors of the television docudrama *The Execution of Private Slovik*, a recreation of the events leading to the only American execution, by a firing squad, of a deserter in World War II, believe this debate is spurious. Their defense of the form echoes most members of the Hollywood and New York television creative community:

> Shakespeare put words in the mouth of Julius Caesar, as did Shaw and Thornton Wilder. Playwrights and novelists have pillaged history

for centuries, turning the quick and the dead into spokesmen for their own philosophies. . . . . The objections to these liberties have been minimal. But television brings with it a strong element of credibility that historians and other critics of the medium feel changes the perception of the audience in a significant way; . . . there are those who are convinced that the TV viewer cannot easily distinguish between reality and dramatic truth, especially when they cohabit the same piece of furniture; . . . is it only permissible to play hob with the truth when a suitable number of centuries have intervened and none of the actors wears business suits?[23]

Critic Michael Arlen, writing about *Washington Behind Closed Doors*, disagrees, noting that the docudramatic serial clearly represented the administration of President Richard Nixon shortly after its demise (Jason Robards played the fictitious Richard Monckton) and thereby "lays deliberate claim to authenticity," which it should not do. Arlen nevertheless concedes the work was the best in the genre's short history and, as biographical criticism, may have revealed much more about the personalities of Nixon and his White House associates than could any straight documentary. Arlen's way out of this conundrum seems to be to clearly label the work "fiction." He wrote, "There should be room in our historical narrative for such a marvellously evocative (though perhaps not precisely factual) interpretation as Robards' depiction of Nixon-Monckton's strange humorous humorlessness, where an actor's art gave pleasure, brought out character, and took us closer to truth."[24] The trouble with this resolution is that good biographical criticism is precisely that. If it is revelatory, it should be accepted as truthful.

Critics of docudrama who claim a "distortion of history" treat history as if it can somehow be separated from ideology. It cannot. History is always naturalized and therefore ideological—it is what those in control wish it to be. Political analyst Richard Reeves was correct when he argued that docudrama should be treated as a political event.[25] For, as with all television, what is given and what is left out offer a distinction of vast importance. Television production is expensive. All presentations of history are not equal in terms of their impact. Access to presentation of oppositional history is important, and such access is today not granted, except on an occasional public-television series such as *Visions*, which presented such controversial docudramas as one about life in a U.S. World War II internment camp in which Japanese-Americans were forced to live; and on cable-television's public-access channels, which to date have very limited viewerships. Barring such access as a producer, the critic must examine the choices made in docudramatic presentations for their ideological consequences, and engage dominant cultural producers in a dialogue regarding those choices.

NOTES

1. Northrop Frye, *Anatomy of Criticism* (Princeton, N.J.: Princeton University Press, 1957), p. 47.

2. Ibid.

3. Peter Brooks, *The Melodramatic Imagination* (New Haven: Yale University Press, 1976), p. 201.

4. Ibid., p. 204,

5. Ibid.

6. Orrin E. Klapp, *Heroes, Villains, and Fools: The Changing American Character* (Englewood Cliffs, N.J.: Prentice-Hall, 1962), p. 19.

7. Ibid., p. 8.

8. Ibid., p. 17.

9. Ibid., pp. 16-17.

10. David Thorburn, "Television Melodrama," in *Television as a Cultural Force*, ed. Richard Adler and Douglass Cater (New York: Praeger, 1976), p. 85.

11. Raymond Williams, *Television: Technology and Cultural Form* (New York: Schocken Books, 1974), pp. 86-94 passim.

12. Richard Levinson and William Link, *Stay Tuned* (New York: Ace, 1983), pp. 74-75.

13. C. Wright Mills, *The Power Elite* (New York: Oxford University Press, 1956), p. 138.

14. In a survey of top corporate executives and members of boards of directors of six leading electronic-media corporations—RCA/NBC, CBS, ABC, Time, Inc., Westinghouse, and Warner Communications—conducted by the author in 1983, we were able to isolate and profile 76 members of the boards. This limited survey confirmed the description offered by Mills a quarter of a century earlier. Of the 76 board members, 38 hold undergraduate, advanced, or professional degrees from Ivy League universities. One-sixth hold degrees from Harvard, and one-tenth from Yale. Of the remaining 38 directors, a significant number attended prestigious midwestern and western private educational institutions, notably Northwestern, the University of Chicago, and Stanford. Of the 76 directors, only six, or 7.9 percent, are women, with no more than one woman on any board. This is an educated, genteel, and clubbish man's world defined by conservative politics, social elitism, and the tight economic control of the interlocking directorate. At the lower levels of control, it is a world in which a corporate "team" is really a set of cliques in which, as Mills put it, "the prideful grace of individuality is not at a premium." One learns the art of conformity well before advancing to the upper reaches of the powerful organization—he is, above all, a corporate man, with a proper birthright and education.

15. Tom Wolfe, *The Electric Kool-Aid Acid Test* (New York: Bantam Books, 1969), pp. 34-35.

16. Joseph Campbell, *The Hero with a Thousand Faces* (New York: Pantheon Books, 1949), p. 29.

17. Mills, *Power Elite*, p. 59.

18. Michael J. Arlen, "Smooth Pebbles at Southfork," in *The Camera Age* (New York: Farrar, Straus and Giroux, 1981), p. 50.

19. Mills, *Power Elite*, p. 163.

20. Dennis Porter, "Soap Time: Thoughts on a Commodity Art Form," in *Television: The Critical View*, ed. Horace Newcomb (New York: Oxford University Press, 1982), pp. 125-26, 130.

21. Bradley S. Greenberg et al., "The Soaps: What's On and Who Cares?" *Journal of Broadcasting* 26 (Spring 1982):519-35.

22. Ralph Nader, "Television Presents False Image of Unions," *Athens News*, March 2, 1981, p. 3.

23. Levinson and Link, *Stay Tuned*, pp. 146-47.

24. Michael Arlen, "Getting the Goods on President Monckton," *The New Yorker*, October 3, 1977, p. 115ff.

25. Richard Reeves, "How I Became a Supporter of and Appalled by Docudrama, and a Fan of the Talented, Frustrated, Confused Men and Women Who Would Like to Make Television Better if Only So They Wouldn't Have to Apologize for What They Do—Write and Produce the Stuff America Loves," *Panorama*, March 1980, p. 39.

7

TELEVISION NEWS
AND
THE TELEVISION DOCUMENTARY

It would be both naive and presumptuous for the author to present an exhaustive overview of the development of television news and the television documentary in so limited a context as a single chapter of a television survey. Therefore, the author has chosen to limit his discussion on news and the documentary to an exploratory analysis of the myths that operate in both the newsgathering and the presentational apparatus itself and in the products of that apparatus—the stories which draw upon real events and people in the world.

There are many significant issues for current and future academic discussion of television news and the documentary, all deserving of careful consideration and detailed research, both critical and empirical. As these issues specifically impact on the discussion in this chapter, they will be addressed within the context of myth analysis.

There is a continuing debate that has produced volumes of literature on such journalistic issues as the importance of organizational imperatives versus personal journalistic bias in news-content determination and presentation; and the relative importance of the so-called reality (or mirror) theory and the "collage" explanations for news determination (advanced by the news professionals themselves) as against the organizational and personal-bias explanations (advanced by critical sociologists).[1] There is the question as to how much of television news is "show," in which entertainment values predominate (especially at the local level as news consultants reorganize and standardize the presentational-packaging elements of the newscast), and how much is "substance."[2] Further, granted that there is, to a degree, substance in all news presentations—including story content and packaging—if the substance is broadly defined as cultural information, the debate then moves to whether journalists are essentially objective in their journalistic practice (often defined as being fair and open to correction), or consciously adversarial (variously defined as being personal or polemical, depending on the politics of the definer). At a deeper level still, the question is raised as to whether so-called objectivity is possible in any case, given the ideological frames within which journalists must operate or against which they must rebel.[3] There are frequent debates regarding the ethicality of the television journalist's becoming involved in the story she is covering and thus either being forced or choosing to take an ideological stand by virtue of her involvement.

From various ethnographic observations of the network-television newsgathering process,[4] and from content analyses of news programs, it can be suggested that, to varying degrees, news organizations and the corporate chiefs to whom they must report have developed identifiable ideological perspectives that at least indirectly impact on the newsgathering process; that individual journalists have personal biases cultivated from years of experience in personal worlds that on the surface exhibit ethnic, racial, sexual, religious, economic, political, and geographic uniqueness, but underneath manifest a consistent motif of aggressiveness and achievement orientation tempered by a slight dissatisfaction with the monotony of the middle-class lifestyle and a certain skepticism that comes from an education that stresses the development of the critical faculties; and that both organizations and individuals operate in cultures which at any given moment provide certain dominant ideological frames that impact on reportage as they set limits to the journalistic discourse and determine the relationship of the journalistic apparatus to the government in power (e.g., which news organizations and reporters get access to the President of the United States, or which reporters are allowed scoops on breaking stories). The degrees to which each of these characteristics impacts on journalistic practice and in what combinations is the focus of important ongoing debate and research.

THE TELEVISION-NEWSGATHERING APPARATUS

The precise nature of the process of gathering and publishing news depends in large measure on one's definition of news. The assignment editor sends television reporters into the field to cover stories which may or may not make it to the air that day or evening, thus committing corporate funds to the process on what may seem like a speculative basis. But the odds are very good that, because of years of experience with the news formula, the news one went after will emerge. News is, at this simplest level, what the television-news department covers and airs on a given day. The screening out of that which is news from that which is clearly not news has already been accomplished before the raw remote videotaped footage and the reporter's or cameraperson's notes are relayed back to the newsroom (in the case of live news coverage, there are revealing moments when the newsgathering organization's selection process is publicly displayed and opened to a critique when the news doesn't materialize).

The frames within which news is defined are implicit and seem to become embedded in an undeclared yet commonly understood news-department agenda. This agenda, particularly on the local level, is often set by a combination of forces—of news executives at the local level responding to vague notions of the cultural composition, and the nature of the social interactions, within their coverage area, gathered in the past through periodic surveys of the community's opinion leaders (excluding more militant community forces), regarding important issues of local public concern, and by the group-station owners' reliance on news consultants who test and market formulas for successful news presentation. (The group-station owners are generally absentee managers who tend to resort to the same policies for all the stations in their group.) From this combination of perceived public interest, which is markedly centrist, and style, which is markedly entertaining, the news "package" emerges—it holds the news program together, giving it form and direction, and supposedly separates it from the competition. Beyond questions of form is the basic issue of the articulation of an overriding news philosophy. What do these various corporate enterprises consider "news"?

There is clearly no agreement among scholars and journalism critics as to a definition of news, yet the divergence of opinion is enlightening as we see the various definitions compete in the news packages we receive on our television screens. Let's first examine the competing definitions of news, then briefly look at the television-news frames that employ, whether explicitly or implicitly, these definitions.

University of Chicago sociologist Robert E. Park defined news as a part of our communications that calls for a change of attitudes concerning events of importance to a community—events whose significance is still under consideration and discussion. Journalism historian Frank Luther Mott defined news as an accurate, unbiased account of the significant facts of some timely happening. A synthesis of these definitional frames leads us to the definition of news as the provision of significant facts relevant to the formation of an opinion, or to the change of an attitude on some current public issue of importance to a community of persons. That community may be a group of workers, a neighborhood, city, county, state, region, nation, continent, or world. A public issue is one about which there already exists some division of opinion. Mott's call for an "accurate, unbiased account" is, of course, moot if one acknowledges the influence of ideology in the structuring of public discourse—accuracy and lack of bias will be claimed by different positions within the public debate in an effort to enforce or counteract an ideology. No journalist can divorce himself from the community of persons, and he thus cannot, in reality, stand apart from the world he covers. The resolution of debate is really a matter where whoever disseminates news either directly or indirectly determines its ideological slant.

In contrast to news, this traditional definitional scheme views human-interest content as that which describes, in a dramatic narrative style, some human experience in a manner that enables the reader, listener, or viewer to make a sympathetic personal identification with the subject. Facticity is not necessarily a requirement of the human-interest story, although the story should be grounded in real events and involve real people as subjects.

In such a contrived dichotomy between news and human-interest content, we find a verbal wall constructed between the truth of the accurate news report, which presents facts and lets us decide which side we will support, and the probing, interpretive psychological or biographical reportage that may be interesting but is subject to charges of sensationalism and questions regarding its veracity. Thus, public issues abstracted from everyday experience and presented by middle-class public officials within an aura of authority are treated with a certain reverence while the depiction of everyday experience, with its images of human suffering, frustration, and general despair, is open to question regarding reporters' motives. (ABC reporter/muckraker Geraldo Rivera was frequently criticized for his overly liberal ideological bias as he reported on the disenfranchised and degraded minority cultures in American society, as if his work was something less than news.)

This definitional framework places the journalist in an essentially subservient role vis-a-vis the dominant political institutions—

as "faithful messenger" of the political elites—whose task becomes, as Walter Lippmann described it, to simply "signalize" events about to unfold. Such a view of the newsgathering apparatus is by no means shared by all critics. Ron Powers, the Pulitzer prize-winning former television critic for the *Chicago Sun-Times* (who, as of this writing, was presenting critiques of television and television journalism on *CBS Sunday Morning*), takes a radically different view of the journalist's role in this process. Powers describes the function of news, which he admits he is narrowly defining, as monitoring and reporting "the conduct of public officials and others who exercise power over private citizens, toward the goal of assuring openness, accountability, and the intelligent administration of community life."[5] Powers, unlike Park and Mott in their more generalized definitions of news, sees the newsgathering apparatus operating to rebalance a system of social relations unbalanced by dominant-subordinate power relationships that are revealed in human experience. He adds that contemporary television newsgathering does not perform "the vigorous, adversary, check-on-government intervening role that American journalism has traditionally performed."[6] Far from the "signaling function," Powers concludes that the best American journalism "traditionally proceeded from the assumption that it is mining areas that the public did not even know existed."[7]

Journalism critic Edward Jay Epstein warned, however, of the inherent dangers of journalistic interventionism—of the journalist perceiving her role as public crusader, a role which can easily lead, wrote Epstein, to the myth of journalistic revelation of truth, in which the journalist, acting as "little David," punctures "the official veil of secrecy" and, in the height of melodrama, brings Goliath—monolithic government—to his knees.[8] Epstein believes that such a journalistic mythos conceals the actual relations of the process of revealing truth —a process in which the journalist, removed by at least one step from the context in which an actual event occurred, can best function honestly as a conduit for the release of information to publics.

With this debate unsettled regarding both the very definition of news and the proper role of journalistic practice in the conduct of human affairs, the activities of the television-newsgathering apparatus unfortunately become all too easily defensible.

Journalistic practice is significantly more complex than the tale of the "news hound" hot on the trail of an eye-popping story, although taken in by the contemporary mythology of the embattled star reporter seeking to blast through walls of governmental deception, duplicity, and euphemism, one might not recognize the competing pressures that delimit the journalistic endeavor. The reporter, whether print or broadcast, is, first of all, institutionalized by the very fact of his or her being hired to report for a particular organization, and by subservience to the needs of that organization as determined by the decisions of editors who assign the reporter stories and particular beats and thus determine at the outset the very quality of the relationship of the reporter to the subject matter (i.e., many reporters, especially electronic-media ones, have little or no special knowledge of their subject that insures that coverage will be limited to information from press handouts and that sources will not be seriously challenged; of course, the reporter can grow into the beat over time). Second, the ambitious young reporter is trying to make a name for himself or herself—to climb the middle-class ladder of achievement, success, and public recognition that has been firmly embedded in the reporter's subconscious following years of survival training administered through the culture's dominant educational apparatus, which, in journalism education, assumes the importance of the by-line as a token of professional existence and achievement. In the struggle which ensues, between the journalistic institution—which seeks to report news to fill the holes between ads and to avoid any major conflict with other institutions, especially those of the powerful, centralized executive branch of the federal government and large corporations—and the reporter, who seeks his distinctly middle-class spot in the community of publicly recognized journalism professionals, the institution often reaches a position of wary tolerance of the superstar, superego investigative journalist who will produce the Pulitzer Prize-winning or Columbia-Dupont Award-winning expose of corruption. The prize is, of course, subsequently appropriated by the institution, which uses it as a mantle of prestige and respectability.

TELEVISION NEWS AND MYTH

The television medium is ideally suited to the transmission of the mythic world of news. Its combination of a simplified press, which fulfills needs for rudimentary political and economic information (e.g., how much the viewer can expect to pay for a loaf of bread, given the current international monetary crisis); the photograph, which presents the personal world of the community, the family, and personal life to the literate and the nonliterate alike; and the motion picture, which satisfies the need for curiosity and entertainment, establishes a readily accessible and understandable (and ultimately a palatable) context for the unfolding of our contemporary struggles.[9]

In television journalism much more than in print journalism, the symbol of truth becomes the image of the journalist himself—the aggressive advocate willing to challenge authority—rather than the story or editorial itself. Style predominates over content or context. The defender of the public's right to know satisfies the medium's insatiable demand for melodramatic personae who clearly and simplistically represent the just cause. These journalist-heroes allow viewers to vicariously watch the unapproachable bureaucrat or the arrogant general (who never answered letters of complaint or phone calls) brought to his knees by the crafty and efficient journalist—the modern-day personification of the Homeric epic hero who, like Odysseus, is condemned to a life of wandering, skepticism, and continual tests of his ability to outwit the dangerous adversary. The television audience revels in the myth of the individual in news, manifested in the reporter as "independent spirit," unafraid to take on the powerful on their own turf.

The mise-en-scene of the journalistic quest reveals first the reporter, standing alone in front of a backdrop, such as the immobile, ponderous architecture of the government building signifying stasis and impenetrability (or why would the reporter be standing outside?). The reporter then moves inside to the office of the interviewee, with its bookshelves lined with innumerable specialized reports that obviously were written to camouflage the clear and simple truth the reporter, and the viewer, are seeking. The reporter has now pierced the veil of secrecy, like Superman, who can see the enemy through concrete walls, and has brought us all closer to the correct solution to the investigative problem. At this point the reporter is "living the myth" as Tom Wolfe once said regarding his own status as star journalist.

One the the major characteristics of the myth of the individual in television news is that heroes are more efficient that are villains. The individual hero-correspondent, who has used his craftiness and wit to outsmart the institution and to penetrate the institutional barriers that hide the conspiracy or deception, now reveals his efficiency by trapping the reluctant interviewee into ostensible admissions of guilt or into internal contradictions in his answers (if the source refuses to appear on camera, the journalist may implicate the institution in an implied cover-up; he does this by aurally berating the institution for its sphinxlike failure to cooperate with the investigation while simultaneously flashing a picture of the institution's imposing headquarters—the physical and intellectual barrier to the truth—in the background). This aggressive journalistic dance, when extended to its extreme, features, in the words of critic Michael Arlen, the correspondent as "prosecutor" in a courtroom-style melodrama. Arlen discussed a CBS *60 Minutes* investigation of corruption in Wyoming as an example of the myth at work.[10] Arlen saw television news and expecially the news magazine, of which *60 Minutes* is the most visible representative, as succumbing to the mystique of "the thrill of the chase," with the interview subjects serving as "quarry." The *60 Minutes* correspondents were increasingly drawn into "prosecutorial scenarios" in the 1970s, in which the reporter personified "judgmental righteousness." Here we find aggressive correspondents in search of a story upon which a moral judgment can be passed. What becomes important in this realm of prosecutorial journalism is "the *appearance* of a story: the dramatic texture of televised confrontation."[11] By using a technique in which allegations of misconduct are framed as dramatic questions, *60 Minutes* reporter Dan Rather was able to "prove" that everyone, from the Rock Springs, Wyoming, police chief to the state's governor "knew about" prostitution in the energy boomtown (and by implication were "guilty" of condoning prostitution). Rather then attempted to demonstrate how the governor of Wyoming might be linked to organized crime. Rather, as it turned out, relied on a questionable source for evidence to support this allegation (Rather set the source up as "a superb investigator"). However, "facts" turned out to be, in Arlen's subsequent personal investigation of the Wyoming reports, "inaccurate, or incompletely presented or ambiguous."[12] The newsgathering process was paramount here. Rather's inquisitorial style convinced the viewer that he was on top of the story so that his findings must be correct. The efficient, provocative interrogation of sources became the key part of the story, what Arlen termed "the seductive flow of the news-gathering drama."[13]

In another television-news context—the evening news report—the myth of the individual, of the larger-than-life journalist-hero, is further established in the persona of the anchorperson. The networks' public-relations campaigns promoting their anchorpersons project an image of the anchor as nearly omniscient and omnipresent. Before his death, Frank Reynolds was touted by ABC as "uniquely qualified to bring you the world"—Reynolds clearly operated on a plane considerably above that of the traditional newsreader or the contemporary print journalist, at least in the world of public relations.

In American television the news anchor, through his introductions to every story in the newscast, assumes a central role in all stories, usurping authority from the correspondent in the field (the anchor will go on location for the big story, e.g., the assassination of Egyptian President Anwar Sadat, or the Apollo moon launch, further relegating the correspondent to a minor position in the news operation by implication that he is not qualified to do the big stories). The anchor is the presence that connects the newcast, the voice that orders the chaos of the everyday world. The anchor is the loner of the myth of the individual. He stands outside the group of correspondents, sources, and viewers, secure in his lair—the television studio—diligently observing the world outside. He is above the fray, yet deeply involved in it. He does more than read us the news—he guides us through the world as his news organization has defined it that day. In the presentation of news, critic Raymond Williams noted, the anchorperson presents "a studied informality" with less emphasis on reading a script (a formal gesture) and more emphasis on "personal presentation" via eye contact through a teleprompter.[14] The personal gaze becomes the anchor's heroic signature as he confronts the world of danger and mystery. We live vicariously through his journey. Anchors become "arbiters of correct reactions to the news."[15] The anchor is detached one moment, cynical, amused, folksy, or self-righteous the next. After we are led through this range of emotional reactions to the world, we reach our final destination—the newscast's end, the drama's epilogue. The anchor-hero, having survived the dangerous world, signs off with a verbal coat of arms by which we identify his standing and worldly position. Walter Cronkite's famous "And that's the way it is," and Chet Huntley's and David Brinkley's "good night, David; good night, Chet" offer a note of finality and confident closure, a sign that they are still in control. In a nonnewscast context, Edward R. Murrow's "good night, and good luck" sign-off injected a more open-ended and cautious response to his world—his hero-character was not so self-assured as today's electronic journalists, perhaps because Murrow sensed, correctly, that the world of everyday experience was beyond the control of the journalistic apparatus. Murrow was the strong, worldly-wise, tired hero of the traditional epic, not today's corporate hero for whom efficiency would always overcome ambiguity.

The anchor's sign-off leads us to a discussion of another myth revealed in the television-news presentation—the myth of the puritan ethic. The sign-off not only works to consolidate the anchor's position of power and control over news; it also leaves the viewer with the "illusion of hard work accomplished."[16] Reporters and news anchors must believe in this myth by the very nature of their occupation. Just as their work is to bring order to the world of dangerous events and personal confrontations, so too is the "work" of their news subjects celebrated in stories with such themes as: "putting their lives back together after the disaster," or "a return to normal after the aborted coup d'etat," or "a mother working two jobs to put her sons through college so they can have a better life than she." Work is rarely viewed for what it is in our society—by and large, an alienating experience to so many unskilled or semiskilled laborers, and increasingly to the white-collar proletariat—the clerical-information workers of the computer age—as well. Rather, work is presented as evidence of the human will to survive and make a better life—a distinctly middle-class vision of the world. The stories are framed as highly individualized accounts of survival symbolic of the human condition and are thereby cut off from their more concrete and therefore more powerful social and ideological contexts. Rarely do we get an adequate exploration or analysis of the increased susceptibility of the lower socioeconomic classes to physical danger in the workplace or in inadequate housing, unsafe transportation, or lack of sufficient police protection outside the work environment; or of their desertion by the educational apparatus that teaches them at best how to cope in the technological world; at worst, how to fail. Instead, the success of those who have escaped these conditions through hard work is celebrated, while the basic structure of oppression is ignored.

The illusion of hard work is reinforced in the presentational elements of the newscasts themselves. In many newscasts, both local and national (e.g., the old CBS/Cronkite set and the *ABC World News Tonight* set), the working newsroom becomes the backdrop for the report. In the background of the establishing shots, we see people moving to and fro, seemingly preparing the news (the newscast, of course, is already prepared and very tightly scripted). At one particularly successful local news operation, CBS affiliate WBNS-TV in Columbus, Ohio, the newsroom becomes a special place to which the viewer is taken for a sneak preview of upcoming stories. Weatherperson Joe Holbrook is shown fiddling with a weather computer, the high-tech machine reinforcing the reporter's status as a hard-working expert in charge of his machinery. We cut to working-anchor Dave Kaylor in the bowels of the newsroom, shirt sleeves rolled up, preparing copy for the next half-hour's newscast. Here we are confronted with the old image of the hard-nosed reporter at his typewriter. All that's missing is the green eyeshade.

The calculated presentation of the journalist as a hard worker, a direct formatting change designed to counter the critical outrage over "happy-talk" and "tabloid" news, should not be taken as a total ruse; many journalists do work very hard. The issue is one of the nature of the work itself. With all that hard work done, why are television newscasts generally so stylized and devoid of cognitive substance?

An amazing spoof of the working newsroom was mounted by the Los Angeles Metromedia independent-television-station KTTV in the mid-1970s. Titled *Metronews, Metronews* (one surmises, after the *Mary Hartman, Mary Hartman* model of soap-opera spoof-celebration), the half-hour newscast featured two informal anchors—one in an army fatigue shirt, the other in a rumpled white shirt and tie with sleeves rolled up—who wisecracked their way through the day's events in a mock-tabloid style using what appeared to be parodies of soft news features (one was never certain just how seriously the show took itself). The show's coup was its newsroom setting, which looked like a real newsroom with a water cooler, file cabinets, old desks, teletype machines, and messages scrawled on slips of paper and tacked up here and there. *Metronews* clearly confronted, through its style, the fake show-business world of the legitimate newscast. The informality of the *Metronews* anchors, who were really happy (and who seemed to border on being stoned), pointed to the contrived happy informality of "happy-talk" news. The telephone to the newsroom, a standard set piece, into which one anchor was seen talking as we returned from a commercial break, was dead—"nobody there," he exclaimed as he hung up.

The reward for the journalist's hard work is a combination of prestige and significant pecuniary compensation. At the highest levels of contemporary electronic journalism, the network news anchors, this reward is substantial. In television's early days, salaries were good, but not mind-boggling. In 1948, NBC paid John Cameron Swayze $25,000 a year to read news on the nightly *Camel News Caravan*, a 15-minute network newscast, while CBS paid Douglas Edwards $30,000 for his nightly news program. In contrast, in 1983, according to CBS *60 Minutes*, ABC paid its anchor Peter Jennings about $1 million; NBC paid anchor Tom Brokaw $1.7 million; and CBS paid Dan Rather, the strong ratings leader in the competition, $2 million —some 67 times as much as fellow CBSer Douglas Edwards had earned some 35 years earlier.[17]

The anchors have developed their journalistic skills through many years of print-and electronic-news practice. They have made the right moves in the corporate news game, have been "team players."

Now that they are millionaires, what impact do they have on news management? Have their years of hard work and newsgathering experience paid dividends in terms of personal control over the news apparatus? Both NBC's Brokaw and ABC's Jennings say they take an active role in their nightly newscasts. Brokaw, the "managing editor" of the *NBC Nightly News*, works with the program's executive producer to construct the newscast, and writes about 60 percent of the program; but, he noted, "it's not a big deal, . . . it's mostly lead-ins to the correspondents." Jennings, ABC *World News Tonight*'s "senior editor," says he has "an editorial presence." He helps determine the day's news coverage with his executive producer, and he writes the beginning and end of the broadcast and edits introductions to stories prepared by news-staff writers in New York.[18] Clearly, the pecuniary rewards seem linked less to current journalistic activities than to the anchorperson's presence, demeanor, and ability to attract and hold an audience in a fierce competitive battle wherein one rating point— 833,000 homes—is worth nearly $25 million in annual advertising revenue.[19]

In this world of high finance and prestige, there always exists a possibility that the network electronic journalist-superstar will fall out of touch with "the people" as he spends the preponderant amount of his working, and in many cases socializing, hours with top national- and foreign-government officials. "The people," described by Brokaw as a "large mass, looking at us in a distracted way,"[20] are the true target audience for both the network and local evening-news programs. Audience studies have repeatedly found network and local news viewers to be below the national average educational level and generally older. The network news image makers, most likely unconsciously, work hard to project an atmosphere that is pure upscale suburban middle landscape—the mental landscape in which the majority of newspersons themselves dwell. Network reporters and anchors appear as highly successful, self-important personages, taking themselves too seriously. This image building does, however, serve a useful purpose in the larger world of network-affiliate relations, for the patronizing ambience of the national news, which exudes "responsibility," compensates for the tent-show atmosphere of so much local news, which gathers higher ratings than serious news but runs the risk of alienating government regulators. Local news generates carry-over for the network news that follows. What is therefore of primary importance is getting the "average Joe" to turn on the set for the fires, rapes, and murders, then keep him watching while the serious world events are presented in a truncated, easily digestible form by the serious people. The affiliates have made money and have kept the Federal Communications Commission off their case, the people have been entertained, and the networks have secured their carry-over into their prime-time shows.

The suburban middle landscape in network news is reflected in news values, dress, and presentational codes. This landscape is presented in news not as a geographic place (the suburb is exceedingly difficult to locate geographically any more, but it is there) but as a state of mind to which an appearance is correlated. Most of the spokespersons, both journalists and sources, seem to come from this place irrespective of their personal life histories or the nature of the story being reported. Their dress and their mannerisms point, above all, to their "belonging."

Values-and-lifestyle research would classify the successful news anchor, male or female, as part achiever—a prosperous, middle-aged materialist—and part "belonger"—a patriotic, traditional, and stable person generally quite happy with his or her life. Critic Edwin Diamond provided his own version of the "anchor model": "middle-aged, mid-American, white males, . . . the men the old Life magazine used to refer to as 'the command generation.' "[21] They look and sound authoritative, but not too authoritative—the Walter Cronkite persona. Edward R. Murrow was too authoritative, too intense for the night-after-night presence of news anchoring, but his intensity was ideal for the clear focus and closure of documentary work. The anchors write and report well, but not too well; otherwise they sound erudite and are relegated to providing commentary, à la Eric Severeid and Bill Moyers. They are not too young, not too old (ABC's Peter Jennings spent four years as ABC anchor in the mid-1960s but was too young to command the necessary presence; ten years later, in 1978, now more mature, he returned to the anchor slot at ABC in their triple-anchor format, and in 1983 he took sole possession of ABC's anchor). They are good looking, but not too handsome. They are, above all, loyal to their corporation. And they have an "unceasing drive to win."[22] As CBS anchor Dan Rather said while being interviewed for a *60 Minutes* segment on network-television news anchors, part of his desire to be a network anchorperson was "to run something on your own." This entrepreneurial spirit is a prerequisite for the successful anchor, who is clearly now a corporate person, but one who also maintains his individual pride and the sense of skepticism that got him to this point in his career as a serious professional.

He knows the limits to which he can bend the corporate apparatus and still maintain his professional integrity and personal status.

This perfect combination of fierce competitive drive, good looks, cool controlled informality, and substantial talent, which is nonetheless unthreatening to one's associates, is rare, and makes the ideal anchor a valuable commodity. Sociologist Orrin Klapp classified this classic American-hero character type as the "group servant"—a defender of the dominant order who, through tireless work, rights wrongs, and saves the weak from the strong. This hero is what Klapp terms a "compensatory type" helping people put up with a reality different from the ideal.[23] The television anchor, while he may not actually accomplish such feats, gives the appearance of such accomplishment. Compensation is particularly relevant, given the context of news, which so often presents to the viewer a vision of the urban frontier, which is, according to critic Tony Schwartz, "almost unbelievably grim," especially at the local, metropolitan level. This vision is "one dominated by film of burning buildings and smoke-blackened firemen; stretchers being loaded into ambulances and tight-lipped detectives pacing around cordoned-off crime scenes."[24] The same images are also prevelent in national and international news coverage as minor wars pop up all over the globe and American military forces and news correspondents are shipped off to become involved.

No longer the youthful independent spirit—the lone individual doing battle with the unyielding institution—but still personifying the myth of the individual in large measure, standing above the fray, guiding our view of the world, and teaching us how to react, the mature anchor now must also play a role of a reasonable arbiter of reality for millions of Americans; he must be strong and fair, decisive and warm. Above all, he must be trusted by tens of millions of average people. Dan Rather's warm, middle-class gentility is reminiscent of Steve Douglas, Ozzie Nelson, and Ward Cleaver, three famous denizens of television's suburban middle landscape. But Dan didn't exude such an aura until the sweater; before the sweater, we knew Dan as that tough White House correspondent who directly challenged Richard Nixon during the famous press conferences surrounding Watergate, and as the contentious, aggressive interrogator of *60 Minutes*. His image for millions of viewers was cool if not cold—a bit too hard edged for the nightly exposure as news anchor. The sweater—a V-neck pullover—gave him, in the words of *Washington Post* critic Tom Shales, the "trust-me, you've-got-a-friend, hello-out-there-in-television-land sense."[25] *The CBS Evening News with Dan Rather,* which had lost much of its substantial ratings lead over NBC and ABC since Rather took over for Cronkite in March 1981, surged ahead once again, regaining Cronkite's commanding lead. Dan's sweater was Walter's pipe in disguise. The V-neck sweater became the talk of journalistic circles. Everywhere, anchors bought sweaters. Was the sweater a tremendous public-relations coup? Not to hear Rather tell the story, a story right out of *Leave It To Beaver*. It appears he had a cold in early winter and wore his V-neck sweater, which his wife had given him 11 years before, around the office. One night he kept it on for the newscast and his wife said it looked great on the air. The rest is history. What made the sweater so vital? One CBS executive hypothesized to Shales that Rather's handsomeness and perfection were putting some viewers off, making people feel inadequate by comparison. Rather, it is reported, went out and bought three new sleeveless sweaters and two long-sleeve sweaters, "off the rack."

The stories which reinforce this image of warm middle-class gentility are those which deal with culture and civility and act to set straight once again the world of bad news and human degradation. We see this clearly manifested in the lifestyle reports of *CBS Sunday Morning with Charles Kuralt* and occasionally on the tail end of the nightly newscast (PBS's new entry into the competition, *The MacNeil/ Lehrer News Hour*, has adopted Kuralt's video-postcard motif as well as the "trip-to-the-art-gallery" report). The world of arts reportage, showing aficionados attending legitimate galleries or blockbuster museum retrospectives such as the 1983 Manet exhibit at the New York Metropolitan Museum of Art, serves to reinforce the power of corporate patronage under the illusion of democratic access to culture. As critic John Berger wrote, "The majority of the population do not visit art museums. . . . [They] take it as axiomatic that the museums are full of holy relics which refer to a mystery which excludes them, ... that original masterpieces belong to the preserve (both materially and spiritually) of the rich."[26] What is set straight in the world of news and of suburban-middle-landscape culture is the dominance of the corporate elite and the subservience of the people.

There can be no doubt that the news, especially local news and national network news in major markets, is a middle-class corporate venture. As critic George Comstock noted:

> News and public affairs programming, unlike entertainment, are the products of the disseminators. . . . The daily selection and treatment of events are the responsibility of the news staff. These decisions are made autonomously of management. Yet news cannot escape the

values of management, which reside in popularity. Journalists may manufacture the news, but management manufactures the newsmen and their tools. Formats and personnel are the creatures of management, as is the budget to do the job. Thus news, like entertainment, becomes honed to the exigencies of competition.[27]

When we involve management, the critique of news must include not only matters of style, but also related matters of technique, for management, not willing to trust its aesthetic or gut feel, and not prone to bold experimentation, turns to the modern-day management tools—viewer surveys and news consultants—to generate information about news presentation. Not even the sacrosanct anchor is spared such quantitative, detached scrutiny. From the use of data on what viewers want to see as their news, it is a small step to the concept of news packaging—the employment of rigid formulas to structure and order the presentation of each day's messy world according to some notion of audience acceptability.

Technique operates on many levels in television news. As a manifestation of the myth of eternal progress—of a technically sophisticated America in charge of her destiny—technique is most clearly visible in an ostensibly neutral technological context, represented by the progress of computer graphics on local weather (which lend an air of authority to the performance of the weatherperson via his association with sophisticated machinery); live minicam reports from the field on breaking stories (most of which seem yet to break or have already broken as the correspondent tries desperately and, often on the local level, comically, to inject his personality into the report to save it from absurdity); computer-generated reports on battle tactics (especially intriguing were the continual graphics displays during the 1982 Falkland Islands war between Britain and Argentina—the viewer became engrossed in a real-life version of the video game as little graphic Exorcet missiles were fired from graphic fighter planes, hit their targets, the graphic British ships, and the ships exploded like so many images in an old comic book); those incredible twirling graphics, in so many local news openings, designed to give the cast a modern, "with-it" look (one feels the world tumbling and swirling about until it rights itself as the anchors appear on the screen and things quickly settle down); and the promotional bumpers before the commercials—graphics which provide teasers for upcoming stories. Viewers have generally reacted very favorably to such technical improvements in news presentation, saying that these technical feats enliven the show, making it more interesting to watch. This, of course, would be expected, given the atmosphere of entertainment that pervades today's daily news broadcasts.

Technique moves beyond simple fascinating electronic blips and live reports. The "human technique" of which Jacques Ellul has written is manifested in the pseudoscientism of war reportage, as war becomes body counts; of politics, as issues become poll results; and of economics, as the economy becomes indexes and graphs. The network newspersons try their best to balance numbers with stories about individuals who are included in those numbers. This "personal touch" obscures what is lost in the antinomy of data and living beings—namely, the intelligent discussion of issues related to existing social relations. The world of data-as-news is a world of "unassimilated facts"[28]—of "scenes," as critic Michael Arlen once described television generally. Closure in this world is structural, not conceptual. Each story, especially if it deals in relatively difficult abstractions, must be closed that night and filed away to be discussed again at some future time. Exceptions to this type of closure are voyeuristic journeys into violence, sex crimes, murder trials, and death-row watches, coverage of which continues in a serial format until the stories reach their conclusions.

Most local newscasts use technique in their story ordering within the news segment. It is predictable and, to the viewer, comfortable. The news generally moves from a description of the grave events of the day (fires, murders, auto accidents, natural disasters, and acts of terrorism are grist for the local news headlines whether they are local or not); to the description of more mundane affairs—the ones that really affect our lives, but to which few of us pay much attention because they are buried in the middle of the news and they lack exciting visuals—affairs such as the city council's resolution of the traffic signal dispute; and finally to the upbeat (from the pathos of the WCBS-TV "Our Block" motif, which often features hapless people, such as the elderly citizens of the South Bronx, struggling to hold their lives together—the-will-to-survive theme that tugs at so many middle-class and working-class heartstrings, to the contrived humor of "the story about the man with the winged cat").

Technique operates behind the scenes in television news as well, most notably in the activities of the audience survey and the regimes of the infamous news consultants. Here is where most of the damage is done, out of sight of viewers and critics. Networks have used Q-scales developed by market researchers to rate newspersons and television personalities generally according to a viewer's positive response to a performer's personality. According to the Q-scale, CBS anchor Dan

Rather was found to be almost as warm, compassionate, and honest as Walter Cronkite (although not warm enough until the sweater) while Rather's major competition for the CBS anchor position, savvy veteran Washington correspondent Roger Mudd, scored "cold" in comparison. CBS executives denied the Q-scale played a role in their anchor decision. Local news operations have increasingly relied on news consultants such as Frank N. Magid Associates, and McHugh and Hoffman (the major competitors for consultancy supremacy in television news) to help them find ways to improve their news presentation. McHugh and Hoffman is generally credited with developing the lurid tabloid-news format featuring large doses of sex, violence, and corruption coverage, which transformed San Francisco station KGO from a loser to a striking news success in a very short time. Other news operations followed suit and San Francisco went from a town whose local news operations were nationally respected to the site of the nightly peep show. Generally, the formula for news success, the consultants determined, was reduction of the maximum length of a story to 90 seconds, regardless of the story's news value and relative importance to the community, and the attractive newsreader.[29] The revolving-door approach to news talent resulted, as Kansas City anchorwoman Christine Craft of KMBZ discovered to her dismay and anger in 1981 when she was demoted from anchor to reporter because she was not pretty enough and not deferential to her male colleagues. Ms. Craft sued the station and was awarded damages in a jury trial. News consultants poll viewers and tailor the news and the news personalities to fit viewers' desires. They fine-tune their clients' image through the use of technique. They are paid handsomely. Their clients, on the whole, realize increased profitability by following their advice.

As Jacques Ellul wrote, "Technique . . . clarifies, arranges, and rationalizes. . . . It is efficient and brings efficiency to everything."[30] Certainly television news is no exception. Here all is order, efficiency, and comfort as the familiar persona of the anchorperson night after night, aided by slick technical visualization and easily understood symbology, conjures up scenes of events from far and near via satellites, helicopters, microwave dishes, and minicams and entertains us while providing the barest hint of the day's happenings. That, after all, is what we have come to expect and what we have told the television news consultants we want. We have learned to march complacently in place in front of our TV screens as the world out there muddles on.

The Clash of Myths in Television News

Beneath the smooth exterior of the television-news presentation are hints of the real conflicts that exist in contemporary social relations, but seem somehow to escape the watchful eye of the video camera and reporter. They are there nonetheless, and can be discovered through an analysis of the complex clash of myths that subtly pervades television-news content, despite institutional attempts to present a world of clear-cut antagonisms dependent for their resolutions on the force and power of the dominant culture.

As soon as television journalists announce their professional status, namely, their objectivity, we discover perhaps the most basic clash of myths in television news. As critic William Henry wrote, "American TV news, like the rest of American journalism, is scrupulously 'objective'—which means it does not challenge the prevailing biases of a predominantly white, Judeo-Christian, imperial, internationalist, capitalist society."[31]

Objectivity, which many journalists prefer to define as overall fairness in presenting various positions in a controversy of immediate concern to a community or nation, and an openness to correction, is in reality a subterfuge that conceals presentational inequities favoring the dominant cultural position in any argument. This is most clearly evident in the clash of the myths of the suburban middle landscape and the urban frontier as represented in social conflict. Critic Jeff Greenfield described the atmosphere in which these two myths collided as television news was forced to deal with the social unrest of the 1960s: "A largely unwilling participant, . . . the medium was communicating events over which *it had little or no control*—against its clear institutional interests. . . . The cultural upheaval of fashion and taste—rooted in the power of rock-and-roll music—was an upheaval ignored on the national airwaves until its presence was unavoidable."[32] (Italics mine.) Rock and roll, political assassinations, burning cities, police brutality, and violent demonstrations on college campuses and at a national political convention—all of these powerful symbolic images were manifestations of the urban frontier. The news was certainly incongruous in the context of the reassurance of the suburban middle landscape of television comedy so popular during the early years of the decade and of the rural middle landscape of childlike escapism of the middle and late years of that same decade.(Newscasts and live coverage of news events could thus easily be considered by viewers to be staged or distorted because the predominant television-entertainment frames showed a much less troubled world.) One can argue with Greenfield's conclusion that television had "little or no control" over the events it was communicating. The television-news apparatus indeed worked hard, if subconsciously, to draw clear ideological lines between legitimate authority and anarchic protest. The voice of legitimate authority was heard resonating in the suburban middle landscape in the form of "reasoned responses of the arranged studio discussion," which had much greater persuasive power than "unreasoned, merely demonstrative, responses" of street confrontations.[33] The oppositional elements who were forced to resort to protest demonstrations to make their points took to the streets in the urban frontier. These political "happenings" often became violent, and the film crews provided millions of viewers with powerful scenes of the conflict shot from behind police lines. The point of view the images revealed showed us an unruly urban frontier in which young people wearing clown makeup, army fatigue shirts, torn blue jeans, and draped in American flags, threw rocks, bottles, and human feces at law-enforcement agents. When scenes of violent confrontation were presented, they provoked charges from news critics, such as Vice-President Spiro Agnew, that the television networks advocated radical change. On the contrary, as Edward Epstein pointed out, this bias toward change was "not ideologically motivated but an inevitable outcome of the search for a mass audience" through the construction of "highly simplified melodramas, built around conflict, and illustrated with visual action."[34] Clearly Epstein is closer to the truth in this debate, but he discounts use of the strong pull of the network news apparatus to balance coverage to the point that order inevitably predominates. Cronkite's liberal indignation at the thug tactics used by Chicago Mayor Richard Daley's police against CBS news correspondents, such as Rather, who covered the 1968 Democratic National Convention was clearly substantively motivated rather than some search for a mass audience. Cronkite's remarks set up a clear-cut conflict of ideas; yet it was quickly followed by Cronkite's invitation to the Chicago boss to appear in the CBS anchor booth to respond. Cronkite, the voice of reason, had backed down. The CBS news organization appeared to be apologizing, both to the mayor and to the American people, for Cronkite's justifiably passionate condemnation of the suppression of journalistic activity the night before. Daley appeared calm and authoritative. Everything was civilized. The confrontation was defused and the antiwar demonstrators protesting in front of the Conrad Hilton Hotel—the convention headquarters hotel—appeared by contrast to be overreacting. Cronkite's attempt at fairness and balance in the end confused the entire issue. As the protesters shouted that "the whole world is watching," the television news frames were pro-law and order. By emphasizing law-enforcement activities during the urban riots of 1965 and 1967 in Watts, Detroit, Newark, and other metropolitan areas, and by stressing interviews—many with whites in black neighborhoods—television news deflected substantive matters of blacks' "underlying grievances and tensions" and thereby failed to present a meaningful sociohistorical context for these confrontations.[35]

The myths of the individual and the puritan ethic lead the television news person ever closer to the status system that contains the politician. The ultimate fusion of journalism and politics comes at times like 1968, when the journalist whose reasoned voice seemed to rise above political demagoguery was touted as a potential presidential nominee: Walter Cronkite, the "most trusted man in America," seemed capable of running the country; indeed, on his February 27, 1968, evening newscast, Cronkite declared that the Vietnam War was lost and the only "rational" thing to do was to negotiate a settlement. He sounded more of a leader than our leaders.

Regardless of the journalist's sympathy with the cause of the underdog and tendency toward the more liberal stance, the status world of the hard-working achiever/belonger is far removed from the dirty nonstatus world of the street demonstrations. The urban frontier provides visual fuel for the nightly news report. The fire is put out by the boys from the suburban middle landscape. The technique embodied in the slick package and the instant report—the myth of eternal progress—reassures the viewer that the "radical messiness of reality" is under control.[36]

The myth of the individual as it operates in television news contains subtle internal contradictions. The basic operating frame of the myth is clear: An individual meets an institution in a confrontation. The results are far more complicated and hinge on characterization. When the individual is a superstar journalist, the likely outcome is that the individual will emerge victorious. When the individual is the common man, the likely outcome is that the individual will be wronged by the institution and rendered seemingly helpless, but will be saved through the intervention of the journalist as moral defender of the truth (thus demonstrating that democracy works; i.e., that a free and unfettered press protects men from abuses of power). If the institution in question is government, the institution is likely portrayed as unresponsive, anonymous, bureaucratic, and inefficient—in short, the institution is at fault. If the institution is a giant corporation, the wrong done to the individual is blamed not on the capitalist institution itself, heartless greed, or corruption, but rather, on individual mismanagement. If the bad manager is fired or if a more effective management strategy is initiated, the wrong will disappear. It is little wonder that the hard-working aggressive star journalist would implicitly view the problem as one of managerial ineptitude rather than as one of basic systemic structural deficiency, for his or her success had depended in large measure on his or her corporateness—a basic belief in efficient management and the value of creative entrepreneurial solutions to human problems. Entrepreneurial flair and style will inevitably produce the better mousetrap and the better social solution; bureaucratic hesitation, bungling, and lack of imagination will produce failed social programs. Admittedly this antinomy is presented here in broad brush strokes, but it can be argued that such a frame operates in television news in the broadest sense as well with particular exceptions now and then.

When things get so hot in the urban frontier that the men and women from the suburban middle landscape cannot seem to bring them under control, the television-news apparatus may invoke one of its most powerful myths—the myth of the rural middle landscape—to deflect attention from the chaos. This version of the myth is "Waltonesque"—the strong mature rural citizen coping with the evil world crashing all around him by maintaining pure country values, including the sanctity of the extended family and the value of hard work not for achievement, but for a higher moral purpose. The rural middle landscape speaks to a moral victory. Charles Kuralt's eloquent "On the Road" profiles of strong-willed, commonsensical country folks lent substantial credibility to the myth. In contrast to the rural middle landscape, the urban frontier, when it is New York City, may lose morally. But its portrayal in television news assures that it will win a cultural victory. The suburban-middle-landscape mind-set of the news packagers assures such victory by deflecting pressing questions of human degradation and social injustice in the name of the vibrancy of urban culture—the American melting-pot ideal which produces great authors from the slums. However, when the urban frontier is Los Angeles (the great television entertainment capital), it pales in comparison with the rural middle landscape both morally (it is the epitome of the self-centered, egotistic "me generation" of which Tom Wolfe wrote) and culturally (it is inhabited by ostentatious kooks disguised as creative people; it has no urbanity in the New York sense, but rather, harbors Hollywood pretenders to the cultural throne of Broadway).

Network television news is a New York affair, with deference to the nation's political capital, which, unfortunately it would seem, was moved to Washington—that humid, rather uncultured marshland full of military personnel and glorified clerk-typists—nearly two centuries ago. While the roots of many of the anchors and correspondents are in southern or midwestern culture, those places have become merely origins from which occasionally a strong sense of morality will well up in condemnation of a generally uncivilized world. The world in which these people now live and work is at a far remove from those roots—it is a world of achievement, success, public prestige, and corporate control.

THE DOCUMENTARY: CONTROL AND DEMYSTIFICATION

The television documentary has taken on many forms in its three-decade history, including the television argument (Peter Davis's *The Selling of the Pentagon*, CBS, 1971); the personal television essay (*Bill Moyers Journal*); the television history (Allistair Cooke's *America: A Personal History of the United States*, NBC, early 1970s); television exposition (Dr. Jacob Bronowski's *The Ascent of Man*, BBC, aired on PBS, 1975); the television magazine (CBS's *60 Minutes*; NBC's *First Camera*; and ABC's *20/20*); and vérité (Frederick Wiseman's *Welfare*, WNET/PBS; Craig Gilbert's *An American Family*, PBS, 1973; and Peter Davis's *Middletown*, PBS, 1982).

Most television-documentary work has used a correspondent/narrator structure that packages various scenes into a clear linear presentation. The layer of external explanation is provided in both the on-camera speech and the voiceover narration of the correspondent or narrator, who generally follows a script and an interview framework developed beforehand by the documentary's producer/director/writer. The tone of the documentary may be that of Edward R. Murrow's and producer David Lowe's moral indignation in *Harvest of Shame* (CBS, 1960)—a powerful exposé of the terrible living and working conditions of migrant farm laborers who feed the nation; that of cynical distrust, as in producer Peter Davis's and correspondent Roger Mudd's *The Selling of the Pentagon* (CBS, 1971), which focused on the highly questionable motives and fiscal waste of the U.S. military's public-relations activities; or of irony, as in the controversial 1970 PBS documentary *Banks and the Poor*, which accused the banking industry of consciously perpetuating the miserable conditions in our urban ghettos, and which, in a devastating indictment of governmental conflict of interests, superimposed a crawl listing 98 members of

Congress, who owned shares or were directors of banks, over a shot of the capitol, while the "Battle Hymn of the Republic" played in the background. These critically acclaimed efforts were a needed antidote to the nightly scenes that passed as news on the local and network newscasts. They attempted to transcend the pattern of reassurance that had come to characterize the "soft" evening news. The best work in the documentary form was hard-edged, clear-cut, and provocative. The primary weakness with this narrative format, however, was the tendency for viewers to feel that once these social injustices and institutional excesses of power had been exposed and righteously condemned, the social problems would be resolved. (Such was obviously not the case as ten years after *Harvest of Shame*, NBC's Martin Carr produced *Migrant*, which demonstrated that conditions for migrant workers hadn't changed despite Murrow's exhortations.) The narrative closure encouraged such a feeling of accomplishment.

Since 1959 the three commercial television networks have packaged their documentary work in competing series, beginning with *CBS Reports*, and followed shortly by *NBC White Paper* and *ABC Close-Up*. The forerunner to these efforts was the provocative Edward R. Murrow-Fred Friendly documentary series on CBS, *See It Now*, which began in 1951. PBS, founded in 1967, aired the *Realities* series (which was canceled after the 1970 season because of the congressional uproar over *Banks and the Poor*). Ratings for these programs have always been considered failures by commercial television network executives. *The Selling of the Pentagon*, which was aired February 23, 1971, and is considered by many as the hardest-hitting and most exciting investigative documentary of 1970s television, was seen by 5,350,000 homes. Like most documentaries, it came in last in the week's rating race. In contrast, its entertainment competition, *Marcus Welby, M.D.* was seen in 17,250,000 homes. *The Guns of Autumn* (CBS, 1975; Irv Drasnin, producer) was seen in 8,490,000 homes. It so angered the National Rifle Association that hate mail poured into CBS. Its ideological impact went far beyond its general popularity level. While these viewership figures are small compared to prime-time entertainment programs, they still reveal a significant national interest in such programming despite network executives' assertions to the contrary. Particularly low in the ratings are documentary works dealing with foreign affairs (e.g., the Communist party in Italy or the economic and social decline of Britain). Most viewers seem to be turned off by discussion of complex economic questions, especially in the international arena, where the immediate ramifications to the individual are more difficult to interpolate. More successful are documentaries which broadly survey domestic problems such as violence and crime.

In absolute numbers, documentaries on the commercial television networks have declined significantly in recent years. In 1975, for example, 61 documentaries were presented (28 on CBS, 18 on ABC, and 15 on NBC). In 1976, a presidential-election year, the total fell to 36 (15 on CBS, 13 on NBC, and eight on ABC). In the September-April period of the 1982-83 season, only 14 documentaries had been aired. These constituted 10.7 percent of all network specials. The average Nielson rating for the documentary in the 1982-83 season was 8.0. The average share was 13.6 (about one in seven homes that were watching television at the time were tuned to a documentary—certainly not a negligible figure). A further analysis of the 1982-83 season's data reveals that nine of the 14 documentaries were aired in the 10:00-11:00 p.m. time slot (EST)—the last hour of prime-time, when audiences were beginning to decline. Two were aired in the early 7:00-8:00 p.m. time slot (EST) on Sunday. Thus, only three documentaries, or about one-fifth of the total, were aired in the heart of prime time. There were no documentaries aired between September 22, 1982, and December 4, 1982—the "new season."[37] Documentaries have been, and are more than ever, second-class citizens in the world dominated by melodramatic and comedic television entertainment.

In contrast to the typical documentary, the network news magazine, led by CBS's *60 Minutes*, has been a ratings success, and sometimes a huge success (*60 Minutes* has been in the top ten network programs since 1977). During the six-week period, April 7-May 12, 1983, *60 Minutes* averaged a 23.2 rating and 39.75 share—three times that of the average documentary aired during the 1982-83 season. ABC's *20/20* averaged a respectable 17.2 rating and 29 share during that six-week period (a level considered acceptable by network entertainment-program standards for renewal), or twice that of the average documentary. Especially revealing is the April 1983 reading for the *20/20* time slot (ABC, Thursday, 10:00-11:00 p.m., EST). On April 7, 14, and 29, *20/20* had a 29 share each night. On April 21, ABC substituted an *ABC Close-Up* documentary entitled "Banking." The *20/20* audience deserted in droves—the 29 share was nearly cut in half, down to 17. This suggests that viewers may watch the television news magazine more for the personalities of the correspondent-performers than for the substance, or that the substance of the magazine is less conceptually difficult and more entertainingly packaged than the traditional investigative documentary.[38] While *60 Minutes* and

20/20 demonstrate that audiences are not turned off by controversy, in which both magazines wallow, they may be turned off by the level of abstraction inherent in the serious discussion of economics, politics, and ideology.

The long-form, 60- or 90-minute documentary has suffered hard times in competition with the news magazine. CBS's vice-president for public-affairs broadcasts, John Sharnik, told critic John Culhane in 1977, "It's hard to drum up enthusiasm around here for some things when '60 Minutes' has taken off the cream."[39] By covering two or three stories in abbreviated form each week, the news magazine leaves the viewer with the feeling that all that need be said has been said on the subject (the same sense of closure one feels with traditional long-form narrative documentaries), while eating up potential topics at a rapid clip.

And when a long-form documentary project is undertaken, which may engage a producer and staff for a year and a half, the end result may be years of aggravation for the creative forces who worked hard to produce a meaningful piece. As one documentary producer told Culhane, "If the show is controversial enough . . . the producer finds that everything he did in the course of the film is subject to the minutest investigation. . . . The networks sometimes back you up and sometimes don't."[40]

The producer/director/writer and the correspondent of a highly controversial documentary may get pressure from outside their organization. While *The Selling of the Pentagon* was still on the air, CBS started getting angry telephone calls. CBS News President Richard Salant was called before the House Commerce Committee, and eventually the full House of Representatives, to answer questions about the documentary. CBS President Frank Stanton refused Representative Harley Staggers's subpoena for the outtakes of the documentary. The documentary was rebroadcast a month later with a 15-minute critical response from Vice-President Spiro Agnew, Secretary of Defense Melvin Laird, and Representative F. Edward Hebert, chairman of the House Armed Services Committee. Guards were placed at CBS studios in New York and Washington as a caller threatened to assassinate correspondent Mudd. In May 1971 Marine Colonel John MacNeil, who claimed CBS rearranged parts of a speech he had given in Peoria, Illinois, to publicly embarrass him on the documentary, filed a $2 million libel suit against CBS, Inc. and WTOP-TV in Washington, D.C., which carried the documentary. The same month, CBS won an Emmy Award for *The Selling of the Pentagon*. Clearly, the network backed its documentary workers in this case even though some questionable film-editing practices were employed, including the excision of qualifying phrases of some interviewees and the joining of statements, made in a number of different contexts, as the single answer to a question.

Eleven years later, CBS was faced with another libel suit over one of its investigative documentaries. This time the response was markedly different. Broadcast in January 1982 on CBS, *The Uncounted Enemy: A Vietnam Deception* featured a heated interview between CBS's Mike Wallace and retired U.S. Army General William Westmoreland. The 90-minute documentary's thesis was that in 1976, Westmoreland led a military conspiracy to sustain U.S. support for a faltering war by grossly underreporting enemy troop strength. *TV Guide* reporters investigated the documentary and questioned CBS's evidence. CBS News President Van Sauter conducted an internal investigation, upon receipt of which he publicly admitted that the broadcast contained factual errors. He labeled use of the word "conspiracy" as "inappropriate." CBS set up an ombudsman to hear complaints about future newsgathering practices. Although not mentioning him by name in the public admissions of guilt, Sauter found producer/director/writer George Crile negligent in "combining answers from several questions on the same subject into one answer," thus violating network guidelines. Sauter said the documentary should have included more remarks from officials who disputed the charge against the top-level military strategists. All this was not sufficient for Westmoreland, who filed a $120 million libel suit against CBS in September 1982. Claiming that CBS News "credibility" was at stake, Sauter had publicly called into question the techniques and, by implication, the ideological motives of the CBS documentary-production apparatus. The old balancing act had once again managed to divert attention from the issues at hand, namely, Westmoreland's conduct of the war in which over 50,000 Americans lost their lives. CBS News had apologized to city boss Richard Daley in 1968 before millions of Americans. Fourteen years later, CBS News was in essence apologizing to the man who drove us deeper into the morass of Southeast Asia. In both cases, the newsgathering apparatus had gotten so close to some real ideological questions (police as "thugs" and generals as "conspirators" in a lie that cost thousands of young men their lives) that a violent discourse ensued, but the network news operations, ever conscious of their status with their news sources in high places in government, hid behind the blind cloak of objectivity and balance. Clearly, different men in different political climates will react differently, regardless of the general tendency toward a particular type of behavior. News in general, and Salant and Stanton in particular, were more testy in the 1971 era of *The Selling of the Pentagon*—a time when Nixon's inherent distrust of all newsgatherers except those at the *Washington Star* and ABC produced a contentiousness among the press corps and press executives—than in 1982 when newsmen seemed strangely lulled by Reagan's public-relations posturing and his "sincere" warmongering.[41]

If the traditional network documentary, with its built-in layers of control through clear narrative structure, is exposed to charges of conscious manipulation from those whose ideological positions it challenges, the vérité documentary—a form in which the documentarian rejects external narration and instead ideally lets the subjects reveal themselves through their everyday activities, filmed or taped by the unobtrusive camera/observer—gives the appearance of objectivity. Of course, objectivity is impossible because the editing of thousands of feet of film or hours of videotape superimposes a structure on the work. The essential difference between the two forms is the latter's acceptance of life's complexity, ambiguity, and lack of closure. The vérité work ends, but the personal lives it revealed and the relationships among people and between people and institutions continue. Vérité thus seems to leave more room for viewer response and subsequent action because of the inherent continuation in the work itself. Vérité's weakness, however, is that the subsequent plan of action is often vague or nonexistent because the social relations explored in the work are not clearly explicated within a well-developed conceptual frame. While the traditional television narrative documentary may leave the viewer complacent, feeling the problem is under control because the network documentarian has discovered and properly framed the problem, the vérité documentary, with its very structure encouraging a nihilistic response, may leave the viewer cynical and frustrated. Neither response is optimal.

The vérité form is ideally suited to penetrating the veil of contemporary mythology, and herein lies its potential as a counterideological tool. By burrowing beneath the surface of the standardized public images of heroic character types presented in television entertainment, it can reveal the ugly blemishes which contextualize the myth. Whether focusing on social institutions, as Frederick Wiseman has done repeatedly and with powerful results, or focusing on individuals and intimate social groups such as families, as Craig Gilbert and Peter Davis have done in their work, the myths are opened up to the intense gaze of the unrelenting camera eye. Vérité can be a provocative tool since it cannot occur unless it is admitted into its subject's world and thereby becomes privy to the primary-source context of everyday experience—the place where mythology is manifested. Unlike news coverage or the tightly scripted traditional television documentary in which the correspondent enters the context for a brief moment, does a stand-upper or a few interviews, and leaves the scene, vérité is, at its best, cultural anthropology. While it could easily become voyeuristic, vérité's professed role is as a chronicler of and, by the very nature of its relationship with its subject, a participant in the social acts of the time.

Since the vérité form is synonymous with hand-held camera work, run-on scenes, and lengthy exposition, it is generally thought unsuited for commercial television network broadcast, with its time constraints and demand for careful narrative control. Most independent vérité work that has been aired has received its support from PBS, and especially from the New York flagship WNET. Two important examples of vérité's ability to unmask myth were aired nearly a decade apart on public television. Both explored, in vastly different ways, the reality behind the myth of the suburban middle landscape. The first, *An American Family*—a 12-part vérité series focusing on the Loud family of Santa Barbara, California—was produced by Craig Gilbert and aired in 1973. *An American Family* revealed the vacuousness in the anomic social relations of the suburban middle landscape. The second, the "Family Business" episode of *Middletown*, a six-part vérité series documenting life in Muncie, Indiana, was produced by Peter Davis, whose credits include *The Selling of the Pentagon* and the theatrical release *Hearts and Minds*, and directed by Tom Cohen. Aired in 1982, "Family Business" revealed the pathos of the Howie Snyder family as they struggled courageously to keep alive the great American Dream of the successful small entrepreneur, embodied in their suburban Shakey's Pizza Parlor franchise. They were deeply in debt to the central corporation and on the verge of foreclosure. The great American Dream was nothing but an empty slogan in the hollow lives of the Louds. In the lives of the Snyders, it was something to be cherished but its veracity was increasingly in doubt.

Conceived and produced by Gilbert, with cameraperson Alan Raymond and soundperson Susan Raymond (who were to produce *The Police Tapes* for PBS in 1976), *An American Family* documented the final stages of the disintegration of the 20-year marriage of William and Patricia Loud. The family was filmed from May 30, 1971, to January 1, 1972 in Santa Barbara and New York City. More than 300 hours of film were edited down. The serial cost over $1 million to make. The Louds and their five children were filmed in their lovely suburban house with its lovely swimming pool; 35 Wooddale Lane in Santa Barbara, California, became, for a few months, the stage upon which was acted out the promises and perils of the Great American Dream. It was the heart of the suburban middle landscape, a world right out of the film *The Graduate*, with heavy drinking, boredom, a twice-a-week Mexican maid, and gross materialism. When the scene shifted to New York City, 20-year-old homosexual son Lance was camped at the Hotel Chelsea on Twenty-third street—once a haven for some of America's great artists, now an overpriced boardinghouse for suburban avant-garde groupies. Lance constantly telephones home for money. The Louds' other children seem nondirected, bored—the forerunners of the "valley girls." Eighteen-year-old Kevin seems pleasant enough but vacuous. Seventeen-year-old Grant wants to be a rock star. Bill wants him to work at manual labor, but he would rather play. Fifteen-year-old Delilah tap dances in the third episode. She is going through adolescence. Thirteen-year-old Michele is shy, gentle—the warmest in the family. Admittedly, the children are frozen in time in the film. They will change and mature. But the scenes question the base upon which they will grow and mature.

Bill drinks too much, has numerous affairs with other women, and seems dissatisfied with his children. He blames Lance's failure on Pat for her allowing doctors to induce labor. Pat, a Stanford graduate, is interested in fashion, manners, and money. She blames Lance's failure on Bill for his not being closer to his son. Bill is busy trying to keep his strip-mining machinery business from going downhill. Rather than pursuing the great American Dream, he seems to be chased unrelentlessly by its ghost.

This is a far cry from Mayfield and *Leave It To Beaver*. The Louds' reality has order, but the order has nothing to do with mutual trust. Their order is that of routine. Love, which all of these people seem to desperately need, escapes their relationships. As Anne Roiphe wrote of the series, "The Louds have escaped the small-town mores of an earlier America" into a world with no central core of beliefs and little conscious understanding of work structures.[42]

But curiously, *An American Family* did share some of the attributes of *Beaver*. For during the filming, the Vietnam War raged on and Pakistan decimated Bangladesh, yet the Louds didn't notice. Theirs was a world, like that of Ward, June, Wally, and the Beaver, in which the view was cut off at the edge of town or at the perimeter of the front yard.

The Louds, who volunteered to be filmed and were paid no money for their participation, were bitter upon seeing the results. While critics generally were effusive in their praise of the work, Bill Loud accused Gilbert and the Raymonds of New York leftist leanings. Pat felt easterners lived too close together and seemed to be in an unending state of psychoanalysis.[43] Pat wrote an articulate and poignant "Letter to the Forum For Contemporary History," dated February 23, 1973, 13 months after the completion of filming. In it she stressed the horror of being constantly dissected, especially when "shows are being taped for replay in class, and ... students are assigned to play one of the various roles within the family."

Reviews were generally scornful of the Louds. Pat felt critics treated her family as "objects and things instead of people." On one level, the Louds had become symbols, examples of contemporary bourgeois America. On a more personal level, Pat Loud wrote, "It has denuded us of such honor and dignity as we owned." The mirror, she felt, was distorted. Pat continued in her letter, "Like Kafka's prisoner, I am frightened, confused and saddened by what I see. I find myself shrinking in defense not only from critics and detractors, but from friends, sympathisers and finally, myself." The Louds didn't like what they saw. Pat concluded, "We have been ground through the big media machine, and are coming out entertainment . . . did we, *family and network alike*, serve up great slices of ourselves—irretrievable slices—that only serve to entertain briefly, to titillate, and diminish into nothing?"[44] (Italics mine.) Fashion-conscious, status-conscious Patricia Loud seemed to have awakened from her suburban-middle-landscape dream. If so, the documentary effort was successful in human terms.

Following the airing of *An American Family*, Bill and Pat Loud became talk-show celebrities, their media "slices" not yet fully consumed.

If *An American Family* showed us all the warts of the myth of the suburban middle landscape in the era of the "me generation," Peter Davis's and Tom Cohen's *Family Business* showed us a moving personal struggle to hold onto the elusive great American Dream in an economic world that was constantly eating away at the outdated nineteenth-century promise of the independent entrepreneur. The protagonists, the Howie Snyder family, were part of the new entrepreneurial class—the franchisees. They operated a Shakey's Pizza

Parlor in Muncie, Indiana—pure American middle landscape. The ma-and-pa-and-sons operation is characterized in the vérité piece by pride in their work, and the dream of sharing its financial rewards. Howie, a Marine Corps veteran is a natural-born entertainer, singing and clowning his way through the grueling work routine of long days and nights. Director Cohen captured the Snyders' despair in many moving scenes, including one in which Howie is talking on the telephone to the invisible parent-corporation's representative, asking, and almost begging for an extension on credit. The corporate operative on the other end of the line does not seem to be moved by Howie's personal stories of hard work and dedication to the company. Shakey's is threatening to foreclose. In the background Howie's wife is crying.

As the work at the pizza parlor drags on, we begin to feel its sweatshop atmosphere and both Howie's courage and, in a profound way, his naiveté emerge. At a family dinner, Howie discusses the possibility of giving up the business but decides he will continue. One son breaks down and sobs as he confronts the idea that his father might be a failure. It is powerful and revealing material, especially as it uncovers relationships between the traditional petit-bourgeois entrepreneur and the new middle-class corporate managers—an internal struggle for control within the suburban middle landscape. Howie Snyder, in the tradition of the small-shop owner, has roots and affiliations with the working class of which he is proud, and he is resentful of the efficient managerial system established in the pizza-franchising apparatus. He can't seem to understand, however, the extent to which he lacks control over his own business. He does not realize that in 1980, 25 percent of retail businesses were franchises and that their owners—businessmen such as himself—were accountable to the corporations who dictated to them how their businesses were to be run, the prices, and the look of the product and business establishment. He knows that on a personal level, Shakey's is threatening to foreclose. But on a social and macroeconomic level, he is overwhelmed by the abstraction. But while Howie has yet to clearly articulate his status in the context of Muncie and his pizza franchise, the viewer is able to see the economics in action.

Critics of vérité argue that the difficulty with the form is that social context is sacrificed in favor of the human, personal story; that the vérité works are little more than upper-West Side Manhattan liberal voyeurism. They argue that explanations of political economy require highly structured documentary work. *Family Business* demonstrates that vérité techniques can be effectively and profoundly used to reveal social processes by going into families' everyday experiences and by selecting families because they represent an idea. Such occasions are both memorable and rare in the world of television news and documentaries.

NOTES

1. For a full accounting of these approaches, see Michael J. Robinson, "Future Television News Research: Beyond Edward Jay Epstein," in *Television Network News: Issues in Content Research*, ed. William Adama and Fay Schreibman, (Washington, D.C.: School of Public and International Affairs, George Washington University, 1978), pp. 197-211.

2. Daniel Menaker, "Art and Artifice in Network News," in *Television: The Critical View*, 3d. ed., ed. Horace Newcomb (New York: Oxford University Press, 1982), p. 240 ff.

3. See John Fiske and John Hartely, *Reading Television* (London: Methuen & Co., 1978), pp. 91-100, for a discussion of the ideological frames which impact on television news. Also see Raymond Williams, *Television: Technology and Cultural Form* (New York: Schocken Books, 1974), especially pp. 44-54.

4. Edward Jay Epstein, *News From Nowhere* (New York: Vantage Books, 1973) is the classic study of the organizational imperatives operating in the news-gathering process in television news, and is based on ethnographic observations of the process, with emphasis on NBC News, which provided Epstein with substantial access to their day-to-day news operations.

5. Ron Powers, "A Modest Proposal," in *The Newscasters* (New York: St. Martin's Press, 1978), p. 236.

6. Powers, "Vamping It," in *Newscasters*, p. 13. It must be noted that this "intervening role" is the exception in American journalistic history. Such journalists as James Franklin, with his editorial campaigns against the Massachusetts colonial government, and the heavy-handed theocracy of Mather in his *New England Courant* in 1721-26, and Horace Greely, with his prolabor and abolitionist editorials in his *New York Tribune* in the mid-nineteenth century, while exemplary advocacy journalists, often stood alone in their eras as other journalists, more conservative, satisfied themselves with reprinting government and later corporate press releases.

7. Powers, "In the Palace of the Ice King," in *Newscasters*, p. 109.

8. Edward J. Epstein, *Between Fact and Fiction* (New York: Vantage Books, 1975), p. 19.

9. Williams, *Television*, pp. 22-23.

10. Michael Arlen, "The Prosecutor," in *The Camera Age* (New York: Penguin Books, 1981), pp. 158-79.

11. Ibid., p. 159.

12. Ibid., p. 172.

13. Ibid., p. 173. A Wyoming Grand Jury, dubbed "the 60 Minutes Grand Jury," met for a year on allegations of government corruption stemming from the *60 Minutes* telecasts, but returned no indictments of top officials, including the governor, the mayor, or the state's Democratic chairman, all linked to corruption by the two *60 Minutes* reports.

14. Williams, *Television*, p. 47.

15. Tom Smucker, "Control Factors: The Legacy of Lawrence Welk," *The Village Voice*, November 9, 1982, p. 56.

16. Menaker, "Art and Artifice," p. 233.

17. CBS, *60 Minutes*, September 26, 1983.

18. Sally Bedell Smith, "The Great Chase in Network News," *New York Times*, November 28, 1983, p. C21.

19. There can be little doubt that network news is a high-stakes enterprise. In 1983 it was estimated that the news budgets of the big-three networks were about $150 million each, and that of Cable News Network approximately $50 million. Each evening 30-minute network newscast cost about $200,000 to produce and each 30-second spot sold for between $35,000 (NBC) and $44,000 (CBS). In view of these figures, an anchor's $2 million annual salary does not seem out of line if his presence nets the network an extra $25 million in revenue over the course of a year.

20. Smith, "The Great Chase," p. C21.

21. Edwin Diamond, "Television's 'Great Anchors'—And What Made Them Rate," *New York Times*, March 23, 1980, sec. 2, p. 35.

22. Ibid., p. 40.

23. Orrin E. Klapp, *Heroes, Villains, and Fools: The Changing American Character* (Englewood Cliffs, N.J.: Prentice-Hall, 1962), pp. 46-48.

24. Tony Schwartz, "What's Wrong With Local TV News?" *New York Times*, February 21, 1982, sec. 2, p. D1.

25. Tom Shales, "The Pull of the Pullover," *Washington Post*, February 8, 1982, p. C1.

26. John Berger, *Ways of Seeing* (London: British Broadcasting System, 1972), p. 24.

27. George Comstock, *Television in America* (Beverly Hills: Sage Publications, 1980), pp. 25-26.

28. William A. Henry III, "News as Entertainment: The Search for Dramatic Unity," in *What's News*, ed. Elie Abel (San Francisco: Institute for Contemporary Studies, 1981), p. 134.

29. Marvin Barnett, *Moments of Truth?* (New York: Thomas Y. Crowell Co., 1975), pp. 90, 94.

30. Jacques Ellul, *The Technological Society*, trans. John Wilkinson (New York: Vintage Books, 1964), p. 5.

31. Henry, "News as Entertainment," p. 135.

32. Jeff Greenfield, "Remembering the 1960's, as Seen on TV," *New York Times*, August 12, 1979, sec. 2, p. 25.

33. Williams, *Television*, p. 53.

34. Epstein, *Fact and Fiction*, pp. 204-5.

35. *Report of the National Advisory Commission on Civil Disorders* (New York: Bantam, 1968), pp. 369-73.

36. Menaker, "Art," p. 234.

37. On the local television level, very few individual independent stations or station groups bother to explore the serious long-form documentary as a way of fulfilling FCC public-interest obligations. The high cost and low return scare the local broadcast entrepreneur away. Even the well-intentioned Westinghouse Group-W documentary unit—the Urban America Unit—which did a series of 20 documentaries over a five-year period under executive producer Dick Hubert, could find very few commercial TV stations outside Group-W to take the works (exceptions were WMAL, Washington, D.C.; WHEC, Rochester, New York: WISN, Milwaukee, Wisconsin; and WCBW, Buffalo, New York). Out of 246 public-television outlets, only 13 put the UAU documentaries on, even when they were offered for free. See Barrett, *Moments of Truth?*, pp. 104-5.

38. Data for 1982-83 are interpolated from "Programming" reports of Petry, a station representative who distributes network ratings summaries to station clients.

39. John Culhane, "Where TV Documentaries Don't Dare to Tread," *New York Times*, February 20, 1977, sec. 2, p. D14.

40. Ibid., p. D15.

41. The libel suit is unsettled as of this writing. For background reports on the controversy, see Jonathan Friendly, "CBS Producer Defends Program on Vietnam," *New York Times*, July 17, 1982, p. 44; William A. Henry III, "Autopsy on a CBS 'Expose,' " *Time*, July 26, 1982, p. 40; and John Corry, "Weighing the Facts in Westmoreland vs. CBS," *New York Times*, September 4, 1983, sec. 2, p. 19.

42. Anne Roiphe, "Things Are Keen But Could Be Keener," in *An American Family* (New York: Warner Paperback Library, 1973), p. 22.

43. Ibid.

44. *An American Family*, pp. 236-38.

8

LIVE TV

Sport and the TV Event

Defenders of television frequently celebrate the medium's ability to present events, as they happen, in real time, live, and they glorify the resultant drama of the unpredictable, an open future in which anything might happen. While there indeed may be some cause to praise live television when compared to the stultifying formal predictability and redundancy of such television genres as melodrama, one should be cautious. Ours is an assembly-line lifestyle, whether we admit it or not, in which repetition and consistency produce on the one hand the boredom of the workplace defined by technique, tasks, and productivity quotients, and on the other hand a sense of security, of the known in a world of increasing confusion complicated by high levels of mobility and value systems that shift as if they rest on a bed of sand. In the world of sport, the joy of the unpredictable, with little personally at stake, allows us to momentarily escape the routine, the predictable, and ride a safe psychic roller coaster of victory and defeat, of quick changes in fortune. Like the Congress or the general on the ridge top, our participation is vicarious, our health assured. From the safety of such a vantage point, we can dream of the upset of the decade, or at least of the season, to put the predictable in its place for a moment, to break the all-too-familiar pattern. We hang on to the hope of the miracle finish, knowing with baseball sage Yogi Berra that "it's not over 'til it's over." In other television contexts, we hope that the streaker who briefly derailed the increasingly gentrified Academy Awards ceremonies one memorable year will someday return to the small screen with some new outrage. Thus, on the surface we have a relatively clear-cut rationale for the culture's reveling in the live television event, whether it focus on sports or on the celebrity processional—we're desperately seeking relief, with no personal risk, from the monotony of our everyday lives; we want a manufactured emotional high er even an emotional low. Then after the joy or the despair quickly wears off, we can return to our own world in which our place is as secure as it was yesterday and the day before. We even have a new line of conversation to help us pass the time—"If only he had called for the hit-and-run, the double play would have been broken up; they oughta get ridda da bum;" or, "I can't believe Redford didn't win for best actor."

In the age of television, and now with cable distribution and program development and what critic Les Brown has named "Television II," the American sport fanatic can stuff himself with the vicarious witnessing of the athletic competition of others from daybreak to daybreak, without a break, for all time. There is an entire round-the-clock cable channel devoted to sport—ESPN; a channel devoted predominantly to sport, the USA Network; and three commercial television networks that, within the framework of increasing competition for advertising revenue, each year expand their coverage of major sporting events until it reaches the point of absurdity, as was the case with NBC's 1983 "Breakfast at Wimbledon" coverage, during which the announcing corps barely had an opportunity to gulp their orange juice and start on their toast and jam before the gentlemen's final came to an abrupt and merciful end, leaving the chagrined Bud Collins and uncomfortable Dick Enberg with four hours to waste as they went backward in the tournament to show videotaped highlights of matches seen on earlier telecasts.

Why this voracious appetite for televised sport, especially at a time when increasingly vocal critics of both the genre and the world of corporate sport that provides the grist for the ravenous television *machina* point to the incredible system of values being promoted through sport to generations of susceptible youth? The answers are complex and intriguing, and can be found in the study of contemporary American mythology.

SPORT—THE MERCENARY WARRIOR MEETS THE JOURNALIST-PUBLICITY AGENT

If heroes, as sociologist Orrin Klapp defined them, are social types providing the society with models people try to approximate, and act further as a "photograph" of the society's previous activities, then the respective public symbols, manifested in our sports heroes, of (1) the individual as character/adventurer/wanderer and seeker of joy and personal fulfillment through the playing of children's games, and of (2) the corporate warrior as a celebrated and expendable public commodity, whose exploits are more the stuff of business data than of legend, bring the major shifts in our twentieth-century culture into clearer focus. Further, if social types such as our public heroes represent the essential dimensions of social control—of that which is to be valued, of the proper order of things and people—then a discussion of sport, the sport hero, the sport journalist, and television must, by implication, refer to ideology and the nature of social relations outside the narrowly defined world of sport.

In the relatively closed world of the rural community, which provides the psychic geography for innumerable stories to fuel our culture's myth of the rural middle landscape, the notion of hero is much more closely linked to a combination of one's particular skills and his or her eccentricity—unusual character traits that transcend normative boundaries and lend themselves to the telling, retelling, and embellishing of stories. One's skills and eccentricity are directly related to cultural traditions of long standing, and the links between folk hero and the culture from which that hero emerged are strong and clear—the hero's exploits return something vital to that culture. The famous pitcher who began by throwing baseballs into a bushel basket out behind the barn and who became the tobacco-chawing major-league strikeout king, but who always came back home at season's end to sit around fishin' with the folks he never really left behind is a recurring rural sport motif—fame never spoils the country boy. While such is obviously not always the case, especially in today's world, sport journalists in past years have filled many a rain delay in a baseball contest with such stories. ABC Sports, in a characteristically excessive manner, in its "Up Close and Personal" profiles, features athletes at home in such bucolic settings as a tiny Italian coastal fishing village or a grassy mountainside in the Alps as they enjoy life's simpler pleasures before the agony of defeat once again came to dominate their consciousness. Today's sports yarns are filled with urban pop psychology focused on the inner struggle to succeed.

Far from the rural world of the eccentric wandering sport hero-artisan with character, pride, and the simple values necessary to derive pleasure by spending the bulk of one's productive adult years in pursuit of children's games is today's era of the incorporated sport celebrity and the attendant journalistic celebration of wealth and power at the expense of character. The artistry of sport forms the common boundary between the two eras, but the old-time "magic" is now replaced by technique. Secretly the baseball fan delights in the possibility that the aging 300-game-winning pitcher sweating out there on the mound brushing the bill of his cap and his moist hair on a sultry summer's eve has invoked divine intervention by tossing up a spitter or two, since he cannot strike 'em out anymore with a fast ball (the younger hurlers have the smoke, timed by the computerized speed gun at 95 miles per hour, as if baseball and the Indy 500 were synonymous). The spitter and the knuckler are mystic tokens of the human in sport; and above all, our heroes, to achieve such heroic status, must exhibit human characteristics they then are able to transcend as they reach their exalted positions.

Along with the newfound worship of technique—of speed and power and consistency—comes the celebration of celebrity and a new phase of sport in the television era. C. Wright Mills defined celebrity as "the names that need no further identification, [who are] recognized with some excitement and awe, [and who] are the material for the media of communication and entertainment."[1] In this new world of money and power, finesse—Sandy Koufax's miraculous curveball that "falls off the table," or Tom Watson's "surgeon's touch" with the sand wedge, or Bjorn Borg's uncanny accuracy with a two-handed backhand top-spin shot down the line, or Gayle Sayer's wonderful dancelike quality of changing directions of his run in midair—fades into the background as the emphasis shifts to competition, winning, and nationalism. As early as 1954, Mills found, in the celebration of celebrity, "the star system of a society that makes a fetish of competition. . . . It does not seem to matter what the man is the very best at; so long as he won out in competition over all others, he is celebrated."[2]

The celebrants, led by the television sportscasters who specialize in what critic John J. O'Connor called the "superfluous packaged by the hyperbolic,"[3] invoke warlike, pugilistic language in the service of "color." One player or team "demolishes" or "finishes off" the opponent. Because he is a superb tennis player, Borg becomes "the angelic assassin" who outlasts his underdog American opponent Roscoe Tanner, the folksy innocent "hillbilly from [Lookout Mountain] Tennessee," in the 1979 Wimbledon final.[4] The tennis tie breaker, instituted to speed up the game in the television era, is ominously described by the unflappable announcer as "lingering death," a phrase sure to inject agony into the drama of the contest.

This warlike and, in the case of international sporting events, jingoistic character of the television treatment artificially builds dramatic tension and solidifies allegiances. Individual achievement becomes one more datum in the corporate sport record book rather than a mark of personal style. According to critic Karl Meyer, the catalyst in the "long-postponed passing of the Main Street Myth" in our culture has been the contemporary American phenomenon of marketing.[5] Television packages its audience into "metropolitan units," according to Meyer, and like the citizens of the classic Greek city-states (who, it should not be forgotten, built their classic culture on a bed of slavery), Americans have become possessed by the passion for urban display. In addition to such public symbols of urban wealth and eternal progress as the blockbuster museum exhibition (e.g., the King Tut show), the convention center, the city magazine extolling the glory of *your* community, and the downtown rehabilitation/gentrification, our new contemporary tabernacle—the multimillion-dollar sports complex—provides the modern space for the performance of the ritual combat. Television enlarges the public ritual space to the region, and now with superstations such as Ted Turner's WTBS in Atlanta, broadcasting a single team's schedule (the Atlanta Braves, which Turner also owns) to the entire country, we have, at least according to the television hypesters, "America's team." The athlete becomes a public symbol of the city's status in the competitive world of city pride and ultimately of its economic viability (by encouraging tourism). The symbol becomes so important in some instances that bizarre fan behavior results.* Consider, for example, Cincinnatians' attempt to have the ageless baseball hero Pete Rose, of "Grecian formula" fame, proclaimed a city landmark to prevent him from changing teams. He eventually left Cincinnati for the Philadelphia Phillies, who paid him significantly more money.

If cities were expendable to the mercenary warriors who wander from metropolis to metropolis in search of the golden fleece, so too are the athletes themselves expendable in this corporate sports world of winning. Sociobiologist Edward O. Wilson, in his book *On Human Nature*, posits that the contemporary citizen can easily form, break, and reconstitute alliances and accept, without lasting hostility, the annual buying, selling, and trading of professional athletes and even entire teams as mere commodity deals because he has resolved his

---

*Since "fan" is short for "fanatic," one might argue that no behavior exhibited by such a class of persons could be considered bizarre.

environment into personal identity with an "aggressive" ingroup against an enemy—"an elemental physical struggle between tribal surrogates" in which "teamwork, bravery, and sacrifice" transcend the persona of the sport hero.[6]

Television has contributed greatly to both the athlete's and the city's expendability as it has created its own world of sport (*ABC's Wide World of Sports* heralded the emergence of television as a self-contained world). By paying huge sums of money to professional sport leagues to gain the rights to televise their contests (the television networks reportedly paid about $600 million to the National Football League (NFL) for its 1978-81 cycle, or about $5.8 million per team per year),[7] television has provided the sport franchise with the needed capital to engage in a murderous bidding war for the services of the most talented players—this is most clearly evident in baseball's free-agency rules.[8] On the other hand, with the huge amounts of money a quality player can secure from appearances in television advertisements and with product endorsements (today's professional tennis players and Indianapolis 500 race cars bear an uncanny resemblance to walking/rolling billboards), his or her team or even country loyalty becomes secondary because it plays an increasingly secondary role in his or her celebrity status and generation of wealth (which has become increasingly dependent on televisual opportunities). The athlete/businessperson is thus for himself and increasingly a product of television. We now have Panasonic's ad campaign for "ReggieVision," company video equipment endorsed by baseball hero Reggie Jackson, formerly of the New York Yankees but bought by the California Angels. It is true that newspapers and radio have, for decades, created and traded on the celebrity status of our sport hero, but television has made the sport star wealthy, and has transformed his very nature from culture hero to commodity.

The athlete's exploits are translated into statistics that on the surface "provide subplots for the TV audience, and help fill in dead spots in the action,"[9] but, more importantly and less apparently, give the athletes hard data by which to market themselves. And owners have reams of data by which to confirm the positive effect television has had on professional sport. According to critic William Barry Furlong, ". . . the mating of commercial television with pro football had a wonderful synergistic effect. . . . Attendance has quadrupled in the [Pete] Rozelle era—the modern TV era—and the number of franchises has more than doubled while their market value has quintupled."[10]

While much has been gained by athlete, owner, and television network in a peouniary sense, much has also been lost. Minor-league baseball in the United States and lower-level Third and Fourth Division soccer in England have suffered greatly from the video overexposure of the top-level teams. Because of the constant hype of sport celebrity, community teams such as minor-league or semiprofessional teams are considered second-raters unworthy of much support. The once-mythic exploits, the dusty bus trips, and the roadside diners from small town to small town are now viewed as somehow low class and the underpaid struggling athletes are seen as losers rather than as eccentric characters. Only when there is a human-interest story involved do the high-powered sportscasters dip down in the minors, and the story usually involves a once-great major-league player such as former Detroit pitcher Mark "the Bird" Fidrych, whose bad arm forced him out of the big leagues, but whose spirit and tenacity kept him fighting for a comeback. The minor leagues become places for player rehabilitation on the road back to stardom—a sport sanatorium. The movement toward the development of a caste system in the modern sport and television era is increasingly evident, for television favors only the celebrity, the success, the human incarnation of the myth of eternal progress who sets the new record, whether that record be in yards gained or in prize money won.

Television has even changed the tempo of sport. To meet the insatiable demands for advertising revenues, television has given sport the "television time-out" for commercials. This holds up play and chops up the once-flowing event into a new event structured according to television's time signature (baseball, tennis, and boxing, with natural breaks, don't face this problem, while football and basketball, two of America's most enduring television sports, do). The miserable fan at the site of the event feels as if he is watching his television receiver. Indeed, many fans take small battery-powered sets to the contest to get the instant replay or the isolated camera—the best of both worlds.

The networks' pecuniary motives lead to pumping up even the dullest of contests—dull because one team or person is so far ahead of the other that victory, the sine qua non of contemporary sport, is assured. Viewers, who have through the years been trained by the networks to deal with ends and not means or the process of play, must somehow be induced to stay tuned for the advertisements which pay for the spectacle. Some sportscasters, faced with this dilemma

they themselves have helped create, often resort to ridicule of individual athletes' weaknesses to hold attention.

Television, in its quest for the ultimate continuous entertainment, surrounds the sport activity itself with a variety of other, related TV events—a Kentucky Derby special or a Super Bowl special
featuring people partying, cheering on their team and town, with
many from other places adopting the town and the regional trappings
of the successful combatants—these are the true sport groupies. A
favorite adopted team is the Dallas Cowboys—like the Atlanta Braves,
"America's team." The urban-cowboy look and lifestyle became more
than a regional phenomenon on Super Bowl day. And who wouldn't
want to get a little closer to those cheerleaders? Sport becomes a con-
textual element in a larger social ritual of money, sex, drugs, and
power. The dominant ideology's concepts of success are paraded before the television screen in this flow of competition and desire. When
ninth graders were queried regarding revelations that some of their
Dallas Cowboy heroes were involved in buying, selling, and using
cocaine, they seemed disillusioned. However, such cynicism is normal
for that age. By the time they pass adolescence, many will have come
to accept such behavior as the price to be paid for modern superstar-
dom, for the trappings of celebrity as revealed on television include
drug use as part of the daily video ritual. The myth of eternal progress
admits the use of stimulants to improve performance—within limits,
of course.

Atop all of this activity stands the sport celebrity, the isolate, a
man figuratively "without a country," whose motivation to engage in
sport has increasingly become money, whose responsibility to the
social group is the provision of a brief thrill and emotional uplift without any long-term commitment to the community. He comes into the
community like the gunslinger in the mythic Western, does his business—murders the opponent—and departs for other parts and other
battles.

So the star athlete moves from city to city selling his talents to the
highest bidder, and the fan learns to accept this behavior as he has
accepted the larger social system that produces it. The imaginary realm
of the athlete-celebrity is that of the self-as-ego, the "I." The team is
composed of discrete units, of interchangeable individuals, who sell
their labor power for substantial sums, but who, at the same time,
are robbed of their surplus value by the team owners who make large
profits off their players. The stars in turn cause the labor power of
the minor leaguers to command much less remuneration than should

be the case were the community supporting the local team and not staying home, eyes glued to the big boys racing across the television screen. The public image we have learned to accept is that of the individual celebrity who is free to get rich through his initiative. This image is, of course, a mirage. Thus, when the NFL players called a strike in the middle of the 1982 season, the very idea of a union of players representing the interests of individual celebrity-heroes—the symbolic "we"—turned off sports fans and viewers, who were duped into reverence for the abstract imaginary realm of the "I." That all those "greatests" should have to resort to a union negotiator to gain salary increases is incongruous with their telehyped status. It exposes the guile of the club owners who exploit humans for profit. It also exposes the total confusion of spectators regarding the true locus of pecuniary power that defines contemporary sport—namely, the fiscal arrangements made between the giant television corporations and the power elites that own sports teams and players. On occasion one detects a certain spectator cynicism seething just below the surface, as the realization that the athlete has become a prostitute, selling himself on the semiopen market to the highest bidder, sinks in; and further, as the spectator realizes that the athlete can do this because club owners and sport promoters, anxious to make large profits from their operations, encourage this practice. The losers are the fans, who lose a proper perspective of the nature of heroism and community.

The pecuniary motif in contemporary sport is encouraged by those who pompously refer to themselves as sports journalists or sportscasters; a more appropriate term for the majority of these individuals would be sport public-relations agents, whose main function is to elevate the banal.

Just as the outrageous behavior, on and off the field or court, of such bad-boy sport celebrities as baseball manager Billy Martin, owner George Steinbrenner, player Reggie Jackson, and tennis players John McEnroe, Jimmy Connors, and Ille Nastase "was rewarded by even bigger fees and commercial endorsements,"[11] so too did the outrageous behavior of sportscaster Howard Cosell—a provocateur more than an analyst—lead to the emergence of the superstar sportscaster as hype-artist, a celebrity in his own right, who becomes more important than the event and players he is covering. The sportscaster's actions became the event, the controversy. Clearly situated in the age of telenarcissism, the sportscaster-hyperbolist lives through the sport celebrities he covers. The first important modern television tandem was Cosell and heavyweight-champion boxer Muhammad Ali in the

1960s. In those early days, much to his credit and prior to his rise to telecelebrity status, Cosell cried out against racism in sport and in the society generally and he defended Ali's position regarding the draft, a position which had alienated the entire jingoistic U.S. sport establishment. Then, as Cosell began to build his own television-star status through alliances with such great ones as O.J. Simpson, Broadway Joe Namath, and Sugar Ray Leonard, he became less and less involved with sport and more and more involved in himself.

Like so many other sport hyperbolists, Cosell became so involved in the language he used to describe the event that analysis was lost in what John O'Connor called a "numbing polysyllabic onslaught" which served no purpose other than to demonstrate Cosell's erudition, but upon careful semantic scrutiny, proved instead his ineptness. Examples of such linguistic pretensions abound: Reporting the content of an interview he conducted with boxer Michael Spinks, Howard stated, "I had to ask Michael some of the key questions circumscribing his whole career."[12] That is to say, Howard talked to Michael about his life. Or, describing the shift of control of a boxing contest from one fighter to another, Howard let loose with a veritable barrage of words: "a sharp change in the tide of affairs of these two men." Cosell's use of English is analogous to the advertising lingo anthropologist Jules Henry dubbed "parapoetic hyperbole"—the use of high-flown figures of speech that resemble, but are not, poetry to make the subject appear more significant or important or powerful than it is in actuality. Cosell, the self-as-ego, meets the bad-boy athlete self-as-ego. Together they frame the television transaction of sport-celebrities we love to hate, the "big properties" in a web of vaudeville, propaganda, and money.[13]

The mirrors are everywhere distorted as the boundaries between journalism, sport, and commodification blur. Such was the case in the January 1983 NFL playoff game between the Dallas Cowboys and the Green Bay Packers, carried on CBS. John Madden, former Oakland Raider coach and now color man for CBS, was doing this game. We see him in the "Bowling Alley" spot for Miller Lite Beer, bursting through a wall with a bowling ball, as befits his reputation as a brute, and hamming it up. We then cut back to the game, with Madden urging Green Bay's right tackle to block better downfield. It's hard to take Madden seriously, although his analysis, as revealed on the isolated camera, is technically accurate. In that same contest, Cowboy coach Tom Landry, who is continuously held up as a paragon of the humanist-athlete devoted to Christian causes and good sportsmanship, is seen in an American Express advertising campaign spot we shall call "Cowboys and Indians." The famous coach is seen comin' in off the dusty trail. Sporting a long trail coat and a huge ten-gallon hat that reminds one of an old Three Stooges getup, the venerable Cowboy enters an old-West saloon only to be surrounded by Redskins (the Washington variety). He uses his American Express card to buy a drink. The ad is very clever. We cut to the game and a shot of Landry pacing the sidelines in a modern-day sport coat, tie, and hat. The roles both Madden and Landry play in the advertisement are, of course, all in good fun; and why shouldn't one make fun of oneself on television? Howard Cosell made numerous appearances on sitcoms, Bob Hope specials, and celebrity roasts, always playing his inimitable self. He even had his own variety show for a brief time on ABC. All these tele-celebrities are winners, in coaching, journalism, acting, hosting, and toasting—in short they are among our culture's premier entertainers. And that is what televised sport is ultimately all about—the celebration of success according to the dominant version of the American Dream. That dream does not have a spot for losers, except as the butt of public jokes about their ineptness, as is the case with ex-major-league weak batsman Marv Throneberry, now famous as a star of Miller Lite commercials. Losers are hooted out of town from the stands and the press boxes by the likes of Cosell, for association with the loser makes the egocentric telecelebrity vulnerable. There are exceptions. Joe Garagiola, a very minor figure as a major-league catcher, became a major figure as genial host of NBC's *Major League Game of the Week* and now laughs in public about his marginal performance behind the plate and in the batter's box—all the way to the bank, one should add.

The ultimate hypocrisy and the shameless use of ideology to camouflage the true social relations of contemporary professional and even amateur sport in this country are best exemplified by the high moral tone sportscasters such as Cosell take toward the other members of their profession as well as toward athletes. The following examples of such confusion of values are taken from a fascinating interview conducted by Chicago public-television station WTTW's John Callaway, with Cosell as interviewee. The interview was aired nationally on PBS on November 12, 1981. About sport journalism, of which he has been the major national symbol for the past decade, Cosell argued, "I thought about the hypocrisy involved in sports journalism. And I thought about Edward R. Murrow. And then I thought about sports and the sanctity given to it. And I find more personal integrity in doing a movie with [Woody] Allen than in doing a big-time college game with the bought-and-paid-for players who don't even, in most cases, belong in college and who don't ever get degrees."[14] The Super Bowl, according to Cosell, is "another excess in the world of sports"; "a prolonged hype"; "a corporate enterprise—most of the seats and most of the suites are held by the great corporations"; and "Commissioner Rozelle's party, which now costs anywhere from eighty-to-one-hundred-thousand dollars for the print medium, is frankly a disgrace." Of the athletes, Cosell complained:

> All athletes are heroes, to the point where they become surrogate parents in many American homes. When, as a matter of fact, an athlete may be an addict, he may be an alcoholic, he may be a whoremonger . . . and is hardly equipped for heroism because he can hit a baseball or catch a football. And then as wrong after wrong and corruption after corruption is exposed in the sports world, where have the media people been through all of the years? Any why are they so desperately afraid of and resistant to truth in sport?"

Finally, of newspaper sport journalism, Cosell complains, "The very hypocrisy and contradiction of our sports pages in this country is almost self-evident; . . . the sports pages appear now as a series of tout sheets, listing the point spreads and inviting the very gambling that leads to college scandals we talk about."

Cosell, who "symbolized within sports the rise of the television superstar over the print superstar,"[15] has had numerous internecine battles with print sport journalists who claim his bombast, combined with television's need for constant action, is wrecking the image of American sport and sport journalism. Who are we to believe? The overbearing telecelebrity Cosell we see and hear on our television receivers, covering Monday-night football or the Kentucky Derby or the major-league baseball playoffs? Or the moralist we find granting interviews about the sad state of sport and sport journalism in our society? Such an obvious confusion of values borders on the schizophrenic and does nothing for the concerned sport fan except sadly to obfuscate the important issues regarding the nature of sport and the character of those who engage in the public ritual of sport, both players and reporters.

SPORT AND IDEOLOGY—TELEVISION MYTH IS THE UNOFFICIAL TEXT OF THE 1984 OLYMPICS

Amateur athletics are not exempt from the hype and the pecuniary fixations of professional sport. Indeed, the boundary between

the two categories is increasingly blurred and is today seemingly beyond recognition. There are the recruiting violations that repeatedly
plague big-time college football as the drive toward the national
championship and the resultant school prestige and added income for
the school's sports program encourage coaches and recruiters to bend
the rules.

More insidious and more intriguing in the context of this chapter
is the current state of international amateur competition and especially of that most visible context, the Olympic Games. Here, in the
tradition of the Greek Olympiad, idealized by contemporary media,
the athlete, transcending *realpolitik* and ideology, is a mythic competitor in a game which allows him or her to demonstrate grace, agility,
power, finesse, and stamina—all elements of the well-conditioned body
guided by the intelligent, resourceful mind—the stuff of mythic heroes
whose praises were sung by the bards. In the spirit of civilized competition between mutually respectful people, the victor is rewarded
with laurel and is congratulated by the vanquished, who will redouble
his or her effort in an attempt to be victorious at the next games. The
reality, of course, is a jingoistic battle between warriors who often
serve as unwitting pawns in a high-stakes game of international politics and transnational marketing strategies.

The athlete becomes the ideological vehicle—the public token of
the national will. No clearer example of such ideological duplicity can
be found by this author than in a provocative 1983 Miller Beer advertising campaign, which is representative of the corporate approach
to the celebration of athletic success. Miller's "This American Dream"
campaign features one spot, which I shall label "that kid's out there,"
in which we see a young handsome, muscular black runner whose
dream is to win the Olympic 400-meter run. After his daily job, he
goes to a deserted track somewhere in urban America and runs by
himself. At this point, his dream is probably just that, and will remain
so; alas, with institutional support, provided by your friendly neighborhood transnational corporate conglomerate such as Miller, he will
succeed because he is able to train at the Olympic Training Center.

How easily and conveniently this entire commercial fairy tale
ignores the reality of the political-ideological fiasco of the U.S. boycott of the 1980 Summer Olympic Games, held in Moscow, in protest over the Soviets' invasion of Afghanistan and the Soviets' boycott
of the 1984 Summer Olympic Games, held in Los Angeles. In the
former case, the institutions, who had prepared our athletes for those
"apolitical international" games, deserted those athletes by capitulat-
ing to the desires of an administration whose vaguely defined and ill-

conceived foreign policy took precedence over this American Dream. NBC, which was to cover the 1980 games, recovered most of its investment in the games through its insurance with the British firm Lloyds. The athletes were not as fortunate.

What do the Olympic Games mean? To a nation, they may mean pride, or in some cases saving face. To a competitor, they may launch a professional career in some sport such as boxing or hockey or skiing or football (which has recruited on occasion from Olympic track stars), or they may simply be valued for the national-hero status they confer on winning contestants. To a transnational corporation, they may mean large profits through public relations. Motives are often difficult to discern, although a careful scrutiny of the "quest-for-the-gold" hype of American television sportscasters might lead the skeptical observer to conclude that the network sports divisions, in search of dramatic tension and preoccupied with quantification of achievement and margin of victory, have turned the Olympiad and other world-championship amateur competitions into bloody battlegrounds on which national honor and even national legitimacy is won or lost.

The 1984 Summer Olympic Games, Southern California style, meant, above all else, big business. The thrill of victory and the agony of defeat in this competition involved which corporate conglomerate got official sponsorship status, or, to a lesser degree, who became an official licensee or official supplier. The benefit or bottom line, as the moguls like to call it, in this way was "a shinier public image, a bigger market share."[16]

The Los Angeles city government, the host for the games, amended its city charter to prohibit government subsidy of any cost overruns. They turned instead to private industry for financial support. By April 1983, more than $116 million had been generated in corporate sponsorship and advance royalty fees. This was an exclusive of the ABC television-network contract by which ABC paid $225 million for U.S. television rights.

The 1980 Winter Olympic Games in Lake Placid, New York, had 181 official sponsors—companies who pay large sums to the Olympic Committee in exchange for an exclusive in their industry and are allowed to display both the official Olympic symbol and official mascot of the games in their advertising and public-relations materials. In contrast, the 1984 Los Angeles Olympic Organizing Committee (LAOCC), a group of private business and professional people, went after the high rollers by limiting sponsorship to 30 companies and requiring a minimum payment of $4 million for sponsorship.

The major corporations put up huge sums of money for the games, although by their fiscal standards, this is a small price to pay for such patriotic public relations. Atlantic Richfield (ARCO) spent about $30 million in connection with the Los Angeles event, including a gift to the city of $4 million to refurbish the Los Angeles Coliseum and build practice tracks. ARCO Olympic program manager Earl McKinley frankly admitted the purpose of ARCO's participation —to "positively influence the media, politicians, and the community."[17] With businesses, especially oil companies, constantly complaining about unfair media treatment, the linking of sport, politics, and public-relations efforts in such a visible and ostensibly neutral forum is ideal.

Anheuser-Busch, America's largest brewer, contributed about $10 million in sponsorship money and planned to spend about $20 million on advertising related to the games. While it did not declare any of its beers the official Olympic beer, its ads showcase "the free enterprise system."

McDonald's, which won the race to become the official fast-service restaurant of the Olympics (we know what that is a euphemism for), built the new Olympic swim stadium on the campus of the University of Southern California, another $4 million gift to the city. Fuji Photo Film, an American subsidiary of a Japanese transnational corporate conglomerate, beat out Kodak as the official photographic products, with a sponsorship gift of $5 million in cash. Fuji intended to "dispense free film to authorized media staffers."[18] Not content to rest with free gifts to photojournalists, Fuji developed a high-school photography course, the final lesson of which was a photo contest, with the winner receiving a free trip to the Los Angeles Olympic Games. Having infiltrated educational curricula, with the assumed support of the educators, the task was complete.

In addition to money from sponsors, approximately 50 companies became official licensees out of an estimated 3,700 requests. Each licensee signed a royalty agreement for its product, with a minimum guarantee by the licensee of $150,000 to be paid to the LAOOC.

Official suppliers "normally provide a half-million dollars worth of their products to the games in exchange for the promotional exposure," with smaller companies providing less. According to Dan Greenwood, LAOOC vice-president for sponsorship, the smaller contribution is acceptable because the small companies "aren't going to exploit the trademarks that much."[19] Greenwood's frank, if unwitting reference to degrees of exploitation reveals the true nature of these arrangements.

Why should the Olympic Games be any different from any other hyped sport event? Why shouldn't heroism on the field of sport be used to sell beer, hamburgers, gasoline, film, and the glories of the free enterprise system? In the name of ideology, major international athletic competition becomes a televised celebration of the American Dream of material success, of the power of the giant transnational corporate conglomerate that seemingly recognizes neither geographical nor moral boundaries. The 1984 Summer Games are a true television Olympics, with 23 sites spread over 200 square miles of Southern California. While "the freeway Olympics" may be a headache for the live spectators, television viewers, who sit back and enjoy the contests as if they were all in one small physical area—the area of the small screen, are content to sip their official beer and munch on their official burgers, not much caring about complaints of the lack of international camaraderie, itself a form of cruel myth perpetuated by those who seek to legitimize the jingoistic spectacle. Rumor has it that Mayor McCheese was seen practicing for the 400-meter breast stroke in a giant-McLympic-sized pool. All things are in their proper places.

THE TV EVENT—PREDICTABLE AND UNEVENTFUL

If televised sport has become predictable as celebrity hype with attendant values, so too has the nonsport live television event—our country's contemporary ceremonial.

In the TV event, we find the stars of many different celebrity systems drawn together. It is truly a world of champions. It is also "the pinnacle of the prestige system and a big-scale business."[20] Television creates, selects, and celebrates celebrities. Celebrities are put on display. They also use media. As television has gained in both power and prestige, a class of professional celebrities has solidified its power base through continual use of the medium. Entertainers, entertainment businesspersons, champions of sport, famous artists, journalists, and commentators, through their regular appearances in a variety of television contexts, become household words, names of those we come to admire and respect. We await their appearances at our public ceremonials, the televised rituals of awards presentations, national political conventions, celebrity roasts, and tributes from our hallowed national cultural institutions for those ancient artists whose careers have reached their twilights.

We hope to see our celebrities, in the living-room intimacy of television, somehow unmasked—to know something of their human quality while still reveling in the mystique of their status as stars. What we now get, according to critic Michael Arlen, is a television event that is "increasingly fine-tuned and over-directed until [its] point . . . often seems to be no more (and no less) than [its] televisability."[21] The Academy Awards, in the early days of television, before its tremendous visceral power to mold public opinion was clearly understood, featured cigar-smoking, visibly inebriated Hollywood celebrities dressed in outrageous costumes, seated around tables, thoroughly enjoying the party but often losing their composure under the scrutiny of the television camera, which they surprisingly seemed either unaware of or uninterested in. Today's public ceremonial in Tinseltown finds well-behaved, rather conservatively dressed (for Southern California at any rate) young men and women sitting in rows of theater seats in the Dorothy Chandler Pavillion graciously applauding the awardees and "the new 'Internationale' of pop music."[22] The celebrities are confined to brief winners' speeches, the emcees read quickly from the teleprompters, and the commercial breaks are precisely orchestrated in the tightly scripted format. As is the case in the well-planned sovereign processionals for the coronation, marriage, and death of monarchs and their heirs, the event now must, at all costs, run right.

Of course, the only time that the liveness of television really emerges in these increasingly dull video realizations of spectacle is when some brave or slightly demented soul injects the human act by tearing up the script and becoming confrontational; when a Vanessa Redgrave or a Paddy Chayefsky or a Marlon Brando engages in a polemic about the Palestine Liberation Organization, or McCarthy's blacklisting of artists in the 1950s, or the plight of the American Indian; and when the voices of the Hollywood establishment (the dominant entertainment culture), famous faces such as the biblical mug of Charlton Heston, counter that the awards ceremonies are no place for personal politics or ideology (as if the writer, director, or actor were somehow a neutral person with no ideas of his or her own or with no right to state those ideas they do have in a nonnarrative context—at least not during a program sponsored by Revlon or General Motors—and further, as if the television extravaganza itself were outside the realm of ideology and politics—an obvious patently false conception to begin with).

What we are given at presidential tributes to the arts are visions of the cafe society as the Reagans, their invited guests, and millions of bored television viewers who have tuned in for the live event are treated to a pas de deux performed under a grotesque White House chandelier and paraded out as a celebration of American artistic genius, while thousands of progressive cultural workers have found their government-funding support evaporate like a shallow creek bed in a drought.

Our political conventions, especially those of the Democrats, were once vital, fascinating fora for the exercise of the political process, at which party delegates would wrangle, bolt from one faction or another, stage demonstrations, and argue passionately over the language of the party platform. Since the Chicago Democratic Convention of 1968, with the riots in the streets and the rough handling of television journalists in the convention hall itself—all carried live and uncut to an incredulous nationwide television audience—party officials have done all within their power to manipulate the media coverage to prevent any controversy from reaching the American televiewers. The Republican public-relations experts have in fact succeeded in turning their conventions of recent vintage into mirror images of the Academy or Emmy Awards (one might even claim the Grammies) with songs by Donnie and Marie, dancing, polite applause, and mindless public speeches. The conventions even end on time—at the end of prime time—something the Oscars cannot even yet claim.

Television has organized the event as it has sucked the life from the event. The procession of celebrity, while orderly, is dull.

There are larger social questions raised by the relationship of television to our reverence of the professional celebrity. As this chapter has repeatedly emphasized, the professional celebrity in the era of television, while revered by the fan, stands somehow outside the pattern of everyday social relations, although not outside the values of most citizens. Of course, this fact is endemic to the very quality of celebrityhood. The social function of celebrityhood is less apparent. C. Wright Mills finds that an important function of the celebrity in contemporary social relations is the use of the celebrity by the country's "power elite"—the economic, political, and military bosses—to help them avoid the spotlight of public-media attention. In Mills's argument, the professional celebrity becomes an important and necessary media distraction, channeling the energy of the masses into hero worship. Mills suggests that for clearly defined reasons, namely, the continued consolidation of their true economic and political power, the power elite is "quite content to rest uncelebrated."[23] Karl Meyer finds an essential class bias concealed in the myth of eternal progress as manifested in the worship of celebrity and fed to the flock by the latest marketing techniques. For the institutions and their workers who have achieved celebrity status appeal to the needs of demographically upscale audiences. The classic theme of the new city-statism or urban regionalism, according to Meyer, is inequality. Thus "money is available for 'blockbuster' shows but not for humdrum museum conservation; for municipal stadiums and convention centers but not services for the poor; for 'gentrification' of townhouses, while slum areas are redlined."[24]

Our distractions are expensive in a larger social context, for while we sit down to our beer and popcorn and watch the parade of tele-celebrities pass before the camera lens on our "free" television, brought to us by official sponsors, the pecuniary system of social values is solidified and the material gap between the haves inside the set and the have-nots sitting at home watching them widens. The American Dream is to be celebrated in living color with voiceover commentary supplied by the electronic pundits of our age.

NOTES

1. C. Wright Mills, *The Power Elite* (New York: Oxford University Press, 1956), pp. 71-72.

2. Ibid., p. 74.

3. John J. O'Connor, "On 'Chats' and Chatty Sports Announcers," *New York Times*, July 26, 1981, sec. 2, p. D25.

4. John J. O'Connor, "Sportscasting—Over-Explained, Over-Researched, Over-Hyped," *New York Times*, July 29, 1979, sec. 2, p. 25.

5. Karl E. Meyer, "Love Thy City: Marketing the American Metropolis," *Saturday Review*, April 28, 1979, p. 16.

6. Quoted in Meyer, ibid., p. 17.

7. William Barry Furlong, "The Monster Is Lurking Just Over the Hill," *Panorama*, March 1980, p. 51.

8. The NFL has an exemption from antitrust laws, which allows it to pool its television income, rather than each team generating separate income according to the number of television appearances it makes. By pooling or giving equal shares to each team, the NFL attempts to maintain a league-quality balance.

9. Joan M. Chandler, "TV & Sports: Wedded with a Golden Hoop," *Psychology Today*, April 1977, p. 75.

10. Furlong, "Monster," p. 51.

11. David Halberstam, "The Mouth That Roared," *Playboy*, December 1982, p. 130.

12. O'Connor, "On 'Chats'," p. D25.

13. BBC sport coverage, like newsreading on the British network, is markedly different from American television's sport coverage. BBC commentators are less verbose, generally much more insightful, and focus on analysis of the play rather than on the personalities of the players or on their status as multimillionaire celebrities.

14. Cosell did play-by-play of the assassination of a dictator in Allen's film *Bananas*.

15. Halberstam, "Mouth," p. 130.

16. Chris Barnett and Richard J. Pietschmann, "American Business Goes for the Gold," *United: The Magazine of the Friendly Skies*, April 1982, p. 77.

17. Ibid., p. 82.

18. Ibid.

19. Ibid., p. 80.

20. Mills, *Power Elite*, p. 74.

21. Michael J. Arlen, "The Big Parade," *The New Yorker*, April 30, 1979, p. 122.

22. Ibid., p. 123.

23. Mills, *Power Elite*, p. 91.

24. Meyer, "Love Thy City," p. 20.

9

TV RELIGION
AND
THE TV GAME SHOW

The Great American Dream in
the Late Twentieth Century

The television preacher is this culture's most peculiar and most provocative version of the entertainer-celebrity. A true splendid performer, his ego-driven quest for notoriety has served this country's conservative political and industrial elites well, diverting attention from their ideological regime of ever-increasing centralized control of production and capital accumulation by redirecting the barely contained anger of the exploited rural and urban poor toward the alleged evils of twentiety-century social reformers who are, they declare, tampering with both the word of the Lord and each person's "right" to lead his own life. This modern-day theocrat has manufactured a new ideology based in the American Calvinist theological tradition by incorporating the dogmatic idea of the "right ordering" of self, family, and state—of total control of every aspect of everyday life in order to glorify God—and in the late-nineteenth-century conservative American socioeconomic theory of individualism, which held that the government should provide an orderly society in which the individual is protected as he fulfills his destiny, and which accused the secular government of unduly meddling in man's destinies. The television preacher has buttressed his ideology with the myth of the puritan ethic and its promise of reward, through God, for hard work. The result is an intense video celebration of an American social ethos revealed in the mythic constructs of eternal progress, as manifested in entrepreneurial capitalism; of the frontier, with its rugged individualism; and of manifest destiny, with its single-minded philosophy of conquest sanctioned by God—conquest of geography, bank accounts, and souls. In short, the electronic preacher is the exemplification of the Great American Dream of the "now generation," television style. A study of the electronic ministry becomes a study of television's self-reflexivity, of television imitating itself ad nauseam. The video realm of power and progress is clearly revealed in the imaging system that marks the new religion. Establishing shots divulge the conspicuous splendor of the video church, which is, more likely than not, a massive television studio with live audiences supplying the background enthusiasm.

In one particularly elaborate electronic church/studio, the audience dutifully and very politely applauds a pop singer's "easy-listenin'" rendition of some religious tune—pure Lawrence Welk from the golden age of television. Extreme close-ups of these preachers' intense, Rasputin-like gazes and their occasional wistful stares into space, evoking the vision of settlers preparing for the conquest of the American West, captivate millions of sedentary American living-room parishioners. One notorious electronic minister, following AT&T's ad-campaign advice to "reach out and touch someone," goes so far as to lay hands on your television screen. The viewer knows this electronic prophet is working overtime to drive away the devil as he sweats profusely under the Klieg lights, exhorting God to "heal . . . heal . . . heeeeeaaaaalll!"

The fundamentalist social subculture, which today claims a very large following, estimated variously between 55 and 80 million persons throughout the United States,[1] traces its lineage to groups such as the lower-class rural Virginians of the late eighteenth century. According to American cultural historian Russel Blaine Nye, "The small farmers of the Piedmont and the artisans of the towns were rough, proud, individualistic, turbulent people. They were Calvinist or evangelical in their religion, with little sympathy for the gentlemanly deism or Anglicanism of the Tidewater."[2] Today, Virginia boasts a concentration of electronic ministries, from Jerry Falwell's rural Thomas Road Baptist Church in Lynchburg to Pat Robertson's mammoth suburban-style Christian Broadcasting Network operation in Virginia Beach.

With this subculture's roots so closely linked with Calvinist dogma and its notions of the inherent sinfulness of humanity, is it any wonder that so many Americans tune in regularly to be reminded of their debased condition—of their fall from grace—something the television melodrama, and especially soap opera, has specialized in for decades, and to revel in the side-show spectacle of its temporary subjugation as the preacher, resembling a combatant on all-star wrestling, puts an "atomic drop" on the devil and adds a Bruce Lee karate chop for good measure. Television is a medium which, against its own best pecuniary interests exposes the soul in all its banality—"up close and personal," in the words of that indefatigable sports announcer-celebrity Howard Cosell—just as it unflatteringly reveals the wrinkles, which makeup will not hide, in the aging actor's face. It is through the television minister, with his crass pecuniary motives and perspiring insincerity, that the true colors of bourgeois culture stare out at us from behind the curtain of grace.

Not far from the sacred realm of television preaching, in the root cellar of the human imagination, dwells that other modern entertainer-celebrity—the television game-show host. He wears ostentatious haberdashery the television preacher wears, but adds a bit of Southern California-calculated informality, such as a plaid sport jacket or an open-necked shirt and love beads. His on-air attitude is clearly analogous to his teleevangelist counterpart—a curious mixture of smug condescension and used-car-salesman hard sell. He exhorts his prey—the contestants—to bare their souls to the millions in the audience by dressing up in outlandishly degrading costumes or by abandoning all public decorum by uncontrollably gesticulating and feigning excitement at the slightest provocation (the bemused viewer, buying into the entire charade, revels in the possibility that the insane contestant has messed her pants). Their actions are direct confessions of their abject complicity in this debasing public spectacle of greed and narcissism.

The essential difference between these two television forms is that the latter, rather than glorifying the socially conservative work ethic, celebrates instead sloth and chance, although the contestants must work hard—a new form of American work—to be noticed by the host or his agent by exhibiting some provocative or bizarre behavior, and by virtue of such behavior, be selected to appear on the show. Yet the religious show and the game show are similar in many ways, not the least important of which is their promise of instant salvation —that money, either donated in the former instance, or won in the latter, will release the victor from some psychic or physical suffering. These shows are the epic odysseys of our time—electronic journeys of punishment and the quest for release. As critic Edwin Diamond cynically wrote, "On God's television one prays for God's help to get a new car or a higher paying job or a better apartment . . . and the unremitting faith in getting the world's goods makes these programs resemble 'The $20,000 Pyramid' or other television grab shows."[3]

Pat Robertson told his *700 Club* audience one night that Jesus would help them find parking spaces. The money must have flooded in from desperate New Yorkers who hoped that Robertson was on to something.

Aesthetically, the pacing of these shows is remarkably similar, although their formats are distinct. Miracles or clues to the merchandise behind door number two are revealed to the show's participants and the home audience at breakneck speed. There is incessant small talk, periodic singing or music background, and always selling. Don Pardo, rattling off the list of prizes "donated" for the daily jackpot, bears a striking resemblance to the born-again local bible-hour guest breathlessly speaking in tongues. Cries of joy and hallelujahs are heard from the winners, sobs from the losers (although the electronic preachers talk about losers in the past tense). There is continual tension and its subsequent release. This is great television drama.

THE GOSPEL ACCORDING TO JIM BAKKER ET AL.

There was a mood of apprehension at the *Praise The Lord (PTL) Club* in Charlotte, North Carolina, in 1981. Jim Bakker, poor boy from Muskegan, Michigan, who went on the road to preach for the Pentacostal Assembly of God and who was now spiritual leader of a multimillion-dollar television ministry, was under investigation by the Federal Communications Commission for possible misappropriation of funds. It seemed as though Bakker's pleas for financial support for his overseas missions had produced substantial contributions, many of which may have been diverted to domestic projects under Bakker's control. These projects included the continued support of his large electronic ministry and construction of his Christian camp and retreat center—"The Total Image Center"—a $100 million project in Fort Heritage, North Carolina, complete with chalets and a school of evangelism. His Christian financial television empire (the *PTL Club* bought approximately $7.5 million worth of air time on nearly 200 television stations and 3,000 cable systems in 1979) seemed to be on the skids —a common malady claimed by television preachers as they press their pleas for support—having lost 50 affiliates in early 1981. In the backs of the entrepreneurial minds of Jim and his spunky little wife and cohost, Tammy, must have been the old dictum, lately revised to meet the tenor of the times: "He who lives by TV shall die by TV." Like the Roman Empire of old, the electronic church, in the hot battle for souls, may get carried away by the quest and ignore the dangers of overextended supply lines.

Televised religion clearly represents the confusing contemporary social milieu wherein, in the constant clash of traditional values and industrial drives, competition emerges victorious at the expense of cooperation and our cultural orientation gradually and subtly shifts from reciprocity to struggle and survival at the level of the individual, not for the group. This is manifested both in the attitudes and praxis of the electronic minister himself as the survival of his ministry takes precedence over theological issues related to the nature of the Gospel; and in the electronic parishioner, whose salvation is linked to prayer inextricably tied to monetary contributions to support the ministry's regime of communication satellites and opulent university complexes, for which he is recognized individually through such cunning public-relations gimmicks as inclusion of his name in a prayer tower subsequently sealed for eternity. This lends a sense of exclusivity to the religious act, analogous to one's gaining membership in some prestigious country club. And, while the individual souls of the electronic church's faithful major contributors are so saved, the society as a whole, say the electronic preachers, is rapidly going to the dogs, courtesy of Communist sympathizers and homosexuals who undermine family bonds, while traditional respect for the authority of dominant institutions, such as the corporate state apparatus, diminishes.

What is ironic about this incongruous mixture of pecuniary philosophy and traditional values manifested in electronic religion is the resultant transformation of these very traditional values the electronic church extols into their opposites. As cultural anthropologist Jules Henry noted, "Since values like love, truth, the sacredness of high office, God, the Bible, motherhood, generosity, solicitude of others . . . are the foundations of Western culture, anything that weakens or distorts them shades traditional life; . . . as it embraces the traditional values, pecuniary philosophy chokes them to death."[4] This state of affairs, termed by Henry "value deterioration through monetization," occurs when certain cultural forces, such as religion, not ordinarily considered part of the processes of production and selling, are used to make money.

The electronic church is, on its most basic level, a contradiction in terms. Religious values and the hucksterism associated with commercial television entertainment can at best coexist in an uneasy alliance. While it provides an important basic service to one segment of the population—the shut-ins, who would not otherwise enjoy the sense of community offered to the mobile by the neighborhood spiritual center traditionally associated with organized main-line religion of all denominations—the electronic church, needing—or so it claims —the intensive capitalization necessary to play the big-time television game of prestige and profitability, to secure, in short electronic cultural legitimacy, moves beyond this limited social function toward a new role as contemporary polemicist and moral watchdog in the worst traditions of 1950s McCarthyism. The motto of the electronic preacher, who has learned how to milk the dramatic possibilities of television, might well read: "First get their attention; then save 'em." And from what are they being saved? First, from themselves, in the cynical Calvinist tradition. Second, from communism and, according to the ideological scheme, its American offspring—evil liberal secular humanism. The electronic preachers offer hackneyed political dogma sandwiched between clean all-American entertainment, packaged in a late-night talk-show format perfected by that secular humanist Johnny Carson, but minus Carson's wit and sexual innuendo. The neatly scrubbed, racially balanced Gospel singers, who graduated from the "Muzak School of Tunes and Human Factor Engineering," provide the up-tempo ambience for a celebration of success—the great American Dream of eternal progress in the suburban middle landscape. Critic Dick Dabney wrote disapprovingly that TV evangelists were "raising money by selling miracles—and hard-selling them especially to the poor, the ill, and the desperate, . . . [equating] New Testament Christianity with the worship of success."[5] The incongruity of these celebrations of winning is clear to Christian critic Virginia Owens, who wrote, "The original pattern these people profess to imitate was [that of] a vagrant celibate whose own seminar on happiness elevated the mourning meek rather than the smiling success."[6] The winners in this new era of pecuniary religion, who have been saved from themselves and have subsequently come to know both Christ and King Midas, parade through the ether to testify. The stories of human degradation and ultimate salvation are the preludes to the inevitable pitch, which takes a myriad of amazingly inventive forms in the glorious tradition of television ad campaigns, but interestingly without the polish the studio acts and lavish sets seem to portend. The pitches are often made on videotape, and are generally very quiet compared with the preceding razzle-dazzle. In the CBN studios, Pat Robertson asks the viewer to send him $100 or more along with "seven lifetime prayer requests." The viewer's name and requests are then put on microfilm and interred in something called a "prayer pillar," upon which rests a table top and a large King James Bible, in the center of the prayer chapel in the CBN building. The pillar is sealed and the donor's salvation guaranteed—at least for this year.[7] At the PTL Club, Jim Bakker asks the viewer to send him $1,000. In return, this lucky soul receives an illustrated heirloom Bible with a "stamped antique gold cover," with the donor's name printed on it.[8] If you happen to tune in Rex Humbard's television ministry and contribute, but fail to continue your contributions, you may receive a personalized word-processed letter, which reads: "Dear . . .: Last week I knelt at the prayer altar to pray for every member in the Prayer Key Family Book, and I wanted to pray for you . . . but your name was not there." Ernest Angley, the TV faith healer who lays his hands on your television screen, offers a modest package. For only $100, you receive 16 audio cassettes that contain the complete New Testament. This seems the best deal of the lot.

The quiet pitch for financial support becomes the preacher's down-home ruse—a mark signifying he hasn't forgotten his roots. His electronic overhauls remind his followers of the humble rural-middle-landscape mythology that undergirds the entire electronic religious imaging process. The electronic preacher uses this poor-country-boy heritage to great advantage as he stresses his own humble beginnings in the context of his successful rise to power through hard work, single-mindedness of purpose, and prayer. These are stories involving faith, love of family and children, and folksiness. There is Jim Bakker's story, recounted briefly earlier. There is Oral Roberts, poor Oklahoma farm boy who now has a home on the edge of a Palm Springs country club. There is Pat Robertson, a seeming exception to the tale of the self-made Christian. Son of a U.S. Senator from Virginia and a Yale graduate, Robertson has nevertheless made the best of this potentially problematic heritage (after all, the Piedmont farmers of 150 years ago had little respect for the likes of Thomas Jefferson and the Tidewater intelligentsia). He claims he fled his posh Manhattan apartment, his wealth, and his secular emptiness to return to his Virginia roots and his Bible study. Upon conversion, Robertson claims, he gave all his worldly goods to the poor. Yet somehow he sent four children to college, has horses, a beautifully furnished house, and an office described as luxurious.[9] There is Dr. Robert Schuller, genial host of *The Hour of Power*, an Iowa farm boy who came to Southern California in 1955 with $500 and an organ in a rented U-Haul trailer, started a drive-in church on top of a snack bar of the Orange Drive-In Theater, which he used from 1955 to 1961, and now preaches from the $15 million Crystal Cathedral, designed by architect Philip Johnson.

How is it possible for these teleevangelists to be so visibly successful and yet continue to lay claim to their inherent humbleness?

This is accomplished through the contemporary advanced capitalist mechanism of the fringe benefit or perk—that extra benefit beyond salary that freshens the deal. Indeed, if one looks at the teleevangelists' salaries, one gets a highly distorted view of their wealth. According to a Cable News Network special report on teleevangelists, aired in 1981, the average salary for an electronic minister of some visibility was $45,000-$60,000 per year, yet they had "considerable expense accounts" and "rent-free mansions."[10] In 1979 Robert Schuller reportedly had a salary of but $39,000. He was driving a Cadillac Seville donated by a wealthy parishioner.[11] As C. Wright Mills wrote in *The Power Elite*, the new power elite camouflages its wealth in stock options and benefits other than "visible" salary. And, as the newest members of this American power elite, the teleevangelists are no exception to the rule.

This powerful battery of myths—of the humble beginnings and family support in the rural middle landscape; the rugged individualism of the frontier, which encourages the humble minister to venture unafraid into unknown territory in hopes of establishing a viable ministry; the single-mindedness of manifest destiny; and the entrepreneurial success of the "now" suburban middle landscape—coalesce in the vision of the Great American Dream, late twentieth-century style. To understand the power of such a social construct as presented in the lives and words of the teleevangelists, one must recognize that the predominant audience for television worship is rural, southern or southwestern (although there are many provincial viewers in large east-coast metropolitan areas as well), and traditional in its value orientation; but these people are also the children of the camera age, with its constant imaging focused on urban luxury, competition, shifting values, and individual achievement. The ecclecticism of the television church fits comfortably into this seemingly contradictory mythic structure. Like the characters on *Dallas*, whom we love to hate, the electronic church allows us to view ourselves—acquisitive, competitive, successful, anomic, and full of sin—and to reconcile ourselves to the contradictions we observe. We mollify our self-hate; and we send money for this ecclesiastical legerdemain.

All this is a far cry from the individual "justification by faith" of Martin Luther. Indeed, the entire apparatus of the electronic church flies in the face of the Reformation, which asserted the sovereignty of God over both the individual and the religious institution. How does the *700 Club*'s and the *PTL Club*'s pecuniary salvation differ in intent from the medieval Catholic papacy's sale of indulgences to the German city-states to gather money needed to build elaborate basilicas?

As was the case with the church's construction of monuments to its own power, the teleevangelists likewise construct vast media edifices to legitimize their authority and to spread the "word." The Christian Broadcasting Network tapes the *700 Club* in a 400-seat studio with a live audience. The studio cameras, RCA TK-47s, are connected to state-of-the-art one-inch-videotape recording equipment. The studio lighting is computerized. And the studio is but a small part of the $20 million CBN headquarters complex, which includes television studios, corporate offices, and a graduate school in Christian communication. Robert Schuller's Crystal Cathedral is pure Southern California. His weekly *Hour of Power* program is taped there. The song-and-dance extravaganza, reminiscent of the most lavish of Cecil B. DeMille sets, fits perfectly in the all-glass tower. The glass entrance features doors 80 feet high and 12 feet wide. Architect Philip Johnson, the cathedral's designer, noted that "the opening of those doors will look great on TV. Dr. Schuller knows exactly what he's doing."[1][2] The *Praise The Lord Club* of Jim Bakker is taped before a live studio audience in Charlotte, North Carolina, in an extravagant studio complex rivaling that of CBN. Oral Roberts's telecasts, taped at the Maybee Center television complex at Oral Roberts University in Tulsa, Oklahoma—the Disneyland of America religion—use equipment equivalent to that used in the NBC network-television studios in New York. The electronic preachers, being practical men, understand that the television audience has come to expect the very highest technical quality from their religious programs. The local Gospel hour, with its "hot" preacher, taped either in a closet studio with torn draperies, cheap microphones, and uneven lighting, or in a cavernous auditorium with awful acoustics conjuring images of a shoot-out in a warehouse reminiscent of *The Untouchables*, is unacceptable to today's multimillion-dollar religious entrepreneurs. Oral Roberts, in his earlier television faith-healing days, preached in such an environment. But he has grown up with the medium. And the younger electronic preachers followed suit.

As mentioned above, these elaborate facilities confer status on their owners and build credibility, which allows them to continue to spread the word. And the word is "control." The most intelligent and ambitious of the teleevangelists, men such as Pat Robertson and Jerry Falwell, have a clearly conceived world view of theology, economic theory, political theory, and sociology woven together to form an articulate, if highly debatable vision of human nature and contemporary social response to human needs.[13]

The world view articulated by the teleevangelists begins with their fundamentalist theological position—that is, a literal belief in the Bible. The word of the Lord dominates all discussion of lifestyle, politics, and economics. The viewer must come to know Jesus directly. Traditional theology would have this happen as one contemplated, in silence, in the presence of other worshipers, the mystery of the spiritual. Further, the hiddenness of religious meaning, according to traditional theological argument, would, upon one's participation in sacred "initiation rites," be revealed to the true believer.[14] Teleevangelists give this traditional theology a contemporary twist, best expressed by CBN's Pat Robertson through his so-called kingdom principles. According to this scheme, one comes to know Jesus through a combination of prayer and giving. If the viewer gives to Jesus, Jesus will give it back to the viewer. And the most effective and efficient way to give to Jesus is to give money to his slave, the teleevangelist—in this case, Pat Robertson. Through his kingdom principles, Robertson thus encourages his audience "to believe that they can buy miracles."[15] Further, if one is in desperate financial straits and still manages to give to Jesus, through Robertson, out of one's need, that person will achieve even greater power. This, cynically translated, means you give your social-security check to Robertson and his ministry, do without heat, and eat white bread and gravy every day. To the middle class, Robertson preaches a modified version of the kingdom principles; namely, that these upwardly mobile Christians should refrain from purchasing that new house so that they might be able to maintain their contributions to his ministry, and through it to Jesus. The twist here is that by answering Robertson's call to give, economic miracles may flow. The unemployed man may get that job offer he has been desperately seeking. The struggling entrepreneur, on the verge of bankruptcy, may swing that big deal which was always just beyond his grasp. Hope is held out in exchange for an investment in Robertson's ministry, with salvation as a fringe benefit. These people have worked hard, fallen on misfortune, and, through the miracle of Jesus Christ, with the intercession of the teleevangelist, will be saved.

While the Bible suggests Jesus will bring the believer tribulation as a test of his or her moral commitment, the new teleevangelical interpretation has Jesus bringing instead riches, an interpretation appropriate for its television context. The televised religious experience is, first of all, public, not private or communal. It is preformulated and one-way. It is immediate, rational, highly planned, and carefully bud-geted—in short, it has clear secular overtones dictated in large measure by the medium that carries it, and by the culture created in large measure by that medium. As such, the new television religion stands in direct contradistinction to the traditional main-line religion, a stance the teleevangelists are quick to defend.

The television preachers declare that main-line religious theology is at odds with today's "supposedly spontaneous spirituality," is dull, and preaches an increasingly liberal secular doctrine.[16] In contrast, they argue, they offer contemporary religion to which people can re-late. They see little virtue in solitude, humility, or frugality. They are upbeat, preaching personal, if not social, optimism and the ethic of success—what one critic termed "brisk, no-apologies materialism."[17] Jim Bakker can say, with a straight face, "Diamonds are made for Christians, not Satan."[18] Robert Schuller, the champion of "possi-bility thinking," a strange mixture of religion and economics, can pro-fess the "economics of Christianity"—a doctrine aimed at middle-class Christians stressing personal pride, business success, and charisma, the latter defined by one of Schuller's guests, professor David Schwartz, as divine spirit given to mankind, which man must use to make mon-ey.[19] Schuller's program, *The Hour of Power*, is the personification of this Christian ethos. The service is a mixture of pop Christian tunes, in the manner of Barry Manilow, sung by elegantly gowned soloists using wireless hand-held microphones. The imaging is decidedly high-tech. Camera work is flawless and well rehearsed, and relies on dis-solves, through flower arrangements and gently waving palm trees, from a large choir to Schuller's son Robert A., engrossed in prayer. Schuller's son is the warm-up for dad's appearance. The transition between son and father is the inevitable pitch for money, which has included, as a gift for one's contribution, a coffee mug inscribed with Schuller's motto: "If it's going to be, it's up to me."

This new religion has a deeply troubling implicit premise; namely, "An ordinary life is contemptible and . . . there is a magical way out."[20] The premise is revealed in two highly disparate ways. In the Calvinist religious traditions of fundamentalism, we watch "the tele-vised confessions of frailty, guilt, misdemeaner or felony," which "be-come inspiration events, . . . the equivalents of revivalist baptisms."[21] Bakker's *PTL Club* once had a children's puppet segment in which the puppets were singing, "How do you spell relief? J.E.S.U.S." This motley scene was modeled on the advertising jingle for Rolaids antacid tablets. The children were being relieved from original sin. Such analogizing of moral status and indigestion is offensive to the religious and areligious alike because it reduces higher questions of the meaning of being human to the level of over-the-counter commodities. On another level, in the tradition of mid-twentieth-century American individualism, the most important Christians have become the Christian superstars of the public-media world. Singers such as Pat Boone, Robert Goulet, and Roy Rogers and Dale Evans; actors such as Efram Zimbalist, Jr.; athletes such as Sugar Ray Leonard; politicos such as Chuck Colson of Watergate fame and former radical Eldridge Cleaver; and chicken magnates such as Colonel Harlan Sanders, have all appeared to testify on the *700 Club* or another of the Christian "talkies." The world of Christian winners, like the secular world upon which it so consciously models itself, offers a world of champions to the downtrodden viewer—a media world in which the stars of a variety of systems are drawn together to celebrate their success. This is "the star system of a society that makes a fetish of competition."[22] This celebration of celebrityhood draws attention to the economic power and social prestige of the teleevangelist, who is able to achieve the coup of getting top-name talent on his show. And it lessens the blow of economic-class and social-class status inequality associated with celebrityhood by revealing that even these superstar heroes were once humanly weak. As always, spiritual equality is presented as transcending material inequality. This rationale sets the stage for additional requests for financial support.

The realm of superstar media Christianity is reinforced by an entire Christian lifestyle-marketing strategy, which fits nicely into the cool ambience of the suburban middle landscape of the Christian talk show a la *PTL Club* and *700 Club*, and the suave elegance of Schuller's Crystal Cathedral. This new Christian lifestyle is strictly suburban middle landscape. Its psychographic profile would include achievers—prosperous, middle-aged Christian materialists—and emulators—ambitious young Christian adults. The resentful, poor sustainers, who are more likely to relate better to the heavy-handed Elmer Gantryism of a television faith healer like Ernest Angley or Rex Humbard or any of a variety of local or regional "UHF preachers," are outside the purview of this new upper-middle-class Christianity (although these sustainers are attracted to the messages of Pat Robertson and Jim Bakker, who can successfully play both sides of the Christian scene—a tribute to their media performance skills).

The scope of Christian lifestyle marketing is far reaching, with books on Christian cooking, diets, exercise regimes, money-making strategies, athletics, sexuality, and psychology—a perfect mirror of secular culture. There are conference ministries, the "retreat centers," which critic Virginia Owens calls "genial exercises in relaxation."[23] There are Christian lifestyle workshops in such areas as assertiveness training, feminism, and cooking. There is the Christian entertainment industry with its concerts, record companies, agents who book appearances and determine, through market research, the hottest-selling theology of the day, and Christian nightclubs that sell overpriced soft drinks. The mass-produced romance is "going Christian" as Silhouette Books, a $140 million publishing enterprise, released its sixth and newest line of formulaic romantic novellas—this one called "Silhouette Inspirations"—in early 1984. These romances will be, according to the Inspirations editor-in-chief, "entertaining stories about wholesome people who have made a commitment to God in their lives."[24] Twenty-four new titles, each 192 pages long, will be released each year and will be sold in religion sections of secular bookstores.

The image underlying the new Christian lifestyle is "impeccable cultural accommodation"[25] to the secular world, as the teleevangelists seek the financial support needed to fuel their ever-expanding media machines. And it is a small step from lifestyle into direct involvement in the affairs of state. It is in the latter realm that the role of the teleevangelist has stirred bitter controversy, not only between television preachers and secular critics, but also between television preachers themselves.

John Cotton, a seventeenth-century Puritan clergyman and a leader of the Massachusetts Bay Colony wrote that fundamentalism prescribed "perfect rules for the right ordering of a private mans soule . . . a mans family, yea, of the commonwealth too, so farre as both of them are subordinate to spiritual ends."[26] Cotton staunchly defended the colony's policy that men were admitted to citizenship only if they were church members, irrespective of their social status. Cotton was a highly articulate spokesman for a fundamentalist Christian aristocracy and monarchy. Today's most vociferous television ministers would agree with Cotton that the ideal form of government is a Christian theocracy. How this is accomplished, however, is open to dispute. Billy Graham cautioned that television ministers should avoid the political arena, and that television transformed "staid politicians into glib media stars. The same process could devour preachers and their ministries."[27] Graham, a close friend of Richard Nixon, urged teleevangelists to speak to moral issues, not to endorse political causes or support political candidates. Graham's argument is, of course, specious, for morality and politics are inseparable, as Cotton knew so well.

Today, if one needs a "mandate from the people" as well as from God to lead in the political arena, then the most prominent teleevangelists believe they have that mandate, based both on the sheer quantity of declared "born-agains" revealed by recent survey research, and on the fervent qualitative commitment of these people to the born-again dogma. A 1979 Gallup survey, for example, funded by 29 religious groups, found that 34 percent of those interviewed considered themselves born-again Christians.[28] A 1982 Gallup survey, quoted by Graham, found that one-third of the Americans in the sample said they watched religious programs during the seven days prior to the survey, and most said these programs were evangelical. A 1981 Nielsen survey found that during the survey period, 1.36 million households (or about 4 million people) watched Oral Roberts's weekly program *Oral Roberts and You*, 1.26 million households watched Robert Schuller's weekly *Hour of Power*, 690,000 households watched Jerry Falwell's weekly *Old-Time Gospel Hour*, and 413,000 households watched Jim Bakker's *PTL Club*.[29] These programs are among the most successful of the evangelistic shows carried by hundreds of over-the-air television stations throughout the United States. Schuller's program is picked up by about 150 television stations in the United States and Canada, and 82 stations on the U.S. Armed Forces Network; Robertson's *700 Club* is carried by about 150 television stations and about 2,800 cable systems which pick up his CBN channel; Bakker's *PTL Club* is carried by about 200 television stations and 570 cable systems which carry his PTL Television Network. It has been estimated that more than 62 million people worldwide watch Oral Roberts's Christmas and Easter television specials. With such a potential power base, it is little wonder that Falwell, Robertson, and others believe that a political mission is an integral part of the ideology of their ministries.[30]

While each minister has his individual political goals and philosophy, there is a commonality to their basic political thought. The New Christian Right, as the political movement is called, has an implicit political platform. It adheres to the constitutional principle of freedom of speech (i.e., the church should be free to condemn the evils of misguided liberals). It believes in the separation of church and state (i.e., the state should stay out of the church's affairs). And it believes secular authority has lost control, that America is being held captive to the whims of Communists, homosexuals, proabortionists, feminists, liberal politicians and Supreme Court justices, pornographers, and "bloated consumerism." In short, America is diseased. According to CBN's Pat Robertson, we suffer "values confusion" and seek answers for our confusion in pleasure and secular therapies which are doomed to failure. This "embattled view" offered by television ministers would have us believe that our real enemy is "secular humanism," which holds that God is irrelevant to the conduct of our everyday lives, and that secular authorities are playing God by enculturating the nation's children, through amoral secular education, to believe in "moral relativism" and theories of evolution. Further, according to this line of reasoning, liberal politicians "robbed the working class to create for themselves a huge constituency of debased, supine, viscious lumpen" whose existence was destroying the moral fiber of American society.[31] This argument is not new. It was advanced in the early nineteenth century, long before evolutionary theories had been developed, by politically and socially conservative Christians of the Christian benevolent societies. Between 1815 and 1830 nearly a dozen moral reform societies were established to counter threats to social control by irreligious democrats espousing egalitarianism. These groups—the American Tract Society, American Bible Society, American Sunday School Union and others—dreamed of a nonpolitical Christian Party ensuring a one-party system open to moral talent and the natural superiority of Christian leadership.

Robertson is correct that secular education is "amoral." However, his definition is incorrect—the amorality comes in the enculturation of obedient students into a regime of consumption and unproductive leisure and in the preparation of these students for mindless work as white-collar proletarians, enculturation of which Robertson would approve so long as the children were also taught to give money to Jesus through the *700 Club*.

To reinstall a politics of morality in the United States, Robertson offers his "earthly program," which advocates (1) Christians taking control of education from the secular humanists and fighting government attempts to impose racial quotas on generally segregated Christian schools in the South; (2) Christians deserting main-line religious denominations which have become irrelevant; (3) Christians controlling their own media; and (4) Christians assuming power in the federal government. Redemption of individual souls is insufficient according to this regime, which calls for nothing less than the redemption of amoral American institutions themselves, accomplished through the auspices of teleevangelism. If it takes church involvement in politics to remove bureaucrats from control of social welfare programs, that's what must happen. After all, it is argued, it is the church's duty to deal with destiny, not the secular government's duty.

In this battle for control over the destiny of America, Jerry Falwell has declared "[I will] gamble my ministry . . . on saving this country."[32] As spiritual leader of Thomas Road Baptist Church, Chancellor of Liberty Baptist College, and head of Moral Majority, Inc., a political organization approximately one million families strong, Falwell's goals include the election of conservative Christians to political office, and the clean-up of television, which he calls a "vendor of perniciousness."[33] Falwell, along with the Reverend Donald Wildmon, founder of the National Federation for Decency and chairman of the Coalition for Better Television (CBTV) have initiated an organized program of monitoring television programs and rating both them and their sponsors according to the level of decency displayed. Since 1977, they have pressured sponsors of programs they disapproved of to drop their sponsorship. Such "hit lists" of programs and advertisers, while making a mockery of First Amendment principles, are justified by the organization on grounds of moral obligation. This vehement video crusade has been countered in the media by liberal television producer Norman Lear, who founded People For The American Way (PAW). PAW has produced a series of television commercials featuring celebrities such as Mohammad Ali as well as "regular folks" that stressed pluralism, secular humanist individualism, and the tired liberal concept of the free marketplace of ideas. The battle between the dogmatic Christians and the tired liberal pluralist wealthy was tragicomic. Both missed the basic issue of economic inequities existing throughout the society and the invidious control of social discourse regarding the location of control of the means of production of material goods and culture. The debate was about abstract concepts of morality and relative freedoms. Questions of morality as it relates to actual social structures and daily life were largely ignored. It was a debate without substance.

On April 29, 1980, the "Washington for Jesus March," organized by Pat Robertson and others of the New Christian Right, attracted 250,000 born-agains to the nation's capitol. Robertson claimed the March was not political, but rather one of repentence. The fervent marchers had listened to Pat Boone sing at Robert F. Kennedy stadium the previous night. The United States hostage rescue attempt in Iran had just failed and the country was questioning the political leadership ability of its highest elected officials. The message that a tele-evangelist would risk his entire ministry to save America was sweet music to the ears of the disenchanted who watched America lose a war in Vietnam, saw a President resign in disgrace, heard a President declare that there was a "malaise" in this country, and recalled how they sat in their overheated automobiles waiting to buy gasoline after the Arabs had turned off the petroleum. Pat Robertson had been predicting Armageddon in the Middle East both on television and in his CBN newsletter *The Perspective*. It appeared many were listening.

One wonders about the net change when one set of powerful suburban-middle-landscape entrepreneurs and actors is replaced by another set of powerful suburban-middle-landscape entrepreneurs and actors. Both groups wear three-piece pin-stripe bankers suits; drive Cadillacs; live in luxurious mansions; make relatively modest salaries while garnering substantial fringe benefits which make life exceedingly comfortable; and profess to care about the rights of the poor while hiring the best lawyers to find every conceivable tax shelter and loophole and thereby increase the tax burden on these same poor who are being cared for. The difference between the two groups is that one group claims a moral imperative in civil government while the other claims a moral imperative in divine rule. In either case, the Great American Dream of eternal progress is paraded across the airwaves as false hope is encouraged. Which group in closer to the truth?

The New Christianity is cast in the image of the Great American Dream of unproductive leisure and "lifestyle," in which discourse on social relations is bracketed and the language spoken by the electronic church is increasingly pecuniary language, camouflaged by political rhetoric which preaches the need for moral equality while ignoring economic and social inequality and in many ways reinforcing such inequality.

THE GOSPEL ACCORDING TO CHUCK BARRIS

No one speaks pecuniary language better than Chuck Barris, the P.T. Barnum of contemporary television entertainment, whose game shows delighted the perverse entertainment appetites of millions of television viewers in the 1960s and 1970s, and who, at least for the time being, is mercifully absent from the small screen. His early works, *The Dating Game* and *The Newlywed Game*, each with a fifteen-year run, revealed his disdain for authentic human relations. *The Newlywed Game* featured couples revealing their intimate activities on their honeymoons and their first months together to an audience of video voyeurs. In the process, they sometimes revealed some strong reservations they had developed regarding their partner and the marriage— secret thoughts they had withheld from each other in their everyday lives, but now revealed to each other in public. Their confessions were often accompanied by embarrassed glances and occasional open hostility. Barris, whether out of sadistic pleasure or not is hard to say, kept a scorecard of his contestants' marriages and found forty percent had subsequently ended in divorce. This is perhaps not unusual, since the divorce rate during the period in the larger culture was also high. Barris's later works, *The Gong Show* and *The $1.98 Beauty Show* featured contestants, thirsty for television exposure, making absolute fools of themselves for the most minimal of prizes. Barris's work thus may be characterized as the purest form of exploitation of one's fellow human beings—that which preys upon their feelings of insignificance or inadequacy in their everyday lives and allows them a moment of video exposure in exchange for their naive complicity in their own exploitation for their owner's profit. This is nothing other than a slaveowner-slave relationship, where the exploited ephemeral television celebrity is purchased and displayed as a commodity, as a fool, before the invited quests—the millions of television viewers.

Whereas the teleevangelist relies on the display of successful winners to make money, the game show producer relies on losers to the same ends. After watching hundreds, if not thousands, of average Americans being ridiculed on his programs, and after amassing a sizeable personal fortune in the process, Barris does not acknowledge that degradation occurred. Rather, he feels that "95%-97% of these people" were "real, not phony," and were "having a ball." He adds that one cannot "purposely, knowingly humiliate somebody because a person knows in advance that it's coming and they can avoid it if they have any brains at all."[34] This cynical view of the inherent stupidity of his guests is reinforced by Barris's admission that "if I was married, and we love and respected each other, I just know that my wife and I would never go on *The Newlywed Game*."[35]

At his peak Barris, once director of daytime programming at the ABC television network, was producing 11 hours of prime-access-time programming a week through his independent production company. He is probably most famous for *The Gong Show*, which aired from 1976 through 1980 and featured such aspiring "talent" as Murray Langston, the "Unknown Comic," one of the show's better acts, and the infamous Popsicle Girls, which Barris said was his most memorable act. Popsicle Girls were two attractive young women who came out in shorts and halter tops and proceeded to provocatively suck away on Popsicles. The show was "knocked off the network West of Chicago," according to Barris, who was forced to apologize to the president of the television network who had vigorously complained about the show's lack of taste.

Barris went a step further with *The $1.98 Beauty Show* as women, many homely, obviously talentless, and seemingly desperate for attention, competed in a talent contest and a bathing suit competition which was ostensibly a parody of the Miss America Pageant, but was in reality a study of female degradation. Outraged critics called for its quick death. With *The $1.98 Beauty Show*, Barris, "one of the few men who really understands the outrageously exhibitionistic, tabloid-shallow nature of what is the only art form ever devised for accountants,"[36] seemed to have burnt himself out and slithered away from television.

Barris's television of exhibitionism and sexual innuendo is rivalled if not equalled by other representatives of the genre, including quiz shows and game formats featuring celebrities on the skids, such as *The Hollywood Squares*, and the "cynical exploitations of middle-class greed,"[37] *Let's Make A Deal, The $25,000 Treasure Hunt,* and *The New Price Is Right*.

The suburban middle landscape lurks just behind door number two, as *Let's Make A Deal* storms into millions of television households. More than any other daytime game show, *Deal* represented what critic Karl Meyer termed "that epiphany of greed."[38] The show originated in 1965 in its daytime version on NBC. In 1968 it moved to ABC and took with it a loyal following of nine million daytime viewers (the evening version attracted 27 million viewers), and transformed ABC's entire daytime ratings standing. Between 1965 and 1978, the total income from the show earned by its host Monty Hall, the most kissed man in America, and producer and former symphonic oboist Stephan Hatos, was about $45 million. In 1976 alone, the pair earned $11 million. In the 13-year period 1965 to 1978, *Let's Make A Deal* distributed over $31 million in prizes over its 3,800 programs, more than any other game show, and gave product manufacturers thousands of free plugs in the process.

Structurally, this game show format required no skill, not even the rote memorization of early quiz-type programs. It did require chutzpah, however, as Hall selected 31 contestants, known as traders, to appear on the program. Prospective contestants arrived at the studio in outlandish costumes. The more ridiculous, the greater the chance of being recognized and perhaps selected. The lucky 31 would then be given opportunities to win cash and prizes, and would dutifully quake, scream, pogo, or cry upon victory or defeat. Hall would often apply the subtle torture technique to his hapless victims by describing, in the vaguest terms, the prize just won before revealing its true nature. An automobile might turn out to be nothing more than a replica of the Beverly Hillbillies' jalopy. A swimming pool might in fact be a 6-foot plastic wading pool with a rubber duck floating in it. The audience laughed as the contestant squirmed, at first puffed up like a bantam rooster, but soon deflated as he rode Hall's roller-coaster of luck and exploitation. The rudimentary video performance work by the contestants was the heart of the show. However, after a few screenings, the gestures were worn out. One could tell that the contestants had watched other contestants run through the same repertoire and had practiced the successful scream and the winning leap. But millions kept watching. The stinger was the "big deal," which three contestants had a chance to win, but only one would eventually claim. Behind one of the three doors were cars, motor boats, trips to Las Vegas, and cash to spend for the lucky big winner. True, the pathos of *Deal* could not equal that of a famous earlier game show of 1950s vintage, *Queen For A Day*, in which five downtrodden women would spill their stories of misfortune to a sympathetic studio audience and the winner, chosen by studio audience approbation registered on an applause meter—the woman with the biggest tear-jerker—would win a mink coat and an automatic washing machine to help with her five orphaned children's laundry. But *Deal* did provide suspense to the very end. Hall and Hatos were defensive about their show, as well they should be, claiming that "they want the program to be seen as a symbolic statement about the glories of competition and the rewards of American life."[39] And the contestants' motives are clear—they want something for nothing. Everyone, it seems, is deceived, even the viewers at home who must take a secret joy in watching the greedy contestant lose, put in her place for such a public display of tastelessness, while they simultaneously fantasize that they were "there," on television gunning for the big deal. The prizes, right out of the suburban-middle-landscape catalogue, are ones with which we are all familiar— wall-to-wall carpets, trash compacters, gas bar-b-cues, patio furniture, automatic electric organs which play by themselves so you don't have to take lessons to be a musician, and self-polishing linoleum floor covering. "You have just won a replica of Ward Cleaver's house!" Applause.

The ultimate blending of the suburban-middle-landscape game show and that other daytime staple, the suburban-middle-landscape soap opera occurred in a queer, short-lived NBC program titled

Wedding Day, aired in 1981. Critic John J. O'Connor called this program "the ultimate level of exploitation."[40] Far removed from the self-evident fantasy of the get-rich-quick game show, yet tied to the same mythic frame of reference, *Wedding Day* was a voyeuristic celebration of petit bourgeois mediocrity. It was *Goodbye Columbus* done with a straight face. Its attempt to provide a background of everyday life's realism for a ceremony of transition, a wedding rite, without any clear sense of the meaning of relations between people perhaps goes far to comment on the root of the contemporary malady of marriage failure in the larger society. When reduced to the status of soap opera, complete with painfully inept love poetry extracted from the most insipid greeting-card culture, the unoriginality of pecuniary culture is laid bare before us. The show, produced in association with the Osmonds, Donny and Marie, featured hosts Mary Ann Mobley, Miss America 1959, from Mississippi, and Cable News Network reporter Huell Howser, from Tennessee. The Southern charm associated with the civil society and its emphasis on traditional values is as self-consciously exuded as is the obvious discomfort of the participants, who reenact their bachelor party, bridal shower, and wedding ceremony in the television studio before a live studio audience who applauds each successful stage. The ceremony is held on a revolving stage, which turns 180 degrees so the couple can exit to the reception and cut the cake. It is at the reception that, for making complete fools of themselves, they receive their reward—a water skiing boat and a honeymoon trip to a secluded island such as Pango Pango. The cycle now completed, the pay-off gathered in, the couple splits for a happily-ever-after life on the lake. We know, however, from the soap opera context that there will be rocky times ahead of our newlyweds. A stranger with more money—a mysterious physician with a skeleton in his closet, will enter and destroy this happy household. Meanwhile, the hapless viewer can dream on of this elegant material life which simultaneously attracts and repels, which one can never quite achieve no matter the effort.

Where did all this quest for prizes and brief electronic notoriety originate? One might trace the genre to its first highly successful program, *The Quiz Kids* of the radio era. A national favorite from mid-1940 through 1951, and on television until 1956, *The Quiz Kids* featured precocious children answering difficult questions. Like today's *College Bowl* spin-offs, knowledge was equated with memorization of facts and rapid recall under pressure—signifiers of rationality in the age of science and national competition and implicit in the myths of eternal progress and manifest destiny as they guided the outlook of a nation first at war and later in a Cold War. The radio quiz kids toured the country selling war bonds and entertaining the troops at military bases during World War II. The genre reached its peak in the 1950s just before the quiz show scandals revealed the sham behind the glorification of American "genius." It was revealed that "brilliant" contestants on programs such as *Twenty One* and *The $64,000 Question* had been given answers in advance so that more popular contestants could dethrone the unpopular champions and had faked the looks of intense concentration and perplexity to build suspense. The payoff was large, even in those years' dollars. With *The $64,000 Question* and similar programs thus exposed, the nation was forced to examine, if only briefly, television's lack of integrity and its representation of pecuniary social relations in which the currency of exchange consisted of lies and deception. *The Quiz Kids* is back on television, the wounds of the quiz show scandals healed and generally forgotten. This revival, produced at Boston television station WNAC, was syndicated in New York City and eight other markets in 1980. Five contestants, aged 7-14, participated on each show. The three with the top scores were called back the following week. In the true spirit of intellectual competition on television, the producers hoped "that, after a while, viewers will respond to the personality and intellect of the individual contestants and will root for some and against others."[41] Joel Kupperman, an original radio "Quiz Kid" who became a national celebrity and who now teaches philosophy at the University of Connecticut, criticized the whole concept of the programs which "encourage people to come up with fast and superficial answers to questions."[42]

How can a television executive with a conscience allow these travesties to air on his station? The answer is two-fold and simple. First, as a successful product of pecuniary society, a worshipper of the Great American Dream of eternal progress, and an inhabitant of the suburban middle landscape, he can accept these works of television as legitimate celebrations of the American spirit. Monty Hall and Stephan Hatos were obviously sincere when they thus defended *Let's Make A Deal.* The strength of the myth is, after all, the fact that it *is lived* and thus not transparent to those whose lives are deeply involved in its celebration and perpetuation. Second, in a medium "created for accountants," the genre makes ultimate good business sense. It cost $30,000 to $50,000 to produce five episodes—an entire week's worth—of a game show for syndication in 1980. It cost a minimum of $130,000 *per episode* or $650,000 to produce five episodes of an original situation comedy for syndication.[43] This 15-to-one cost ratio lays the matter to rest.

THE GOSPEL ACCORDING TO THE BIBLE BOWL

"Coach" Jack Gray's television ministry originates in Tulsa, Oklahoma, a decidedly upper-middle-class southwestern city exemplifying the new America of wealth and power derived from natural resources. Oral Roberts University and Roberts's City of Faith hospital, dedicated to finding a cure for cancer, are there. Oklahoma is a football state. The citizens are proud of their Oklahoma Sooners, for decades a major college football power appearing at least twice each year on television. In the best traditions of both southern-style fundamentalism with its tent-show revivals, and football with its intense competition and substantial pecuniary rewards for victory, Coach Jack offers us *The Bible Bowl*. This children's show, a mockery of *The Quiz Kids* on the one hand, and of religion on the other, features two teams—"the bible boys" versus "the gospel girls"—who compete for prizes which range from a five dollar bill for a bible boy or gospel girl who gets the correct answer to a question such as "who walked on water?" to first crack at a giant gloppy bowl of ice cream for the winning team at the show's conclusion. Before the opening kick-off, Coach Jack sits in the Christian locker room and discusses the upcoming contest and the religious theme for the day with a cardboard robot that lights up. The kids, all clean, smiling, and eager to please Coach Jack and win that five dollar bill, jump up and down and shut-up on command. A tiny huckster resembling Marjoe Gortner and Jimmy Joe Jeeter of *Mary Hartman, Mary Hartman* does the breaks as Coach Jack prepares the half-time pitch, in which he sells the Bible Bowl board game for only twenty dollars. Later in the contest he takes a time out to ask parents to send money so he may continue his enlightened ministry which brings so much joy to kids.

While this program must be seen to be believed (it has run on the Christian Broadcasting Network since the late 1970s) a certain ideology is obvious to even the most naive among us. In the successful world of the suburban middle landscape, unquestioning obedience to dominant patterns of social control will produce pecuniary rewards. Believe in America, eternal progress, competition, and Jesus and you will be a big winner. You win goods, trips, and even salvation by getting the right answers which are not open to debate.

This rational world of the quick fix, of the person in himself, not for the group has come to define the basis for contemporary social relationships in advanced capitalist America. The teleevangelist and the game show producer and host clearly reveal our own weaknesses to us, and for that perhaps we should be grateful—and, of course, send money.

NOTES

1. Edwin Diamond estimates there are 55 million "born-again" Christians in the United States. See Edwin Diamond, "God's Television," *American Film*," March 1980. Dick Dabney speculates there may be as many as 80 million "conservative" Christians. He does not define this term. See Dick Dabney, "God's Own Network," *Harper's*, August, 1980. A 1979 Gallup survey, funded by 29 religious groups, and quoted in John Mariani, "Television Evangelism: Milking The Flock," *Saturday Review*, February 3, 1979, found that 33 percent of the survey respondents considered themselves "born-again" Christians. This would place the numerical total at around 75 million Americans.

2. Russel Blaine Nye, *The Cultural Life of the New Nation* (New York: Harper & Row, Publishers, 1960), p. 114.

3. Diamond, "God's Television," p. 32.

4. Jules Henry, *Culture Against Man* (New York: Vantage Books, 1963), p. 62.

5. Dabney, "Network," p. 52.

6. Virginia Owens, *The Total Image, or Selling Jesus in the Modern Age* (Grand Rapids, Michigan: William B. Eerdmans Publishing Company, 1980), p. 37.

7. Dabney, "Network," p. 46.

8. Diamond, "God's Television," p. 30.

9. Dabney, p. 38.

10. Cable News Network, "Televangelism," a special report with reporter Jim Clancy, 1981.

11. Mariani, "Television Evangelism," p. 25.

12. Ibid.

13. An excellent discussion of this overarching social theory is contained in Jeffrey K. Hadden, and Charles E. Swann, *The Rising Power of Televangelism* (Reading, Mass.: Addison-Wesley, 1981).

14. Owens, *Total Image*, p. 47. We shall set aside for now the question of what to do with those found "unworthy" of initiation.

15. Dabney, "Network," p. 40.

16. Owens, *Total Image*, p. 62.

17. Diamond, "God's Television," p. 32.

18. Ibid.

19. *Hour of Power*, October 2, 1983.

20. Dabney, "Network," p. 40.

21. Mariani, "Television Evangelism," p. 23.

22. C. Wright Mills, *The Power Elite* (New York: Oxford University Press, 1956), p. 74.

23. Owens, *Total Image*, p. 67.

24. *Publisher's Weekly*, July 21, 1983, p. 66.

25. Owens, *Total Image*, p. 37.

26. Perry Miller and Thomas Johnson, *The Puritans* (New York: American Book Co., 1938), p. 209.

27. Billy Graham, "TV Evangelism: Billy Graham Sees Dangers Ahead," *TV Guide*, March 5, 1983, p. 5.

28. Mariani, "Television Evangelism," p. 23.

29. Peggy Charren and Martin W. Sandler, *Changing Channels* (Reading, Mass: Addison-Wesley Publishing Company, 1983), p. 102.

30. Recent data, compiled from a variety of sources indicates that in 1983 there were over 60 syndicated religious television programs, three major religious cable television networks (CBN, PTL, and Trinity), 38 full-time religious television stations, 66 cable systems owned by religious organizations, 1,400 Christian radio stations, and 125 pending Low-power television applications submitted by the Radio and Television Commission of the Southern Baptist Convention.

31. Dabney, "Network," p. 36.

32. Cable News Network, "Televangelism."

33. Charren, *Channels*, pp. 154-155.

34. Scott Eyman, "Chuck Barris," *Sunday Magazine*, October 12, 1980, p. 53.

35. Ibid.

36. Ibid.

37. Robert Lindsey, "School Is Back in Session for 'The Quiz Kids'," *New York Times*, April 13, 1980, sec. 3, p. 37.

38. Karl E. Meyer, "The Gaming of America," *Saturday Review*, October 28, 1978, p. 37.

39. Ibid.

40. John J. O'Connor, "An Exploitation of the Fanciful," *New York Times*, June 21, 1981, sec. 2, p. D25.

41. Lindsey, "School is Back," p. 37.

42. Ibid.

43. Scott Haller, "Is 'The $1.98 Beauty Show' Really What They Had in Mind?" *TV Guide*, May 10, 1980, p. 14.

10

THE TV TALK SHOW

Commodification and the Individual

Television is today's most powerful means of conferring status. In earlier chapters dealing with comedy and melodrama, we examined the roles of heroes central to fictional television narrative, namely their function as models that provide viewers with clearly-circumscribed rules of behavior. In the chapters on news and sports, we briefly examined the status of news anchors and correspondents, newsmakers, sports announcers, and athletes as television personalities. Whether we call these people heroes, television personalities, or celebrities, they all present us with a public persona which exceeds the boundaries of power, adventure, and glamour known through our everyday experience. We may worship them as ego ideals, seek to emulate their style of dress or coiffure or their mannerisms, or attempt to achieve an electronic status analogous to theirs, if only fleetingly. The concept of "media hero" has wide-ranging implications not only for the viewers entranced by the visible signs of success on television, but also for the media heroes themselves who are brought under television's spell—trapped in an electronic hall of mirrors.

New York Times essayist Russel Baker clearly understood the nature of this television power, which he describes in his poignant parable of inventor Harley Hatchfield's search for personal confirmation through television:

> When Harley Hatchfield died the other day, the obituary writers all
> said he was a failure. I prefer to think of him as a dreamer in the finest

American tradition. Though none of his dreams were realized, he never abandoned dreaming for the sour despair and self-pity into which lesser spirits withdraw from life's great adventure.

His final years were devoted almost entirely to schemes for getting himself televised. He had observed that with the aging of the present century, appearance on television had become the only persuasive evidence of an individual's existence. He himself had come to doubt the existence of anyone who had not been on television.

"In Descartes' time," he told me, "a person could say, "I think, therefore I am.' In our age anybody who thinks can only conclude that he is not, unless masses of people can see him on television and tell him yes, he is, too. In our age, Descartes would have said, 'I am televised, therefore I am.'"

This reasoning led Harley to doubt his own existence. . . .

Not surprisingly, Harley began dreaming of ways to get television to certify his existence. Study of the local news programs led him to conclude that the most certain way would be to arrange to have his wife and five children destroyed in a dreadful fire. In this event, he was fairly certain, the local stations would televise him looking distraught while a reporter asked, "How does it feel having your wife and five children burned to death here today?"

The difficulty was that Harley, being unmarried, did not have the essential wife and children. That led him to undertake his last big project: the development of a wife and five children constructed out of balsawood, horse hair and ball bearings. When he finished them, however, he had become so fond of having them around the house and helping the children with their homework that he hadn't the heart to put them to the torch.

It was not until his death that the television cameras finally came. Attracted by the human interest angle of six balsa wood survivors mourning their loved one, the cameras finally granted existence to Harley, who no longer existed.[1]

The images and sounds captured on videotape or sent hurtling through outer-space and into our living rooms, live, become the legitimizing agents of our time. The power of personal presence becomes at best ancillary to one's media power. This is true not only for advanced capitalist man, but also for pre-capitalist man living in the shadows of modernization and technology.

The distinguished anthropologist and communications theorist Edmund Carpenter described the impact of electronic communications in the lives of rural New Guineans and Ojibwa Indians from the Lake Superior region of North America:

Electricity has made angels of us all—not Angels in the Sunday school sense of being good or having wings, but spirit freed from flesh, capable of instant transportation anywhere.

In New Guinea, when villagers ignore their leader, the government may tape-record his orders. The next day the assembled community hears his voice coming to them from a radio he holds in his own hand. Then they obey him.

Among the Ojibwa Indians, young people eagerly listen to tape recordings of their grandparents' stories, though they don't want to listen to the grandparents telling the same stories in person.[2]

"Televiso, ergo sum"*—I am televised, therefore I am—is our new ontology. There exists an abundance of signs which support this theory of our electronic being. Where the answer to "what do you want to be when you grow up" was once a doctor or a nurse, today it is a rock star or an astronaut or an anchorwoman—all people who owe a great debt to television for granting them electronic status and thereby assuring their success and fame. The Cartesian mind/body dualism today becomes a tape/body dualism. "Is it live, or it it Memorex?" is a moot question since we know that while these two states of being may be equivalent in presence, the latter is significantly more powerful than the former by virtue of its ubiquity and, as Carpenter has pointed out, its otherworldliness. Desiring the power that television promises us, we begin to act out our lives as we think we would were we television personalities. The nature of the relationship between the viewer and the image, of course, helps marketing strategists regulate the flow of new commodities into the marketplace which depends heavily on subtle shifts in lifestyle which are increasingly generated through both fictional and non-fictional media exposure. On a deeper level of commodification than material emulation, we find style finding its way into the social relations delimiting political discourse. Chauncey Gardiner, the hero of Jerzy Kosinsky's novel *Being There*, is an example of Marshall McLuhan's dictum that we become what we behold on our television screens. Gardiner, an illiterate menial, becomes a national political hero because he is an amalgam of all the television he has ever watched. Television, which with the garden he tended, had constituted his entire life experience until his forced entry into the "real" world, framed the discourse available to him. He was pure

---

*We are indebted to Russell Baker for coining this wonderfully expressive turn of phrase in his Harley Hatchfield essay quoted above.

substantive video feedback and thus, ironically, profoundly acceptable to a nation of what Kosinski termed "vidiots" who understood the television iconography on a cursory level. Chauncey was the perfect talk show guest—providing direct answers and offering stale metaphors regarding the relationship of politics to gardening—in short, providing viewers with platitude camouflaged as profundity. Chauncey Gardiner lived and exuded the mythos of the American individual whose surface appearance of freedom masks the institutional control which commodifies and markets that appearance.

This book has attempted to demonstrate that each television form contains elements of the exploitative—the mythic constructs which work to mask essences of true social relations at any given time. As we shall see in regard to the television talk show, the myth of the individual frames the discourse which develops in this particular form. The myth is best expressed in the American ideal of the "independent spirit"—one who acts and stands alone, who follows some solitary path outside a group, but who nevertheless operates within constraints imposed by the dominant culture.[3] The myth admits certain character types as legitimate while excluding others. In contemporary American culture, "idea" persons—those who produce unique utilitarian public commodities such as sophisticated gadgets which make everyday living and even warfare easier; those who manufacture best sellers and other profitable public culture; and those who develop innovative advertising campaigns and new lifestyle designs—are admitted and revered in television's public celebration of importance, while intellectual crackpots and egg heads—social critics and oppositional philosophers and artists— are either excluded or are admitted only to be subjected to ridicule, which functions to reinforce the status of the acceptable "independent spirit." Dreamers are excluded in the name of practicality. Those on the fringes who rebel against conventions and those considered angry commentators are excluded in the name of conformity.

The American "individual" is characterized by decisiveness, action for a cause deemed worthwhile and undertaken with confidence, and the appearance of independence from the pressures exerted by normative institutions to conform to stifling social conventions. While certain of these conventions in dress, behavior, and use of language may be flouted, basic values such as the importance of hard work and quick practical thinking which leads to the bold solution are held as inviolable; thus the mythic regime rests on a bed of cooptation. We think we worship the individualist, when in fact we acknowledge our conformity through our respect for the leadership status of our functionalist hero. One's individualism is repeatedly celebrated by the media hypsters as a badge of personal commitment and integrity, often irrespective of the social results of one's actions—the glorification of image over content. Individualism has become a token of superiority and distinctiveness in a system of increasingly anomic, highly-competitive social relations characterized by pecuniary prestige won by conformity with the codes of personal power established within the capitalist marketplace.

Within a culture, there may not be unanimity regarding who is a hero and who a villain or fool. The alienated rebel who rejects and attacks conventional values with defiance or destructiveness (the Beats of the 1950s, the student radical underground, and the revolutionary urban minority guerillas of the 1960s, and the cult of working class Punk in the 1970s are contemporary American examples) may be hero to repressed, disenfranchised urban street people, and villain or fool to respectable petit bourgeois suburban bureaucrats or corporate executives. One thing is certain—that within the heroic pantheon exist both dominant-culture heroes and minority-culture heroes, both providing models of behavior for those who acknowledge their heroic status, and by implication their class position and politics. Since television restricts the discourse to that sanctioned by the dominant social strata, we find the myth of the individual encompassing the compliant rather than the defiant character type. The latter is relegated to the fringe areas of oppositional culture rather than permitted a functioning position in the mainstream of debate.

Television holds out the promise of ephemeral personal power and public status, but it reserves true power for itself as an apparatus which controls the drama of electronic existence. It grants people status so long as they advance its pecuniary ends. And those who best fit its needs for drama are the "hot" performers—those easily readable individuals who play beautifully against the "cool" hosts who run the show and control the tempo of electronic life.

This chapter will explore the ramifications of being "in the medium"—of flaunting one's individualism—especially in the arena of the talk show on which established celebrities from the entertainment, sport, literary, political, and lifestyle world of image marketing are thrown together with "ordinary folk" who personify the myth of individualism and themselves ascend to ephemeral celebrity status, to be used up and quickly discarded, in television's continual pecuniary search for the glamorous, the exotic, and the bizarre.

TRADITIONAL TELEVISION TALK

While the television talk show has comprised numerous forms—from *The Tonight Show with Johnny Carson*'s celebration of celebrity and the banal to Groucho Marx's *You Bet Your Life*, a talk show trading on ridicule and thinly disguised as a game show—constants have been its repackaging of current fashion and dominant ideology for mass consumption; its lack of silence and contemplation; its rejection of complexity for simplicity; and its substitution of notoriety for substance. The television talk show is, above all, commerce—a finely-tuned barter system. A prominent politician will appear and reap the public relations benefits of addressing an audience substantially larger than any year's worth of non-television public speeches could reach, in exchange for the risk that his extemporaneous speaking style may reveal his inarticulateness or intellectual shortcomings (the risk of the latter is not great however, since the host will rarely, if ever, press substantive matters). A popular entertainer-celebrity will trade some intimate sexual or psychological revelation for a movie or album plug. Persons with advanced academic credentials who claim "expert" status offer their mass-produced popular therapies in exchange for the immediate public adulation they would never achieve were their activities-of-the-mind carefully cultivated through intellectual rigor and years of observation and disciplined analysis. Authors sit through countless minutes of small-talk waiting their turns to take the stage in the "authors' ghetto" of the post-midnight segment of the network late-night talk show, so they may plug their latest tome and boost it toward success on the best-seller list. And a regular citizen who, through some extraordinary or notorious act, has been admitted to ephermeral celebrity status, will subject his motives and integrity to cursory public scrutiny—instant judgment by those not qualified to pass such judgment—and often even the host's ridicule in exchange for a fleeting moment of public recognition. Like drama, the tension created by the possibility of the dangerous revelation lurking in the background of this tightly controlled discourse keeps the viewer's otherwise scattered attention focused on the talk and poised for the inevitable next block of commercials. However, the "dangerous" revelation will rarely if ever be one of direct political or ideological import, but rather a titillating one restricted to the realm of personal impropriety or indiscretion.

An examination of the history of the television talk show reveals five clearly developed major forms. By far the predominant talk form, which has shown great staying power since its emergence in the early years of television is the "entertainer-celebrity-talk-variety" form featuring comedy routines, musical numbers, and banal informal celebrity interviews which are more properly classified as chit-chat. All this is recorded on tape in a large television studio before a studio audience who applauds on cue. In this form, the guest is always subservient to the pecuniary demands of the medium, demands which prevent substantive discourse, and especially discourse which is in opposition to dominant ideological frames. The only thing at stake in this form is the individual's claim to celebrity status, and that, rarely. Celebrity status itself is a given, not to be questioned. As C. Wright Mills noted, celebrities run interference for the "power elite," camouflaging the real locus of power in advanced capitalist society. To question celebrityhood would lead to questions regarding the social role of the television apparatus itself. In this form, entertainment is sacred, providing viewers release from the frightening events and less-than-desirable life conditions of their everyday experience. Fun is functional. Entertainers are elevated to the status of cultural heroes. The form emerged on network television with *Tonight*, hosted by Steve Allen on NBC from 1954 to 1957. Allen and his resident company of singers and commedians kept the 90 minutes of frivolity moving briskly. Steve would open at the piano with a song he often composed. His schtick would include person-on-the-street remotes from outside the NBC New York studios. While talk via the interview was not the major focus of the show, Steve Allen's *Tonight* did set the tone for succeeding versions of the *Tonight* show which would use celebrity talk as an important viewer draw. *The Jack Paar Tonight Show*, which ran on NBC from July 1957 to March 1962, like Allen's show, featured music and comedy. Paar's forte, however, was informal conversation. He became a sort of national antihero with some of his more controversial material. But the staple of this talk show was the amusing interview with the off-beat celebrity, notably Zsa Zsa Gabor and Cliff "Charlie Weaver" Arquette. Of course the premier lighthearted talker is Johnny Carson, who took over *The Tonight Show* in October 1962. Carson avoided the controversial guest. He was much less emotional than Paar, affecting instead a cool, detached Midwestern persona. His version of the late night show, which began in New York, moved to Hollywood in 1971, the perfect backdrop for the mindless activities which night after night lit up the small screens of millions of sleepy American televiewers. Other, less notable representatives of the "entertainer-celebrity-talk-variety" form include shows hosted by "crooners" Mike Douglas and Merv Griffin, both of whom went out of their ways not to offend anyone.

A new entry, *Late Night With David Letterman*, which follows Carson on NBC as of this writing, began in 1982 as a replacement for Tom Snyder's *Tommorow* program. While supposedly a "hip" youthful talk alternative, to date it has yet to demonstrate anything other than the silly irreverence of the more mediocre schtick of the early years of *Saturday Night Live*. An example will demonstrate the general ambience of this talk form.

We were standing outside in a crowded, low-ceilinged hallway waiting to get in to NBC's small seventh floor studio in Rockefeller Center. My connections with one of the show's staffers got me "VIP" tickets. This was the "biggie," Show Number 246. The guests included the man of a thousand personalities and voices, Robin Williams of *Mork and Mindy* notoriety, and reggae superstar Peter Tosh and his group. Outside with us were other VIP friends of the production staff, some of them obviously Robin Williams groupies wearing Mork-style haberdasherie. One particularly obnoxious older character kept chain-smoking Camel cigarettes, crushing the butts on the recently waxed floor, and making lewd adolescent comments to the women NBC pages, who did their best to maintain their composure and ignore him. At last the studio doors were opened and the VIPs were escorted in. The true VIPs get center seats, while the less fortunate VIPs get side-section seats. Never mind. One can see the action better on the overhead monitors anyway. The still-less-fortunate without VIP status get to watch the monitors in the NBC Green Room, and others in one of NBC's screening rooms where NBC execs normally screen programs. Seemingly thousands of others who wanted to see Williams and/or Tosh were turned away. I felt fortunate to be admitted to the inner circle.

Inside the studio, which looks so much larger on TV, are three studio cameras on pedestals, and a portable camera which roves, hand-held, picking up studio audience reaction shots and providing an air of informality to an otherwise very tightly run ship. This contradiction of surface informality and tightly-structured format with carefully-timed segments and commercial breaks best describes the "language" of the late night "entertainer-celebrity-talk-variety" form.

We are all seated now. The show's announcer Bill Wendell does a short warm-up and David Letterman comes out to offer a few lines for the warm-up as well. The Indiana-bred Letterman, tall and thin, wears his double-breasted suit well. This is no 1960s work-shirt George Carlin routine. It feels like a large late-night business, which it is. The guests are there to plug their latest releases: Williams, his new film with Walter Matthau, *The Survivors*, and Tosh, his latest record album. All is in apparent readiness. Director Hal Gurney has the crew functioning like a Swiss watchworks.

The show is on. Letterman pulls out a giant, seven-foot goldfish from behind his desk; I sense shades of Steve Allen schtick—"schmock, schmock!" The diminutive Williams, looking like a little boy in a grown-up's suit, spends his allotted time bantering with Letterman about his new baby. The "adult" discussion of the birthing process is idiotic. Williams, like most celebrity talk show guests, is there to merely display himself for twenty minutes, plug his latest commodity, which is himself, pick up his paltry $431—the appearance fee is certainly not the inducement for appearance—and exit, stage left.

The show amazingly broke down half-way through the taping, the first major technical failure in the show's brief history. Peter Tosh's reggae group had too much equipment to patch into NBC's studio board. For budgetary reasons NBC executives, I was told, refused to give Letterman an additional audio board earlier that afternoon. There was an inexorable delay as the technical staff tried to remedy the problem. The studio audience, perhaps wanting to see the real Robin Williams, if there was one, responded "call out Robin" to Wendell's seemingly insincere question as to how they would prefer to wait it out. Wendell noted matter-of-factly, "Robin left immediately after his segment. He had another engagement. He's a very busy man." Indeed.

The highlight of the show was a periodic feature titled "stupid pet tricks," in which people parade their talented pets in front of a nation of bleary-eyed viewers in hopes that their pet's silly tricks, which usually were doomed to failure due to opening night stage fright, would provide the nation comic relief while simultaneously skyrocketing them to ephemeral celebrityhood. There was the dog who smiles, but wouldn't. The parrot who walks through a box, but instead, on this occasion just stared at the studio audience. The little poodle who sings, but had lost her voice. And the Afghan dog who barked whenever its master counted.

As I left the studio after waiting in vain for the Tosh segment (which was finally taped about three hours later and edited together with the other material), I wondered what made *Late Night* any different from any of the dozen-or-so other late night talkers from television history. All that remained in my mind were traces of commodity, schtick, display, and formatized midwestern informality.

Another talk form is the "visit-to-the-famous," pioneered on television by Edward R. Murrow's *Person To Person* and *Small World* (an international version of *Person To Person*) and resurrected by David Susskind with his *Good Company*, hosted by attorney F. Lee Bailey. In this talk form, the celebrities, who ranged from heads of state to baseball heroes, allowed the television camera to enter their personal space—their homes—while the host would probe their minds for a personal portrait which might reveal sides of their characters previously unknown to their public admirers. The television camera provided the immediate visual element missing from the print portrait. In addition, Murrow's very popular *Person To Person* was live (Murrow had an almost childlike fascination with the technical capabilities of video), which added a sense of drama to the event. *Person To Person* aired on Friday nights from 10:30 to 11:00 on the CBS television network from October 1953 to September 1961 (Charles Collingwood hosted the final two years of the series). Murrow electronically visited two celebrities each week. The celebrity would give Murrow and the television audience a tour of the house. Murrow actually conducted the interview from a CBS television studio (he thereby assumed a perspective similar to that of the viewer and avoided what might be construed to be the journalist's privileged position in this essentially one-way communication transaction—from the powers in New York to the viewers at home). Murrow, who chain smoked on the air—his trademark and ultimately the cause of his death—was "one of us." Murrow's guests included politicians President Harry Truman, Senator Jack Kennedy, and Cuban leader Fidel Castro; actors and actresses Marilyn Monroe, Humphrey Bogart and Lauren Bacall, and Marlon Brando; authors John Steinbeck and Margaret Meade; opera singers Maria Callas; and sports hero Jackie Robinson, the first black major league baseball player. While cinema stars Bogie, Bacall, and Monroe were very much at ease in front of the bulky cameras with their miles of umbilical cables strewn everywhere throughout the house, politicians still seemed nervous with the medium in those early years, although like the movie stars and starlets, our political leaders were eager for the exposure the new medium offered. Senator Jack Kennedy and his wife Jacqueline seemed shy and even awkward when they appeared on the program. Kennedy read a poem and talked about his life as a public figure and the sense of responsibility which a public servant must demonstrate. He and Jackie would grow up very quickly with the medium and the medium, through its live qualities, would document the nation's sorrow only a few years later following Kennedy's assassination.

Susskind and Bailey's *Good Company* lasted but three months on ABC in the fall of 1967. While reminiscent of *Person To Person*, its format contained a basic difference. The fascination with live television of the 1950s had given way to the control of the 1960s. Bailey would go to the celebrity's home with a film crew and shoot the interview. It would then be edited and aired. Bailey's interviewees included figures in the public eye such as *Playboy*'s founder and chief Hugh Hefner, television talk show host Jack Paar, and Illinois Senator Everett Dirksen, the man with a voice which sounded as if it slowly seaped up from the bottom of a well—all television "characters."

As was the case with the "entertainer-celebrity-talk-variety" form, the "visit-to-the-famous" form never questioned the institution of celebrityhood itself; it never asked "why, in this system of social relations, should this person be accorded such status?" Rather, the form merely reveled in the excitement of being admitted to the kingdom of the famous. Murrow opened the visit by asking his host "may we come in . . . through the window . . . in this fashion?" True, the interviews were a step above the mindless chit-chat of the "entertainer-celebrity-talk-variety" form. A senator reading poetry assured that heightened status; no matter that the poetry was uninspired or the reading amateurish. Yet the incongruity of the hard-nosed reporter Murrow—this country's adversarial conscience in his *See It Now* confrontation with Wisconsin senator Joseph McCarthy and his *CBS Reports Harvest of Shame* expose of the plight of our migrant workers—and the tough defense lawyer F. Lee Bailey hosting meek celebrity interviews with the world's major public figures points to the strange amalgam of opinion and entertainment which, on a primary level, frames television's discourse. The basic promise of this talk form could permit a limited video probing of character in a manner consistent with the traditions of literary psychological and biographical criticism. Yet the televised form did not advance toward such revelation of character and motive because the discourse in which the human transaction was framed was television discourse—an underlying "one-to-many" communication pattern according to which the public figure was given a video soapbox to extol the Great American Dream which led him or her to this very position of status and dominance. Celebrityhood, through such a vehicle, feeds back into itself, reinforcing its claim to importance.

More recent manifestations of this form find the celebrity coming to the television studio and engaging in a protracted conversation with the interviewer. Programs included PBS's *The Dick Cavett Show* (1979-1982) which featured nightly interviews with actors, authors, critics, and other public figures; Chicago public television station WTTW's *John Callaway Interviews*; and the late CBS Cable's *Signature*, hosted by Greg Jackson (who took his format to ABC's late night show *The Last Word*, a follow-up to *Nightline*). These programs featured the one-on-one interviewer form. Callaway's interviews are done in extreme close-up in a video attempt to reveal character, while Jackson's interviews employ a Cubist video technique featuring a series of dissolves from a straight-on shot to a left and right-face profile of the interviewee, all done in close-up. Both approaches to visualization are strong and draw the viewer into the conversation. And these interviews were more contentious than the earlier programs. Yet the substance was still relatively mild and the interviewee still controls the talk from his expert position.

This form was carried to its extreme in a highly controversial 1977 case. David Frost's series of interviews with former president Richard Nixon was severely criticized for its unabashed use by Nixon as a vehicle to deny his complicity in the Watergate scandal. CBS and ABC, much to their credit, turned down Nixon's request for a one-million dollar fee to do the interviews on grounds that this was "checkbook journalism." NBC News offered Nixon $400,000, and seemed willing to negotiate this figure upward when Frost beat the network to the draw in 1976 and procured Nixon's services for $600,000 and 10 percent of the profits. The financing for the interviews, according to critic Lee Brown, came in large part from "conservative West Coast businessmen who believed that Nixon had been wronged . . . and wanted him to have a forum to tell his side of the story."[4] Four 90-minute interviews were taped in Nixon's San Clemente, California estate. One-hundred-fifty-five markets carried the syndicated interviews on a barter basis (i.e., Frost gave the program to the stations "free" in exchange for a certain number of national commercial spots on each program which he would then sell to advertisers—in this case, six minutes were negotiated). The interviews were aired in 1977. The programs captured a large audience (45 million viewers for the first interview). While ostensibly a "news interview" program, the interviews caught the public imagination more as a human interest personality profile. Nothing new was learned about the structure of American government or its ideology. Little light was shed on the structural relationships which encourage such malfeasance. The very fact that Nixon agreed to "come out," lent a new legitimacy to his persona— the very act of the television appearance became his individual bold gesture. Far from a mea culpa, the interviews became tools for further Nixon deception.

A gross perversion of the "visit-to-the-famous" form occurred on Tom Snyder's *Tomorrow* program. Snyder organized a video visit with convicted mass murderer Charles Manson in his prison. Snyder, trying to get to the bottom of the infamous matter of the Tate and LaBianca murders, took on the role of psychoanalyst—a role for which he is emminently unqualified. What emerged from this travesty of showmanship was a forced portrait of a paranoid, insignificant little man who should never have been allowed five seconds of the nation's airtime. When the visit was over, one came away with a sense of meaninglessness of purpose—not only with regard to the savage murders but also with regard to the program itself. The interview with Manson was nihilistic and counterproductive. Manson, who all his life sought individual status, *televiso ergo sum*, finally achieved it with Snyder's help. The audience knew nothing more about the influence of social structure on personality which may produce such acts; on the contrary they may well have come away from the highly-publicized program feeling helpless and fatalistic as they saw one "crazy" individual isolated from the social system and therefore from any possible control.

A third traditional television talk form is the serious "long-form-round-table" discussion of substantive social and artistic issues with prominent political figures, intellectuals, and members of the creative community. (I am not including here the weekly Sunday news discussion programs such as *Meet The Press, Face The Nation* or *Issues and Answers*—now *This Week With David Brinkley*—on which individual dominant culture politicos are invited in to provide the "party line" on some issue which headlines that particular week's news while correspondents stumble over one another in a self-conscious attempt to be hard-nosed and adversarial, but instead merely reveal their lack of intellectual acumen through their series of banal questions which come thinly disguised as challenges to their guests. These "public affairs" shows, while pure television talk, are discussed elsewhere in the context of "objective" newsgathering.) The video "long-form-round-table" studio talk form is closely related to its print counterpart, the symposium, in which a group of knowledgeable persons provide a variety of opinions on some topic of common interest. Debate, argumentation, and disagreement among individual thinkers who hold often highly disparate viewpoints on the matter under consideration is the hallmark of this most significant of television talk forms. Ideas rather than surface impressions of personal character or exigent political positions are the currency of this form. As such, its viewer popularity in the age of titillation and the short attention span would not be expected to be very high, although its critical popularity would.

An important program in this form in television's youthful years was David Susskind's *Open End*. Susskind, a producer of significant television drama for anthologies including *Kraft Theater, Armstrong Circle Theater,* and *Kaiser Aluminum Hour,* and the acclaimed series drama *East Side, West Side,* created a critical tour de force in 1958 with *Open End,* which he both produced and hosted. The syndicated program introduced us to a new televisual form as we entered the final phases of the initial age of television program experimentation— the open-ended talk with no set time limit. The program ended when its host and guests ran out of energy. The there was plenty of energy to go around. *Open End* featured such notable political discussants as Soviet premier Nikita Khruschev and then vice-president Richard Nixon, certainly not friends as evidenced by the famous "Kitchen Debate" of 1959. Susskind was often challenging, sometime abrasive, but always sincerely involved in his topics. His *Open End* displayed a serious commitment to the discussion of ideas and a respect for his audience, evidenced by his belief that provocative talk, freely unfolding, could sustain the interest of the concerned viewer. In fact, *Open End* must be considered an important model for the public access talk program two decades later, with its emphasis on letting the conversation unfold unfettered by commercial television's time signature with its advertising constraints and its programmers' belief that viewers will quickly tire of thought. In the mid-1960s, *Open End* became *The David Susskind Show,* and its format was changed to a one-hour closed-ended discussion. As befell other television forms, notably the anthology drama and the extended coverage of congressional hearings on issues of major public concern such as the Kefauver hearings on organized crime and the Army-McCarthy confrontation of 1954, talk was now carefully contained and packaged. The era of bold experimentation in live television ended.

Other talk show hosts would occasionally introduce truly contentious material, although not with the consistency or the depth of *Open End. The Jack Paar Tonight Show* had an occasional serious side. Paar used his program to crusade against Cuban dictator Batista prior to Castro's revolution. Paar, capable of outrage and petulance, walked out of NBC for a month following the network's censure of his famous "water-closet" joke. Tom Snyder's *Tomorrow* would on occasion tackle serious subjects such as drug abuse and draft dodging during the Vietnam War, and would gather panels of psychologists and other experts from time to time to assess the contemporary social scene. But these ventures into the serious were exceptions to the main business of celebrity talk and the showcasing of "oddities" such as Snyder's visit to a nudist camp and his constant baiting of ordinary persons who were invited on the show because of some peculiar special interest they represented.

As we move from the sacred talk realm of entertainer-celebrities, political pundits, and panels of educated experts, we enter a world of common folk whose valiant exploits, despicable deeds, personal tragedies, bizarre inventions, and sometimes even their mere "commonness" earn them a brief moment under the bright lights on the talk circuit. The binding agent in all these talk transactions is that of the end use of people as commodities—the folk are used up to attract an increasingly voyeuristic viewership.

The exploitation of inarticulate, camera-shy common folk as butts for the cynical talk-show comic's jokes flourished with the talk-game program *You Bet Your Life*, hosted by the immensely popular film comedian Groucho Marx. The game of answering trivia questions was but a backdrop to Marx's ridicule of the lifestyle, dress, and awkwardness of the contestants, who were paired in male-female teams. The program aired from 1950 to 1961 on NBC and has since reappeared throughout the country in a highly-popular syndicated strip format. The contestants were amazingly good-natured (or docile) people, willing to endure Marx's insults in order to appear before the nation. This ostensibly harmless, all-in-fun abuse of "the little guy" set the trend for subsequent talk show discourse. The average working person was frequently portrayed in these settings as an "oddball"; his opinions, while maybe interesting, were quaint if not "cracked." This was the view of the rural American we saw emerging in the rural-middle-landscape comedies of the 1960s—a childlike innocent not to be taken seriously.

On a more sinister level, hosts such as Tom Snyder, on *Tomorrow*, and Joe Pyne and Les Crane on their syndicated talk shows would invite guests on the program, then bait them. Snyder would seek out people with odd inventions or abberrant social values and subject them to debates over their worth or their values. Pyne, a disabled war veteran, used his show to attack any liberal he could find, especially homosexuals and anti-Vietnam War protesters (Pyne is an excellent real-world model for the Archie Bunker character). Crane, on the other hand, sought out racists and other bigots for ridicule. There was no fun intended in these dark displays of public antagonism. The shows, in a way, were seemingly little more than set-ups to show off the interrogatory acumen of their hosts; they were exercises in ego which traded on hapless people who were unprepared for the television pressure cooker.

The final, and most interesting traditional television talk form is one best labelled "the video-talk-trial." In this form, the ordinary person, who through some extraordinary or outrageous personal act has become notorious, is paraded before millions of viewers as a surrogate defendant in a public video trial. The defendant must answer questions about his or her morality and values. The studio audience becomes both judge and jury and the talk-trial host, chimera-like, becomes one minute prosecutor and the next defense counsel. In all cases the guests appear of their own volition. They are not coerced by the production staff into appearing, although it might be argued that they are subconsciously coerced by the television apparatus itself through the implicit promise of fame.

This televisual form is best understood through *The Phil Donahue Show*, although it has roots in call-in radio, and especially a notorious early 1970s radio format, duplicated in numerous markets, known as "Topless Radio." The pioneer program was *Feminine Forum*, hosted by Bill Ballance. To understand this form of talk-exploitation, we should examine the media work of both Ballance and Donahue.

Early in 1971, a former all-night disk jockey named Bill Ballance began *Feminine Forum* on KGBS-AM in Los Angeles. After twenty-months of what was dubbed by critics as "sex-talk" or "Topless Radio," Ballance's show was the top-rated program in the nation's largest radio market. An estimated 400,000 people tuned in every day. By early 1973 there were an estimated fifty or sixty stations around the country programming daily radio shows in this format. The format was characterized by its focus on a single sexual topic each day; callers were not pre-screened or pre-taped, which would have dampened spontaneity; only the caller's first name was revealed in order to protect the caller's privacy; the hosts were all men while the preponderance of the callers were women; and the target audience was described as "wives and mothers in their twenties." Storer Broadcasting, which owned KGBS, started versions of *Feminine Forum* on its five other AM radio stations in Cleveland, Detroit, Miami, Toledo, and New York City. Other media owners followed suit, including Metromedia-owned KNEW, San Francisco (with *California Girls*, hosted by Don Chamberlain); Fairchild's KLIF in Dallas with *The Dave Ambrose Show*; and WWDC's *Scott Burton Show* from the nation's capital. By the end of 1972, Ballance's show had become one of the hottest syndication properties in radio, handled by Dick Clark Radio Shows, Inc. (the Dick Clark of *American Bandstand*). It had been placed in 22 markets, including four in Canada and one in Perth, Australia. Pilots for a Bill Ballance television show, to be handled by Clark, were "in the can."[5]

But the radio sex-talk form was not without its influential detractors. FCC Chairman Dean Burch, in a speech to the National Association of Broadcasters annual convention in Washington, D.C. in 1973 heralded the Commission's coming war against indecency in American life by saying "If electronic voyeurism is what the authors of the Communications Act had in mind, I'll eat my copy."[6] The NAB shortly thereafter passed a resolution condemning "tasteless and vulgar program content." And on April 13, 1973, the FCC announced its intention to fine Sonderling Broadcasting Corporation's Oak Park, Illinois radio station WGLD-FM $2,000 for airing its version of the sex-talk form—a program titled *Femme Forum*. The FCC invited Sonderling to appeal its fine through the judicial system in order that a test case could be decided regarding indecency in broadcast programming, but Sonderling refused. Sonderling's refusal to pursue the matter was not an admission of guilt but rather a case of economic exigency. In fact Egmont Sonderling, President of Sonderling Broadcasting in New York, said WGLD's *Femme Forum* was a program dealing "with the problems of modern woman."[7] Ballance, who skyrocketed to fame on the strength of *Feminine Forum*, defended his media work, claiming he helped women who "are conversationally intimate with me because they can't communicate with their husbands. The show brings out a lot of marital discord that has been simmering below the surface."[8] Ray Stanfield, manager of KGBS in Los Angeles, where it all began, said "we do not have a sex-talk show on this station. We have a talented, clever interviewer on the air, talking to callers about man-woman relationships. Sex is an occasional by-product."[9] Despite Stanfield's clinical talk, KGBS changed *Feminine Forum* to the *Bill Ballance Show* and cut the sex-talk, bending to FCC pressure.

Feminine Forum flourished during a period in which media had begun to open up, if usually quite tentatively, to the controversial content area of sexuality. *All In The Family* began its long CBS run in 1971. Richard Levinson's and William Link's television film exploring the human relations of a homosexual father, *That Certain Summer*, had aired on ABC in November 1972. The daytime soap operas were becoming increasingly sexual. Sex manuals for the lay person led the lists of best-selling books. *Maude* developed a two-part episode on abortion (which received nearly two-thousand viewer complaints). What made *Feminine Forum*, and "Topless Radio" generally, more offensive? Its defenders called this two-way talk "cathartic radio"—radio which asked listeners for personal experiences rather than political opinions. This was radio-as-therapy. Euphemism aside, underneath it all was a disingenuousness. Ballance and the other hosts seemed to prey upon the insecurities of these women who wanted so much to hear themselves talking, to confirm their being in the media-world. ("Please turn your radio down" has become the anthem of radio talk—a powerful symbol of the feedback of one ego talking and listening through the talk loop to itself—feeding one's desire for contact, masturbatory contact with one's own media image.) If these were mothers and wives in their twenties who, as Ballance himself noted, could not communicate with their husbands and were feeling isolated and confused, was this self-indulgent talk a legitimate outlet for their frustration? Was there any hope of resolution?

The content of the shows—one day oral sex, the next masturbation, the next the evils of miniskirts, the next the frequency, or lack thereof, of one's orgasms—seemed increasingly mundane as the months wore on. The content was much less intriguing than the very presence of these women whom we knew by first name only, but whose intimate lives we shared in the voyeuristic safety of our radio space. These intimate interludes were far from simple entertainment. When one would call and lay her sexuality on the line before 400,000 listeners, there would be the inevitable irascible next caller who would begin by chastising the hapless woman who had just opened-up, calling into question the woman's morality or even her sanity. On occasion Ballance himself was not above deriding a caller for her narrow-mindedness or ignorance of a sexual subject. This program prided itself on its openness and sincerity—liberal, holier-than-thou buzzwords which easily disguised the callous pecuniary motivations behind this sex-talk. Like the contestants on television's *The $1.98 Beauty Show*, the women callers became audio prostitutes, selling images of their bodies but turning all the money over to the radio apparatus which hustled them on the airwaves. Beyond the practice of radio prostitution, however, was the trial-like atmosphere in which the talk took place. Women were judged by other women whom they had never before met or spoken to. The initial radio meeting was at best superificial—one event taken from a woman's entire experience and cast out on the airwaves as representing her. This unidimensional psychic and moral portrait is at best simplistic and probably quite misleading, given the groundrules of the talk.

What was gained and what was lost in this radio transaction? The stations made substantial profits from advertising revenues generated by these immensely popular programs. Millions of listeners were titillated, and maybe learned some new sexual techniques (one memorable program on oral sex discovered a woman who was revolted at the thought of felatio until she discovered that putting peanut butter on her husband's genitals and licking it off made them both happy). The caller, under the protection of anonymity, achieved ephemeral celebrity status. She was an individual who held the media "floor" for three minutes or so—her thoughts counted and were part of the electronic discourse established by the number one radio show in L.A. Further, she could talk to a man. On the other hand, she had not begun to resolve the problem of her inability to talk with her husband, if Ballance's assessment of the motivations of these women to call is granted. She had revealed intimate details of her life to a disinterested radio entertainer. And she helped legitimize the public media commodification of the isolated psyche. It is little wonder that women's organizations labelled Ballance as "the complete pig."

While Phil Donahue exudes integrity, unlike the sex-talk hosts, his hour-long syndicated daytime talk program *Donahue* in its own way thrives upon personal revelation in a trial-like atmosphere filled with often tense cross-examination and incessant moralizing. *The Phil Donahue Show* began in 1967 on WLWD-TV in Dayton, Ohio, owned by Avco, and soon was syndicated nationally. In 1973, the program was retitled *Donahue* and moved to WGN-TV, Chicago. The show featured celebrity interviews and discussions with experts on topical matters, especially women's issues. The program was highly successful with carriage by 160 stations in the late 1970s. Donahue prepared a half-hour version for prime-access in 1979, and did interview features for NBC's *Today*. In 1982, he prepared an abbreviated fifteen minute version of talk for ABC's *Late Night*. It seemed as if Phil Donahue was everywhere on the nation's television screens in the 1970s and 1980s—early morning, mid-day, evening, and late-night. He had unlocked the secret to immense video popularity.

Like sex-talk, Donahue's programs deal with controversial, sometimes titillating material. The studio audience, resembling the Roman aristocracy at a gladiatorial contest, would get caught up cheering for or against a guest. Sincere men and women with problems who wished to share them with us through television eagerly came to Donahue to open-up their lives. And like sex-talk, when the affair was over, one wondered what was gained, what was lost.

The underlying feeling one carries away from *Donahue* is that of having just attended a cross between a group therapy session with people you have never before met but who seem genuinely deeply troubled and a rambling, undisciplined free-for-all discussion at the local PTA meeting. Critic William Henry labelled *Donahue* the 1970s television manifestation of the mid-1960s; "common-man personality and topicality" which prospered to the extent that it "let the shameful tout their shamelessness."[10] Donahue prodded and poked, challenging his guests, then discretely backing away. His feigned neutrality, camouflaged as "liberal tolerance" of the most aberrant behavior of the common folk, counteracts potential criticism of the program's flirtation with subject matter considered by many moderate people to be taboo. Like Ballance, Donahue shifts the responsibility for moral judgment to members of his audience, those in the studio during the taping and occasionally the phone-in audience. Given limited information about the program's guests, and lacking the necessary professional training to be able to properly evaluate the guests' motivations or to understand the complex questions of law which were often cursorily raised as they related to a case, the audience nevertheless was called upon to interrogate the guest regarding his or her actions. This vapid display of vox populi leaves one feeling quite uncomfortable.

The guest, meanwhile, tries hard to persevere, to reiterate her contentions. Donahue will defend her or empathize with her one moment, then, in the interest of balance, he will turn on her, albeit with a cunning courtesy which belies antagonism. The guest becomes a human yo-yo, literally jerked around to enhance the drama of this video talk-trial. As any lawyer will tell you, trials, even those involving a murder suspect, can be deadly dull; but on television, they must become *Perry Mason* adventures in discovery, fraught with intrigue and the constant revelation of hitherto secreted information.

A particularly telling example of Donahue's video-talk-trial ambience was a program aired in December 1977 in which Mrs. Francine Hughes appeared. Mrs. Hughes had murdered her ex-husband (with whom she had reunited) out of fear, she said, for her life and the lives of her children. Mr. Hughes had physically abused her for thirteen years. She tried to leave him, but had nowhere to go; the police were of little help to her and she did not know of shelters for battered wives. Her situation appeared increasingly hopeless. One night while Mr. Hughes was sleeping, she poured gasoline around the bed, lit a match, and left. She was brought to trial. A jury found her temporarily insane. Her admission to Donahue's circle of topicality was guaranteed by the verdict which on the one hand seemed to permit justifiable homicide by women victims of severe and persistent physical abuse and on the other hand left the judicial floodgates ajar with the temporary insanity verdict, clearly not an acquittal. In addition, the burning, the trial, and the physical abuse constituted high drama.

Mrs. Hughes appeared with her lawyer. She did not seem remorseful over the murder. Rather, she seemed tired and a bit withdrawn. She said she wished only to share her experience with others. As the discussion proceeded, Donahue and many in the studio audience and call-in audience tried to get Mrs. Hughes to show some guilt, to be at least somewhat repentent. In the next breath Donahue and others in the audience defended her right to defend herself. Back and forth and back again. The studio audience became highly polarized, many cheering an audience member who made an impassioned plea for women's rights, many others cheering an audience member who insisted Mr. Hughes should have had some rights as well, namely rights to rehabilitation, and that his execution negated those rights. By the program's mid-point, Mrs. Hughes began to fade into the background, having served her purpose of stirring up the studio audience and thereby guaranteeing heated confrontation.

What was learned from this talk? Nothing about the mechanisms of existing support systems for victims of physical abuse such as secure shelters for battered wives. Nothing about the intricacies of our legal system which allow a verdict of not guilty by reason of insanity. Nothing revealing about the deep, highly-individual emotional world in which Mrs. Hughes had struggled for thirteen years. We received instead impressions, descriptions of a murder; we were given a ticket to a group psychodrama which searches in vain for universal emotional truth which doesn't exist, except on television—a psychodrama enacted by players on stage and in the audience. *Donahue* is serious business.

The video-talk-trial leaves many issues unresolved. Perhaps the most intriguing issue was raised by Jerzy Kosinski in his novel *Being There*. Chauncey Gardiner, a simpleton-gardener who by circumstance became a media-hero, had been invited to appear on a television talk show:

> Chance turned on the TV. He wondered whether a person changed before or after appearing on the screen. Would he be changed forever or only during the time of his appearance? What part of himself would he leave behind when he finished the program? Would there be two

Chances after the show: one Chance who watched TV and another who appeared on it?[11]

The experience of appearing on television talk must be both exhilarating and humbling. Ephemeral celebrityhood is a relationship of relative power—of the host over the guest, and both over the audience; but the relationship is ultimately defined by the levels of meaning generated in the human exchanges that constitute that power. The television talk program "often confuses notoriety with persuasive power, and visibility with impact."[12] When Chance exits the studio, he will leave behind traces of himself: his unintended metaphors linking his garden and world politics and economics which come to symbolize his "quick mind" to gullible viewers suckled on platitudes, and his affability. When Mrs. Hughes exited the studio, she left behind traces of herself: her self-doubt hidden just beneath the veneer of her seeming remorselessness, and her preoccupation with "sharing" her own world. The audience carries away traces of performances which dish up emotion masquerading as answers to difficult questions of social relations.

THE NEW TALK

If the old television talk resulted in the commodification of the individual psyche for the consumption of millions of viewer-voyeurs, the new television talk—a spin-off of the Donahue brand of Midwestern-pious-soul-searching-group psychotherapy—is a delayed video reaction to the self-help generation who seek solutions to complex questions of personal identity in therapies of all kinds, including the generic quick-fix of pop psychology. It is but a short step from the "fix your own plumbing" regimes of the 1950s as seen in those queer old books with line drawings of gaskets and monkey wrenches to the "fix your own head" routines of 1980s California. Television and radio have capitalized on the trend.

"Psychological Radio" is a step beyond Bill Ballance's "Topless Radio." Dr. Toni Grant, a radio psychologist from Syracuse University, took Ballance's job away from him at KABC radio in Los Angeles in 1978. She was first in her time slot with an average listenership of about 150,000 (in 1982). Most of her listeners and callers are women. Dr. Grant insists she mainly gives out information and does not make universal diagnoses or prescribe universal remedies for psychological problems discussed with individual listener/callers. But Dr. Peter Wish, a psychologist and a founding member of the Association for Media Psychology, which drafted guidelines for media psychologists in 1982, argues that psychological radio raises serious ethical issues regardless of the claims of the hosts. Wish notes that there is a tendency for the psychologist to become a media star; that giving advice on the airwaves is distinct from providing therapy; that the media psychologist, in talking to a caller, is working with minimal and incomplete information on her "client"; that the media psychologist is forced to make a snap judgment and a speculative, impersonal diagnosis; and finally there is a distinct danger that some listener will think he has the same problem as the caller when he may not, and may follow the media psychologist's advice to the caller which may not be appropriate in his case.[13]

Psychological radio is entertainment pretending to provide a psychological service. The listener is the recipient of a one-way communication while the client/caller is involved in a very limited two-way conversation with the media psychologist. Some commentators claim that this new talk is progressive because callers not only get psychiatric or medical advice, but also frequently offer encouragement and support for a previous caller, thereby adding to an ongoing discourse.[14] Nonsense! This "discourse" is phony. Without face-to-face, open confrontation, this is nothing but safe media group therapy with no emotional strings attached. The caller, who does not like what she hears from the media psychologist or the next caller, can tune out (she has paid no money as an incentive to stay with the therapy)—a response which probably in many cases produced the caller's current psychological discomfort in the first place.

Psychological radio served as a model for the new psychological television, which has taken a variety of forms on the new specialized, as yet infrequently watched cable television networks. Cable Health Network has developed such psychological programs as *Take Charge*, featuring Lester Coleman, an upbeat media psychologist; *Human Sexuality* with host Sharon Goldsmith, a half-hour interview show aired daily and featuring talks with "real people" about their sexual problems, all of which she believes can be resolved by "relating"; and *Join The Group*, featuring twelve men and women in the 50s and 60s discussing psychological problems associated with aging such as disease, fear of dying, divorce, and children growing up and leaving the nest, and above all emphasizing people "coping." USA Network has *Sonya* with host Sonya Friedman interviewing people about their problems—a cross between *The Merv Griffin Show* and Dr. Joyce Brothers, the pioneer pop TV psychologist/talk show maven.[15] Everyone is a "real person," "coping" and "relating" their way through the complexities of the late twentieth century. The only thing missing is sponsorship by a hot tub manufacturer.

But enough of this pseudo-therapeutic group commiseration. The ultimate new psychological television is a direct one-to-one confrontation in the true realm of television psychodrama. Take, for example, "Dear John" video. A video service named Posterity Pix (because it specializes in videotaped readings of wills) tapes statements that people are reluctant (or afraid) to express in person but will put on tape. According to a *Time* magazine report, "One client could not work up the nerve to tell her husband face-to-face that she intended to leave him, so she taped a 'Dear John' message—and then left."[16]

Television talk, in this most blatant manifestation, is revealing, for we can clearly detect its form reduced to one person, cut-off from meaningful human relationships, taking decisive action which produces the bold solution, leaving behind a video trace of her persona in a one-way communication. This is far from authentic communication as we once knew it. It is fatalistic, and nihilistic. This is the true television talk—a video monologue without commitment—today's electronic mythic realm of the individual.

How far will television talk go? Until December 26, 1982, nothing seemed too outlandish for the form's appropriation. But that day, the boundaries of television talk were stretched. An Associated Press "News Digest" item speaks for itself:

> People considering suicide would be the stars of a TV series proposed by a man who contends that the program, "Second Chance," would save lives.
>
> "We'll set up a suicide hot line, and when a call comes in, we'll send out a psychiatrist or counselor to talk to that person, and we'll also send out a camera," Laurence Schwab said. "The purpose is to talk the person out of suicide."
>
> He said he is trying to recruit investors and make a pilot of the program.
>
> The Suicide Prevention Center in Los Angeles has denounced the proposal as "potentially dangerous for suicidal persons seeking help."
>
> The center issued a statement saying it could "provoke some individuals, who might have been helped, into actually killing themselves, and might attract others to act suicidally because of the publicity involved."
>
> Asked if the program amounted to exploiting the miseries of would-be suicide victims, Schwab replied, "I'll get some money out of it, but not much. What I'm getting out of it is a fantastic sense of accomplishment and a chance to save lives.

"But certainly it's exploitation," he added. "Everything is exploitation. 'Captain Kangaroo' is exploitation. 'Laverne and Shirley' is exploitation. But this is not another one of these comedies or game shows. This is important."[17]

Second Chance turns the myth of the individual on its head. The potential suicide acts and stands alone, a solitary person outside the group. But he violates the unchallengeable moral constraints imposed by Western religion and common law and thus is branded the fool, to be pitied, not revered. He can be hero neither to the dominant culture nor the oppositional culture given the ground rules for this discourse (in the latter case this is so because the potential suicide's action is divorced from any political context to which it might refer). His "worth" becomes his televisability—his value as a dramatic persona. His "life and death" struggle is ideally suited to television's dramatic desire for clarity and rudimentary moral conflict.

Rather than waste money on a media psychologist to attempt to talk the potential suicide out of commiting the act on *Second Chance*, why doesn't the producer simply give the potential suicide a camera and recorder and let him become a video post, taping his own suicide note. Once a number of such messages are "in the can," the producer can put those together that reflect a common theme, say "no one understands my sensitivity," and edit them down to fit between the commercial breaks. Following the tapes, in the show's epilogue, the producer can come on camera, à la Chuck Barris on *The Gong Show*, and tell the viewers who actually carried out the act and who didn't. That shall surely produce enough drama to go around.

NOTES

1. Russell Baker, "Televiso, Ergo Sum," *New York Times*, August 23, 1980, p. 23.

2. Edmund Carpenter, *Oh, What A Blow That Phantom Gave Me!* (Toronto: Bantam Books, 1973), p. 3.

3. Orrin E. Klapp, *Heroes, Villains, and Fools: The Changing American Character* (Englewood Cliffs, N.J.: Prentice-Hall, 1962), pp. 43-45. Klapp sees the independent spirit functioning as a heroic model who offers compensation for average people who are "tired of their roles and welcome a vacation."

4. Lou Brown, *Encyclopedia of Television* (New York: Zoetrope, 1982), pp. 168, 308-309.

5. "Touchiest Topic on Radio Now: Talk About Sex," *Broadcasting*, March 19, 1973, pp. 118-121.

6. "Government and the NAB Close In On Sex Programs," *Broadcasting*, April 2, 1973, p. 27.

7. Ibid., p. 28.

8. "Sex On The Dial," *Newsweek*, September 4, 1972, p. 90.

9. "Touchiest Topic," p. 118.

10. William A. Henry, "From the Dawn of Gab: The Evolution of TV's Most Indigenous Form," *Channels*, May/June 1983, p. 43.

11. Jerzy Kosinski, *Being There* (New York: Bantam, 1971), p. 51.

12. Henry, "Gab," p. 43.

13. Interview with Dr. Peter Wish, *ABC Nightline*, February 12, 1982.

14. Mary Pratt, "No, She Really Loves Eggs: Fighting It Out on Call-In Radio," *Tabloid* (Winter 1983), pp. 27-37.

15. Ross Wetzsteon, "Psychochatter: The Trend of the '80s," *Channels*, May/June 1983, pp. 49-51.

16. "Lights, Cameras, Wills," *Time*, December 1981, p. 72.

17. Associated Press "News Digest" as reported in *The Athens Messenger*, December 26, 1982, p. B-6.

11

TOWARD AN OPPOSITIONAL TELEVISION

Strategies for Change

With rare exceptions, television network executives, program producers, writers, directors, actors, journalists, advertising agency people, commercial directors, and financiers ultimately respond to television as a business, and the works of television as product. These are, by and large, men and women driven by the dream of "the good life"—the great American Dream—a world of money; of freedom from the constraining regimes of ordinary everyday work and leisure; and of status. These men and women live the myth of eternal progress framed by the Puritan ethic: a vision of hard work, and intense competition, with personal prestige and especially wealth the reward for the survivors.

The programs and the commercials they offer us appear to be little more than an assemblage of disparate and contradictory life-styles and beliefs. However, when carefully decoded, the contradictions resolve into well-ordered and potent traditional mainstream values:

1. The sanctity of the "ordinary" American family. This is offered up either ideally, in the strong family bonds evident in the rural-middle-land-scape melodrama and the 1950s and 1960s suburban-middle-landscape comedy; or cynically, by contrast, in 1960s rural-middle-landscape comedy where the oddball family, while loving, is outside the mainstream and therefore not to be taken seriously, or in the suburban-middle-landscape families of the soap opera who, while upscale, are

305

alienated and miserable, their American Dream turning into a nightmare. The traditional urban comedy found it necessary to substitute the work-family for the biological family as a socializing agent in a world where the urban dweller seemed cut off from the security of marriage and family. Even the contemporary single-parent divorced families of today's urban comedies portray the parent constantly searching for a new mate and the stable life of the ordinary family.

2. The triumph of personal initiative over the bureaucratic control and inefficiency of the state. This is offered up in police melodrama in which the police hero, often out of uniform (undercover) and beyond the police bureaucracy, may himself violate the law or police practice, and also may violate the rights of the suspect, in order to produce quick results. It is also evident in the private investigator melodrama, in which the svelte private detective shows up the bumbling, incompetent police. Not only in the tense world of the urban frontier does the individual transcend the legal arm of the state. In the distant, allegorical world of the western frontier, bourgeois cattle barons such as the Cartwrights and bounty hunters such as the romantic Paladin, the heroic knight, take the law into their own hands when the law is found wanting. In all these cases, however, the legal apparatus itself is not being challenged, but rather, the property interests of the wealthy and the political interests of the state are being more efficiently protected by the bold actions of the individual protagonists.

3. One's gain at another's expense. This is constantly and blatantly reinforced in game shows, and insidiously in electronic religion. In the latter instance, it is manifested in the television preacher's dictum that man must depend for truth on God's revelation, and god has revealed that viewers shall give part of their food and rent money to his "servants" here on earth, the teleevangelists.

4. The elevated status of quiet authority in the status hierarchy of power and social control. This is clearly seen in the contrasting forms of the television news interview as it is conducted with management and government officials in quiet television studios in an atmosphere of deference punctured now and then by the necessary, inauthentically "tough" question; and as it is conducted with blue-collar workers during strikes and work disruptions, and with ghetto residents and dissident students during public protests in a man-on-the-street format amid noise and confusion, featuring the halting language of heated extemporaneous speech.

5. The celebration of celebrity. This is most visibly manifested in mindless talk shows, sport interviews, and celebrity roasts, and functions in the larger arena of social relations to deflect attention from the economic and political control of America's power elite.

6. The conversion of history and the deflection of questions of social structure into the "personal." This is evident in television news, documentary, and docudrama. It is also clearly evident in social comedy such as *M*A*S*H* and *All in the Family*. These capitalist-pluralist, "democratic" values organize the large, seemingly random, cacophonous mental landscape of American television. They are offered up through a powerful mythology which we viewers cannot easily articulate. Above all, these values are controlling.

Against this panoramic backdrop of dominant centralized commercial and public television in the United States, scattered and not always clear oppositional ideology now and then appears in such varied forms as community-based video documentary works addressing contemporary community problems related to both the material relations of work and the social relations of ethnic, racial, political, religious, and economic groups; on a rare occasion, a serious critical self-examination conducted by a dominant television news organization which results in a limited condemnation of certain, but certainly not all, dominant television practices; "anti-television" performance art such as the oppositional ideological critiques of popular art texts and the siting of these texts in their economic contexts of production and dissemination, and true two-way, "performer-viewer-performer" television conversation; and the revival and presentation of regional and local folk culture via video histories of cultural spokespersons who are often clearly outside dominant cultural activities.

A major problem is that these forms are rarely foregrounded when they are presented. Rather, they remain lost in the background due to their lack of publicity (including pre-reviews in major print publications), and their inherently subordinate position as interlopers relegated to the outer reaches of UHF (where the world of the click-stop knob is finally replacing the incredibly awkward flow-through UHF tuning apparatus—really an economic device which ensured VHF broadcasters an airwave oligopoly for years), and to those "weird" public access channels which are so laid back that their programs magically appear at 7:23 p.m. (taken as an oppositional strategy itself to reflect on the tight time control of commercial television, this free-form approach acts initially rather to confuse the well-trained viewer).

In an examination of oppositional television work, one must be extremely careful to place the work in context. What work, if any, is allowed on dominant cultural television, commercial or public, and why? What work is automatically excluded? And what programming apparatuses operate in the realm of oppositional television that may tend to duplicate the control mechanisms of dominant television?

I shall only hint here at what I believe to be emerging trends in the development and restriction of oppositional work in television. First, however, a clarification of the terms dominant and oppositional is necessary. Foremost in our discussion, the dominant culture attempts to regulate and control viewer desires in terms of "possession" of material goods, a possession which presupposes their unequal distribution, while the oppositional culture encourages the creation of desires which cannot be regulated in an unequal power relationship by the dominant culture, such as a desire for community to counteract individual alienation, redistribution of wealth, guaranteed health protection, etc. The dominant culture attempts to keep the viewer outside the objects of her desire—the lifestyle of the upper-middle class, for example—and thus outside of power; this is done through the creation of "spectacle" and the placement of the viewer in the position of voyeur who desires, and is allowed limited possession of insignificant objects, of tokens of that lifestyle (this, of course, operates most powerfully in the commercials). Oppositional culture attempts to point out the absurdity of this relationship and incite the viewer to act to break down the unequal power of possession that holds those outside the power center in check. Dominant culture legitimizes those individuals who are wealthy, ostentatious, and wield power over others (the characters of *Dallas* are excellent examples). Oppositional culture attempts to demonstrate how that wealth was achieved, i.e., at whose expense, and how it is being used to continue unequal class and status relationships. Finally, dominant culture, in circumscribing the correct or "proper" alternative positions on issues— channeling resistance by providing an outlet for it—defuses true oppositional positions. Thus *M*A*S*H*, as described in Chapter 5, is "anti-war" but not anti-politics. That is, *M*A*S*H* transcribes the horror of war into a personal revulsion through the characters of the cynical doctors. When the Korean War, and by implication Vietnam, is criticized, the critique centers on bureaucracy—the inability of the generals and civilian negotiators to end the interminable conflict. The politics which controls the discourse within which a war such as Korea or Vietnam comes to make sense to the American people is thereby defused. In a similar vein, the 1983 television movie *The Day After*, which depicted the results of a nuclear conflagration between the Americans and the Soviets is "anti-nuclear war"—we see devastation and individual misery all around—Lawrence, Kansas, the setting for this film, is blown back to the Stone Age. But *The Day After* is not anti-nuclear politics, for nuclear politics presupposes the survivability of the species, in whatever condition, and the film does the same.

Countering the inherent imbalance of the power relationship between dominant television and oppositional television is a major undertaking which will need the highest levels of ideological commitment and staying power. Some tentative yet important examples of work in this vein can serve as models for future efforts.

Community-based video documentary works addressing contemporary community problems have, on occasion, been given air time on local public television stations and, on rare occasions, have gained access to national commercial television. An aesthetic premise, though certainly not a rule, of much if not most of this work is its rough-edged verité style and technical unevenness (although public television finds such work increasingly unacceptable as it goes after ratings like its commercial counterparts). While the rough-edged quality of the work can be an ideological advantage, that is, it can relate formal structure more authentically to content and context, it can also turn-off viewers who are trained in dominant-television watching. Two important thrusts of this type of work bear close examination: (1) works made by workers themselves that address the material conditions of work, and (2) works made by community-based artists/documentarians that address the social and cultural conditions in the community. As oppositional works, both types of work reveal commitment to a ideological position critical of an unjust contemporary social condition.

An important example of the first type of work is a videotape titled *Signed, Sealed and Delivered*, produced by striking postal workers with help from a number of community-based artist/documentarians. *Signed, Sealed and Delivered* documents the struggle of postal workers in New York City to achieve safer working conditions in postal facilities and more humane consideration of their demands by postal officials. The tape, a combination of hand-held black-and-white, hand-held industrial-grade color, and slick local news footage, documents a wildcat strike by the postal workers over intolerable work conditions, the firing of the strikers, the death of a worker who was chewed up by an unsafe conveyor belt at the bulk mail processing facility in New Jersey, and the attempts of workers to achieve justice through Congressional hearings on the work conditions which led to the death and the wildcat strike. The soundtrack features protest songs written especially for this videotape. An extremely powerful document, it was aired on WNET/Thirteen in New York City and submitted to video festivals around the country. *Signed, Sealed and Delivered* demonstrates the use of the video camera as another important tool in workers' struggles.

The work of community-video documentarians such as John Alpert of Downtown Community Television Center (who has also done independent work for NBC News in Southeast Asia and Central America) and Alan and Susan Raymond, who were camera and sound persons for Craig Gilbert's *An American Family* and whose vérité documentary, *The Police Tapes*, was aired nationally on PBS in 1976 in a 90-minute version and subsequently aired on ABC's *Close-Up* series in August 1978 in a cut 60-minute version, is representative of the more significant community-based video documentary work being done today. Their work also points to the subject-matter required in order to receive widespread distribution.

With Rockefeller Foundation funding, Alpert's Downtown Community Television Center produced *Vietnam: Picking Up the Pieces*, which was aired in 1978 as part of WNET's *Visa* series. The work, decidedly pro-Vietnam, describes the rebuilding and reeducation effort in a united Vietnam, as the former South Vietnamese are reintegrated into a society which labored continuously to eradicate prostitution, capitalist opportunism, drug addiction, adult illiteracy, and above all the emotional scars of a protracted war imposed on all the people of Vietnam from the outside, first by the French and later by the United States. Alpert's piece shows the new Vietnam succeeding, but with much rebuilding and social change remaining to be accomplished. Among the American legacies, Alpert points out toward the end of the piece, are 800,000 orphans, many with American fathers, who are now cared for by an order of Vietnamese nuns. The children cry a great deal.

Alpert, working with NBC News, did a "Segment 3" on the nightly news program in which he followed the Sandinistas in Costa Rica as they attempted to overthrow Nicaraguan dictator Somoza. In a powerful interview with one Sandinista following a battle in which counter-revolutionary soldiers are killed, Alpert asks the Sandinista, "Is this victory?" The response, "We need notebooks and papers to write and read . . . and all we get is death." This segment does credit to the network news organization which, on occasion, can rise above the political pressures of the dominant television ideological apparatus. Alpert, an independent, could gain the trust of the Sandinistas and the Vietnamese, who believed he could present their struggle without the dominant news frames distorting the story.

Downtown Community Television Center's work includes reports on poor people being evicted from their apartments in northern New Jersey to make way for the new upscale residents and their co-operatives and condominiums; drug addicts wandering the streets of New York City, stealing and shooting-up; poor homesteaders in Philadelphia who were led to believe they could renovate abandoned houses and thereby become home owners, but who in the end were deceived as the houses on which they spent so much time and love were put on the Sheriff's auction block; and miners striking in South Dakota in an attempt to publicize occupational hazards. Many of these later tapes, while well-intentioned, have serious though not fatal flaws. They take an oppositional stance but ignore debates. They become polemic, often lacking a clearly-drawn political and social context. This tendency to focus on the emotions of the participants and beg the viewer for a reaction rather than to present a carefully-reasoned argument against an institution and convince the viewer of the truthfulness of the oppositional position lessens these works' significance. Nevertheless, the works do exhibit commitment and encourage a response, even if the nature of that response is sometimes left floating free, cut-off from the social context in which the work was constructed.

The Raymonds' documentary, *The Police Tapes*, is an important example of the battle between the good intentions of the cultural workers who make the tape and the pressures, explicit or otherwise, which cause the ultimate defusion of oppositional work as it enters the dominant television apparatus. The work appears "oppositional," and some segments, taken by themselves, are clearly oppositional. Yet, taken in its entirety (in the 90-minute version with which I am familiar), the work becomes not so much an indictment of the politics which maintains the ghetto, as it is a quiet celebration of police work (for this reason, its airing on ABC's *Close-Up* is understandable). Yet, the black-and-white vérité technique and the subject matter—police wandering the streets of the 44th Precinct in the notoriously dangerous South Bronx area of New York City—lend the work a depressing quality and convince the viewer that "the system" has broken down. We see an Hispanic murder victim, killed during a robbery by two Blacks, lying in a pool of blood on the floor of a social club. We see a Latino boy dead under a car, stabbed fourteen times in a family dispute. People in the street are screaming. An Officer, Renko-like, yells "aw . . . shut up!" We hear police describe the "trance-like state" of murderers and we hear police assert that people with limited property will fight, and even kill, to defend it. We hear talk of the "animals out there." We hear the officers continually criticize the court apparatus for letting convicted felons back out on the streets. We hear their frustration with plea-bargaining arrangements. Yet we marvel at their constraint. There is no police brutality, no corruption, no one is "on the take" or involved in drugs.

Like vérité work generally, *The Police Tapes* is absent a narrator. Thus context is provided by that footage which is ultimately shot and assembled in the final edit. As discussed in Chapter 7, vérité work can be provocative, but it must "be there" to reveal crucial moments of ideological conflict. *The Police Tapes* is important in revealing the stark reality of ghetto conditions. It is not clear at all about causes, politics, or economics. Its inherent drama will attract an audience (ABC knew this), and its aesthetic will seem provocative. Yet, beneath it all its ideology is easily incorporated into the dominant conception of police work.

In that rare instance of network critical self-examination we find in an occasional documentary, it is assumed that relatively small audiences will be tuned in, even though the size of these audiences in absolute numbers is substantial (five-to-10 million people). The most provocative efforts at self-critique are, of course, to be admired. Yet one must also be careful to question the motivations behind such work, and beyond that to explicate the total ideological frame of the work. Such work should be encouraged, but it is in no way beyond further critique. The 1973 documentary *You and the Commercial*, an installment of the *CBS Reports* series, serves as an excellent example both of the strengths and the limitations of such work. Narrated by Charles Kuralt and produced by Irv Drasnin, *You and the Commercial* featured Federal Trade Commission condemnation of deception in television advertising, especially that aimed at children, analysis of the underlying myths of the television commercial by psychoanalyst Erich Fromm (see Chapter 3), and some profound interviews with leading advertising agency executives, one of whom admitted that he, like all of us, was "a sucker" for an ad. Representatives for television's largest advertisers refused to appear on the program. While the harsh light of publicity explicitly avoided CBS, who appeared in this context as the Don Quixote of television (after all, it just ran the commercials, it didn't make them), by implication CBS would have to shoulder at least some of the responsibility for the public dissemination of the commercials. Clearly, an institution engaged, for profit, in selling audience to advertisers by attracting viewers to the programs sandwiched in between the commercials will not seek to alienate the source of its profits. How did CBS News manage to play both sides? It created the illusion of alienating its sponsors. By first questioning the motives of advertisers and then by ending the documentary with the warning *caveat emptor*, CBS had circumscribed the correct position regarding the power of the ads—they may suck you in, but its *your* responsibility to ignore them—and thereby defused a truly oppositional position, which might have included a call for an FTC ban on all ads targeted at children (a position later taken by Action For Children's Television), and an effort to hold ad agencies and their clients increasingly culpable for willful negligence in the inaccurate representation of their products or services.

"Anti-television" performance is an important oppositional strategy. This form can develop in many different ways. What links the differences is a common focus: the control exerted by dominant television performance—a one-way communication, "them-to-us." They are telling us what is acceptable, what we should value, and we are listening to them tell us. They, of course, are those who work for the dominant television system: networks, local over-the-air broadcast stations, multiple system cable owners and their local origination cable channels. They are managers, news directors, performers. The two-minute-editorial-response-by-"qualified"-spokesman routine at the tail end of the six o'clock news won't cut it. Paper Tiger Television, a group of New York political artists, has expanded the editorial response for cable access television. A series of *Paper Tiger* videotapes offers, with wit and political insight, an oppositional video "reading" or critique of the texts of dominant cultural print and electronic media. Brian Winston's "reading" of *TV Guide* lets the viewer in on the skeleton-in-the-closet, that is, what is not revealed between the lines. Winston's reading of *TV Guide* is particularly provocative and representative of the best of the series. Winston points out, for example, how Walter Anenberg, founder of *TV Guide* and many other magazines, including *Seventeen*, and philanthropist who had communications colleges built in his name at major American universities as monuments to himself, maintained his vast wealth. Winston pointed out Anenberg's 1939 conviction for tax evasion. The piece becomes a witty and clear indictment of the camouflage of capitalist ethics through the contrived publicity of public service. It speaks not only to *TV Guide* and its founder, but to the television system on which the magazine depends for survival.

In another installment of *Paper Tiger Television*, Elayne Rapping "reads" romance novels. Rapping, sitting in a tacky laundramat set, is folding clothes. In the background we see slides of a laundramat alternating with covers from romances. Rapping offers a cogent feminist critique of the social relations depicted in these books. She highlights the fact that in these cover pictures, as well as in the stories themselves, "man is on top, woman is on the bottom." Rapping notes that Xerox and Scholastic Publications produce romances geared to 12-15 year old girls. The stories, which present "sexual feelings" and "kissing," but no more, are really training manuals for an adulthood of "enormous consumer product spending" which is so prevalent as decor in the adult romances. While Rapping's reading flirts with a "rap," her preparation, obvious intelligence, sincerity, and the laundramat setting make this engaging television. Unfortunately, it is still "one-way." Call-in audience response would intensify the effort by involving, for example, the viewer who reads romance novels.

Another form of "anti-television" performance confronts the medium on its own turf. Coca Crystal's Manhattan cable public access weekly one-hour talk show *If I Can't Dance You Can Keep Your Revolution* says "fuck you" to Dick Cavett, Johnny Carson, Mike Douglas, Phil Donahue, and David Letterman. Coca smokes a joint, talks with callers about politics, and generally breaks down the centrist, stereotypically Middle-American ambience of the television talk show.

Crystal's work has the freedom of public access. Its viewers will be those already committed to this form of wide-open talk. What of those other viewers who do not yet understand the terms according to which the confrontation between traditional- and anti-television performance is being waged? Video and performance artists such as Douglas Davis have worked hard to clarify the language of oppositional performance, of "performance-against-performance." In one particular piece, "How To Make Love To Your Television Set," Davis explores the meaning of talking back. Davis had performed this work prior to being invited by Warner QUBE in Columbus, Ohio to perform it in the Summer of 1979. (The QUBE system in Columbus had gained national attention as the first interactive cable television system in the United States, and artists were intrigued by its potential. Subscribers to QUBE can respond to questions asked from the QUBE studios by pressing one of several buttons on a response console. They can also order up programs in a similar manner. Their responses and program selections are fed into a central computer at the cable head end.) Davis wanted to use QUBE to engage in a more personal two-way communication than merely pressing buttons in response to questions. He would subject himself to the will of the viewer by following the viewer's phoned-in directions for his video performance in the studio. The program was live. Anything could happen. In this way, a mutual trust could be built between the two human beings linked via television and telephone. But was QUBE really ready for interaction in the human, rather than the computer sense of the term? Not quite. Davis was restricted to the talk-show format of the *Columbus Alive* program. He was engaged in a brief discussion of his work and asked to do a brief demonstration of "interaction" (How, after all, does one demonstrate interaction? One merely interacts). The show's hostess was pleasant and at first calm, although there was an atmosphere of apprehension in the studio and control room. What if someone asked Davis to do something outlandish? There were a few crank calls and a few calls from viewers who seemed intrigued by the possibility of directing the evolving discourse. Then an unexpected ideological breakthrough occurred. The hostess took another call. Although she didn't know it at the time, the caller was a male student in a television criticism class watching the performance from an off-studio viewing area. He wanted to break down traditional television performance barriers. He politely asked not Davis, but the hostess to "come over to the TV monitor in the studio and do what I ask." The hostess seemed to interpret the caller's gesture in sexual terms, not an unlikely response. The student's warm sincerity was transformed by the voyeuristic, commodified television frame. Interaction was impossible in this context. The hostess was no longer in control of the discourse. She sensed her status as an "object" yet could not or would not relate that status to the larger realm of televised commodification.

To counter the distorted history offered by the national-centralized dominant television, many cable public access channels have attempted to redirect attention to the vast wealth of regional and local history and culture—history and culture which speaks directly in some cases, indirectly in others of social struggle against racism, of the capitalist/labor struggle in the mines and fields and sweat shops, and of the rich heritage of the family as a social and work unit. Among the pioneers in this "video history" project are Austin Community Television (ACTV) in Texas, and Appalshop in Kentucky. These organizations have compiled videotapes, films, and audiotapes of community elders who recall the social struggles and recount the development and maintenance of indigenous folk culture in their regions and communities. Each tape or film is a statement which links the present to its history via the eyewitness and thereby counters the tendency of dominant television to naturalize that history, that is, to render the past in terms of the power relationships of the present.

Until 1980, the control by dominant television over the domain of electronic public art had remained unshaken. However, in the last few years there is some evidence of the erosion of popular support for commercial television. A report appearing in the April 13, 1983 edition of *Variety* revealed the results of a National Association of Broadcasters study of viewer attitudes. The results were overwhelmingly negative, according to *Variety*. Based on 500 in-depth interviews at home and 1,000 telephone interviews, the report found that people rated television less important in their lives than in 1977, less entertaining, and less of a technical marvel. Viewers saw television encouraging bad behavior and language. Half of the viewers said they were watching less television than in 1977, one-sixth the same amount, and only one-third more. More importantly, the drop-off in viewing was found across all demographic and socioeconomic groups. This means that that traditionally heavy viewers in poorer socioeconomic classes are beginning to turn away from the system of constant electronic control to which they have been subjected for decades. What has happened to produce such a result? While it certainly may be speculated that current dominant television fare is artistically vapid, the turning-away from television might also be attributed to a desire for work more relevant to the lives of viewers. The NAB study found that over 50 percent of the respondents said they wanted the new cable television technology for "participating in discussion or asking questions of political figures."[1] This feeling of a need for a political dialogue via television is highly encouraging. But how likely is it that these disenchanted viewers will witness an expanded, opened political system as a result of the revolution in electronic technology? Current indications are that this sophisticated technology can and will be used for further control of the minds of the television audience.

ART, IDEOLOGY AND TECHNOLOGY

The increasing technological sophistication in electronics has resulted in the miniaturization of hardware and increased portability, greatly expanded data storage capacity and ease of accessing data, better image resolution, and expanded person-machine interactive capability. The dream of a home information center is today a reality. While we have all this electronic technology at our fingertips, however, we cannot neglect to question who established the technology in the first place and who establishes the information parameters for the software, for those questions lead us into crucial issues of ideology.

The most basic social manifestation of the electronics revolution is the proliferation of consumer-grade home video recording and playback equipment. Relatively low-cost compared to broadcast quality equipment and easy to operate, this home video technolgy—VCRs, video disc players, single tube color cameras—allows recording program materials off the air, playing pre-recorded materials purchased or rented from distributors or video clubs, and making one's own personal videotapes. The viewer can directly control his own video environment as an active programmer and program producer. Video cartridge games and home computer terminals with data storage and video display capability are additional inputs to this self-contained privatized video environment. While this emerging video system is important as an alternative to the dominant one-way, non-participatory television, and while the business and leisure implications of the technology are profound, one cannot ignore the fact that the system requires a substantial personal monetary investment to purchase, maintain, and upgrade, and could well exacerbate the existing unbalanced access to information according to economic class.

Throughout the 1970s, as portable video equipment became more affordable, artists were beginning to break through traditional television's programming barriers by circumventing commercial broadcasters and uncovering public television and a variety of cablecasting distribution alternatives. But many of the hundreds of independent producers working in film and video have charged that public television is simply not open to new or controversial material. Others who have, on occasion, had their work broadcast argue that their compensation has been woefully inadequate. Accomplished artists who must make a living from their art are thus relegated to the status of enlightened slave laborers subsidizing the top-heavy bureaucracy of the cultural apparatus put in place to ostensibly serve the public interest.

Alongside the independents grew up regular folks who desired to participate more directly in their communities' affairs through video. In the United States, the National Federation of Local Cable Programmers (NFLCP) has, since the mid-1970s, spearheaded a drive to establish public access channels on local cable television systems throughout the country. Composed of local government officials, enlightened cable system operators (who are a rare find), and community access workers employed by a variety of institutions ranging from local governments to non-profit community group coalitions, the NFLCP has encouraged citizens to get involved in making their own tapes about their communities' activities and problems. In addition, NFLCP advocacy teams have helped local governments secure cable franchise agreements beneficial to their communities.

While community video access can be a significant step toward a more responsive medium, some crucial philosophical issues remain to be resolved regarding the movement's intentions and ideological position. If access is a producer's medium (i.e., let any program produced by a community group or an individual, no matter its technical quality, ideology, or moral posture, be aired on a first-come, first-served basis) will viewers be attracted to the access channel and stay tuned? Limited evidence suggests viewers will not tune in poorly produced, ill-conceived "home movies" and will quickly lose interest in the channel itself. On the other hand, if access is a viewer's medium (i.e., for a program to be aired, it should at least conform to average standards of technical quality as well as have substance), will video novices with ideas but little production background—the people for whom the idea of access was originally intended—thereby be screened out of the communication process? Some members of the video access movement suggest structuring access channels to satisfy both elements—a channel programmed by access "professionals" which would air more sophisticated, i.e., higher technical quality material, and another channel which would air all other video efforts. However, by establishing what in essence would be a hierarchy of access programming, the access movement could fall into the information control trap of the dominant television system—the main reason for which the access movement was founded in the first place.

In 1977, improved cable television distribution technology was linked with a centralized computer at the cable head end to produce Warner-Amex's pioneering two-way interactive cable television system called QUBE (described above). The viewer at last could almost instantaneously communicate back to the program's producers. The cable operator still controlled the conversation, however, determining both the questions asked of the viewer and the range of responses the viewer could make. QUBE has produced some curious interactive events over the past few years. Perhaps the most questionable affair was a live QUBE survey (in conjunction with PBS) following the 1980

PBS airing of the documentary *Choosing Suicide*. The program was a video autobiography of 62-year-old artist Jo Roman who chose to end her life rather than to slowly die of cancer. After a very moving production we immediately were switched to a PBS television studio where moderator Hugh Downs asked QUBE viewers in Columbus, Ohio questions such as "Do You Agree With Jo Roman's Decision?" Answer "Yes," "No," or "Not Sure." Within thirty seconds we had an answer, which was 48 percent Yes, 32 percent No, and 20 percent Not Sure. Without knowing either the number of respondents or their demographics, we are given an opinion, or what Downs called "an electronic show of hands." Equally amazing is the small percentage of "Not Sures" responding to an amazingly complex and difficult question of ethics. Within the context of the documentary, such a video "conversation" seemed voyeuristic. It resembled a Roman circus at which the spectators are asked to rule on the fate of the losing combatant without questioning the morality of the event itself. While the potential of QUBE's two-way system is great—it could bring viewers the participation in political dialogue they said they want from the new technologies—it has yet to be even remotely realized, and there seems little evidence to date that the dominant television apparatus has much interest in actualizing this potential; there seems to be no profitability in such discourse. In addition, serious questions remain regarding the desireability of feeding personal information to a system for storage and subsequent easy retrieval for use in a variety of ways unknown to the viewers.

Cable television technology allowed the growth of community video access as additional channels were made available for communicating. Multiple-channel cable systems rendered problematic the notion of the scarcity of available broadcast channels—a regulatory argument long proffered by the Federal Communications Commission and gladly accepted by commercial broadcasters whose profit margins depend in large measure on principles of scarcity of supply and increase in demand. Today the scarcity argument has been technologically nullified within the broadcast spectrum itself. The FCC has authorized the licensing of up to 4,000 new Low-Power Television stations (LPTV's) over the next few years. These are low-cost operations which can function in much the same way as cable access channels, but whose signals travel through the air covering a radius of from 10 to 20 miles. The first LPTV station, in Bemidji, Minnesota, went on the air on December 12, 1981. For as little as $20,000 one can put a ten-watt VHF-LPTV station on the air (the cost would increase as production equipment was purchased for local origination of material). The LPTV technology becomes accessible to non-traditional broadcasters with controversial ideas but little corporate capital. Many of these LPTV stations can be linked by satellite to form a specialized network. The Spanish International Network has developed plans to link more than a dozen of its licensed LPTV stations in such a network; other, more profit-oriented LPTV entrepreneurs have similar plans. LPTV offers an important potential for unique programming and information for specialized audiences, including neighborhoods (especially inner city neighborhood), ethnic communities, and isolated rural areas. At the same time, the possibility for abuse is very real, especially if there is a concentration of ownership of stations and if the owners turn such stations into "feeder" units designed to broadcast reruns of old TV series sandwiched between commercial blocks. The FCC has placed no restriction to date on the number of LPTV stations a licensee can own, although it has decided that in awarding licenses to competing applicants in a community, it will give preference to applicants who own no other LPTV station (the FCC's handling of the LPTV question has been incredibly confused, and there is little guarantee that the guidelines I have described above will be the ones operating as you read this). Big names in the LPTV hunt already include ABC, NBC, Sears (through its Allstate Insurance subsidiary), and Federal Express.

The communications satellite technology which now transmits so much of our communications, including television and radio signals, telephone messages, business, civilian government, and military data, becomes increasingly sophisticated. Direct broadcast satellite (DBS) technology will offer the individual a relatively low-cost reception technology through which one can receive transmissions directly at home or at the office. Ideally, DBS offers access to information freed from the control of intermediary programming bureaucrats such as television station programmers or cable system operators, both of whom constantly make moral-ideological decisions based on the dominant culture's conception of community norms and the suitability of programs for their viewers. But, while DBS receiving technology is relatively inexpensive compared to traditional communication satellite reception, the message transmitter must still pay substantial amounts to access a satellite transponder to send messages, and will have to spend equal or greater amounts of money for pre-air publicity to gain any visibility in a gigantic multi-channel potpourri of programming. Since the potential availability of transponders is limited physically, the laws of supply and demand will likely harm independent producers who are not economically competitive. Independent artists and progressive political groups will have to work hard to form cooperatives which pool resources to buy their own transponder or to lease time on others' transponders. While attempts have been made to organize progressives to fund satellite distribution, to date nothing has materialized. An example of the problem is the attempt to establish the Vanguard Cable Television Network. Carver, Matthew, and Smith, leading progressive direct-mail advertisers, established Vanguard Cable Television in 1982 to manage the network and represent a coalition of public interest groups. Interest was expressed by the American Civil Liberties Union (ACLU), Common Cause, and by Norman Lear's People for the American Way (PAW) which had been running ads countering the politics of the Moral Majority. The network also intended to air programs sponsored by "progressive" for-profit publications such as *Washington Monthly* or *New Republic*. The intent was to satellite telecast 3½ hours of programming weekly in the initial phases, including progressive news with Vanguard's own news team, public interest group programs and spots, and work acquired from progressive independent artists and political groups. As of this writing, the network has not materialized. Many groups on the Left felt that too much power would be vested in the operators—Vanguard Cable Television. This reflects continuing problems in Left television, namely lack of adequate funding and failure of the plurality of Left groups to reach a consensus on the mechanisms for control of the information apparatus. To them, centralization smacks of dominance and questionable motives on the part of those who organize such ventures, whether politically progressive or not.

All of these new television strategies have been initiated because the technology of electronic communication has permitted lower-cost production and distribution through an ever-increasing abundance of available channels, and because there were so many groups who were for years effectively closed out of our electronic communications system. Their pent-up frustration through years of enforced electronic silence craves an outlet. Yet regardless of channel capacity, the cost to access a channel and promote oppositional work so it may reach large numbers of viewers is still problematic. In addition to cost problems, before we can assume an enlightened nation of activist television workers, it is necessary to cultivate the true critical viewer who would welcome oppositional work. This book is one modest attempt in that direction.

CULTIVATING THE CRITICAL VIEWER

The critical viewer who sees "the fraudulence of a proposition in advertising," or the controlling myth of eternal progress through acquisitiveness operating in prime time soap opera, or the overimportance attached to the heroic splendid performer—whether athlete, politician, or electronic preacher—is not likely to buy that product or complacently stand outside the centers of capitalist power as the "correct" ideological positions are circumscribed for him. The critical viewer is rather a potential anarchist practicing, on one level, an ethics of non-power, characterized by freedom, transgression, play, conflict, and serious cultural negotiation, and in Jacques Ellul's words, embodying the notion that "man accept *not* to do what he is capable of doing,"[2] namely organizing himself, through technique, into an efficient, unthinking consuming machine. "Noise," considered to be dysfunctional in traditional communications theory, is, according to this strategy, highly functional since it serves to critique, through decidedly human acts of non-power, a society characterized by the non-act of consuming—a society in which we have become heteronymous alienated spectators of our own history, existing through products and outside the "web of human relations."[3] These acts of non-power, however, while important personal gestures of defiance, will not, in the long term, threaten the stability of advanced capitalism. Individuals must rather be organized into activist organizations with clear group goals, tactics, and strategies.

The individual critical viewer described above must, as a first step, fight neutralization by our culture's dominant institutions. Neutralization occurs naturally through a process of incorporation, of hegemonic domination of entire ways of thinking and being. The educational institution, many critics argue, has become such an agent of incorporation. British social critic Raymond Williams wrote that "Education transmits necessary knowledge and skills, but always by a particular selection from the whole available range, and with intrinsic attitudes, both to learning and social relations, which are in practice virtually inextricable."[4]

Bringing television and television studies into both the traditional and the non-traditional "classroom"—into our educational institutions and into lifelong learning situations via public television and community public and educational cable access channels—is clearly more than a reluctant act of admitting "popular art" into the established curricula of traditional educational structures. Television studies brings another set of critical strategies into cultural play, strategies which are extremely relevant to our everyday experience in which the pervasive medium of television has created a universe of discourse, a language of common symbols and commonly held beliefs which control the nature of our cultural negotiation. The culture critic must ask: In what manner does this negotiation occur in and outside the classroom? Is this negotiation confined by what Louis Althusser termed the Educational Ideological State Apparatus in which the limiting and pervasive ideology of advanced capitalism encourages a view that the given material and social history is impenetrable and immutable? Or is it possible to open up the dominant ideology to serious critique, to the elaboration of residual and emergent oppositional ideologies and cultural formations,[5] encouraging the use of television as an important tool in the struggle for social change, change in which the inequities of social class stratification, the unequal distribution of the benefits of the "good life," and the condition of individual "unfreedom" will be eliminated?

Clearly, the general character of cultural negotiation depends on the role of the individual teacher. Samuel Bowles and Herbert Gintis argue for the role of the teacher as social activist. Instead of encouraging naive spontaneity, as in the "free school" environment, or student rebellion against harsh school authority, they argue that educators should instead highlight contradictions in the social system through the application of dialectical educational philosophy. They clearly delineate the ground for such a dialectic:

> The struggle between working people and capital has its counterpart in educational conflict. . . . employers and other social elites have sought to use the schools for the legitimation of inequality through an ostensibly meritocratic and rational mechanism for allocating individuals to economic positions; they have sought to use the schools for the reproduction of profitable types of worker consciousness and behavior through a correspondence between the social relationships of education and those of economic life. On the other hand, parents, students, worker organizations, blacks, ethnic minorities, women and others have sought to use schools for their own objectives: material security, culture, a more just distribution of economic reward, and a path of personal development conducive not to profits but to a fuller, happier life.[6]

Television, with its powerful symbolic texts accessible to students of all backgrounds and classes, can prove quite useful by providing cultural material that highlights such a dialectic. Hard-hitting investigative social-activist community video documentary contains particularly relevant texts open to deconstruction, as does the best of vérité work; but so too do the dominant television genres of comedy, melodrama, news, sport, electronic religion, game and talk programs, and commercials.

By engaging in serious critique, however, the secondary and middle-school teacher, unlike their relatively protected university counterparts, may face overt political pressure from school principals, boards of education, and PTAs with vested interests in maintaining the dominant ideologies. Thus the teacher must be able to overcome an "inner vulnerability," for, according to Jules Henry, "behind many intellectual failures is indeed a failure of nerve."[7] Nerve must be steady for the teacher to move beyond mere description of the way things are to an enlightened interpretation of why they are perceived to be that way, even if the explanation calls into question the nature of the educational apparatus itself. Interpretation must occur in an educational environment open to the challenge of oppositional ideologies— an environment characterized by open enrollment, free tuition, no tracking which separates advantaged and disadvantaged students, and teachers who do not isolate themselves as unapproachable "professionals," but rather take active roles in counter-hegemonic instruction by forming "alliances" with students, especially those of working classes, and by respecting students' insights developed through their prolonged and intensive television experiences.[8] While teachers who operate in this manner may be branded subversives, in fact they are upholding the ideals of enlightened education which encourages active open debate of ideas and advocacy of principles by educated autonomous individuals.

NOTES

1. David Bergmann, "In Search of The Hardcore Fan," *Variety*, April 13, 1983, p. 47.

2. Jacques Ellul, "The Power of Technique and the Ethics of Non-Power," in *The Myths of Information: Technology and Postindustrial Culture*, ed. by Kathleen Woodward (Madison, Wisconsin: Coda Press, Inc., 1980), p. 245.

3. Jan Pierre Dupuy, "Myths of the Informational Society," in *The Myths of Information*, p. 11.

4. Raymond Williams, *Marxism and Literature* (London: Oxford University Press, 1977), pp. 117-118.

5. Ibid., pp. 121-127. Examples include the residual ideology of rural "purity"—of community—in opposition to the personal isolation produced by

urban industrial capitalism, and the residual religious ideology of service to others without reward; both are areas the dominant culture has neglected or undervalued. An example of an emergent oppositional cultural form is the radical student and working class press which warns, among other things, against the incorporation of working class lifestyles into popular advertising. This press has to date been unable to find an appropriate open distribution vehicle in American television, except for an occasionally progressive public access cable channel. Radio, through community radio stations, has with some regularity opened its doors to such oppositional forms. One result of this openness was the lawsuit involving indecent language in the WBAI-Pacifica case.

6. Samuel Bowles and Herbert Gintis, *Schooling in Capitalist America* (New York: Basic Books, Inc., 1976), p. 101.

7. Jules Henry, *On Sham, Vulnerability and Other Forms of Self-Destruction* (New York: Vantage Books, 1973), p. 105.

8. Bowles and Gintis, *Schooling*, passim.

Index

About the Author

HAL HIMMELSTEIN is Associate Professor of Television and Radio at Brooklyn College of the City University of New York. He has previously taught at Fordham University, Ohio University, and the University of Kansas.

Dr. Himmelstein has published in the areas of popular television, artists' television, and the social environment. His book on the state of American television criticism, *On The Small Screen*, published by Praeger in 1981, was chosen as an Outstanding Academic Book, 1981-82, by *Choice* Magazine. His articles on television and his artist interviews have appeared in *Access*, *1982 Almanac: The Annual of the International Council of the National Academy of Television Arts and Sciences*, and *Wide Angle*.

Dr. Himmelstein holds a B.A. and an M.A. from the University of Kansas, and a Ph.D. from Ohio University.

DATE DUE	
APR 17 1996	
APR 0 2 2001	
NOV 24 2001	

GAYLORD   PRINTED IN U.S.A.